FAUST

JOHANN WOLFGANG VON

GOETHE

FAUST

A TRAGEDY

PARTS ONE & TWO

FULLY REVISED

Translated from the German by

MARTIN GREENBERG

Introduction by W. Daniel Wilson

Yale UNIVERSITY PRESS

New Haven and London

Yale University Press books may be purchased in quantity for
educational, business, or promotional use. For information, please
e-mail sales.press@yale.edu (U.S. office) or sales@yaleup.co.uk
(U.K. office).

Set in Minion type by Westchester Book Group.
Printed in the United States of America.

ISBN: 978-0-300-18969-8 (paperback)
Library of Congress Control Number: 2013956843

A catalogue record for this book is available from the British Library.

This paper meets the requirements of ANSI/NISO Z39.48-1992
(Permanence of Paper).

To the memory of Robert Warshow, boyhood
friend, college mate and dear companion spirit in
manhood, so early, so very early cut off

And to the memory of Herbert Howarth, no
sooner united by understanding, sympathy and
affection than snatched away

—Martin Greenberg

.

CONTENTS

Introduction by W. Daniel Wilson, ix

Translator's Note, xix

FAUST: A TRAGEDY

Part One, 3

Part Two, 169

Notes, 443

INTRODUCTION

W. Daniel Wilson

Goethe's *Faust* is considered not only the most important work of Germany's greatest writer, but a seminal text of world literature. Its legacy is immense both in Germany and beyond. The impact of the wider Faust tradition, which began with the 1587 chapbook history of Dr. Johann Faustus and boasted such canonical works as Christopher Marlowe's *Dr. Faustus* (1604), is often difficult to distinguish from that of Goethe's play. But his work definitely inspired such seminal works—to mention only music and novels—as Schubert's haunting song *Gretchen at the Spinning Wheel* (1814) and Charles Gounod's opera *Faust* (1859), as well as Thomas Mann's challenging multi-layered work *Dr. Faustus* (1947) and Mikhail Bulgakov's anti-Stalinist novel *The Master and Margarita* (first published 1967). And its continuing vitality is expressed in a lively filmic reception.

Goethe worked on *Faust* off and on over sixty years of a long life. Born in 1749 into the family of an independently wealthy Frankfurt patrician, he enjoyed private tutoring and the consciousness of belonging to the privileged. His early literary work is part of the first German youth literary movement, the Sturm und Drang or "Storm and Stress," which became an English expression for youthful revolt. These writers took up social themes, but the political situation in German-speaking lands, which were not a unified country but hundreds of tiny to large semi-independent territories, precluded political action, so the young men had to be content with radical gesturing.

Part One of *Faust* owes its socially critical theme—the burning issue of infanticide—to this movement, which rediscovered sixteenth-century figures like Doctor Faustus and the independent knight Götz von Berlichingen, the subject of the play (1773) that instantly made the brash young author into a household name in Germany. In the next year, Goethe's first novel, *The Sufferings of Young Werther,* scandalized theologians who felt that it encouraged suicide. It was banned in several places in Germany and cemented Goethe's fame or indeed infamy.

The newly installed eighteen-year-old duke of the small duchy of Saxe-Weimar-Eisenach, Carl August, was so impressed with the brash writer that he invited him to Weimar, then a town of only some 8,000 inhabitants and capital of a duchy of about 100,000 souls. Goethe ended up staying for the rest of his life in this provincial corner of Thuringia that quickly became a literary center, attracting other leading writers. What began as wild antics with the duke—apparently part of Goethe's project to 'humanize' him and benefit society—quickly settled into a post as a top adviser and administrator, which took up practically all of Goethe's energies for nine years. So little did he publish that the literary world wrote him off. In 1786, Goethe "fled" (his own term) to Italy, where he spent the better part of two years, generously supported by the duke, immersing himself in classical art and cultivating new sources of creative energy. When he returned to Weimar, a new accommodation allowed him to play a minor role in matters of state and devote himself more fully to writing and, for a while, directing the court theater. Goethe had been moving for some time toward a more 'classical' aesthetic, inspired by ancient Greek and Roman literature and a stress on balance, harmony, and moderation. His 'high' classical phase was the result of a felicitous and intensely productive friendship, beginning in 1794, with the writer Friedrich Schiller (1759–1805). Schiller had distanced himself from his own early Sturm und Drang phase and developed a theoretical underpinning for what we today call "Weimar Classicism." While outside of Germany Goethe is—with a great deal of justification—viewed as a romantic writer, in Germany the late blossoming of its literature (late compared with France or England) resulted in a classical moment contemporaneous with romanticism. Weimar Classicism is partly defined politically, by a vigorous opposition to the French Revolution that touched practically everything Goethe wrote in the 1790s, including his work on *Faust* late in that decade (see Mephistopheles' arcane allusions in the scene Witch's Kitchen). Though Goethe began *Faust* around 1772 or even earlier, he published only a fragment of *Part One* in 1790 (the earliest version, which scholars called *Urfaust,* was only discovered in 1885). This version, most notably, lacked a very large part of the final published work, particularly around the apparently difficult issue of how Faust came to terms with the devil. But in the late 1790s this version fed the early romantic writers' conviction that Goethe was their leading light: after all, Faust's sustaining principle is *striving,* a very romantic boundlessness with a focus on process rather than goal. Goethe worked further on *Part One* largely around 1797, when he still benefitted from collaboration with Schiller, and finished it in 1806 (it was published in 1808). *Part Two* is largely the work of the older Goethe. He completed it in 1831, but instructed that it should be published only after his death, which came a year later at the age of 82. Goethe was increasingly alienated from the reading public and predicted—rightly—that few would understand or approve of some of the "very earnest jokes" in the work, as he wrote in his last letter of 17 March 1832. There are reports that the Berlin court was scandalized by the homoerotic brazenness of the penultimate scene, Burial.

German scholars have made a minor industry writing on this play and have uncovered various possible 'influences.' There is no evidence that Goethe knew the 1587 Faust chapbook, but he did know other, orthodox Christian literary treatments, in particular the traveling puppet plays of the legend, which Goethe probably saw as a boy, and which were loosely based on Marlowe. For *Part One,* a major inspiration was the domestic tragedy (bürgerliches Trauerspiel), which focused on conflicts between father and daughter regarding her sexuality and choice of marriage partner. This theme combined with Goethe's own experiences, particularly his probable knowledge of the execution of Susanna Margaretha Brandt for infanticide in Frankfurt in 1772. Infanticide often resulted from fear of the public shaming inflicted by religious authorities in cases of childbirth out of wedlock. For the Sturm und Drang writers, it was a burning and paradigmatic example of the conflict of individual needs with repressive social norms. Goethe's tragedy of Margarete, or as she is sometimes known in the play, Gretchen (a diminutive that perhaps falls short of capturing the fullness of her character), is Goethe's unique addition to the Faust story and gives *Part One* much of its elemental human appeal. The story is given ironic poignancy by an infanticide case in Weimar in November 1783. Duke Carl August, in line with contemporary legal reforms, wanted to eliminate the death penalty for infanticide in Saxe-Weimar. He consulted his three-member Privy Council, which included Goethe. Along with at least one other councillor, Goethe voted to retain the death penalty, and a woman whose fate had been awaiting this decision, Johanna Catharina Höhn, was executed soon thereafter. The case has aroused the kind of heated controversy that only Goethe can attract in Germany. This much is clear: Goethe's vote was crucial. He and the duke were fully familiar with the extensive contemporary arguments for eliminating the death penalty for this crime.[1] The Höhn case cannot, however, be deployed directly in interpreting Goethe's intentions in *Faust,* as it occurred after he had already written almost all of this part of the play—only the haunting image of Margarete in Walpurgis Night, with a red line on her throat that suggests beheading, was written later and may reflect the disturbing Höhn case. At most, it is evidence of the gulf between the writer and the politician.

Goethe's use of the infanticide motif lays the blame for this prototypical women's crime squarely at the feet of contemporary social and religious norms. In the play, the brutal social reprobation is represented by Margarete's sanctimonious and self-satisfied brother Valentin and by the other young women who condemn one of their pregnant peers. But this social critique merges into a uniquely complex interpretive problem regarding the individual responsibility of Faust and indeed Margarete herself. It has often been pointed out that Faust has at least seven deaths on his conscience by the end of the play—in league with Mephistopheles, he has not only wiped out an entire family (Margarete, her child, mother and brother) but in *Part Two* literally 'blindly' acquiesces in the murder of Baucis and Philemon, along with the stranger who tries to defend them.[2] Yet, amazingly, Goethe seems to let Faust off the hook, 'pardoning' him in the end. Many readers have shaken their heads at Faust's redemption, and perhaps rightly so.

Three things must be kept in mind. First, though he calls the work a tragedy, Goethe generally felt himself to be unsuited to the tragic mode: "I was not born to be a tragic writer," he wrote in 1831, "since my nature is conciliatory."[3] Second, Goethe clearly portrays Faust's behavior as repugnant. The reader is 'distanced' from Faust by a series of theatrical devices. In *Part One,* we have the three preliminary metatexts (dedicatory verses, Prelude in the Theater, and Prologue in Heaven, all of them reflecting on the action to come) and at the end a disembodied voice, presumably of the Lord from the Prologue.[4] Third, and most elementally, Faust unmasks himself when he stridently insists, multiple times in the space of a few verses (in his last speech in A Cavern in the Forest), that he "had to" destroy Margarete—but there is no visible necessity to this project other than his own self-absorbed quest. Goethe is not Faust, and arguments that the author "celebrates" Margarete's "destruction and sacrifice"[5] run entirely counter to these distancing devices.

At the same time, Goethe was doubtless invested in this striving, restless spirit, who represents much in the author's own secular outlook and scorn for mindless activity and groundless knowledge.[6] Part of Goethe's purpose was to represent precisely the kind of boundless, self-sufficient quest and questioning so repugnant to conservatives as something admirable, and this plan called for Faust not to be punished. It has also been argued that Margarete should not be reduced entirely to the status of 'victim.' She consciously enters into a sexual relationship with a mysterious man with no visible roots, identified only as a 'traveler' (as she calls him at the beginning of Garden, a seminal scene for showing how stubbornly Faust looks past the everyday reality of Margarete's life) and possibly a nobleman (as she surmises at the beginning of the scene Evening)[7] whom she could never hope to marry. And indeed she never brings up marriage explicitly, though she does test Faust's religious faith as a possible preliminary and fantasizes a wedding wreath in her final delusion. This sexual flaunting of the norms of her restricted, narrow world contrasts with an intriguing interpretation that—not implausibly—marshals modern psychology to portray Margarete as the object of a concerted campaign by Mephisto and Faust to 'shame' her into submission (for example, with the gift of jewels fit for nobility, which only serve to remind her of her low station), and sees shame as a primary cause of her insanity.[8]

After the wrenching tragedy of Margarete, *Part Two* has seemed to many readers a letdown, a confusing foray into a multitude of settings. Much of it, however, returns to some of the themes from the early Faust legend, including the appearance of Helen of Troy—a low magical trick in Goethe's sources, but an imaginative confrontation of ancient and modern in Goethe's version. After the strangely modern issues of the responsibility of the scholar and scientist touched on in *Part One,* the second part seems almost like a panoply of further issues that still agitate us: gender relations, the economics of money, revolution, war, imperialism/colonialism, utopian thought, instrumental rationality, homosexuality, and more. But there are also more universal issues like the nature of evil and morality in a secular age, the relation of art and ethics, and idealism vs. realism. Critics who stress the modernity of the play have increasingly turned with appreciation to *Part Two*. Goethe's interlocutor Johann Peter Eckermann reports the poet saying on 17 February 1831 that *Part Two*, in contrast to *Part One*, has "almost nothing subjective; here we see a higher, broader, brighter, less passionate world, and those who haven't got round in the world and experienced something will not be able to make sense of it." Readers of any age, though, can certainly learn something from a character that has variously been figured as an Enlightenment thinker, a libertine, or a man corrupted by power—the last of these, indeed, is at the core of his relation to Mephistopheles.

While *Part One* is written largely in Knittelvers, a kind of rhymed doggerel verse from sixteenth-century popular literature, *Part Two* is an encyclopedic array of verse forms, and indeed in the amorous dialogue between Faust and Helena the form itself—rhyming—becomes the topic of the work, suggesting that Goethe meant his forms to sustain symbolic significance. Superficially, *Part Two* seems to suit the conventional demands of "Aristotelian" drama, with five acts. *Part One* retains many traces of its Sturm und Drang origins, when experimentation with Shakespeare-inspired breaches of "Aristotelian" demands were common coin: the quickly paced shift through representative scenes from the Margarete story looks forward to early twentieth-century expressionist Stationendrama (a drama of "stations" in the action), from which non-essential parts of the story are omitted and must be inferred. Indeed, the use of the distancing devices mentioned above, particularly the Prelude in the Theater, suggests a metadramatic pre-Brechtian 'epic theatre.' The question of whether the play—particularly *Part Two*—was intended to be performed at all or rather meant as a 'closet play' (for reading only) continues to exercise critical discussion. In the twenty-first century, in any case, directors have begun to stage the entire work, often over more than one day; Peter Stein's uncut Hannover production in 2000 was the most celebrated and controversial of these.[9]

For much of the prudish nineteenth century, Goethe was considered an immoral "heathen" (indeed, he called himself that), and *Faust* contributed to that reading. In the English-speaking world, that reputation even scared off some translators from the work. Goethe had discreetly replaced some vulgar remarks by Mephistopheles in the Walpurgis Night with dashes, and later directors followed his lead by sometimes even omitting any mention of sexual desire. More disturbing for some readers were theologically heterodox remarks. In the twentieth century, this bowdlerizing was replaced by ideologically driven distortions of the work. Particularly during the First World War and the National Socialist periods, Faust was mobilized to represent the German character with its supposed striving for self-fulfillment that entailed contempt for the usual moral restraints. This interpretation willfully overlooked the signals of distancing mentioned earlier and essentially equated Goethe with Faust. The first scholar to mount a sustained critique of this sort of distortion, writing in 1962 under the alias Hans Schwerte, inaugurated the 1960s left-wing paradigm called "critique of ideology."[10] From the communist camp, scholars in the German Democratic Republic (East Germany) interpreted Faust's lines just before his death, culminating in "To stand with free men, on ground that is free!" as prefiguring humanist socialism. East German leader Walter Ulbricht even envisioned the workers' struggle for a socialist state in the GDR as a third part of *Faust*.[11] Most recent scholarship is characterized by sober analysis of some of the work's faults (the Walpurgis Night's Dream, included largely for the sake of polemic, is a case in point) and recognition of the problematic nature of Faust's character.

Martin Greenberg's translation, here presented in newly revised form, has rightly been celebrated for its colloquial idiom. It is also one of the few translations that bring to life Goethe's often funny rhymes, while not slavishly attempting to rhyme the very same words as in the original. Greenberg also tackles the difficult task of reproducing Goethe's metrical schemes, so that English readers can come as close as possible to sensing the impact of the original German lines. His talent comes particularly to bear on *Part Two*, with what he calls "its tremendous poetic exuberance, its fantasticality, its Shakespearian boldness." His notes give necessary information—particularly for *Part Two* with its dizzying classical references—without overwhelming the reader with *Faust* scholarship. The translation brings Goethe's seminal text to life for twenty-first-century readers.

NOTES

1. See W. Daniel Wilson, "Goethe, His Duke and Infanticide: New Documents and Reflections on a Controversial Execution" and "'The 'Halsgericht' for the Execution of Johanna Höhn in Weimar, 28 November 1783," *German Life and Letters* 61 (2008), pp. 7–32, 33–45. The documents of the Höhn case and others have been collected in: *"Das Kind in meinem Leib": Sittlichkeitsdelikte und Kindsmord in Sachsen-Weimar-Eisenach unter Carl August: Eine Quellenedition 1777–1786*, ed. Volker Wahl (Weimar: Hermann Böhlau, 2004).
2. See, most forcefully, Rüdiger Scholz, *Die beschädigte Seele des großen Mannes: Goethes Faust und die bürgerliche Gesellschaft*, 2nd ed. (Würzburg: Königshausen & Neumann, 2011).
3. Letter to Zelter, 31 Oct. 1831, cited by Albrecht Schöne in Goethe: *Sämtliche Werke, Briefe, Tagebücher und Gespräche*, ed. Friedmar Apel et al., vol. 7: *Faust*, ed. Albrecht Schöne, pt. 2: *Kommentar*, 3rd ed. (Frankfurt: Deutscher Klassiker Verlag, 1994), p. 17.
4. See Schöne, pp. 151 f.
5. Barbara Becker-Cantarino, "Witch and Infanticide: Imaging the Female in *Faust I*," *Goethe Yearbook* 7 (1994), pp. 1–22, here p. 18.
6. See T. J. Reed, "Goethe as Secular Icon," *The Present Word: Culture, Society and the Site of Literature*, ed. John Walker (Oxford: Legenda, 2013), pp. 44–51.
7. Faust's clothing seems to mark him as noble; Goethe may have intended him to be dressed, like Mephistopheles, as a noble "Junker" (*Faust's Study [II]*), and Goethe said of him in 1818 that he was to appear as a "knight" (see Schöne, p. 282).
8. Peter Matussek, "*Faust I*," *Goethe Handbuch*, 4 vols., ed. Bernd Witte et al., vol. 4: *Dramen*, ed. Theo Buck (Stuttgart: Metzler, 1996), pp. 352–90, here pp. 377–81.

9. For more on recent theater and *Faust* see *Goethe's* Faust: *Theatre of Modernity,* ed. Hans Schulte, John Noyes, and Pia Kleber (Cambridge: Cambridge University Press, 2011), particularly pp. 197–323, including an interview with Stein (pp. 267–79).

10. Hans Schwerte, *Faust und das Faustische: Ein Kapitel deutscher Ideologie* (Stuttgart: Klett, 1962). In 1995 it was revealed that Schwerte was Hans Ernst Schneider, a former SS officer who changed his identity after the war and became not only a leading figure in leftist German studies, but president of the University of Aachen. However, this strange story does not detract from the value of his critique of Faust interpretations particularly in National Socialist Germany.

11. See Daniel J. Farrelly, *Goethe in East Germany, 1949–1989: Toward a History of Goethe Reception in the GDR* (Columbia, SC: Camden House, 1998), pp. 8–9.

TRANSLATOR'S NOTE

This revision keeps to the purpose of my original translation: to provide an English *Faust* in a "language really used by men." Those are William Wordworth's words in which he laid down early in the nineteenth century the standard for his poetry that by the beginning of the twentieth had become the standard of modern poetry. Goethe anticipated Wordsworth in linguistic realism. "No other poem in modern literature of comparable length and complexity [as *Faust*] stays so close to the vernacular," wrote Barker Fairley, a superior Goethe scholar of a past generation notable, especially among scholars, for the excellence of his English. I have profited from the criticism of reviewers, friends, and time, more especially from time, the most just critic. She got to work early with her criticisms. When I received the author's copy of my translation of *Faust: Part One* (published in 1992) I sat down at once, as writers do, with the arrival of a first copy from the publisher and began to read, to read words that were only too familiar. Yet after no long while I found myself reaching for a pencil to correct this and amend that. And so it went, off and on, these twenty years. A word here, a phrase there, and often enough whole passages. Sometimes, exasperatingly, a single sentence proved impossible, utterly intractable. How many times did one rewrite it! And did one get it right after all?

Does translating Goethe sound like hard work? It is. And it is also a great pleasure. One was working with great poetry, with greatness. That is surely what you would call a good sort of job, under a superior employer. Unlike an employee, however, you enjoy complete independence. The goal is fixed for you, but the German matter to be englished is completely in your hands, to do with as you think best. What *is* the goal? To make something in English that is a match for the German. "Match" is David Belos's term (in *Is That a Fish in Your Ear?*) for what has always been a difficult thing to name satisfactorily, a translation's relation to its foreign-language original. "Match" tells you that the translation is not the original magically metamorphosed into an English replica, that translating *Faust* is not a matter of finding an English that is somehow Goethe still uttering his own words. I have known the most sophisticated people to wish that a translation were just as good—meaning exactly like—the work it translates and complaining that it wasn't. I can't forbear quoting at this point a piece of wit of G.K. Chesterton's quoted by Jorge Luis Borges. He, Chesterton, "said that he did not know Persian but that Fitzgerald's translation [of the *Rubaiyat*] was too good a poem to be faithful to the original."

A match is a likeness, not a copy. It can't be a copy because of the differences between languages, between German and English profound differences in the way the two languages think and work, and other differences. Maybe in prose translation copies are (sometimes) possible. Not in verse. In translating poetry you are thrown very much upon your own resources. In prose you have the foreign sentence before you to follow more or less closely in the way it builds its structure of meaning. (Not that that is easily done!) But in poetry so much more goes into the construction: meter or the musical movement of the language; a diction that is more than suitable, that is *right*, in which you must continually invent to be true; if rhymed verse, a felicity you sometimes hit right off but usually must try for again and again—a general harmony of sound and movement and meaning. This calls on all your powers of language and imagination. It means you must presume in some sort to be the poet yourself, the poet who creates in English a match, a likeness, of the German *Faust*. The work is creative. Yet in the English-speaking world the conception is ingrained, though regularly contested, that translation is mechanical.

English is the dominant international language, not from eternity but since about the end of the nineteenth century, succeeding French. English speakers expect what they read to be in English. If it isn't, then let somebody turn it into English. The translator's position in the publishing business is quite ambiguous. He is not a principal like an author, although all the words are his, the work is his work. His remuneration is nowhere near a principal's, so niggardly in fact that one would be embarrassed to name it. Literary translation is understood to be an avocation, though not by the translator, who is expected to pay himself (as he does) in the coin of his own love for his work. But one doesn't bring up the subject of pay in a translator's note. In most countries translators are well respected, in some celebrated, in Japan extremely, in Germany and Russia greatly; most languages recognize translation as an art.

Faust I and *Faust II* differ strikingly. Goethe concurred in J. P. Eckermann's observation that *Faust* begins as a tragedy and ends as an opera. *Part One* subverted the classical idea of tragedy, which takes the fate of great ones in a great world for its subject, to embrace a narrow provincial small town inhabited by not very pleasant little people, among them however a lower-middle-class girl with a soul fully equal to tragedy. There is a dark sense of constrictedness, confinement, imminence. Gretchen's love for Faust only darkens the atmosphere with its calamitous presentiment.

The overcast *Part One* belongs to Goethe's youth. The brilliant *Part Two* belongs to his maturity and old age. It opens with a great burst of light and color and sound and with a reborn hero—or rather protagonist; Faust is no hero. Magic produces some wonders in *Part One*; *Part Two* is crammed with wonders. A few songs, both lively and sad, punctuate the tragic of the first part. Song doesn't punctuate, it flows and overflows in the second. An extraordinary diversity of verse accomodates the extraordinary diversity of matter, historical, mythological, geographical, political, geological, aesthetic, moral,

xxii   TRANSLATOR'S NOTE

and so on. This enlivens the poetry and taxes the efforts, sometimes desperate, of the translator. Goethe spoke of *Faust: Part Two's* having "so various and diversified a life"—life, not thought. He thought in concrete images, disliked abstractions. It is left to critics and commentators, to the tireless Goethe scholarship, to unearth the abstract meanings buried in the concrete poetic matter of *Faust*.

The surprise in *Faust II* is to find that it is full of jokes, a continuing jokiness. One did not think of Goethe as a humorist. They are, however, "serious jokes"—so he referred to them and so they are. There is an anticipation of them in the hardly humorous *Part One* when Evil (Mephistopheles), which we think of as a mighty power, makes its first appearance—as a dog, an ignominious dog. And moreover of the kind with the silly-sounding name of "poodle." Evil a poodle! It is mockery (the German *Pudel* a little less so). Goethe was inclined to think—did think—that the idea of evil was a way by which religion bamboozled innocent mankind. It was Nature he believed in, that knows nothing of good and evil. The humor here is both flagrant and subtle, as is the case with the great variety of jokes in *Part Two*. I make a rough classification of them into farcical, satirical, and outrageous. Outrageous is the near conversion of Mephisto to the party of Heavenly Love by sexy, hip-switching angels near the very end of the work. It is astonishing, and a good part of the humor is one's astonishment. And evil is again mocked.

There is a particular kind of Goethesque humor that depends on disallowing the law of contradiction. In the Witch's Kitchen scene in *Part One*, disbelieving Faust dismisses the elaborate ceremony by which he is being rejuvenated as nothing more than hocus-pocus, vulgar tricks. Of course tricks, Mephisto says, you're being much too difficult, of course hocus-pocus; she's a sorceress, how else would she get her potion to work?

A witty example that takes the form of ontological contradiction occurs in Act IV of *Part Two*, in the war over the rulership of the Empire. The Emperor sees "an eagle soaring in the heavens / Hard after it one of those frightful griffins"—the griffin, half lion, half eagle, being one of the creatures in Part Two's fabulous bestiary and the eagle the imperial symbol. Faust reassures him:

Watch, do! I am sure the omen's favorable.
The griffin after all is just a fable,
So how should he imagine himself able
Ever to trade blows with a real-life eagle?

But how is it that a *fable* is pursuing a real-life eagle in the first place? And that he more than imagines, he does in fact attack the eagle, attacks so far that he suffers defeat and falls to earth, just like a real griffin, though there are none?

It's a joke. It's a serious joke because of its ontological instability, its wavering (to use one of Goethe's favorite words). *Faust I* is no such joke; when it settles into the story or Gretchen's seduction it is a tragedy—Gretchen's, not Faust's. *Faust II*'s world is one of uncertainty, where all is reflection, image, as Faust declares at its start, and nothing is the thing itself. This uncertainty, however, isn't problematic for Goethe as it is for Kleist and four decades later for Kafka. Goethe isn't able to reach so far as to grasp the essence of things but he does reach something, indirectly, a reflection of the essence in the phenomenal immediate, a likeness of what is beyond reach. So we have a world, a real world, and not a dream in *Faust*.

What shall one say about this rich, various, coruscating, complex world? I abdicate in favor of George Santayana (in *Three Philosophical Poets*): The later Goethe indicated "a philosophy of life . . . namely that he who strives strays, yet in that straying finds his salvation. This idea left standing all that satirical and Mephistophelian wisdom of which the whole poem abounds, the later parts no less than the earlier. Frankly, it is a moral that adorned the tale, without having been the seed of it, and without ever expressing fairly the spirit which it breathes. *Faust* remained an essentially romantic poem, written to give vent to a pregnant and vivid genius, to touch the heart, to bewilder the mind with a carnival of images, to amuse, to thrill, to humanize. . . ."

One last—troubled—word. Faust's final exploit is the reclamation of the Empire's marshy shore region so as (he declares near death) to "open up space for millions in which to work and live" (living space, *Lebensraum*, to use the word of the later German-Nazi agitation for territorial expansion of the Reich). However, says Baucis, the feminine half of the old couple that still keep their cottage and stand of linden trees from Faust's grasp, "the work had something ill about it." Men toiled in vain during the daylight hours; slave labor gangs magically accomplished all by night to the accompaniment of the wails of slave laborers dying in the dark. Faust, now owner of vast lands and an all-powerful trade and business magnate, is driven nearly mad by the old couple's ownership of the linden grove, which he obsessively covets to complete his "possession of the world [*Weltbesitz*]." Because he has wished to be a just squire, he tells Mephisto, he hesitated to evict the couple. Mephisto: "After all the populations you've resettled!" Faust gives the order to dispossess them, and his thugs burn the old couple's cottage to the ground, with them inside. Faust now has possession of the world, although he deplores the violence his henchmen used to give him it. Mephisto, looking backward to biblical times, comments: "Naboth's vineyard once again."

But the passage of time has produced a comparison, surprising, shocking, that is apter than Mephisto's biblical one. I ask the reader's patience: to Hitler and National Socialism. Consider the following phrases in the narrative of Faust's brutal seizure of Baucis' and Philemon's tiny neighboring realm: *Lebensraum*, slave labor gangs, slave laborers dying in the dark, resettled populations, innocents burned alive, *Weltbesitz* [*Heute gehört uns Deutschland, morgen die ganze Welt*]. Is this language an uncanny anticipation? Or a fortuitous conjunction of elements already there? The comparison may be rough, but it is well founded on Goethe's dismissal of evil and the elevation of what he calls striving—action, deeds, no matter if good or bad—above all the purposes of existence that the human spirit is in eternal contention with itself about. The Lord in the Prologue in Heaven declares that striving man is bound to err. What kind of word is "err" for Faust's crimes, for his many *murders*? The destruction of the old couple is a horror and I think, belatedly I think, of the immeasurable German horrors waiting to be enacted in the not so distant future. Only Mephisto—only the Devil!—with his sardonic mutters contradicts the satisfaction with which Faust goes ahead and exterminates a peaceful neighbor. It is true that as Goethe's mouthpiece, Mephisto in his mutterings is Goethe muttering too. By no means does Faust go uncriticized; he is continually being criticized. But he goes unjudged. He is saved from judgment, and shortly after the murders of Baucis and Philemon (and an unnamed third in the cottage) his soul, purged and purified a second time (having had a Lethean cleansing at the start of *Part Two*) is borne on high to the regions of the Goethean blessed. Faust is saved twice, and justice is mocked twice. Does this mockery foreshadow the terrible mockery of justice to come one hundred years later and the acquiescence in it of other men of refined humanistic spirit, so many?

My warm thanks to Sarah Miller of the Yale University Press for her expert editorial guidance and also for her patience. And to Margaret Otzel for her generous encouragement and ever helpfulness.

FAUST

DEDICATION

Come back, have you, you figures shifting, spectral,
Who first appeared to me when I was young?
Try, shall I, this time to hold on to you all,
That wild idea, its pull is still as strong?
Nearer and nearer, out of mist and vapor,
You close in round me—all right, I surrender!
Your ghostly troop is steeped in such enchantment,
My heart is beating with a youth's excitement.

What lively scenes you bring back, days how happy,
Beloved shadows come again to life;   10
First love, first friendships, like some old, old story
All but forgotten, come back with them, and grief
Comes back, and sighing I retrace life's labyrinthine
Wandering course, naming the dear ones ill fortune
Cheated of golden hours and hurried away
Into the darkness before me, out of the day.

They will not hear it, what's about to follow,
Those hearts who were the first to hear me sing,
All that brave company are scattered now,
That first applause has long ceased echoing,   20
My song is poured out to the anonymous crowd
Whose very praises fill me with misgiving.
Among those whom once my poetry delighted,
If any live, they wander who knows where, benighted.

And a yearning, unfelt, unroused for so long,
For that solemn spirit world, seizes me,
Like an Aeolian harp my renewed song
Trembles into sound uncertainly,

A shudder shakes my frame, my eyes brim over till
My too strict heart, relenting, is turned gentle;
What's all around me, mine, looks leagues away,
And vanished ghosts are my reality.

PART

ONE

"In the beginning was the Deed!"

PRELUDE IN THE THEATER

Manager, Poet, Clown

MANAGER. You two who've always stood by me
    When times were hard and the playhouse empty,
    What do you think we may hope for
    From this tour of ours through German country?
    I'd like to please the crowd here, for
    They're really so easy-going, so patient,
    The posts are up, the floorboards laid,
    And all looking forward to the entertainment.   40
    Staring about, composed, at ease,
    They hope for a real surprise, each one,
    I know with this audience how to please,
    But I've never been in a fix like this one.
    It's true what they're used to is pretty bad
    But Lord, what a terrible lot they've read.
    So how surprise them with something lively and new,
    A piece with some meaning that amuses them too?
    I don't deny what pleases me most
    Are droves of people, a great host,   50
    Trying with all their might to squeeze
    Through the strait gate to our paradise,
    When it's daylight still, not even four,
    Using elbow and fist to get to the ticket seller,
    Like starving men rushing the baker's door—

For the sake of a seat prepared to commit murder.
Who works such a wonder on such a mixture
Of people? Why, of course it's the poet,
So fall to, dear colleague, and let's see you do it!
POET. Don't talk to me about that crazy crowd,   60
One look at them and all my wits desert me!
Oh shield me from that shoving, shouting horde
That swallows you up against your will completely!
No, lead me to some quiet, remote place
Where poets only know real happiness,
Where love and precious friends inspire and nurse
The blessed gift that is the power of verse.
    Oh dear, what struggles up from deep inside us,
Syllables our lips shape hesitantly
Into scenes ineffective now, and now effective,   70
Is drowned out in the present's hurlyburly;
Years must pass till, seen in time's perspective,
Its shape and soul shine forth as they are truly.
What's all flash and glitter lives a day,
The real thing's treasured by posterity.
CLOWN. Posterity! Oh that word—don't let's start a row!
If all *I* ever thought of was the hereafter,
Who'd set the audience laughing in the here and now?
To be amused, that's their hearts' desire.
Having a clown on the stage who knows what his business is   80
Is not to be sneezed at—it matters to know how to please.
When yours is the stuff to delight and content a whole
      theaterful,
You don't sourly mutter the public's a mob, always changeable.
What you want's a full house, the sign out saying Standing
      Room Only,
For the bigger the house, the better the response you can
      count on,

So be a good fellow and show us what true drama is really.
Your imagination, let it pour out like a fountain,
Its wonders matched by wisdom, good sense, feeling,
By passion too—but mind you, show us some fooling!
MANAGER. But what's the first requirement? Plenty of action!   90
They're spectators so what they want to see is things happen.
If you've got business going on every minute
That catches people's attention, their roving eyes rivet,
Then you don't have to worry, they're yours, they're won over,
When the curtain comes down they'll shout "Author! Author!"
With a public so large you need an abundance to please
    them all.
Something for everyone, that's how to seize them all,
The last thing you want is to be classically economical.
In the theater today only scenes and set pieces do,
The way to succeed is to serve up a stew,   100
You can cook it up fast, dish it out easy too.
Now tell me, what good is your artistic unity,
The public will only make hash of it anyway.
POET. You don't understand—all that's just hackwork,
A true artist never stoops to such stuff!
Those fine purveyors of cheap patchwork
For you are the measure of dramatic truth.
MANAGER. Go ahead, scold me. I don't mind your censure.
To do a job right you use the tools that are called for.
Remember, it's soft wood you've got to split,   110
Consider the people for whom you write:
One's here because he's bored, another
Comes stuffed from eating a seven-course dinner,
But worst by far are the ones who come to us
Straight from reading the latest newspapers.
The crowd arrives here distracted, distrait,
Thinking of this and that, not of a play.

The reason they come is mere curiosity,
The ladies exhibit their shoulders and finery,
Put on a great show without asking a salary. 120
Oh, the dreams poets dream in their ivory tower!
Flattered, are you, to see the house full?
Well, take a good look at our clientele,
The half vulgar and loud, half unmoved and sour,
One's mind's on his card game after the play,
Another's on tumbling a girl in the hay.
It's for people like that you fools torture the Muses?
Listen to me: You'll never go wrong
If you pile it on, pile it on, and still pile it on.
Bewilder, confound them with all your variety, 130
The public's the public, they're a hard lot to satisfy.
But goodness, how worked up you seem to be!
What's wrong? I can't tell if it's anguish or ecstasy.
POET. Go out and find yourself some other lackey!
You expect the poet, do you, frivolously,
For the sake of your blue eyes to debase
Nature's finest gift to the human race?
How does he teach humankind feeling,
Master the elements, every one?
I'll tell you, by the music pealing 140
Forth from his breast orphically,
Which then by reflux back on him returning
Reverberates as Nature's deep-voiced harmony.
When Nature winds life's endless thread
Indifferently on the bobbin, when
The noisy cries of her countless creatures
No music make, uproar instead,
Who melodizes the monotonous din
And makes all move in living measures?
Who calls each mute particular 150

To sing its part in the general chorus
In a glorious concord of myriad voices?
Who links our passions to wild tempests,
Our solemn moods to fading sunsets?
Unrolls before the feet of lovers
A lovely carpet of spring flowers?
Twines green leaves meaning nothing at all
To crown those proven most worthy of all?
Assures us of Olympus, upon it assembled the gods?—
That revelation of man's powers, the poet, does!   160
CLOWN. Then go on and use them, your marvelous powers!
Go at your business of making verses
The way you go at a love adventure:
A chance encounter, you're attracted, linger,
And little by little you find yourself caught.
You're so happy, later you're not;
First you're enraptured, then it's nothing but trouble,
And before you know it it's a whole novel,
Write the play we want that way, you know how to do it!
Jump right into life's richness and riot,   170
All of us live life, few have an idea about it,
And my, how it interests wherever you scratch it!
Color, confusion, a wild hurlyburly,
With a glimmer of truth amid errors' obscurity,
And there you have it, exactly the right brew
To refresh everyone, make them think a bit too.
Then the best of our youth will flock here to listen,
Gripping their seats in anticipation.
The sensitive soul will find in your play
Food to feed his melancholy;   180
One thing touches one man, another another,
The end result is, all discover
What's in their hearts. The young are still ready

To laugh at a good thrust, let their tears flow in pity,
Warmly respond to lofty ambitions,
Cherishing still their bright dreams and illusions.
You'll never please those whose race is run,
For them there are no more surprises,
But the youth for whom all's just begun,
They will shower you with praises.   190
POET. Then give me back those times again
　　When I, too, was a leaf uncurled
　　And song after song poured out of me
　　Like a fountain flowing uninterruptedly;
　　When mist still veiled the morning world
　　And a bud was a promised miracle,
　　When I plucked the thousand flowers that filled
　　The vales with their rich spectacle.
　　The nothing I owned was more than enough,
　　By fictions delighted, impelled toward truth,   200
　　Oh give me back that unquelled ardor,
　　The happiness whose depth is pain,
　　The strength of hate, love's superpower,
　　Oh give me back my youth again!
CLOWN. Youth, my dear colleague, you need in the following cases:
　　When the enemy's crowding you hard in the fight,
　　When pretty girls in summer dresses
　　Kiss and squeeze you with all their might,
　　When running hard, you glimpse in the distance
　　The wreath that rewards the fleetest foot,   210
　　When after the madly whirling dances
　　With drinking you wear the night out.
　　But to sweep the old familiar harp strings
　　Boldly yet with fine grace too,
　　To make by pleasing indirections
　　For the end your drama has in view—

That's a job for you old fellows,
And we respect you for your skill;
Age doesn't make us childish, God knows,
Just finds us the same old children still.   220
MANAGER. We've talked enough, now let me see
Your tardy quill produce results,
Our business is to stage a play,
Not waste the time in compliments.
And please—don't say you're not in the mood,
It never arrives if you hesitate timidly.
You say you're a poet, good, very good,
Let's hear it, then, your poetry.
You know what's wanted, good strong stuff—
To work now, work, go right at it,   230
What's put off today, tomorrow's put off;
How precious to us is every minute.
A resolute spirit, acting timely,
Seizes occasion by the short hairs,
It won't let go but hangs on grimly,
Once committed, it perseveres.

You know how on our German stage
We're free to try whatever we please,
So don't imagine I want you to save
Me money on paint and properties.   240
Hang out heaven's big and little lamps,
Scatter stars over the canvas sky,
Let's have fire and flood and dizzying steeps,
All sorts of birds and beasts—do the thing liberally.
And thus on a narrow platform you're able
To go all the way round Creation's great circle
At a brisk enough pace, yet deliberately as well,
From Heaven, through this our world, down to Hell.

PROLOGUE IN HEAVEN

The Lord. The Heavenly Host. Then Mephistopheles. The three Archangels advance to front.

RAPHAEL. The sun as always sounds his music
 In contest with each brother sphere,   250
 Marching round and around, with steps terrific,
 His appointed circle, year after year.
 To see him lends us angels strength,
 But what he *is*, oh who can say?
 The inconceivably great works are great
 As on the first creating day.

GABRIEL. And swift, past all conception swift,
 The jeweled globe spins on its axletree,
 Celestial brightness alternating
 With shuddering night's obscurity.   260
 Against the rock-bound littoral
 The sea is backwards seething hurled,
 And rock and sea together hurtle
 With the eternally turning world.

MICHAEL. And tempests vying, howling, riot
 From sea to land, from land to sea,
 Linking in tremendous circuit
 A chain of blazing energy.
 The thunderbolt makes ready for
 The thunderclap a ruinous way—   270
 Yet Lord, your servants most prefer
 The stiller motions of your day.

ALL THREE. From seeing this we draw our strength,
 But what You *are*, oh who can say?
 And all your great works are as great
 As on the first creating day.

MEPHISTOPHELES. Lord, since you've stopped by here again,
    liking to know
  How all of us are doing, for which we're grateful,
  And since you've never made me feel *de trop,*
  Well, here I am too with your other people.   280
  Excuse, I hope, my lack of eloquence,
  Though this whole host, I'm sure, will think I'm stupid.
  Coming from me, high-sounding sentiments
  Would only make you laugh—that is, provided
  Laughing is a thing Your Worship still did
  About suns and worlds I don't know beans, I only see
  How mortals find their lives pure misery.
  Earth's little god's shaped out of the same old clay,
  He's the same queer fish he was on the first day.
  He'd be much better off, in my opinion, without   290
  The bit of heavenly light you dealt him out.
  He calls it Reason, and the use he puts it to?
  To act more beastly than beasts ever do.
  To me he seems, if you'll pardon my saying so,
  Like a long-legged grasshopper all of whose leaping
  Only lands him back in the grass again chirping
  The tune he's always chirped. And if only he'd
  Stay put in the grass! But no! It's an absolute need
  With him to creep and crawl and strain and sweat
  And stick his nose in every pile of dirt.   300
THE LORD. Is that all you have got to say to me?
  Is that all you can do, accuse eternally?
  Is nothing ever right for you down there, sir?
MEPHISTOPHELES. No, nothing, Lord—all's just as bad as ever.
  I really pity humanity's myriad miseries,
  I swear I hate tormenting the poor ninnies.
THE LORD. Do you know Faust?
MEPHISTOPHELES.   The Doctor?

THE LORD.   My good servant!

MEPHISTOPHELES. You don't say! He serves you, I think, very
        queerly,
    Finds meat and drink, the fool, in nothing earthly,
    Drives madly on, there's in him such a torment,   310
    He himself is half aware he's crazy;
    Heaven's brightest stars he imperiously requires
    And from the earth its most exciting pleasures;
    All, all, the near at hand and far and wide,
    Leave your good servant quite unsatisfied.

THE LORD. If today his service shows confused, disordered,
    With my help he will see the way clear forward;
    When the sapling greens, the gardener can feel certain
    Flower and fruit will follow in due season.

MEPHISTOPHELES. Would you care to bet on that? You'll lose,
        I tell you,   320
    If you'll give me leave to lead the fellow
    Gently down my broad, my primrose path.

THE LORD As long as Faustus walks the earth
    I shan't, I promise, interfere.
    While still man strives, still he must err.

MEPHISTOPHELES. Well thank you, Lord—it's not the dead and gone
    I like dealing with. By far what I prefer
    Are round and rosy cheeks. When corpses come
    A-knocking, sorry, Master's left the house;
    My way of working's the cat's way with a mouse.   330

THE LORD. So it's agreed, you have my full consent.
    Divert the soul of Faust from its true source
    And if you're able, lead him along, Hell bent
    With you, upon the downward course—
    Then blush for shame to find you must admit:
    For all his dark impulses, imperfect sight,
    A good man always knows the way that's right.

MEPHISTOPHELES. Of course, of course! Yet I'll seduce him from it
Soon enough. I'm not afraid I'll lose my bet.
And after I have won it,   340
You won't, I trust, begrudge me
My whoops of triumph, shouts of victory.
Dust he'll eat
And find that he enjoys it, exactly like
That old aunt of mine, the famous snake.
THE LORD. There too feel free, you have carte blanche.
I've never hated your likes much;
I find of all the spirits of denial,
You jeerers not my severest trial.
Man's very quick to slacken in his effort,   350
What he likes best is Sunday peace and quiet;
So I'm glad to give him a devil—for his own good,
To prod and poke and incite him as a devil should.
[*To the Angels*] But you who are God's true and faithful
     progeny—
Delight in the world's wealth of living beauty!
May the force that makes all life-forms to evolve,
Enfold you in the dear confines of love,
And the fitfullness, the flux of all appearance,
By enduring thoughts give enduring forms to its transience.
[*The Heavens close, the Archangels withdraw.*]
MEPHISTOPHELES. I like to see the Old Man now and then,   360
And take good care I don't fall out with him.
How very decent of a Lord Celestial
To talk man to man with the Devil of all people.

NIGHT

In a narrow, high-vaulted Gothic room, Faust, seated restlessly in
an armchair at his desk.

FAUST. I've studied, alas, philosophy,
     Law and medicine, recto and verso,
     And how I regret it, theology also,
     Oh God, how hard I've slaved away,
     With what result? Poor foolish old man,
     I'm no whit wiser than when I began!
     I've got a Master of Arts degree,   370
     On top of that a Ph.D.,
     For ten long years, around and about,
     Upstairs, downstairs, in and out,
     I've led my students by the nose
     With what result? that nobody knows,
     Or ever shall know, the tiniest crumb!
     Which is why I feel completely undone.
        Of course I'm cleverer than these stuffed shirts,
     These Doctors, M.A.s, scribes and priests,
     I'm not bothered by a doubt or a scruple,   380
     I'm not afraid of Hell or the Devil—
     But the consequence is, my mirth's all gone;
     No longer can I fool myself
     I'm able to teach anyone
     How to be better, love true worth;
     I've got no money or property,
     Worldly honors or celebrity;
     A dog wouldn't put up with this life!
     Which is why I've turned to magic,
     Seeking to know, by ways occult,   390
     From ghostly mouths spells difficult,

So I no longer need to sweat
Painfully explaining what
I don't know anything about;
So I may penetrate the power
That holds the universe together,
Behold the source whence all proceeds
And deal no more in words, words, words.

O full moon, melancholy-bright,
Friend I've watched for, many a night,   400
Till your quiet-shining circle
Appeared above my book-heaped table,
If only you might never again
Look down from above on my pain,
If only I might stray at will
In your mild light, high on the hill,
Haunt with spirits upland hollows,
Fade with you in dim-lit meadows,
And soul no longer gasping in
The stink of learning's midnight oil,   410
Bathe in your dews till well again!

Oh misery! Oh am I still
Stuck here in this dismal prison?
A musty goddamned hole in the wall
Where even the golden light of heaven
Can only weakly make its way through
The painted panes of the gothic window;
Where all about me shelves of books
Rise up to the vault in stacks,
Books gray with dust, worm-eaten, rotten,   420
With soot-stained paper for a curtain;
Where instruments, retorts and glasses
Are crammed in everywhere a space is;

And squeezed in somehow with these things
My family's ancient furnishings
Make complete the sad confusion—
Call this a world, this world you live in?

Can you still wonder why your heart
Should clench in your breast so anxiously?
Why your every impulse is stopped short   430
By an inexplicable miserv?
Instead of the living house of Nature
God created man to dwell in,
About you all is dust, mold, ordure,
Bones of beasts and long dead men.

Up! Fly to the open countryside!
And do you have a better guide
Than this mysterious book inscribed
By Nostradamus's own hand?
What better help to master the secrets   440
Of how the stars turn in their orbits,
From Nature learn to understand
The spirits' power to speak to spirits.
Sitting here and racking your brains
To puzzle out the sacred signs—
What a sterile, futile business!
You hover, spirits, all around me—
Announce yourselves if you can hear me!

[*He opens the book and his eye encounters the sign of the
Macrocosm.*]

The pure bliss flooding all my senses,
Seeing this! Through every nerve and vein   450
I feel youth's fiery, fresh spirit race again.

Was it a god marked out this sign
By which my agitated bosom's stilled,
By which my bleak heart's filled with joy,
By whose mysterious agency
The forces of Nature about me stand revealed?
Am *I* a god? All's bright as day!
By these pure tracings I can see,
At my soul's feel, great Nature unconcealed.
And the sage's words I understand them finally: 460
"The spirit world is not barred shut,
It's your closed mind, your dead heart!
Stand up unappalled, my scholar,
And bathe your breast in the rose of aurora!"

[*He contemplates the sign.*]

How all is woven one, uniting
Each in the other, living, working!
Heavenly powers rise, descend,
Passing gold vessels from hand to hand!
On wings that scatter sweet-smelling blessings
Everywhere they post in earth,   470
And make a universal harmony sound forth!
Oh, what a show! But a show, nothing more.
How, infinite Nature, lay hold of you, where?
Where find your all-life-giving fountains?—breasts that sustain
The earth and the heavens which my shrunken breast
Yearns for with a feverish thirst—
You flow, overflow, must I keep on thirsting in vain?

[*Morosely, he turns the pages of the book and comes on the sign
of the Spirit of Earth*]

How different an effect this sign has on me!
O Spirit of Earth, how near, how much nearer to me!
Already fresh life-blood pours through every vein,   480
Already I'm aglow as if with new wine—
Now, now I possess the courage to dare
To adventure into the wide world, bear
Earth's ill, earth's well, and bravely battle
The howling storms, when the ship splits, not to tremble.

The air grows dark overhead—
The moon's put out her light.
The oil lamp's nearly dead.
Vapors rise, red flashes dart
Around my head—fright,   490
Shuddering down from the vault,
Seizes me by the throat!
Spirit I have invoked, hovering near:
Reveal yourself!
Ha! How my heart beats! All of my being's
Fumbling and groping amid never felt feelings!
Appear! Oh, you must! Though it costs me my life!

[*He seizes the book and pronounces the Spirit's mystic spell.
A red flame flashes, in the midst of which the Spirit appears.*]

SPIRIT. Who's calling?
FAUST. (*Averting his face*) Overpowering! Dreadful!
SPIRIT. Potently you've drawn me here,   500
     A parched mouth sucking at my sphere.
     And now—?
FAUST.   But you're unbearable!
SPIRIT. You're breathless from your implorations
     To see my face, to hear me speak.

I've yielded to your supplications
And here I am.—Well, shrinking, weak,
I find the superman! You call, I come,
And you're struck dumb. Is yours the breast
Inside of which an entire world was nursed
Into existence, a creation   510
On which you doted with mad elation,
Puffed up to think yourself the equal
Of us spirits, on our level?
Wherever is that fellow Faust
Who urged himself just now with all
His strength on me, made such a fuss?
You're Faust? The one who at my breath's
Least touch, shudders to his depths,
A thing that wriggles off, scared, a worm!

FAUST.   *I* shrink back from you, an airy flame?   520
    I'm him, yes Faust, your equal, the same.

SPIRIT.   In flood tides of life, in tempests of doing,
    Up and down running,
    The here with there joining,
    Birth with the grave,
    An eternal ocean,
    A weaving, reweaving,
    A life aglow, burning,
    So seated before time's humming loom,
    I weave the Godhead's living costume.   530

FAUST.   We're equals, I know! I feel so close to you, near,
    You busy spirit ranging everywhere!

SPIRIT.   You equal the spirit you think I am,
    Not me! [*Vanishes.*]

FAUST.   [*Deflated*] Not you?
    Then who?
    Me, made in God's own image,

Not even equal to you?

[*A knocking*]

Death! My famulus—I know that knock.

Finis my supremest moment—worse luck!

That visions richer than I could have guessed   540

Should be scattered by a shuffling dryasdust!

[*Wagner in dressing gown and nightcap, carrying a lamp. Faust turns around impatiently.*]

WAGNER. Excuse me, sir, but that was your voice, wasn't it,

    I heard declaiming? A Greek tragedy,

    I'm sure. Well, that's an art that comes in handy

    Nowadays. I'd love to master it.

    People say, how often I have heard it,

    Actors could really give lessons to the clergy.

FAUST. Yes, so parsons can make a stage out of the pulpit—

    Something I have seen in more than one case.

WAGNER. Oh dear, to be so cooped up in one's study all day,   550

    Seeing the world only now and then, on holiday,

    Seeing people from far off, as if through a spyglass—

    How persuade them to any effect in that way?

FAUST. Unless you really feel it, no, you cannot—

    Unless the words your lips declare are heartfelt

    And by their soul-born spontaneous power,

    Seize with delight the soul of your hearer.

    But no! Stick in your seats, you scholars!

    Paste bits and pieces together, cook up

    A beggar's stew from others' leftovers   560

    Over a flame you've sweated to coax up

    From your own little heap of smoldering ashes,

    Filling with wonder all the jackasses,

    If that's the kind of stuff your taste favors.

But you'll never get heart to cleave to heart
Unless you speak from your own heart.

WAGNER. Still and all, a good delivery is what
Makes the orator. I'm far behind in that art.

FAUST. Advance yourself in an honest way,
Don't play the fool in cap and bells!   570
Good sense, good understanding, they
Are art enough, speak for themselves.
When you have something serious to say,
What need is there for hunting up
Fancy words, high-sounding phrases?
Your brilliant speeches, smartened up
With bits and pieces collected out
Of a miscellany of commonplaces
From all the languages spoken by all the races
Are about as bracing as the foggy autumnal breeze   580
Swaying the last leaves on the trees.

WAGNER. Dear God, but art is long,
And our life—much shorter.
Often in the middle of my labor
My confidence and courage falter.
How hard it is to master all the stuff
For dealing with each and every source,
And before you've traveled half the course,
Poor devil, you have gone and left this life.

FAUST. Parchment, tell me—that's the sacred fount   590
You drink out of, to slake your eternal thirst?
The only true refreshment that exists
You get from where? Yourself—where all things start.

WAGNER. But sir, it's such a pleasure, isn't it,
To enter into another age's spirit,
To see what the sages before us thought
And measure how far since we've got.

FAUST. As far as to the stars, no doubt!
    Your history, why, it's a joke;
    Bygone times are a seven-sealed book.   600
    What you call an age's spirit,
    What is it? Nothing but your own poor spirit
    With the age reflected as you see it.
    And it's pathetic, what's to be seen in your mirror.
    One look and I head straight for the exit.
    A trash can, strewn attic, junk-filled cellar,
    At best a blood-and-thunder thriller
    Improved with the most high-minded sentiments
    Exactly suited for mouthing by marionettes.
WAGNER. But this great world, the human mind and heart,   610
    They are things all want to know about.
FAUST. Yes, know as the world knows knowing!
    Who wants to know the real truth, tell me?
    Those few with vision, feeling, understanding
    Who failed to stand guard, most unwisely,
    Over their tongues, speaking their minds and hearts
    For the mob to hear—you know what's been their fate:
    They were crucified, burnt, torn to bits.
    But we must break off, friend, it's getting late.
WAGNER. I love such serious conversation, I do!   620
    I'd stay up all night gladly talking to you.
    But sir, it's Easter Sunday in the morning
    And perhaps I may ask you a question or two then, if you're
        willing?
    I've studied hard, with unrelaxing zeal,
    I know a lot, but I want, sir, to know all. [*Exit.*]
FAUST. [*Alone*] Such fellows keep their hopes up by forever
    Busying themselves with trivialities,
    Dig greedily in the ground for treasure
    And when they turn a worm up—what ecstacies!

That banal, commonplace human accents   630
Should fill air just now filled with spirit voices!
Still, this one time you've earned my thanks,
Oh sorriest, oh shallowest of wretches!
You snatched me from the grip of a dejection
So profound, I was nearly driven off
My head. So gigantic was the apparition,
It made me feel no bigger than a dwarf—

Me, the image of God, certain in my belief
Soon, soon I'd behold the mirror of eternal truth,
Whose near presence I felt, already savoring   640
The celestial glory, stripped of my mortal clothing;
Me, higher placed than the angels, dreaming brashly
With the strength I possess I could flow freely,
Godlike creative, through Nature's live body—
Well, it had to be paid for: a single word
Thundered out knocked me flat, all my vain conceit curbed.
No, I can't claim we are equals, presumptuously!
Though I was strong enough to draw you down to me,
Holding on to you was another matter entirely.
In that exalted-humbling moment of pure delight   650
I felt myself at once both small and great.
And then you thrust me remorselessly back
Into uncertainty, which is all of humanity's fate.
Who'll tell me what to do? Not to do?
Still seek out the spirits to learn what they know?
Alas, what we do as much as what's done to us,
Obstructs the way stretching clearly before us.
The noblest conceptions our minds ever attained
Are violated more and more and profaned;
When we've gained a bit of the good of this world for our prize,   660
Then the better's dismissed as delusion and lies;

Those radiant sentiments, once our breath of life,
Grow dim and expire in the madding crowd's strife.

Time was that hope and brave imagination
Boldly reached as far as to infinity,
But now misfortune piling on misfortune,
A little, confined space will satisfy.
It's then, heart deep, Care builds her nest,
Dithering nervously, killing joy, ruining rest,
Masking herself as this, as that concern   670
For house and home, for wife and children,
Fearing fire and flood, daggers and poison;
You shrink back in terror from imagined blows
And cry over losing what you never in fact lose.

Oh no, I'm no god, only too well do I know it!
A worm's what I am, wriggling through the soot
And finding its nourishment in it,
Whom the passerby treads underfoot.

These high walls, every shelf crammed, every niche,
Dust is what shrinks them to a stifling cell,   680
This moth-eaten world with its all kinds of trash,
They are the reasons I feel shut up in jail.
And here I'll discover what it is that I lack?
Devour thousands of books so as to learn, shall I,
Mankind has always been stretched on the rack
With now and then somebody, somewhere's been happy.
You, empty skull there, smirking so, I know why—
What does it tell me, if not that your brain,
Whirling like mine, sought the bright sun of truth,
Only to wander, night-bewildered, in vain.   690
And all this apparatus, you mock me, you laugh
With your every wheel, cylinder, cog and ratchet,

I stood at the door, sure that you were the key,
Yet for all the bit's cunning design I couldn't unlatch it.
Mysterious even in broad daylight,
Nature lets no one part her veil,
And what she keeps hidden, out of sight,
All your levers and wrenches can't make her reveal.
You, ancient stuff I've left lying about,
You're here, and why?—my father found you useful,   700
And you, old scrolls, have gathered soot
For as long as the lamp's smoked on this table.
Much better to have squandered the little I got
Than find myself sweating under the lot.
It's from our fathers, what we inherit,
To possess it really, we've got to earn it.
What you don't use is a dead weight,
What's worthwhile is what you spontaneously create.

But why do I find I must stare in that corner,
Is that bottle a magnet enchanting my sight?   710
Why is everything all at once brighter, clearer,
Like woods when the moon's up and floods them with light?

Vial, I salute you, exceptional, rare thing,
And reverently bring you down from the shelf,
Honoring in you man's craft and cunning—
Quintessence of easeful sleeping potions,
Pure distillation of subtle poisons,
Do your master the kindness that lies in your power!
One look at you and my agony lessens,
One touch and my feverish straining grows calmer   720
And my tight-stretched spirit bit by bit slackens.
The spirit's flood tide runs more and more out,
My way is clear, into death's immense sea,

The bright waters glitter before my feet,
A new day is dawning, new shores calling to me.

A fiery chariot, bird-winged, swoops down on me,
I am ready to follow new paths and higher,
Aloft into new spheres of purest activity—
An existence so exalted, so godlike a rapture,
Does the worm of a minute ago deserve it?   730
No matter. Never falter! Turn your back bravely
On the sunlight, sweet sunlight, of our earth forever,
Tear wide open those dark gates boldly
Which the whole world skulks past with averted heads.
The time has come to disprove by deeds,
Because the gods are great, man's a derision,
To cringe back no more from that black pit
Whose unspeakable tortures are your own invention,
To struggle toward that narrow gate
Around which all Hell flames in constant eruption,   740
To do it calmly, without regret,
Even at the risk of utter extinction.
And now let me lift this long forgotten
Crystal wine cup out of its chest.
You used to shine bright at the family feast,
Making the solemn guests' faces lighten
When you went round with each lively toast.
The figures artfully cut in the crystal
Which it was the duty of all at the table,
In turn, to make up rhymes about,   750
Then drain the cup at a single draught—
How they recall many nights of my youth!
But now there's no passing you on to my neighbor
Or thinking up rhymes to parade my quick wit;
Here is a juice that is quick too—to intoxicate,

A brownish liquid, see, filling the beaker,
Chosen by me, by me mixed together,
My last drink! Which now I lift up in festive greeting
To the bright new day I see dawning!

[*He raises the cup to his lips. Bells peal, a choir bursts into song.*]

CHORUS OF ANGELS.

    Christ is arisen!   760
    Joy to poor mortals
    By their own baleful,
    Inherited, subtle
    Failings imprisoned.

FAUST. What deep-sounding burden, what tremelo strain
    Arrest the glass before I can drink?
    Does that solemn ringing already proclaim
    The glorious advent of Holy Week?
    Already, choirs, are you intoning
    What angels' lips sang once, a comforting chant,   770
    Above the sepulcher's darkness sounding,
    Certain assurance of a new covenant?

CHORUS OF WOMEN.

    With spices and balm, we
    Prepared the body,
    Faithful ones, we
    Laid him out in the tomb,
    Clean in linen we wound him
    And bound up his hair,
    Oh, what do we find now?
    Christ is not here.   780

CHORUS OF ANGELS.
> Christ is arisen!
> Blest is the man of love,
> He who the anguishing.
> Bitter, exacting test,
> Salvation bringing, passed.

FAUST. But why do you seek me out in the dust,
> You music of Heaven, mild and magnificent?
> Sound out where men and women are simple,
> Your message is clear but it leaves me indifferent,
> And where belief's lacking no miracle's possible.   790
> The spheres whence those glad tidings ring
> Are not for me to try and enter,
> Yet all's familiar from when I was young
> And back to life I feel myself sent for.
> Years ago loving Heaven's embrace
> Flew down to me in the Sabbath stillness,
> Oh, how the bells rang with such promise,
> And fervently praying to Jesus, what bliss!
> A yearning so sweet, not to be comprehended,
> Drove me out into green wood and field,   800
> In me an inner world expanded
> As my cheeks ran wet from eyes tear-filled.
> Your song gave the signal for the games we all joined in
> When the springtime arrived with its gay festival,
> Innocent childhood's remembered emotion
> Holds me back from the last step of all—
> O sound away, sound away, sweet songs of Heaven,
> Earth claims me again, my tears well up, fall!

CHORUS OF DISCIPLES.
> Only just buried,
> Ascended already.   810

Who lived sublimely,
On high rose in glory!
Joy of becoming, his,
Near to creating's bliss.
He on the earth's hard crust
Left us, his own, his best,
To languish and wait—
Oh, how we pity,
Master, your fate!

CHORUS OF ANGELS.

Christ is arisen   820
From the bowels of decay,
Strike off your fetters
And shout for joy,
By good works praising him,
By loving, upraising him.
Feeding the least of all,
Preaching him east and west to all,
Promising bliss to all.
You have the Master near,
You have him here.   830

OUTSIDE THE TOWN GATE

All sorts of people out walking.

SOME APPRENTICES. Where are you fellows off to?
OTHERS. To the hunters' lodge over that way.
FIRST BUNCH. Well, we're on our way to the old mill.
ONE APPRENTICE. The river inn—that's what I say.
SECOND APPRENTICE. But the way there's unpleasant, I feel.

SECOND BUNCH. And what about you?

THIRD APPRENTICE.   I'll stick with the rest of
    us here.

FOURTH APPRENTICE. Let's go up to the village. There, I can promise
    you
      The best-looking girls, the best tasting beer,
      And some very good roughhousing too.

FIFTH APPRENTICE. My, but aren't you greedy!   840
      A third bloody nose—don't you care?
      I'll never go there, it's too scary.

SERVANT GIRL. No, no, I'm turning back, no, I won't stay.

ANOTHER. We're sure to find him at those poplar trees.

FIRST GIRL. Is that supposed to make me jump for joy?
      It's you he wants to walk with, wants to please,
      And you're the one he'll dance with. Fine
      For you. And for me what? The spring sunshine!

THE OTHER. He's not alone, I know, today. He said
      He'd bring his friend—you know, that curlyhead.   850

A STUDENT. Those fast-stepping girls there, look at the heft of them!
      Into action, old fellow, we're taking out after them.
      Beer with body, tobacco with a good rich taste,
      And red-cheeked housemaids in their Sunday best
      Are just the things to make your Hermann happiest.

A BURGHER'S DAUGHTER. Oh look over there, such fine looking
    boys!
      Really, I think they are simply wretches.
      They have their pick of the nicest girls,
      Instead they run after overweight wenches.

SECOND STUDENT. [*To the first*] Hold up, go slow! I see two more,   860
      And the pair of them dressed so pretty, so proper.
      But I know that one! She lives next door,
      And her, I can tell you, I think I could go for.
      They loiter along, eyes lowered decorously.

After saying no twice, they'll jump at our company.
FIRST STUDENT. No, no—all that bowing and scraping, it makes me
    feel ill at ease,
If we don't get a move on we'll lose our two birds in the bushes;
The work-reddened hand that swings the broom Saturday
On Sunday knows how to give the softest caresses.
A BURGHER. No, you can have him, our new Mayor,   870
Since he took office he's been a dictator,
All he's done is make the town poorer,
Every day I get madder and madder,
When he says a thing's so, not a peep, not a murmur
Dare we express—and the taxes climb higher.
A BEGGAR. [*Singing*]
    Good sirs and all you lovely ladies,
    Healthy in body and handsome in dress,
    Turn, oh turn your eyes on me, please,
    And pity the beggarman's distress!
    Must I grind the organ fruitlessly?   880
    Only the charitable know true joy.
    This day when the whole world dances merrily,
    Make it for me a harvest day.
ANOTHER BURGHER. On a Sunday or holiday nothing in all my
    experience
Beats talking about war and rumors of war,
When leagues away, in Turkey, for instance,
Armies are wading knee deep in gore.
You stand at the window, take long pulls at your schooner,
And watch the gaily colored boats glide past,
And then at sunset go home in the best of humor   890
And praise God for the peace by which we're blest.
THIRD BURGHER. Yes, neighbor, yes, exactly my opinion.
Let them go and beat each other's brains in,
Let them turn the whole world upside down,

As long as things are just as always in our town.

OLD CRONE. [*To the Burghers' Daughters*]

How smart we all are! And so pretty and young,

I'd like to see the man who could resist you.

But not so proud, my dears. Just come along,

Oh I know how to get what you want for you.

BURGHER'S DAUGHTER. Agatha, come! The awful fright!   900

I'm afraid of being seen with that witchwoman.

It's true that last St. Andrew's Night

She showed me in a glass my very own one.

HER FRIEND. And mine she showed me in a crystal sphere

Looking a soldier, with swaggering friends around him,

And though I watch out everywhere,

I have no luck, I never seem to find him.

SOLDIERS.

> Castles have ramparts,
> Great walls and towers,
> Girls turn their noses up   910
> At soldier-boy lovers—
> We'll make both ours!
> Boldly adventure
> And rake in the pay!
>
> Hear the shrill bugle
> Summon to battle,
> Forward to rapture
> Or forward to ruin!
> Oh what a struggle!
> Our life—oh how stirring!   920
> Haughty girls, high-walled castles,
> We'll make them surrender!
> Boldly adventure
> And rake in the pay!

—And after, the soldiers
　　Go marching away.

Faust and Wagner.

FAUST. The streams put off their icy mantle
　　Under the springtime's quickening smile,
　　Hope's green banner flies in the valley;
　　White-bearded winter, old and frail,　　930
　　Retreats back up into the mountains,
　　And still retreating, down he sends
　　Feeble volleys of sleet showers,
　　Whitening in patches new-green plains.
　　But the sun can bear with white no longer,
　　When life stirs, shaping all anew,
　　He wants a scene that has some color,
　　And since there's nowhere yet one flower,
　　Holiday crowds have got to do.

　　Now face about and looking down　　940
　　From the hilltop back to town,
　　See the brightly colored crowd
　　Pouring like a spring flood
　　Through the gaping, gloomy arch
　　To bask in the sun all love so much.
　　They celebrate the Savior's rising,
　　For they themselves today are risen:
　　From airless rooms in huddled houses,
　　From drudgery at counters and benches,
　　From under cumbrous roofs and gables,　　950
　　From crowded, suffocating alleys,
　　From the mouldering dimness of the churches,
　　They hurry to where all is brightness.
　　And look there, how the eager crowd
　　Scatters through the fields and gardens,

How over the river's length and breadth
Skiffs and sculls are busily darting.
And that last boat, packed near to sinking,
Already's pulled a good ways off.
Even from distant mountain slopes   960
Bright colored clothes wink back at us.
Now I can hear it, the village commotion,
Out here, you can tell, is the people's true heaven,
Young and old crying exultingly—
Here I am human, here I can be free!

WAGNER. To go for a walk with you, dear Doctor,
Is a treat for my mind as well as honoring me,
But by myself I'd never come near here,
For I can't abide the least vulgarity.
The fiddling, shrieking, clashing bowls,   970
For me are all an unbearable uproar,
All scream and shout like possessed souls
And call it music, call it pleasure.

PEASANTS. [*Singing and dancing under the linden tree*]
The shepherd dressed up in his best,
Pantaloons and flowered vest,
        Oh my, how brave and handsome!
Within the broad-leaved linden's shade
Madly spun both man and maid,
            Tra-la! Tra-la!
            Tra-la-la-la! Tra-lay!   980
        The fiddle bow flew and then some.

He flung himself into their midst
And seized a young thing round the waist,
        While saying, "Care to dance, ma'am?"
The snippy miss she tossed her head,
"You boorish shepherd boy!" she said,

Tra-la! Tra-la!
Tra-la-la-la! Tra-lay!
"Observe, do, some decorum!"

But round the circle swiftly wheeled,   990
To right and left the dancers whirled,
    Till all the breath flew from them.
They got so red, they got so warm,
They rested, panting, arm in arm,
        Tra-la! Tra-la!
        Tra-la-la-la! Tra-lay!
    And breast to breast—a twosome.

"I'll thank you not to make so free!
We girls know well how men betray,
    What snakes lurk in your bosom!"   1000
But still he wheedled her away—
Far off they heard the fiddle play,
        Tra-la! Tra-la!
        Tra-la-la-la! Tra-lay!
    The screaming, uproar, bedlam!

OLD PEASANT. Professor, welcome! Oh how kind
    To join us common folk today,
    Though such a fine man, learned mind,
    Not to scorn our holiday.
    So please accept our best cup, sir,   1010
    Brimful with the freshest beer.
    We hope that it will quench your thirst,
    But more than that, we pray and hope
    Your sum of days may be increased
    By as many drops are in the cup.
FAUST. Friends, thanks for this refreshment, I
    In turn wish you all health and joy.
    [*The people make a circle around him.*]

OLD PEASANT. Indeed it's only right that you
  Should be with us this happy day,
  Who when our times were hard, a true   1020
  Friend he proved in every way.
  Many a one stands in his boots here
  Whom your good father, the last minute,
  Snatched from the hot grip of the fever,
  That time he quelled the epidemic.
  And you yourself, a youngster then,
  Never shrank back; every house
  The pest went in, you did too.
  Out they carried many a corpse,
  But never yours. Much you went through;   1030
  Us you saved, and God saved you.
ALL. Health to our tried and trusty friend,
  And may his kindness have no end.
FAUST. Bow down to him who dwells above
  Whose love shows us how we should love.
  [*He continues on with Wagner.*]
WAGNER. What gratification must be yours
  To win such popular applause.
  Lucky the man, thanks to his gifts,
  Who can count on handsome emoluments!
  Who wins himself such benefits.   1040
  Fathers point you out to their boys,
  The fiddle stops, the dancers pause,
  And as you pass between the rows
  Of people, caps fly in the air. Why,
  Next you know they'll all be on their knees
  As if the host itself were passing by.
FAUST. A few steps more to that rock where we'll rest
  A bit, shall we, from our walk. How often
  I would sit alone here, musing, thinking, sighing,

And torture myself with praying, fasting, crying.   1050
So much hope I had then, such great trust—
I'd wring my hands, I'd weep, fall on my knees,
Believing God, in this way forced
To look below, must call a halt to the disease.
But now these people's generous praise of me
I find a mockery. If only you could see
Into my heart, you would realize
How little worthy father and son were really.
    My father was an upright man, a lonely,
Brooding soul who searched great Nature's processes   1060
With a head crammed full of the most bizarre hypotheses.
Shutting himself with fellow masters up in
The vaulted confines of their vaporous Black Kitchen,
He mixed together opposites according
To innumerable recipes. A bold Red Lion,
Handsome suitor he, took for wedding
Partner a pure White Lily, the two uniting
In a tepid bath; then being tested by fire,
The pair precipitately fled
From one bridal chamber to another,   1070
Till there appeared, within the glass,
The young Queen, dazzlingly dressed
In every color of the spectrum:
The Sovereign Remedy—a futile nostrum.
The patients died; none stopped to inquire
How many there were who got better.
    So with our infernal electuary
We killed our way across the country.
I poisoned, myself, by prescription, thousands,
They sickened and faded; yet I must live to see   1080
On every side the murderers' fame emblazoned.
WAGNER. But why be so distressed, there is no reason.

If an honest man with conscientious devotion
Practises the arts his forebears practised,
It's understandable, it's what's to be expected.
A youth who is respectful of his father
Listens and soaks up all he has to teach;
If when grown, he lengthens science's reach,
His son in turn can reach goals even farther.

FAUST. Oh, he's a happy man who hopes   1090
To keep from drowning in these seas of error!
What we know least, we need the most,
And what we do know is no use whatever.
But such cheerlessness blasphemes
The quiet sweetness of this shining hour,
Look, how the sunset's level beams
Gild those cottages in their green bower,
The brightness fades, the sun makes his adieu,
Hurrying off to kindle new life elsewhere—
If only I had wings to rise into   1100
The air and follow ever after!
Then I would see the whole world at my feet,
Quietly shining in the eternal sunset,
The peaks ablaze, the valleys gone to sleep,
And babbling into golden stream the silver runlet.
The savage mountain with its plunging cliffs
Should never balk my godlike soaring,
And there's the ocean, see, already swelling
Before my wondering gaze, with its sun-warmed gulfs.
But finally the bright god looks like sinking,   1110
Whereupon a renewed urgency
Drives me on to drink his eternal light,
The day always before, behind the night,
The heavens overhead, below the heaving sea . . .

A lovely dream!—and meanwhile it grows dark.
Oh dear, oh dear, that our frames should lack
Wings with which to match our soaring spirit,
Yet every soul there is, no matter whose it,
Knows feelings that strive upwards, onwards, straining,
When high above, lost in the azure evening,   1120
The skylark pours out his shrill rhapsody,
When over fir-clad mountain peaks
The eagle on his broad wings gyres silently,
And passing over prairies, over lakes,
The homeward-bound crane labors steadily.

WAGNER.   Well, I've had more than one odd moment, I have,
But I have never felt those impulses you have.
Soon enough you get your fill of woods and things,
I don't really envy birds their wings.
How different are the pleasures of the intellect,   1130
Sustaining one from page to page, from book to book,
And warming winter nights with dear employment
And with the consciousness your life's so lucky.
And goodness, when you spread out an old parchment,
Heaven's fetched straight down into your study.

FAUST.   You know the one great driving force,
May you never know the other!
Two souls live in me, alas,
Irreconcilable with one another.
One, lusting for the world with all its might,   1140
Grapples it close, greedy of all its pleasures,
The other rises up, up from the dirt,
Up to the blest fields where dwell our great forbears.

O beings of the air if you exist,
Holding sway between the heaven and earth,
Come down to me out of the golden mist

And translate me to a new, a vivid life!
Oh, if I only had a magic mantle
To bear me off to foreign lands, strange people,
I'd never trade it for the costliest gown   1150
Or for a cloak however rich and royal.
WAGNER. Never call them down, the dreadful swarm
  That swoop and hover through the atmosphere,
  Bringing mankind every kind of harm
  From every corner of the terrestrial sphere.
  From the North they bare their razor teeth
  And prick you with their arrow-pointed tongues,
  From the East, sighing with parched breath,
  They eat away your dessicated lungs.
  And when from Southern wastes they gust and sough.   1160
  Fire on fire on your sunk head heaping,
  From the West they send for your relief
  Cooling winds—then drown fields just prepared for reaping.
  Their ears are cocked, on trickery intent,
  Seem dutiful while scheming to defeat us,
  Their pretense is that they are heaven sent
  And lisp like angels even as they cheat us.
  However, come, let's go, the world's turned gray
  And chilly, evening mists are rising,
  At nightfall it's indoors you want to be.   1170
  But why should you stand still, astonished, staring?
  What can you see in the dusk to find upsetting?
FAUST. Don't you see that black dog in the stubble
  Coursing back and forth?
WAGNER.   I do. I saw that one
  A while back. What about him?
FAUST.   Look again.
  What kind of creature is it?
WAGNER.   Kind? A poodle—

Worried where his master is and always
Sniffing about to find his scent.

FAUST.   Look, he's
Circling around us, coming near and nearer.
Unless I'm much mistaken, a wake of fire   1180
'S streaming after him.

WAGNER.   I see nothing
But a black-haired poodle. Your eyes are playing
Tricks on you, perhaps.

FAUST.   I think I see
Him winding a magic snare, quietly,
Around our feet, a noose which he'll pull tight
In the future when the time is right.

WAGNER. He's circling us because he's timid and uncertain,
He's missed his master, come on men unknown to him.

FAUST. The circle's getting tighter, he's much closer!

WAGNER. You see!—a dog, and no ghost, sir.   1190
He growls suspiciously, he hesitates,
He wags his tail, lies down and waits.
Never fear, it's all just dog behavior.

FAUST. Come here, doggie, come here, do!

WAGNER. A silly poodle, a poor creature,
When you stop, he stops too,
Speak to him, he'll leap and bark,
Throw something and he'll fetch it back,
Go after your stick right into the river.

FAUST. I guess you're right, it's just what he's been taught,   1200
I see no sign of anything occult.

WAGNER. A dog whose conduct is so good, so clever,
Why, even a philosopher would stoop to pet him.
Some student trained him, he proved an apt scholar—
Sir, he deserves you should adopt him.

[*They enter at the Town Gate*]

FAUST'S STUDY [I]

FAUST. [*Entering with the poodle*]
Behind me lie the fields and meadows
Shrouded in the lowering dark,
In dread of what waits in the shadows
Our better soul now starts awake.
Our worser one, unruly, reckless,   1210
Quietens and starts to nod;
In me the love of my own fellows
Begins to stir, and the love of God.

Quiet, poodle! Stop! A dozen
Dogs you seem, all sniffing at the doorsill!
Here's my own cushion for you to doze on
Behind the stove—if you are gentle.
Just now when we came down the hillside
You gambolled like the friendliest beast.
I'm glad to take you in, provide   1220
Your keep—provided you're a silent guest.

When once again the lamp light brightens
With its soft glow your narrow cell,
Oh in your breast how then it lightens,
And deeper in your heart as well.
Again you hear the voice of reason
And hope revives, it breathes a fresh,
You long to drink the living waters,
Mount upwards to our being's source.

You're growling, poodle! Animal squealings   1230
Hardly suit the exalted feelings
Filling my soul to overflowing.
We're used to people ridiculing

What they hardly understand,
Grumbling at the good and the beautiful—
It makes them so uncomfortable!
Do dogs now emulate mankind?
  Yet even with the best of will
I feel my new contentment fail.
Why must the waters cease so soon   1240
And leave us thirsting once again?
Oh, this has happened much too often!
But there's an answer to it all:
I mean the supernatural,
I mean our hope of revelation,
Which nowhere shines so radiant
As here in the New Testament.
I'll look right now at the original
And see if it is possible
For me to make a true translation   1250
Into my beloved German.
[*He opens the volume and begins.*]
"In the beginning was the Word"—so goes
The text. And right off I am given pause,
A little help, please, someone, I'm unable
To see the *word* as first, most fundamental.
If I am filled with the true spirit
I'll find a better way to say it.
So: "In the beginning *mind* was—right?
Give plenty of thought to what you write,
Lest your pen prove too impetuous.   1260
Is it mind that makes and moves the universe?
Shouldn't it be: "In the beginning
Power was," before it nothing?
Yet even as I write this down on paper

Something tells me don't stop there, go farther.
The Spirit's prompt in aid; now, now indeed,
I know for sure: "In the beginning was the *Deed*!"

If this cell's one that we'll be sharing,
Poodle, stop that barking, yelping!
You're giving me a splitting headache,   1270
I can't put up with such a roommate.
One of us
Has got to quit the premises.
It goes against the grain with me
To renege on hospitality,
But there's the door, dog, leave, goodbye.

But what's that I'm seeing,
A shadow or real thing?
It beggars belief—
My poodle's swelled up huger than life!   1280
He heaves up his hulk—
No dog has such bulk!
What a spook I have brought
In my house without thought.
He looks, with his fierce eyes and jaws,
Just like a hippopotamus—
But I've got you, you're caught!
For a half-hellhound like you are,
Solomon's Key is what is called for.

SPIRITS. [*Outside the door*]

    Someone is locked in there!   1290
    No one's allowed in there!
    Like a fox hunters snared,
    Old Scratch, he shivers, scared.
    Be careful, watch out!

> Hover this way, now that,
> About and again about,
> And you'll soon see he's out.
> If you can help him,
> Don't let him sit there,
> All of us owe him   1300
> For many a favor.

FAUST.   Against such a creature my first defense,
> The Spell of the Four Elements:

> Salamander, glow hot,
> Undine, wind about,
> Sylph, vanish quick,
> Kobold, to work.

> Ignorance
> Of the elements,
> Their power and properties,   1310
> Denies you mastery
> Over the demonry.

> Up go in flames,
> Salamander!
> Babbling streams, flow together,
> Undine!
> Glitter meteor-beauteous,
> Airy Sylph!
> Household help bring us,
> Incubus!   1320
> Come out, come out, enough's enough.

None of the four
Is in the cur,
Calmly he lies there grinning at me;
My spells glance off him harmlessly.

—Now hear me conjure
With something stronger.

> Are you, grim fellow,
> Escaped here from Hell below?
> Then look at this symbol   1330
> Before which the legions
> Of devils and demons
> Fearfully bow.

How his hair bristles, how he swells up now!

> Creature cast into darkness,
> Can you make out its meaning?
> —The never-begotten One,
> Wholly ineffable One,
> Carelessly-pierced-in-the-side One,
> Whose blood in the heavens   1340
> Is everywhere streaming,

> Behind the stove by me sent,
> Bulging big as an elephant,
> The entire cell filling,
> Into mist himself willing—
> No, no! Not through the ceiling!
> At my feet fall, Master's bidding,
> My threats, as you see, are hardly idle,
> With holy fire, out I'll rout you, I will!
> Wait if you wish   1350
> For my triune light's hot flash,
> Wait till you force me
> To use my potentest sorcery.

[*The mist clears, and Mephistopheles, dressed as a traveling
student, emerges from behind the stove.*]

MEPHISTO. Why all the racket? What's your wish, sir?

FAUST. So it's you who was the poodle!

    I have to laugh—a wandering scholar.

MEPHISTO. My greetings to you, learned doctor,

    You really had me sweating hard there.

FAUST.

    And what's your name?

MEPHISTO.   Your question's trivial

    From one who finds words superficial,   1360

    Who strives to pass beyond mere seeming

    And penetrate the heart of being.

FAUST. With gentry like yourself, it's common

    To find the name declares who you are

    Very plainly. I'll just mention

    Lord of the Flies, Destroyer, Liar.

    So say who you are, if you would.

MEPHISTO. A humble part of that great power

    Which always means evil, always does good.

FAUST. Those riddling words mean what, I'd like to know.   1370

MEPHISTO. I am the spirit that says no, no,

    Always! And how right I am! For surely

    It's right that everything that comes to be

    Should cease to be. And so they do. Still better

    Would be nothing ever was. Hence sin

    And havoc and ruin—all you call evil, in sum—

    For me's the element in which I swim.

FAUST. A part, you say? You look like the whole works to me.

MEPHISTO. I say what's so, it isn't modesty—

    Man in his world of self's a fool,   1380

    He likes to think he's all in all.

    I'm part of the part which was all at first,

    A part of the dark out of which light burst,

    Arrogant light which now usurps the air

And seeks to thrust Night from her ancient chair,
To no avail. Since light is one with all
Things bodily, making them beautiful,
Streams from them, from them is reflected,
Since light by matter's manifested—
When by degrees all matter's burnt up and no more.   1390
Why, then light shall not matter any more.

FAUST. Oh, now I understand your office:
Since you can't wreck Creation wholesale,
You're going at it bit by bit, retail.

MEPHISTO. And making, I fear, little progress.
The opposite of nothing-at-all,
The *something*, this great shambling world,
In spite of how I exert myself against it,
Phlegmatically endures my every onset
By earthquake, fire, tidal wave and storm: 1400
Next day the land and sea again are calm.
And all that *stuff*, those animal and human species—
I can hardly make a dent in them.
The numbers I've already buried, armies!
Yet fresh troops keep on marching up again.
That's how it is, it's enough to drive you crazy!
From air, from water, from the earth
Seeds innumerable sprout forth
In dry and wet and cold and warm!
If I hadn't kept back fire for myself,   1410
What the devil could I call my own?

FAUST. So against the goodly, never-resting,
Beneficent creative force,
In impotent spite you ball your fist and
Try to arrest life's onward course?
Look around for work that's more rewarding,
You singular son of old Chaos!

MEPHISTO. Well, it's a subject for discussion—
    At our next meeting. Now I wish
    To go. That is, with your permission.   1420

FAUST. But why should *you* ask *me* for leave?
    We've struck up an acquaintance, we two,
    Drop in on me whenever you please.
    There's the door and there's the window,
    And ever reliable, there's the chimney.

MEPHISTO. Well . . . you see . . . an obstacle
    Keeps me from dropping *out*—so sorry!
    That witch's foot chalked on your doorsill.

FAUST. The pentagram's the difficulty?
    But if it's that that has you stopped,   1430
    How did you ever manage an entry?
    And how should a devil like you get trapped?

MEPHISTO. Well, look close and you'll see that
    A corner's open: the outward pointing
    Angle's lines don't quite meet.

FAUST. What a stroke of luck! I'm thinking
    Now you are my prisoner.
    Pure chance has put you in my power!

MEPHISTO. The poodle dashed right in, saw nothing,
    But now the case is the reverse;   1440
    The Devil can't get out of the house!

FAUST. There's the window, why don't you use it?

MEPHISTO. It's an iron law we devils can't flout,
    The way we come in we've got to go out,
    We're free as to entrée but not as to exit.

FAUST. So even in Hell there's law and order!
    I'm glad, for then a man might sign
    A contract with you gentlemen.

MEPHISTO. Whatever we promise, you get, full measure,
    There's no cutting corners, no skulduggery—   1450

But it's not a thing to be done in a hurry;
Let's save the subject for our next get-together.
And as for now, I beg you earnestly.
Release me from the spell that binds me!
FAUST. Why rush off, stay a while, do.
I'd love to hear some more from you.
MEPHISTO. Let me go now, I swear I'll come back,
Then you can ask me whatever you like.
FAUST. Trapping you was never my thought,
You trapped yourself, it's your own fault.   1460
Who's nabbed the Devil must keep a tight grip,
You don't grab him again once he gives you the slip.
MEPHISTO. Oh, all right! To please you, I
Will stay and keep you company,
Provided with my arts you let me
Entertain you in my own way.
FAUST. Delighted, go ahead. But please
Make sure those arts of yours amuse!
MEPHISTO. You'll find, my friend, your senses in one hour
More teased and roused than all the long dull year.   1470
The songs the fluttering spirits murmur in your ear,
The visions they unfold of sweet desire,
Oh they are more than just tricks meant to fool.
By Arabian scents you'll be delighted,
Your palate tickled, never sated,
The ravishing sensations you will feel!
No preparation's needed, none.
Here we are. Let the show begin!
SPIRITS.
Open, you gloomy
Vaulted ceiling above him,   1480
Let the blue ether
Look benignly in on him,

And dark cloudbanks scatter
So that all is fair for him!
Starlets are glittering.
Milder suns glowing,
Angelic troops shining
In celestial beauty
Hover past smiling,
Bending and bowing.   1490
Ardent desire
Follows them yearning;
And their robes
Veil the fields, veil the meadows,
Veil the arbors where lovers
In pensive surrender
Give themselves to each other
For ever and ever.
Arbor on arbor!
Vines clambering and twining!   1500
Their heavy clusters,
Poured into presses,
Pour out purple wines
Which descend in dark streams
Over beds of bright stones
Down the vineyards' steep slopes
To broaden to lakes
At the foot of green hills.
Birds blissfully drink there,
With beating wings sunwards soar,   1510
Soar towards the golden isles
Shimmering hazily
On the horizon,
Where we hear voices
Chorusing jubilantly,

Where we see dancers
Whirling exuberantly
Over the meadows,
Here, there and everywhere.
Some climb the heights,   1520
Some swim in the lakes,
Others float in the air—
Joying in life, all,
Beneath the paradisal
Stars glowing with love
Afar in the distance.

MEPHISTO. Asleep! Well done, my every airy youngling!
    Into a drowse you've sung him, never stumbling,
    I am in your debt for this performance.
    —As for you, sir, you were never born   1530
    To keep the Prince of Darkness down!
    Let sweet dream-shapes crowd round him in confusion,
    Drown him in a deep sea of delusion.
    But from this doorsill-magic to be freed
    A rat's tooth is the thing I need.
    No point to conjuring long-windedly,
    There's one rustling nearby, he'll soon hear me.

    The lord of flies and rats and mice,
    Of frogs and bedbugs, worms and lice,
    Commands you forth from your dark hole   1540
    To gnaw, beast, for me that doorsill
    Whereon I dab this drop of oil!
    —And there you are! Begin, begin!
    The corner that is pointing in,
    That's the one that shuts me in;
    One last crunch to clear my way.
    Now Faustus, till we meet next—dream away!

FAUST. [*Awakening*] Deceived again, am I, by tricks,
　　Those vanished spirits just a hoax,
　　A dream the Devil, nothing more,　　　　　　　　　　1550
　　The dog I took home just a cur?

FAUST'S STUDY [II]

Faust, Mephistopheles.

FAUST.　A knock, was that? Come in! Who is it this time?
MEPHISTO.　Me.
FAUST.　　　　　Come in!
MEPHISTO.　　　　　　　　You have to say it still a third time.
FAUST.
　　All right, all right—come in!
MEPHISTO.　　　　　　　　　　Good, very good!
　　We two shall get along, I see, just as we should.
　　I've come here dressed up as a Junker Why?
　　To help you drive your blues away!
　　In a scarlet suit, all over gold braid,
　　Across my shoulders a stiff silk cape,
　　A gay cock's feather in my cap,　　　　　　　　　　1560
　　At my side a gallant's bold blade—
　　And bringing you advice that's short and sweet:
　　Put fine clothes on like me, cut loose a bit,
　　Be free and easy, man, throw off your yoke
　　And find out what real life is like.
FAUST.　In any clothes, I'd feel the misery
　　Of this cramped, suffocating life on earth.
　　I'm too old to live for amusement only,
　　Too young to wish for nothing, wait for death.
　　The world—what has it got to say to me?　　　　　　1570

Renounce all that you long for, all—renounce!
That's the truth that all pronounce
So sagely, so interminably,
The non-stop croak, the universal chant:
You can't have what you want, you can't!
I awake each morning, how? Horrified,
On the verge of tears, to confront a day
Which at its close will not have satisfied
One smallest wish of mine, not one. Why,
Even the hope of a bit of pleasure, some pleasantness,   1580
Withers in the atmosphere of mean–spirited fault–finding,
My lively nature's quick inventiveness
Is thwarted by cares that seem to have no ending.
And when the night draws on and all is hushed,
I go to bed not soothed at last, but apprehensively,
Well knowing what awaits me is not rest,
But wild and whirling dreams that terrify me.
The god who who dwells inside my breast,
Able to stir me to my depths, so powerfully,
The master strength of all my strengths,   1590
Is impotent to effect a single thing outside me.
And so I find existence burdensome, wretched,
Death eagerly desired, my life hated.
MEPHISTO. Yet the welcome men give death is never wholehearted.
FAUST. Happy the man, even as he conquers gloriously,
    Death sets the blood-stained laurel on his brows,
    Happy the man, after dancing the night through furiously,
    Death finds him in a girl's arms in a drowse.
    If only, overwhelmed by the Spirit's power,
    In raptures I had died right then and there!   1600
MEPHISTO. And yet that very night, I seem to remember,
    A fellow didn't down a drink I saw him prepare.
FAUST. Spying around, I see, is what you like to do.

MEPHISTO. I don't know everything, but I know a thing
    or two.
FAUST. If a sweet, familiar harmony
    When I was staggering, staggered me,
    Beguiled what's left of childhood feeling
    From a time when all was gay and smiling—
    Well, never again, I pronounce a curse on
    All false and flattering persuasion,   1610
    All tales that cheat the soul, constrain
    It to endure this house of pain.
    First I curse man's mind for thinking
    Much too well of itself; I curse
    The show of things, so dazzling, glittering,
    That assails us through our every sense;
    Our dreams of fame, of our name's enduring,
    Oh what a sham, I curse them too;
    I curse as hollow all our having,
    Curse wife and child, peasant and plow;   1620
    I curse Mammon when he incites us
    With dreams of treasure to reckless deeds,
    Or plumps the cushions for our pleasure
    As we lie lazily at ease;
    Curse comfort sucked out of the grape,
    Curse love on its pinnacle of bliss,
    Curse faith, so false, curse all vain hope,
    And patience most of all I curse!
SPIRIT CHORUS. [*Invisible*]
        Pity, oh pity!
        Now you have done it—   1630
        Spoiled
        The lovely world!
        One mighty blow
        And down it falls

Smashed
By demigod's fist.
We sweep the rubble
Away into nothing,
And mourn
The beauty gone.   1640
Omnificent
Son of the earth,
Rebuild it,
Magnificent,
Inside your heart,
With a clear head and strong,
Singing a new song.
Come,
Make a fresh start!

MEPHISTO. Lesser ones, these are   1650
   Of my order,
   Active be, cheerful,
   Is their sage counsel.
   Out of your loneliness,
   Weak–blooded languidness,
   Their voices draw you
   Into the wide world before you.

   Stop making love to your misery,
   It eats away at you like a vulture!
   Even in the meanest company   1660
   You'd feel a man like any other.
   Not that I'm proposing to
   Thrust you down among the rabble.
   I'm not your grandest devil, no.
   But still, throw in with me—that way, united,
   Together life's long road we'll travel,

And my, how I would be delighted!
I'll do your will as if my will,
Every wish of yours fulfill,
By your leave   1670
Be your bond servant, be your slave.

FAUST. And in return what must I do?

MEPHISTO. There's plenty of time for that, forget it.

FAUST. No, no, the Devil must have his due,
He doesn't do things for the hell of it,
Just to see another fellow through.
So let's hear the terms, what the fine print is,
Having you for a servant's a tricky business.

MEPHISTO. I promise, I will serve your wishes—here,
A slave who does your bidding faithfully;   1680
But if we meet each other—there,
Why, you must do the same for me.

FAUST. That "there" of yours—it doesn't scare me off;
If you pull this world down about my ears,
Let the other one come on, who cares?
My joys are part and parcel of this earth,
It's under this sun that I suffer,
And once it's goodbye, last leave taken,
Then let whatever happens happen,
And that is that. About the hereafter   1690
We have had enough palaver,
More than I want to hear, by far:
If still we love and hate each other,
If some stand high and some stand lower,
Et cetera, et cetera.

MEPHISTO. In that case, an agreement's easy.
Come, dare it! Come, your signature!
Oh, how my tricks will tickle your fancy!
I'll show you things no man has seen before.

FAUST. You poor devil, really, what have you got to offer?   1700
    The mind of man in its sublime endeavor,
    Tell me, have you ever understood it?
    Oh yes indeed, you've bread, and when I eat it
    I'm hungry still; you've yellow gold—it's flighty,
    Quicksilver-like it's gone and my purse empty;
    Games of chance no man can win at, ever;
    Girls who wind me in their arms, their lover,
    While eyeing up a fresh one over my shoulder;
    There's fame, last failing of a noble nature,
    It shoots across the sky a second, then it's over.   1710
    Oh yes, do show me fruit that rots as you try
    To pick it, trees whose leaves bud daily, daily die!
MEPHISTO. Marvels like that? For a devil, not so daunting,
    I'm good for whatever you have in mind.
    —But friend, the day comes when you find
    A share of your own in life's good things,
    And peace and quiet, are what you're wanting.
FAUST. If ever you see me loll at ease,
    Then it's all yours, you can have it, my life!
    If ever you fool me with flatteries   1720
    Into feeling satisfied with myself,
    Or tempt me with visions of luxuries,
    That's it, the last day that I breathe this air,
    I'll bet you!
MEPHISTO.   Done! A bet!
FAUST.   A bet! I swear!
    If ever I plead with the passing moment,
    "Linger a while, you are so fair!"
    Then chain me up in close confinement,
    Then serving me no more's your care,
    Then let the death bell toll my finish,
    Then unreluctantly I'll perish,   1730

The clock may stop, the hands fall off,
And time for me be over with!

MEPHISTO. Think twice. Forgetting's not a thing we do.

FAUST. Of course, quite right—a bet's a bet,
This isn't anything I'm rushing into.
But if I stagnate, fall into a rut,
I'm a slave, no matter who to,
To this one, that one, or to you.

MEPHISTO. My service starts now—no procrastinating!—
At the dinner tonight for the just-made Ph.D.s.   1740
But there's one thing: you know, for emergencies,
I'd like to have our arrangement down in writing.

FAUST. In black and white you want it, pedant!
You've never learnt a *man's* word's your best warrant?
It's not enough for you that I'm committed
By what I promise till the end of days?
—Yet the world's a flood sweeps all along before it,
And why should I feel my word holds always?
A strange idea, but that's the way we are,
And who would want it otherwise?   1750
That man's blessed who keeps his conscience clear,
He'll regret no sacrifice,
But parchment signed and stamped and sealed,
Is a bogey all recoil from, scared.
The pen does in the living word,
Only sealing wax and vellum count, honor must yield.
Base spirit, say what you require!
Brass or marble, parchment or paper?
Shall I use a quill, a stylus, chisel?
I leave it up to you, you devil!   1760

MEPHISTO. Why get so hot, make extravagant speeches?
Ranting away does no good.

A scrap of paper takes care of the business.
And sign it with a drop of blood.
FAUST. Oh, all right. If that's what makes you happy,
    I'll go along with the tomfoolery.
MEPHISTO. Blood's a very special ink, you know.
FAUST. Are you afraid that I won't keep our bargain?
    With every inch of me I'll strive, I'll never slacken!
    So I've promised, that's what I will do.   1770
    I had ideas too big for me,
    Your level's mine, that's all I'm good for.
    The Spirit laughed derisively,
    Nature won't allow me near her.
    Thinking's done with for me, I'm through,
    Learning I've loathed since long ago.
    —Then fling ourselves into the dance
    Of sensual extravagance!
    Bring on your miracles, each one,
    Inscrutably veiled in your sorcery!   1780
    We'll plunge into time's racing current,
    The vortex of activity,
    Where pleasure and distress,
    Setbacks and success,
    May come as they come, by turn-about, however;
    To be always up and doing is man's nature.
MEPHISTO. No limits restrain you, do just as you like,
    A little taste here, a nibble, a lick,
    You see something there, snatch it up on the run,
    Let all that you do with gusto be done,   1790
    Only don't be bashful, wade right in.
FAUST. I told you, I'm not out to enjoy myself, have fun,
    I want frenzied excitements, gratifications that are painful,
    Love and hatred violently mixed,

Anguish that enlivens, inspiriting trouble;
Cured of my thirst to know at last,
I'll never again shun anything distressful.
From now on my wish is to undergo
All that men everywhere undergo, their whole portion,
Make mine their heights and depths, their weal and woe,   1800
Everything human encompass in my single person,
And so enlarge my one self to embrace theirs, all,
And shipwreck with them when at last we shipwreck, all.

MEPHISTO. Believe me, I have chewed and chewed
At that tough meat, mankind, since long ago,
From birth to death work at it, still that food
Is indigestible as sourdough.
Only a God can take in all of them,
The whole lot, for He dwells in eternal light,
While we poor devils are stuck down below   1810
In darkness and gloom, lacking even candlelight,
And all *you* qualify for is, half day, half night.

FAUST. Nevertheless I will!

MEPHISTO.   All right, all right.
Still, one thing worries me.
The time allotted you is very short,
But art has always been around and shall be,
So listen, hear what is my thought:
Hire a poet, learn by his instruction.
Let the good gentleman search his mind
By careful, persevering reflection,   1820
And every noble trait he can find,
Heap on your head, his honored creation:
          The lion's fierceness,
          Mild hart's swiftness,
          Italian fieriness,
          Northern steadiness.

Let him master for you the diffcult feat
Of combining magnanimity with deceit,
How, driven by youthful impulsiveness, unrestrained,
To fall in love as beforehand planned.   1830
Such a creature—my, I'd love to know him!—
I'd call him Mr. Microcosm.

FAUST. What am I, then, if it can never be:
The realization of all human possibility,
That crown my soul so avidly reaches for?

MEPHISTO. In the end you are—just what you are.
Wear wigs high-piled with curls, oh millions,
Stick your legs in yard-high hessians,
You're still you, the one you always were.

FAUST. I feel it now, how pointless my long grind   1840
To make mine all the treasures of man's mind;
When I sit back and interrogate my soul,
No new powers answer to my call;
I'm not a hair's breadth more in height,
A step nearer to the infinite.

MEPHISTO. The way you see things, my dear Faust,
Is superficial—I speak frankly.
If you go on repining weakly,
We'll lose our seat at life's rich feast.
Hell, man, you have hands and feet,   1850
A headpiece and a pair of balls,
And savors from fruit fresh and sweet,
That pleasure's yours, entirely yours.
If I've six studs, a sturdy span,
That horsepower's mine, my property,
My coach bowls on, ain't I the man.
Two dozen legs I've got for me!
    Sir, come on, quit all that thinking,
Into the world, the pair of us!

The man who lives in his head only's   1860
Like a donkey in the rough
Led round and round by the bad fairies,
While green grass grows a stone's throw off.
FAUST. And how do we begin?
MEPHISTO.   By clearing out—just leaving.
A torture chamber this place is, and that's the truth.
You call it living, to be boring
Yourself and your young men to death?
Leave that to Dr. Bacon Fat next door!
Why toil and moil at threshing heaps of straw?
Anyhow, the deepest knowledge you possess   1870
You daren't let on to before your class.
—Oh now I hear one in the passageway!
FAUST. I can't see him—tell him to go away.
MEPHISTO. The poor boy's been so patient, don't be cross;
We mustn't let him leave here *désolé*.
Let's have your cap and gown, Herr Doctor.
Won't I look the fine professor!
[*Changes clothes.*]
Count on me to know just what to say!
Fifteen minutes's all I need for it—
Meanwhile get ready for our little junket!   1880

                                        Exit Faust.

MEPHISTO. [*Wearing Faust's gown*] Despise learning, heap contempt
        on reason,
The human race's best possession,
Only let the lying spirit draw you
Over into mumbo-jumbo,
Make-believe and pure illusion—
And then you're mine for sure, I have you,
No matter what we just agreed to.

    Fate's given him a spirit knows no measure,

On and on it strives, relentlessly,
It soars away disdaining every pleasure,   1890
Yet I will drag him deep into debauchery
Where all proves shallow, meaningless,
I'll have him writhing, ravening, berserk;
Before his lips' insatiable greediness
I'll dangle food and drink; he'll shriek
In vain for relief from his torturing dryness!
And even if he weren't the Devil's already,
He'd still be sure to perish miserably.

           [Enter a student.]

STUDENT. Allow me, sir, but I am a beginner
And come in quest of an adviser,   1900
One whom all the people here
Greatly esteem, indeed revere.
MEPHISTO. I thank you for your courtesy.
But I'm a man, as you can see,
Like any other. I wonder, shouldn't you look further?
STUDENT. It's you, sir, you, I want for adviser!
I came here full of youthful zeal,
Eager to learn everything worthwhile.
Mother cried to see me go;
I've got an allowance, it's small, but will do.   1910
MEPHISTO. You've come to the right place, my son.
STUDENT. But I'm ready to turn right around and run!
It seems so sad inside these walls,
My heart misgives me. I find all's
Confined, shut in, there's nothing green,
Not even a single tree, to be seen.
I can't, on the bench in the lecture hall,
Hear or see or think at all!
MEPHISTO. It's a matter of getting used to things first.
An infant starts out fighting the breast,   1920

But soon it's feeding lustily.
Just so your appetite'll sharpen by the day
The more you nurse at Wisdom's bosom.
STUDENT. I'll cling tight to her bosom, happily,
    But where do I find her, by what way?
MEPHISTO. First of all, then—have you chosen
    A faculty?
STUDENT.   Oh well, you see,
    I'd like to be a learned man.
    The earth below, the heavens on high—
    All those things I long to understand,   1930
    All the sciences, all nature.
MEPHISTO. You've got the right idea; however,
    It demands close application.
STUDENT. Oh never fear, I'm in this heart and soul;
    But still, a fellow gets so dull
    Without time off for recreation,
    In the long and lovely days of summer.
MEPHISTO. Time slips away so fast you need to use it
    Rationally, and not abuse it.
    And for that reason I advise you: 1940
    The Principles of Logic *primo*!
    We will drill your mind by rote,
    Strap it in the Spanish boot
    So it never shall forget
    The road that's been marked out for it
    And stray about incautiously,
    A will-o'-the-wisp, this way, that way.
    Day after day you'll be taught
    All you once did just like that,
    Like eating and drinking, thoughtlessly,   1950
    Now needs a methodology—
    Order and system: *A, B, C!*

Our thinking instrument behaves
Like a loom: every thread,
At a step on the treadle's set in motion,
Back and forth the shuttle's sped,
The strands flow too fast for the eye,
A blow of the batten and there's cloth, woven!
Now enter your philosopher, he
Proves all is just as it should be: 1960
A being thus and *B* also,
Then *C* and *D* inevitably follow;
And if there were no *A* and *B*,
There'd never be a *C* and *D*.
They're struck all of a heap, his admiring hearers,
But still, it doesn't make them weavers.
How do you study something living?
Drive out the spirit, deny it being,
So there're just parts with which to deal,
Gone is what binds it all, the soul.   1970
With lifeless pieces as the only things real,
The wonder's where's the life of the whole—
Encheiresis naturae, the chemists then call it,
Make fools of themselves and never know it.

STUDENT. I have trouble following what you say.
MEPHISTO. You'll get the hang of it by and by
    When you learn to distinguish and classify.
STUDENT. How stupid all this makes me feel;
    It spins around in my head like a wheel.
MEPHISTO. Next metaphysics, a vital part   1980
    Of scholarship, its very heart.
    Exert your faculties to venture
    Beyond the boundaries of our nature,
    Gain intelligence the brain
    Has difficulty taking in,

And whether it goes in or not,
There's always a big word for it.
    Be very sure, your first semester,
To do things right, attend each lecture;
Five of them you'll have daily,   1990
Be in your seat when the bell peals shrilly;
Come to class with your homework done,
The sections memorized, each one,
So you are sure nothing's mistook
And nothing's said not in the book.
Still, note down all, not one word lost,
As if it came from the Holy Ghost.
STUDENT. No need to say that to me twice,
    They help a lot, notes do, all right.
    What you've got down in black and white   2000
    Goes home with you, to a safe place.
MEPHISTO. But your faculty—you've still not told me.
STUDENT. Well, I don't believe the law would hold me.
MEPHISTO. I can't blame you, law is no delight.
    What's jurisprudence?—a stupid rite
    That's handed down, a kind of contagion,
    From generation to generation,
    From people to people, region to region.
    Good sense is treated as nonsensical,
    Benefactions as a botheration.   2010
    O future grandsons, how I wince for you all!
    As for the rights with which we're born—
    Not a word!—as if they were unknown.
STUDENT. I hate the stuff now more than ever!
    How lucky I am to have you for adviser.
    Perhaps I'll take theology.
MEPHISTO. I shouldn't want to lead you astray,
    But it's a science, if you'll allow me to say it,

Where it's easy to lose your way.
There's so much poison hidden in it   2020
It's very nearly impossible
To tell what's toxic from what's medicinal.
Here again it's safer to choose
One single master and echo his words dutifully—
As a general rule, put your trust in *words*,
They'll guide you safely past doubt and dubiety
Into the Temple of Absolute Certainty.

STUDENT. But shouldn't words convey ideas, a meaning?

MEPHISTO. Of course they should! But why overdo it?
It's exactly when ideas are wanting,   2030
Words come in so handy as a substitute.
With words we argue pro and con,
With words invent a whole system.
Believe in words! Have faith in them!
No jot or tittle shall pass from them.

STUDENT. Forgive me, I've another query,
My last one and then I'll go.
Medicine, sir—what might you care to tell me
About that study I should know?
Three years, my God, are terribly short   2040
For so vast a field for the mind to survey.
A pointer or two would provide a start
And advance one quicker on one's way.

MEPHISTO. [*Aside*] Enough of all this academic chatter,
Back again to devilry!
[*Aloud*] Medicine's an easy art to master.
Up and down you study the whole world
Only so as to discover
In the end it's all up to the Lord.
Plough your way through all the sciences you please,   2050
Each learns only what he can,

But the man who understands his opportunities,
Him I call a man.
You seem a pretty strapping fellow,
Not one to hang back bashfully,
If you don't doubt yourself, I know,
Nobody else will doubt you, nobody.
Above all learn your way with women
If you mean to practise medicine.
The aches and pains that torture them   2060
From one place only, one, all stem—
Cure there, cure all. Act halfway decent
And you'll find the whole sex acquiescent.
With an M.D. you enjoy great credit,
Your art, they're sure, beats others' arts;
The doctor, when he pays a visit,
For greeting reaches for those parts
It takes a layman years to come at;
You feel her pulse with extra emphasis
And your arm slipping with an ardent glance   2070
Around her slender waist,
See if it's because she's so tight-laced.
STUDENT. Oh, that's much better—practical, down to earth!
MEPHISTO. All theory, my dear boy, is gray,
And green the golden tree of life.
STUDENT. I swear it seems a dream to me!
Would you permit me, sir, to impose on
Your generous kindness another day
And drink still more draughts of your wisdom?
MEPHISTO. I'm glad to help you in any way.   2080
STUDENT. I mustn't leave without presenting
You my album. Do write something
In it for me, would you?

MEPHISTO. Happily.

[*Writes and hands back the album.*]

STUDENT. [*Reading*] *Eritis sicut Deus, scientes bonum et malum.*

[*Closes the book reverently and exits.*]

MEPHISTO. Faithfully follow that good old verse,

    That favorite line of my aunt's, the snake,

    And for all your precious godlikeness

    You'll end up how? A nervous wreck.

Enter Faust.

FAUST. And now where to?

MEPHISTO. Wherever you like.

    First we'll mix with little people, then with great,   2090

    The pleasure and the profit you will get

    From our course—and never pay tuition for it.

FAUST. But me and my long beard—we're hardly suited

    For the fast life. I feel myself defeated

    Even before we start. I've never been

    A fellow to fit in. Among other men

    I feel so small, so mortified—I freeze.

    Oh, in the world I'm always ill at ease!

MEPHISTO. My friend, that's all soon changed, it doesn't matter;

    With confidence comes *savoir-vivre.*   2100

FAUST. But how do we get out of here?

    Where are your horses, groom and carriage?

MEPHISTO. By air's how we make our departure,

    On my cloak—you'll enjoy the voyage.

    But take care, on so bold a venture,

    You're sparing in the matter of luggage.

    I'll heat some gas, that way we'll rise up

    Quickly off the face of earth;

    If we're light enough we'll lift right up—

    I offer my congratulations, sir, on your new life!   2110

AUERBACH'S CELLAR IN LEIPZIG

Drinkers carousing.

FROSCH. Faces glum and glasses empty?
　　I don't call this much of a party.
　　You fellows seem wet straw tonight
　　Who always used to blaze so bright.
BRANDER. It's your fault—he just sits there, hardly speaks!
　　Where's the horseplay, where're the dirty jokes?
FROSCH. [*Emptying a glass of wine on his head*]
　　There! Both at once!
BRANDER.　　　　　　　O horse and swine!
FROSCH. You asked for it, so don't complain.
SIEBEL. Out in the street if you want to punch noses!
　　—Now take a deep breath and roar out a chorus   2120
　　In praise of the grape and the jolly god Bacchus.
　　Come, all together with a rollicking round-o!
ALTMAYER. Stop, stop, man, I'm wounded, cotten, quick, someone
　　　　fetch some,
　　The terrible fellow has burst me an eardrum!
SIEBEL. Hear the sound rumble above in the vault?
　　That tells you you're hearing the true bass note.
FROSCH. That's right! Out the door, whoever don't like it!
　　With a do-re-mi,
ALTMAYER. And a la-ti-do,
FROSCH. We will have us a concert!   2130
　　[*Sings.*]
　　　　Our dear Holy Roman Empire,
　　　　How does the damn thing hold together?
BRANDER. Oh, but that's dreadful, and dreadfully sung,
　　A dreary, disgusting *political* song!

Thank the Lord when you wake each morning
You're not the one must keep the Empire running.
It's a blessing I'm grateful for
To be neither Kaiser nor Chancellor.
But we, too, need a chief for our group
So let's elect ourselves a pope.   2140
To all of us here I'm sure it's well known
What a man must do to sit on that throne.

FROSCH. [*Singing*]

>   Nightingale, fly away, o'er lawn, o'er bower,
>   Tell her I love her ten thousand times over.

SIEBEL. Enough of that love stuff, it turns my stomach.

FROSCH. Ten thousand times, though it drives you frantic!
[*Sings.*]

>   Unbar the door, the night is dark!
>   Unbar the door, my love, awake!
>   Bar up the door now it's daybreak.

SIEBEL. Go on, then, boast about her charms, her favor,   2150
But I will have the latest laugh of all.
She played me false—just wait, she'll play you falser.
A horned imp's what I wish her, straight from Hell,
To dawdle with her in the dust of crossroads;
And may an old goat stinking from the Brocken
Bleat "Goodnight, dearie," to her, galloping homewards.
A fellow made of honest flesh and blood
For a slut like that is much too good.
What kind of love note would I send that scarecrow?—
A beribboned rock tossed through her kitchen window.   2160

BRANDER. [*Banging on the table*]

Good fellows, your attention! None here will deny
I know what should be done and shouldn't at all.
Now we have lovers in our company
Whom we must treat in manner suitable

To their condition, our jollity,
With a song just lately written. So mind the air
And come in on the chorus loud and clear!
[*He sings.*]
>   A rat lived downstairs in the cellar,
>   Dined every day on lard and butter,
>   His paunch grew round as any burgher's,   2170
>   As round as Dr. Martin Luther's.
>   The cook put poison down for it.
>   Oh, how it groaned, the pangs it felt,
>   *As if by Cupid smitten.*

CHORUS. [*Loud and clear*]
>   *As if by Cupid smitten!*

BRANDER.
>   It rushed upstairs, it raced outdoors
>   And drank from every gutter,
>   It gnawed the woodwork, scratched the floors,
>   Its fever burned still hotter.
>   In agony it hopped and squealed,   2180
>   Oh, piteously the beast appealed,
>   *As if by Cupid smitten.*

CHORUS.
>   *As if by Cupid smitten!*

BRANDER.
>   Its torment drove it, in broad day.
>   Out into the kitchen,
>   Collapsing on the hearth, it lay
>   Panting hard and twitching.
>   But that cruel Borgia smiled with pleasure,
>   That's it, that's that rat's final seizure,
>   *As if by Cupid smitten.*   2190

CHORUS.
>   *As if by Cupid smitten!*

SIEBEL. You find it funny, you coarse louts,
    Oh, quite a stunt, so very cunning,
    To put down poison for poor rats!
BRANDER. You like rats, do you, find them charming?
ALTMAYER. O big of gut and bald of pate!
    Losing out's subdued the oaf;
    What he sees in the bloated rat
    'S the spitting image of himself.
        [*Faust and Mephistopheles enter.*]
MEPHISTO. What your case calls for, Doctor, first,   2200
    Is some diverting company,
    To teach you life affords some gaiety.
    For these men every night's a feast
    And every day a holiday;
    With little wit but lots of zest
    All spin inside their little orbit
    Like young cats chasing their own tails.
    As long as the landlord grants them credit
    And they are spared a splitting headache.
    They find life good, unburdened by travails.   2210
BRANDER. They're travelers is what your Brander says,
    You can tell it by their foreign ways,
    They've not been here, I'll bet, an hour.
FROSCH. Right, right! My Leipzig's an attraction, how I love her,
    A little Paris spreading light and culture!
SIEBEL. Who might they be? What's your guess?
FROSCH. Leave it to me. I'll fill their glass,
    Gently extract, as you do a baby's tooth,
    All there's to know about them, the whole truth.
    I'd say we're dealing with nobility,   2220
    They look so proud, so dissatisfied, to me.
BRANDER. They're pitchmen at the Fair, is what I think.
ALTMAYER. Maybe so.

FROSCH.   Now watch me go to work.

MEPHISTO. [*To Faust*]

    These dolts can't ever recognize Old Nick

    Even when he's got them by the neck.

FAUST. Gentlemen, good day.

SIEBEL.   Thank you, the same.

    [*Aside, obliquely studying Mephistopheles*]

    What the hell, the fellow limps, he's lame!

MEPHISTO. We'd like to join you, sirs, if you'll allow it.

    But our landlord's wine looks so-so, I am thinking,

    So the company shall make up for it.   2230

ALTMAYER. Particular, you are, about your drinking?

FROSCH. Fresh from Dogpatch, right? From supper

    On cabbage soup with Goodman Clodhopper?

MEPHISTO. We couldn't stop on this trip, more's the pity!

    But last time he went on so tenderly

    About his Leipzig kith and kin.

    And sent his very best to you, each one.

                                    Bowing to Frosch.

ALTMAYER. [*Aside to Frosch*]

    Score one for him. He's got some wit.

SIEBEL. A sly one, he is.

FROSCH.   Wait, I'll fix him yet!

MEPHISTO. Unless I err, weren't we just now hearing   2240

    Some well-schooled voices joined in choral singing?

    Voices, I am sure, must resonate

    Inside this vault to very fine effect.

FROSCH. You know music professionally, I think.

MEPHISTO. Oh no—the spirit's eager, but the voice is weak.

ALTMAYER. Give us a song!

MEPHISTO.   Whatever you'd like to hear.

SIEBEL. A new one, nothing we've heard before.

MEPHISTO. Easily done. We've just come back from Spain,

Land where the air breathes song, the rivers run wine.
[*Sings.*]

> Once upon a time a King   2250
>   Had a flea, a big one—

FROSCH. Did you hear that? A flea, goddamn!
I'm all for fleas, myself, I am.

MEPHISTO. [*Sings*]

> Once upon a time a King
>   Had a flea, a big one,
> Doted fondly on the thing
>   With fatherly affection.
> Calling his tailor in, he said,
>   Fetch needles, thread and scissors,
> Measure the Baron up for shirts,   2260
>   Measure him, too, for trousers.

BRANDER. And make it perfectly clear to the tailor
He must measure exactly, sew perfect stitches,
If he's fond of his head, not the least little error, ·
Not a wrinkle, you hear, not one, in those breeches!

MEPHISTO.

> Glowing satins, gleaming silks
>   Now were the flea's attire,
> Upon his chest red ribbons crossed
>   And a great star shone like fire,
> In sign of his exalted post   2270
>   As the King's First Minister.
> His sisters, cousins, uncles, aunts
>   Enjoyed great influence too—
> The bitter torments that that Court's
>   Nobility went through!
> And the Queen as well, and her lady's-maid,
>   Though bitten till delirious.
> Forbore to squash the fleas, afraid

> To incur the royal animus.
> But we free souls, we squash all fleas   2280
> The instant they light on us!

CHORUS. [*Loud and clear*]
> *But we free souls, we squash all fleas*
> *The instant they light on us!*

FROSCH. Bravo, bravo! That was fine!

SIEBEL. May every flea's fate be the same!

BRANDER. Between finger and nail, then crack! and they're done for.

ALTMAYER. Long live freedom, long live wine!

MEPHISTO. I'd gladly drink a glass in freedom's honor,
> If only your wine looked a little better.

SIEBEL. Again! You try, sir, our good humor.   2290

MEPHISTO. I'm sure our landlord wouldn't take it kindly.
> For otherwise I'd treat this company
> To wine that's wine—straight out of our own cellar.

SIEBEL. Go on, go on, let the landlord be my worry.

FROSCH. You're princes, you are, if you're able
> To put good wine upon the table;
> But a drop or two, hell, that's no trial at all,
> To judge right what I need's a real mouthful.

ALTMAYER. [*In an undertone*] They're from the Rhineland.
> I would swear.

MEPHISTO. Let's have an auger, please.

BRANDER.   What for?   2300
> Don't tell me you've barrels piled outside the door!

ALTMAYER. There's a basket of tools—look, over there.

MEPHISTO. [*Picking out an auger, to Frosch*]
> Now gentlemen, name what you'd have, please.

FROSCH. What do you mean? We have a choice?

MEPHISTO. Whatever you wish. I will produce.

ALTMAYER. [*To Frosch*] Licking his lips already, he is!

FROSCH. Fine, fine! For me—a Rhine wine any day.
   The best stuff's from the fatherland, I say.
MEPHISTO. [*Boring a hole in the table edge at Frosch's place*]
   Some wax to stop the holes with, quick!
ALTMAYER. Hell, it's just a sideshow trick.   2310
MEPHISTO. [*To Brander*]
   And you?
BRANDER.   The best champagne you have, friend, please,
   With lots of sparkle, lots of fizz.

   [*Mephistopheles goes round the table boring holes at all the
   places, which one of the drinkers stops with bungs made of wax.*]

   You can't always avoid what's foreign,
   About pleasure I'm nonpartisan.
   A man who's a true German can't stand Frenchmen,
   But he can stand their wine, oh yes he can!
SIEBEL. [*As Mephistopheles reaches his place*]
   I confess your dry wines don't
   Please me, sweet is what I want.
MEPHISTO. Tokay for you! Coming up shortly!
ALTMAYER. No, fellows, slow down, just look at it calmly—   2320
   The whole thing's meant to make fools of us.
MEPHISTO. Ei me! With noble guests such as you are,
   That would be going a bit far.
   Do you imagine I'd be so obtuse?
   So what's your pleasure, I'm waiting—speak.
ALTMAYER. Whatever you like, just don't take all week.
MEPHISTO. [*All the holes are now bored and stopped; gesturing
      grotesquely*]
   Grapes grow on the vine,
   Horns on the head of the goat,

O vinestock of hard wood,
O juice of the tender grape!   2330
And a wooden table shall,
When summoned, yield wine as well!
O depths of Nature, mysterious, secret,
Here is a miracle—if you believe it!
Now pull the plugs, all, drink and be merry!
ALL. [*Drawing the bungs and the wine each drinker asked for gushing
      into his glass*]
Sweet fountain, flowing for us only!
MEPHISTO. But take good care you don't spill any.
[*They drink glass after glass.*]
ALL. [*Singing*]
Lovely, oh lovely, I must be dreaming!
A party so cannabalistically cozy—
Five hundred pigs swilling slops!   2340
MEPHISTO. The people are free! What a time they're having!
FAUST. I'd like to go now. Nincompoops!
MEPHISTO. Before we do, you must admire
Their swinishness in all its splendor.
SIEBEL. [*Spilling wine on the floor, where it bursts into flame*]
All Hell's afire, I burn, I burn!
MEPHISTO. [*Conjuring the flame*]
Peace, my own element, down, down!
[*To the drinkers*]
Only a pinch, for the present, of the purgatorial fire.
SIEBEL. What's going on here? For this you'll pay dear!
You don't seem to know the kind of men you have here.
FROSCH. Once is enough for that kind of business!   2350
ALTMAYER. Throw him out on his ear, but quietly, no fuss!
SIEBEL. You've got your nerve, trying out upon us
Stuff like that—damned hocus-pocus!
MEPHISTO. Quiet, you tub of guts!

SIEBEL.   Bean pole, you!

Now he insults us. I know what to do.

BRANDER. A taste of our fists is what: one-two, one-two.

ALTMAYER. [*Drawing a bung and flames shooting out at him*]

I'm on fire, I'm on fire!

SIEBEL.   It's witchcraft, no mistaking!

Stick him, the rogue, he's free for the taking!

[*They draw their knives and fall on Mephistopheles.*]

MEPHISTO. [*Gesturing solemnly*]

    False words, false shapes

    Addle wits, muddle senses!   2360

    Let here and otherwheres

    Exchange places!

[*All stand astonished and gape at each other.*]

ALTMAYER. Where am I? What a lovely country!

FROSCH. Such vineyards! Do my eyes deceive me?

SIEBEL. And grapes you only need to reach for!

BRANDER. Just look inside this green arbor!

What vines, what grapes! Cluster on cluster!

[*He seizes Siebel by the nose. The others do the same to each other, and raise their knives.*]

MEPHISTO. Unspell, illusion, eyes and ears!

—Take note the Devil's a jester, my dears!

[*He vanishes with Faust; the drinkers recoil from each other.*]

SIEBEL. What's happened?

ALTMAYER.   What?

FROSCH.   Was that your nose?   2370

BRANDER. [*To Siebel*] And I'm still holding on to yours!

ALTMAYER. The shock I felt—in every limb!

Get me a chair, I'm caving in.

FROSCH. What happened? That man, and his wine—so strange!

SIEBEL. If only I could lay hands on that scoundrel,
    I'd give him something in exchange!
ALTMAYER. I saw him, horsed upon a barrel,
    Vault straight out through the cellar door—
    My feet feel leaden, so unnatural.
    [*Turning toward the table.*]
    Well—maybe some wine's still trickling here.   2380
SIEBEL. Lies, all lies! Deluded! Dupes!
FROSCH. I was drinking wine, I'd swear.
BRANDER. But what was it with all those grapes?
ALTMAYER. Now try and tell me, you know-it-alls,
    There's no such thing as miracles!

WITCH'S KITCHEN

*A low hearth, and on the fire a large cauldron. In the steam rising
up from it, various figures can be glimpsed. A she-ape is seated by the
cauldron, skimming it to keep it from boiling over. The male with their
young crouches close by, warming himself. Hanging on the walls and
from the ceiling are all sorts of strange objects, the household gear of a
witch.*

Faust, Mephistopheles.

FAUST. Why, it's revolting, all this crazy witchery!
    Are you telling me that I'll be born a new man
    Here amid this lunatic confusion?
    Is an ancient hag the doctor who will cure me?
    And the mess that that beast's boiling, that's the remedy   2390
    To cancel thirty years, unbow my back?
    If you can do no better, the outlook's black

For me, the hopes I nursed are dead already.
Hasn't man's venturesome mind, instructed by Nature,
Discovered some sort of potent elixer?

MEPHISTO. Now you're speaking sensibly!
There is a natural way to recover your youth;
But that's another business entirely
And not your sort of thing, is my belief.

FAUST. No, no, come on, I want to hear it.   2400

MEPHISTO. All right. It's simple: you don't need to worry
About money, doctors, necromancy.
Go out into the fields right now, this minute,
Start digging and hoeing, with never a stop or respite,
Confine yourself and your thoughts to the narrowest sphere,
Eat nothing but the plainest kind of fare,
Live with the cattle as cattle, don't think it too low
To spread your own dung on the fields that you sow.
So there you have it, the sane way, the healthy,
To keep yourself young till the age of eighty!   2410

FAUST. Yes, not my sort of thing, I'm afraid,
Humbling myself to work with a spade;
So straitened a life would never suit me.

MEPHISTO. So it's back to the witch, my friend, are we?

FAUST. That horrible hag—no one else will do?
Why can't *you* concoct the brew?

MEPHISTO. A nice thing that, to waste the time of the Devil
When his every moment is claimed by the business of evil!
Please understand. Not only skill and science
Are called for here, but also patience: 2420
A mind must keep at it for years, very quietly,
Only time can supply the mixture its potency.
Such a deal of stuff goes into the process,
All very strange, all so secret.

The Devil, it's true, taught her how to do it.

But it's no business of his to brew it.

[*Seeing the apes*]

See here, those creatures, aren't they pretty!

That one's the housemaid, that one's the flunkey.

[*To the apes*]

Madam is not at home, it seems?

APES.

        Flew up the chimney   2430

        To dine out with friends.

MEPHISTO. And her feasting, how long does it usually take her?

APES. As long as we warm our paws by the fire.

MEPHISTO. [*To Faust*] What do you think of these elegant folk?

FAUST. Noisome enough to make me choke.

MEPHISTO. Well, just this sort of causerie

    Is what I find most pleases me.

    [*To the apes*]

    Tell me, you ugly things, oh do.

    What's that you're stirring there, that brew?

APES. Beggars' soup, it's thin stuff, goes down easy.   2440

MEPHISTO. Your public's assured—they like what's wishy-washy.

HE-APE. [*Sidling up to Mephistopheles fawningly*]

        Roll, roll the dice quick,

        And this monkey make rich,

        Have himself at last luck,

        The rich have too much.

        With a few dollars and cents

        The credit I'd have for sense!

MEPHISTO. How very happy that monkey would be

    If he could buy chances in the lottery.

[*Meanwhile the young apes have been rolling around a big ball to which they now give a push forward.*]

HE-APE.

    The world, sirs, behold it!   2450
    Down goes the up side,
    Up goes the down side,
    And never a respite.
    Touch it, it'll ring,
    It's like glass, fractures easily.
    When all's said and done,
    A hollow, void thing.
    See, it shines bright here,
    Here even brighter.
    —Oops, ain't I nimble!   2460
    But you, son, be careful
    And keep a safe distance,
    Or it's your last day.
    The thing's made of clay,
    A knock, and it's fragments.

MEPHISTO. What is that sieve for?

HE-APE. [*Taking it down*]

    If you came here to thieve,
    It would be my informer.

[*He scampers across to the she-ape and has her look through it.*]

    Look through the sieve!
    Now say, do you know him?   2470
    Or you daren't name him?

MEPHISTO. [*Approaching the fire*] And this pot over here?

APES.

    Oh, you're a dolt, sir,
    Don't know what a pot's for!
    Nor a kettle neither.

MEPHISTO. What a rude creature!

HE-APE.

    Here, take this duster,

Sit down in the armchair.
[*Presses Mephistopheles down in the chair.*]
FAUST. [*Who meanwhile has been standing in front of a mirror, going
forward to peer into it from close up and then stepping back*]
What do I see? What a marvellous vision
Shows itself in this magic glass!   2480
Love, land me your wings, your swiftest to pass
Through the air to the heaven she must dwell in!
Unless I stay firmly fixed to this spot,
If I dare to move nearer the least bit,
Mist blurs the vision and obscures her quite.
Woman unrivaled, beauty absolute!
Can such things be, a creature made perfectly?
The body so indolently stretched out there
Surely epitomizes all that is heavenly.
Can such a marvel inhabit down here?   2490
MEPHISTO. Of course when a god's sweated six whole days
And himself cries bravo in his works praise,
You can be certain the results are first class.
Look all you want now in the glass,
But I can find you just such a prize,
And lucky the man, his bliss assured,
Brings home such a beauty to his bed and board.

[*Faust continues to stare into the mirror, while Mephistopheles,
leaning back comfortably in the armchair and toying with the feather
duster, talks on.*]

Here I sit like a king on a throne,
Scepter in hand, all I'm lacking's my crown.
APES. [*Who have been performing all sorts of queer, involved
movements, with loud cries bring Mephistopheles a crown*]
Here, your majesty,   2500

If you would,
Glue up the crown
With sweat and blood!

[*Their clumsy handling of the crown causes it to break in two and they cavort around with the pieces.*]

Oh no, now it's broken!
We look and we listen.
We chatter, scream curses,
And make up our verses—
FAUST. [*Still gazing raptly into the mirror*]
Good God, how my mind reels, it's going to snap!
MEPHISTO. [*Nodding toward the apes*]
My own head's starting to spin like a top.
APES.
And if by some fluke   2510
The words happen to suit
Then the rhyme makes a thought!
FAUST. [*As above*] My insides burn as if on fire!
Come on, we must get out of here.
MEPHISTO. [*Keeping his seat*] They tell the truth, these poets do.
You've got to give the creatures their due.

[*The cauldron, neglected by the she-ape, starts to boil over, causing a great tongue of flame to shoot up the chimney. The Witch comes riding down the flame, shrieking hideously.*]

THE WITCH. It hurts, it hurts!
Monkeys, apes, incompetent brutes!
Forgetting the pot and singeing your mistress—
The servants I have! Utterly useless!   2520
[*Catching sight of Faust and Mephistopheles*]

What's going on here?
Who are this pair?
What's all this about?
Sneaking in when I'm out!
Hellfire burn
Them to a turn!

[*She plunges the spoon into the cauldron and scatters fire over Faust, Mephistopheles and the apes. The apes whine.*]

MEPHISTOPHELES. [*Turning the duster upside down and hitting out violently among the glasses and jars with the butt end*]
In pieces, in pieces,
Spilt soup and smashed dishes!
It's all in fun, really—
Beating time, you old carcass,   2530
To your melody.
[*The witch starts back in rage and fear.*]
Can't recognize me, rattlebones, old donkey, you?
Can't recognize your lord and master?
Why I don't chop up you and your monkey crew
Into the littlest bits and pieces is a wonder!
No respect at all for my red doublet?
And my cock's feather means nothing to you, beldam?
Is my face masked or can you plainly see it?
Must I tell *you* of all people who I am?
THE WITCH. Oh sir, forgive my discourteous salute!   2540
But I look in vain for your cloven foot,
And your two ravens, where are they?
MEPHISTO. All right, this time you're let off—I remember
It's been so long since we've seen each other.
Also, the world's grown so cultured today,
Even the Devil's been caught up in it;

The Northern bogey has made his departure,
No horns now, no tail, to make people shiver,
And as for my hoof, though I can't do without it,
Socially it would raise too many eyebrows—   2550
So like a lot of other young fellows
I've padded my calves to try and conceal it.

THE WITCH. [*Dancing with glee*]
    I'm out of my mind with delight, I swear!
    My lord Satan's dropped out of the air.

MEPHISTO. Woman, that name—I forbid you to use it.

THE WITCH. Why not? Whyever now refuse it?

MEPHISTO. Since God knows when it belongs to mythology,
    But that's hardly improved the temper of humanity.
    The Evil One's no more, evil ones more than ever.
    Address me as Baron, that will do,   2560
    A gentleman of rank like any other,
    And if you doubt my blood is blue,
    See, here's my house's arms, the noblest ever!
    [*He makes an indecent gesture.*]

THE WITCH. [*Laughing excessively*]
    Ha, ha! It's you, I see now, it's clear—
    The same old rascal you always were!

MEPHISTO. [*To Faust*] Observe, friend, my diplomacy
    And learn the art of witch-mastery.

THE WITCH. Gentlemen, now, what is your pleasure?

MEPHISTO. A generous glass of your famous liquor,
    But please, let it be from your oldest supply;   2570
    It doubles in strength as the years multiply.

THE WITCH. At once! Here I've got, as it happens, a bottle
    From which I myself every now and then tipple,
    And what is more, it's lost all its stink.
    I'll gladly pour you out a cup.
    [*Under her breath*]

But if the fellow's unprepared, the drink
Might kill him, you know, before an hour's up.
MEPHISTO. I know the man well, he'll thrive upon it.
I wish him the best your kitchen affords.
Now draw your circle, say the right words,   2580
And pour him out a brimming goblet.

[*Making bizarre gestures, the witch draws a circle and sets down
an assortment of strange objects inside it. All the glasses start to ring
and the pots to resound, providing a kind of musical accompaniment.
Last of all, she brings out a great tome and stands the apes in the
circle to serve as a lectern and to hold up the torches. Then she signals
Faust to approach.*]

FAUST. [*To Mephistopheles*]
What can I hope for here, would you tell me?
That junk of hers, her arms waving crazily,
All the vugar tricks she's performing,
Well do I know them, I don't find them amusing.
MEPHISTO. Jokes, just jokes! It's not all that serious,
Really, you're being much too difficult.
Of course hocus-pocus! She's a sorceress—
How else can her potion produce a result?
[*He presses Faust inside the circle.*]
THE WITCH. [*Declaiming from the book, with great emphasis*]
Listen and learn!   2590
From one make ten,
And let two go,
And add three in,
And you are rich.
Now cancel four!
From five and six,
So says the witch,

Make seven and eight—
Thus all's complete.
And nine is one   2600
And ten is none
And that's the witch's one-times-one.

FAUST. I think the old woman's throwing a fit.

MEPHISTO. We're nowhere near the end of it.
I know the book, it's all like that,
The time I've wasted over it!
For a thoroughgoing paradox is what
Bemuses fools and wise men equally.
The trick's old as the hills yet it's still going strong;
With Three-in-One and One-in-Three   2610
Lies are sown broadcast, truth may go hang;
Who questions professors about the claptrap they teach—
Who wants to debate and dispute with a fool?
People dutifully think, hearing floods of fine speech,
It can't be such big words mean nothing at all.

THE WITCH. [*Continuing*].
The power of science
From the whole world kept hidden!
Who don't have a thought,
To them it is given
Unbidden, unsought,   2620
It's theirs without sweat.

FAUST. Did you hear that, my God, what nonsense,
It's giving me a headache, phew!
It makes me think I'm listening to
A hundred thousand fools in chorus.

MEPHISTO. Enough, enough, O excellent Sibyl!
Bring on the potion, fill the stoup,
Your drink won't give my friend here trouble,
He's earned his Ph.D. in many a bout.

[*The Witch very ceremoniously pours the potion into a bowl;
when Faust raises it to his lips, a low flame plays over it.*]

Drink, now drink, no need to diddle,   2630
It'll put you into a fine glow.
When you've got a sidekick in the Devil,
Why should some fire frighten you so?
[*The Witch breaks the circle and Faust steps out.*]
Now let's be off, you mustn't dally.

THE WITCH. I hope that little nip, sir, hits the spot!

MEPHISTO. [*To the Witch*] Madam, thanks. If I can help *you* out,
Don't fail, upon Walpurgis Night, to ask me.

THE WITCH. [*To Faust*] Here is a song, sir, carol it now and then,
You'll find it assists the medicine.

MEPHISTO. Come away quick! You must do as I say.   2640
To soak up the potion body and soul,
A man's got to sweat a bucketful.
And after, I'll teach you the gentleman's way
Of wasting your time expensively.
Soon yours the delight outdelights all things—
Boy Cupid astir in you, stretching his wings.

FAUST. One more look in the mirror, let me—
That woman was inexpressibly lovely!

MEPHISTO. No, no, soon enough, before you, vis-à-vis,
Yours the fairest of fair women, I guarantee.   2650
[*Aside*] With that stuff in him, old Jack will
Soon see a Helen in every Jill.

A STREET

Faust. Margarete passing by.

FAUST. Pretty lady, here's my arm,
    Would you allow me to see you home?
MARGARETE I'm neither pretty nor a lady,
    Can find my way home quite unaided.
    [*She escapes his arm and passes by.*]
FAUST. By God, what a lovely girl,
    I've never seen her like, a pearl!
    A good girl, too, with a quick wit,
    Her manner modest and yet pert.   2660
    Those red, ripe lips and cheeks abloom
    Will haunt me till the crack of doom.
    The way she looked down, so demure,
    Had for me such allure!
    The way she cut short my come-on
    Charmed me—charmed by a turn-down!
                 Enter Mephistopheles.
FAUST. Get me that girl, do you hear, you must!
MEPHISTO. What girl?
FAUST.   The one who just went past.
MEPHISTO. Oh, her. She's just been to confession
    To be absolved of all her sins.   2670
    I sidled near the box to listen:
    She could have spared herself her pains,
    She is the soul of innocence
    And has no reason, none at all,
    To visit the confessional.
    Her kind is too much for me.
FAUST. She's over fourteen, isn't she?

MEPHISTO. Well, listen to him, an instant Don Juan,
　　　Demands every favor, his shyness all gone,
　　　Conceitedly thinks it offends his honor　　　　　　　　2680
　　　To leave unplucked every pretty flower.
　　　But it doesn't go so easy always.
FAUST. My dear Doctor of What's Proper,
　　　Spare me your lectures, I beg you, please.
　　　Let me tell it to you straight:
　　　If I don't hold that darling creature
　　　Tight in my arms this very night,
　　　We're through, we two, come twelve midnight.
MEPHISTO. Impossible! That's out of the question!
　　　I require two weeks at the least　　　　　　　　　　2690
　　　To spy out a propitious occasion.
FAUST. With several hours or so, at the most,
　　　I could seduce her handily—
　　　Don't need the Devil to pimp for me,
MEPHISTO. You're talking like a Frenchman now.
　　　Calm down, there's no cause for vexation.
　　　You'll find that instant gratification
　　　Disappoints. If you allow
　　　For compliments and billets doux,
　　　Whisperings and rendezvous,　　　　　　　　　　　2700
　　　The pleasure's felt so much more keenly.
　　　Italian novels teach you exactly.
FAUST. I've no use for your slow-paced courting,
　　　My appetite needs no supporting.
MEPHISTO. Please, I'm being serious.
　　　With such a pretty little miss
　　　You mustn't be impetuous
　　　And assault the fortress frontally.
　　　What's called for here is strategy.

FAUST. Something of hers, do you hear, I require!   2710
    Come, show me the way to the room she sleeps in,
    Get me a scarf, a glove, a ribbon,
    A garter with which to feed my desire!

MEPHISTO. To prove to you my earnest intention
    By every means to further your passion,
    Not losing a minute, without delay,
    I'll take you to her room today.

FAUST. I'll see her, yes? And have her?

MEPHISTO.   No!
    She'll be at a neighbor's—you *must* go slow!
    Meanwhile alone there, in her room   2720
    You'll steep yourself in her perfume
    And dream of the delights to come.

FAUST. Can we start now?

MEPHISTO.   Too soon! Be patient!

FAUST. Then find me a pretty thing for a present.

                                 Exit.

MEPHISTO. Presents already? The man's proving a lover!—
    Now for his gift, I know there's treasure
    Buried in many an out-of-the way corner.
    Off I go to reconnoiter!

EVENING

A small room, very neat and clean.

MARGARETE. [*As she braids her hair and puts it up*]
    I'd give a lot to know, I would,
    Who the gentleman was today.   2730
    He seemed a fine man, decent, good,

And from a noble house, I'm sure;
It shows on him as plain as day—
To be so bold! Who else would dare?

Exit.

Mephistopheles, Faust.

MEPHISTO. Come in now, in!—but quietly, take care.
FAUST. [*After a silent interval*] Leave, please, leave me on my own.
MEPHISTO. [*Sniffing around*] Not every girl keeps things so spic
        and span.

Exit.

FAUST. Welcome, evening's twilight gloom,
    Stealing through this holy room.
    Possess my heart, oh love's sweet anguish,   2740
    That lives in hope, in hope must languish.
    How still it's here, how happily
    It breathes good order and contentment,
    What riches in this poverty,
    What bliss there is in this confinement!
    [*He flings himself into a leather armchair by the bed.*]
    Receive me as in generations past
    You received the happy and distressed.
    How often, I know, children crowded around
    This chair where their grandfather sat enthroned
    Perhaps my darling too, a round-cheeked child,   2750
    Grateful for her Christmas present, held
    Reverentially his shrunken hand.
    I feel, dear girl, where you are all is comfort,
    Where you are, order, goodness all abound.
    Maternally instructed by your spirit,
    Daily you spread the clean cloth on the table,
    Sprinkle the sand on the floor so carefully—
    O lovely hand! Hand of a lovely angel

That's made of this home something heavenly.
And here—!
[*He lifts a bed curtain.*]
                    I tremble, frightened, with delight!   2760
Here I could linger hour after hour.
Here the dear creature, gently dreaming, slept,
Her angel substance slowly shaped by Nature.
Here warm life in her tender bosom swelled,
Here by a pure and holy weaving
Of the strands, was revealed
The angelic being.

But me? What is it brought me here?
See how shaken I am, how nervous!   2770
What do I want? Why am I so anxious?
Poor Faust, I hardly know you any more.

Has this room put a spell on me?
I came here burning up with lust,
And melt with love now, helplessly.
Are we blown about by every gust?

And if she came in now, this minute,
How I'd pay dear, I would, for it.
The big talker, Herr Professor,
Would dwindle to nothing, grovel before her.
MEPHISTO. [*Entering*] Hurry! I saw her, she's coming up.   2780
FAUST. Hurry indeed, I'll never come here again!
MEPHISTO. Here's a jewel box I snatched up
    When I—but who cares how or when.
    Put it in the closet there,
    She'll jump for joy when she comes on it.
    It's got a number of choice things in it,
    Meant for another—but I declare,

Girls are girls, they're all the same,
The only thing that matters is the game.
FAUST. Should I, I wonder?
MEPHISTO.   *Should* you, you say!   2790
Do you mean to keep it for yourself?
If what you're after's treasure, pelf,
Then I have wasted my whole day,
Been put to a lot of needless bother.
I hope you aren't some awful miser—
After all my head-scratching, scheming, labor!
[*He puts the box in the closet and shuts it.*]
Come on, let's go!
Our aim? Your darling's favor,
So you may do with her as you'd like to do.
And you do what? Only gape,   2800
As if going into your lecture hall,
Looming before you in human shape
Stood physics and metaphysics, ancient, stale.
Come on!
                                                        Exit

MARGARETE. [*With a lamp*] How close, oppressive it's in here.
[*She opens the window.*]
And yet outside it isn't warm.
I feel, I don't know why, so queer—
I wish Mother would come home,
I'm shivering so in every limb.
What a foolish, frightened girl I am!   2810
[*She sings as she undresses.*]
There was a king in Thule,
No truer man drank up,
To whom his mistress, dying,
Gave a golden cup.

Nothing he held dearer,
And mid the feasting's noise,
Each time he drained the beaker
Tears started in his eyes.

And when death knocked, he tallied
His towns and treasure up,   2820
Yielded his heirs all gladly,
All except the cup.

In the great hall of his fathers,
In the castle by the sea,
He and his knights sat down to
Their last revelry.

Up stood the old carouser,
A last time knew wine's warmth,
Then pitched his beloved beaker
Down into the gulf.   2830

He saw it fall and founder,
Deep, deep down it sank,
His eyes grew dim and never
Another drop he drank.

[*She opens the closet to put her clothes away and sees the jewel box.*]

How did this pretty box get here?
I locked the closet, I'm quite sure.
Whatever's in the box? Maybe
Mother took it in pledge today.
And there's the little key on a ribbon.
I think I'd like to open it!   2840

—Look at all this, God in Heaven!
I've never seen the like of it!
Jewels! And *such* jewels, that a fine lady
Might wear on a great holiday.
How would the necklace look on me?
Who is it owns these wonderful things?
[*She puts the jewelry on and stands in front of the mirror.*]
I wish they were mine, these fine earrings!
When you put them on, you're changed completely.
What good's your pretty face, your youth,
Nice to have but little worth.   2850
Men praise you, do it half in pity,
What's on their minds is money, money.
Gold is their god, all—
Oh us poor people!

OUT WALKING

Faust strolling up and down, thinking. To him Mephistopheles.

MEPHISTO. By true love cruelly scorned! By Hellfire fierce and fiery!
    If only I could think of worse to swear by!
FAUST. What's eating you, now what's the trouble?
    Such a face I've not seen till today.
MEPHISTO. The Devil take me, that's what I would say,
    If it didn't so happen I'm the Devil.   2860
FAUST. Are you in your right mind—behaving
    Like a madman, wildly raving?
MEPHISTO. The jewels I got for Gretchen, just imagine—
    Every piece a damned priest's stolen!
    The minute her mother saw them, she
    Began to tremble fearfully.

The woman has a nose! It's stuck
Forever in her prayerbook,
She knows right off, by the smell alone,
If something's sacred or profane;   2870
One whiff of the jewelry was enough
To tell her something's wrong with the stuff.
My child—she cried—and listen well to me,
All property obtained unlawfully
Does body and soul a mortal injury.
These jewels we'll consecrate to the Blessed Virgin,
And for reward have showers of manna from Heaven.
Our little Margaret pouted, loath—
Why look a gift horse in the mouth?
And surely the one who gave her it   2880
So generously, was hardly wicked.
Her mother sent for the priest, and he,
Seeing how the land lay,
Was mightily pleased. You've done, he said,
Just as you should, mother and maid;
Who overcometh is repaid.
The Church's maw's remarkably capacious,
Gobbles up whole realms, everything precious,
Nor once suffers qualms, not even belches;
The Church alone is able to digest   2890
Goods illegitimately possessed.

FAUST. That's the way the whole world over,
From a King to a Jew, so all do ever.

MEPHISTO. So then he pockets brooches, chains and rings
As if they were the cheapest household things,
And gives the women as much of a thank-you
As a body gets for a mouldy potato.
In Heaven, he says, you will receive your reward:
The women, uplifted, are reassured.

FAUST. And Gretchen?

MEPHISTO.   Sits there restlessly,   2900
    Her mind confused, her will uncertain,
    Thinks about jewels night and day,
    Even more about her unknown patron.

FAUST. I can't bear that she should suffer;
    Find her new ones immediately!
    Poor stuff, those others, hardly suit her.

MEPHISTO. Oh yes indeed! With a snap of the fingers!

FAUST. Do what I say, march, man—how he lingers!
    Insinuate yourself with her neighbor.
    Damn it, devil, you move so sluggishly!   2910
    Fetch Gretchen new and better jewelry!

MEPHISTO. Yes, yes, just as you wish, Your Majesty.

                                        Exit Faust.

    A lovesick fool! To amuse his girl he'd blow up
    Sun, moon, stars, the whole damned shop.

THE NEIGHBOR'S HOUSE

MARTHE. [*Alone*] May God that man of mine condone!
    He's done me wrong—like a bird
    Flew right off without a word
    And left me here to sleep alone.
    I never gave him cause for grief
    But loved him as a faithful wife.   2920
    [*She weeps.*]
    Suppose he's dead—oh I feel hopeless!
    If only I had an official notice.
                    Enter Margarete.

MARGARETE. Frau Marthe!

MARTHE.   Gretel, what's wrong, tell me!

MARGARETE. My knees are shaking, near collapse!
    Just now I found another box
    Inside my closet. Ebony,
    And such things in it, much more splendid
    Than the first ones, I'm dumbfounded!
MARTHE. Never a word to your mother about it,
    Or the priest will have all the next minute.   2930
MARGARETE. Just look at this, and this, and this here!
MARTHE. [*Decking her out in the jewels*]
    Oh, what a lucky girl you are!
MARGARETE. But I mustn't be seen in the streets with such jewelry,
    And never in church. Oh, it's too cruel!
MARTHE. Come over to me whenever you're able,
    Here you can wear them without any trouble.
    March back and forth in front of the mirror—
    Won't we enjoy ourselves together!
    And when it's a holiday, some such occasion,
    You can start wearing them, with discretion.   2940
    First a necklace, then a pearl earring,
    Your mother, she'll never notice anything,
    And if she does, why, we'll think of something.
MARGARETE. Who put the jewelry in my closet?
    There's something that's not right about it.
    [*A knock.*]
    Dear God above, can that be Mother?
MARTHE. [*Peeping through the curtain*]
    Please come in!—No, it's a stranger.
                    Enter Mephistopheles.
MEPHISTO.   Good women, pardon, with your permission!
    I beg you to excuse the intrusion.
    [*Steps back deferentially from Margarete.*]
    I'm looking for Frau Marthe Schwerdtlein.   2950
MARTHE. I'm her. And what have you to say, sir?

MEPHISTO. [*Under his breath to her*]
    Now I know who you are, that's enough.
    You have a lady under your roof,
    I'll go away and come back later.
MARTHE. [*Aloud*] Goodness, child, you won't believe me,
    What the gentleman thinks is, you're a lady!
MARGARETE. A poor girl's what I am, no more.
    The gentleman's kind—I thank you, sir.
    These jewels don't belong to me.
MEPHISTO. Oh, it's not just the jewelry,   2960
    It's the Fräulein herself, so clear-eyed, serene.
    —So delighted I'm allowed to remain.
MARTHE. Why are you here, if you'll pardon the question.
MEPHISTO. I wish my news were pleasanter.
    Don't blame me, the messenger:
    Your husband's dead, he sent his affection.
MARTHE. The good man's dead and gone, departed?
    Then I'll die too. Oh, I'm broken-hearted!
MARGARETE. Marthe dear, it's too violent, your sorrow!
MEPHISTO. Hear the sad story I've come to tell you.   2970
MARGARETE. As long as I live I'll love nobody, no!
    It would kill me with grief to lose my man so.
MEPHISTO. Joy's latter end is sorrow—and sorrow's joy.
MARTHE. Tell me how the dear man died.
MEPHISTO. He's buried in Padua, beside
    The blessed saint, sweet Anthony,
    In hallowed ground where he can lie
    In rest eternal, quietly.
MARTHE. And nothing else, sir, that is all?
MEPHISTO. A last request. He enjoins you solemnly: 2980
    Let three hundred masses be sung for his soul!
    As for anything else, my pocket's empty.
MARTHE. What! No jewel, nice souvenir,

Such as every journeyman keeps in his wallet,
And would sooner go hungry and beg than sell it?
MEPHISTO. Nothing, I'm sorry to say, Madam dear.
　　However—he never squandered his money,
　　And he sincerely regretted his sins,
　　Regretted even more he was so unlucky.
MARGARETE. Why must so many be so unhappy!　　　　2990
　　I'll pray for him often, sing requiems.
MEPHISTO. What a lovable creature, there's none dearer!
　　What you should have now, right away,
　　Is a good husband. It's true what I say.
MARGARETE. Oh no, it's not time yet, that must come later.
MEPHISTO. If not now a husband, meanwhile a lover.
　　What blessing from Heaven, which one of life's charms
　　Rivals holding a dear thing like you in one's arms.
MARGARETE. With us people here it isn't the custom.
MEPHISTO. Custom or not, it's what's done and by more than some.　3000
MARTHE. Go on with your story, more's surely to come.
MEPHISTO. He lay on a bed of half-rotten straw,
　　Better at least than a dunghill, and there
　　He died as a Christian, knowing well
　　Much remained outstanding on his bill.
　　"Oh how," he cried, "I hate myself!
　　To abandon my trade, desert my wife!
　　It kills me even to think of it.
　　If only she would forgive and forget!"
MARTHE. [*Weeping*] I did, long ago! He's forgiven, the dear man.　3010
MEPHISTO. "But she's more to blame, God knows, than I am."
MARTHE. Liar! How shameless! At death's very door!
MEPHISTO. His mind wandered as the end drew near,
　　If I'm anything of a connoisseur here.
　　"No pleasure," he said, "no good times, nor anything nice;
　　First getting children, then getting them fed,

By fed meaning lots more things than bread,
With never a moment for having my bite in peace."
MARTHE. How could he forget my love and loyalty,
My hard work day and night, the drudgery! 3020
MEPHISTO. He didn't forget, he remembered all tenderly.
"When we set sail from Malta's port," he said,
"For wife and children fervently I prayed.
And Heaven, hearing, smiled down kindly,
For we captured a Turkish vessel, stuffed
With the Sultan's treasure. How we rejoiced!
Our courage being recompensed,
I left the ship with a fatter purse
Than ever I'd owned before in my life."
MARTHE. Treasure! Do you think he buried it? 3030
MEPHISTO. Who knows what's become of it?
In Naples, where he wandered about,
A pretty miss with a kind heart
Showed the stranger such good will,
Till the day he died he felt it still.
MARTHE. The villain! Robbing his children, his wife!
And for all our misery, dire need,
He would never give up his scandalous life.
MEPHISTO. Well, he's been paid, the man is dead.
If I were in your shoes, my dear, 3040
I'd mourn him decently a year
And meanwhile keep an eye out for another.
MARTHE. Dear God, I'm sure it won't be easy
To find, on this earth, his successor;
So full of jokes he was, so jolly!
But he was restless, always straying,
Loved foreign women, foreign wine,
And how he loved, drat him, dice-playing.
MEPHISTO. Oh well, I'm sure things worked out fine

If he was equally forgiving.   3050
With such an arrangement, why, I swear,
I'd marry you myself, my dear!

MARTHE. Oh sir, you would? You're joking, I'm sure!

MEPHISTO. [*Aside*] Time to leave! This one's an ogress,
She'd sue the Devil for breach of promise!
[*To Gretchen*]
And what's your love life like, my charmer?

MARGARETE. What do you mean?

MEPHISTO. [*Aside*]   Oh you good girl,
All innocence! [*Aloud*] And now farewell.

MARGARETE. Farewell.

MARTHE.   Quick, one last matter.
If you would. I want to know   3060
If I might have some proof to show
How and when my husband died
And where the poor man now is laid?
I like to have things right and proper,
With a notice published in the paper.

MEPHISTO. Madam, yes. To attest the truth,
Two witnesses must swear an oath.
I know someone, a good man, we
Will go before the notary.
I'll introduce you to him.

MARTHE.   Do.   3070

MEPHISTO. And she'll be here, your young friend, too?—
A very fine fellow who's been all over,
So polite to ladies, so urbane his behavior.

MARGARETE. I'd blush for shame before the gentleman.

MEPHISTO. No, not before a king or any man!

MARTHE. We'll wait for you tonight, the two of us,
Inside my garden, just behind the house.

A STREET

Faust, Mephistopheles

FAUST. Well, speak! It's on? When will I have her?
MEPHISTO. Bravo, bravo, aren't you on fire!
    Very shortly Gretchen will be all yours;   3080
    This evening you will meet her at her neighbor's.
    The worthy Mistress Marthe, I confess,
    Needs no instruction as a procuress.
FAUST.
    Well done.
MEPHISTO.   But something we must do for her.
FAUST. One good turn deserves another.
MEPHISTO. All it is is swear an oath
    Her husband's laid out in the earth
    At Padua in consecrated ground.
FAUST. So we must make a trip there—very smart!
MEPHISTO. Sancta simplicitas! Whoever said that?   3090
    Just swear an oath, is all. You frowned?
FAUST. If that's the best you're able, count me out.
MEPHISTO. The saintly fellow! Turned devout.
    Declaring falsely—Heaven forbid!—
    Is something Faustus never did.
    Haven't you pontificated
    About God and the world, undisconcerted,
    About man, man's mind and heart and being,
    As bold as brass, without blushing?
    Look at it closely and what's the truth?   3100
    You know as much about those things
    As you know about Herr Schwerdtlein's death.
FAUST. You always were a sophist and a liar.

MEPHISTO. Indeed, indeed. If we look ahead a little further,
    To tomorrow, what do we see?
    You swearing, oh so honorably,
    Your soul is Gretchen's, for ever and ever.
FAUST. My soul, and all my heart as well.
MEPHISTO.   Oh noble, great!
    You'll swear undying faith and love eternal,
    Go on about desire unique and irresistable,   3110
    About longing, boundless, infinite.
    That, too, with all your loving heart.
FAUST. With all my heart! And now enough.
    What I feel, an emotion of such depth,
    Such turbulence—when I try to find
    A name for it and nothing comes to mind,
    And cast about, search heaven and earth
    For words to express its transcendent worth,
    And call the fire in which I burn
    Eternal, yes, eternal, yes, undying,   3120
    Do you really mean to tell me
    That's just devil's doing, deception, lying?
MEPHISTO.
    Say what you please, I'm right.
FAUST.   One word more, one only,
    And then I'll save my breath. A man who is unyielding,
    Sure, absolutely, he's right, and has a tongue in his mouth—
    Is right. So come, I'm sick of arguing.
    You're right, and the reason's simple enough:
    I must do what I must, can't help myself.

A GARDEN

Margarete with Faust, her arm linked with his: Marthe with Mephistopheles. The two couples stroll up and down.

MARGARETE. You are too kind, sir, I am sure it's meant
    To spare a simple girl embarrassment.   3130
    A traveler finds whatever amusement he can,
    You've been all over, you're a gentleman—
    How can anything I say
    Interest you in any way?
FAUST. One word of yours, a single look's
    Worth all the science in our books.
    [*He kisses her hand.*]
MARGARETE. No, no, sir, please, you mustn't! How could you kiss
    A hand so ugly—red and coarse?
    You can't imagine all the work I do:
    My mother must have things just so.   3140
    [*They walk on.*]
MARTHE. And you, sir, I believe you constantly travel?
MEPHISTO. Business, business! It is so demanding!
    Leaving a place you like, oh, it is dismal,
    But on you've got to go, it's just unending.
MARTHE. How fine when young and full of ginger
    To roam the world, go everywhere,
    But grim days come, come even grimmer,
    When no one likes what lies in store—
    Likes crawling to his grave a lonely bachelor.
MEPHISTO. When I look at what's ahead, I tremble.   3150
MARTHE. Then think about it while you're able.
          (*They walk on.*)
MARGARETE. Yes, out of sight is out of mind.
    It's second nature with you, gallantry;

But you have friends of every kind,
Cleverer by far, oh much, than me.
FAUST.   Dear girl, believe me, what's called cleverness
Is mostly shallowness and vanity.
MARGARETE.   What do you mean?
FAUST.   God, isn't it a pity
That unspoiled innocence and simpleness
Should never know itself and its own worth,   3160
That meekness, lowliness, those highest gifts
Kindly Nature endows us with—
MARGARETE.   You'll think of me for a moment or two,
I'll have hours enough to think of you.
FAUST.   You're alone a good deal, are you?
MARGARETE.   Our family's very small, it's true,
But still it has to be looked to.
We have no maid, I sweep the floors, I cook and knit
And sew, do all the errands, morning and night.
Mother's very careful about money,   3170
All's accounted for to the last penny.
Not that she really needs to pinch and save,
We could afford much more than others have.
My father left us a good bit,
With a small dwelling part of it,
And a garden just outside the city.
But lately I've lived quietly.
My brother is a soldier. My little sister died.
The trouble that she cost me, the poor child!
But I loved her very much, I'd gladly do   3180
It all again.
FAUST.   An angel, if at all like you.
MARGARETE.   All the care of her was mine,
And she was very fond of her sister.
My father died before she was born,

And Mother, well, we nearly lost her;
It took so long, oh many months, till she got better.
It was out of the question she should nurse
The poor little crying thing herself.
So I nursed her, on milk and water.
I felt she was my own daughter,   3190
In my arms, upon my lap,
She smiled and kicked, grew round and plump.
FAUST. The happiness it must have given you!
MARGARETE. But it was hard on me so often, too.
Her crib stood at my bedside, near my head,
A slightest movement, cradle's creak,
And instantly I was awake;
I'd give her a bottle or take her into my bed.
If still she fretted, up I'd raise,
Walk up and down with her swaying and crooning,   3200
And be at the washtub early the next morning.
To market after that and getting the hearth to blaze,
And so it went day after day, always.
Home's not always cheerful, be it said,
But still—how good your supper, good your bed.
[*They walk on.*]
MARTHE. It's very hard on us poor women.
You bachelors don't listen, you're so stubborn.
MEPHISTO. What's needed are more charmers like yourself
To bring us bachelors down from off the shelf.
MARTHE. There's never, sir, been anyone? Confess!   3210
You've never lost your heart to one of us?
MEPHISTO. How does the proverb go? A loving wife,
And one's own hearthside, are more worth
Than all the gold that's hidden in the earth.
MARTHE. I mean, you've had no wish, yourself?
MEPHISTO. Oh, everywhere I've been received politely.

MARTHE. No, what I mean is, hasn't there been somebody
　　Who ever made your heart beat? Seriously?
MEPHISTO. It's never a joking matter with women, believe me.
MARTHE. Oh, you don't understand!
MEPHISTO. 　　　　　　　　　So sorry. Still, 　　　　　　　　3220
　　I can see that you are—amiable.
　　[*They walk on.*]
FAUST. You recognized me, angel, instantly
　　When I came through the gate into the garden?
MARGARETE. I dropped my eyes. Didn't you see?
FAUST. And you'll forgive the liberty, you'll pardon
　　My swaggering up in that insulting fashion
　　When you came out of the church door?
MARGARETE. I was shocked. Never before
　　Had I been spoken to like that.
　　I'm a good girl. Who would dare 　　　　　　　　　　　　3230
　　To be so free with me, so smart?
　　It seemed to me at once you thought
　　There's a girl who can be bought
　　On the spot. Did I look a flirt?
　　Is that so, tell! Well, I'll admit
　　A voice spoke "Isn't he nice?" in my breast,
　　And oh how vexed with myself I felt
　　When I wasn't vexed with you in the least.
FAUST. Dear girl!
MARGARETE. 　　　Just wait.
　　[*Picking a daisy and plucking the petals one by one*]
FAUST. 　　　　　　　　　What is it for, a bouquet?
MARGARETE. Only a little game of ours.
FAUST. 　　　　　　　　　　　　A game, is it? 　　　　　　3240
MARGARETE. Never mind. I'm afraid you'll laugh at me.
　　[*Murmuring to herself as she plucks the petals*]
FAUST. What are you saying!

MARGARETE. [*Under her breath*]

           Loves me—loves me not—

FAUST. Oh, what a creature, heavenly!

MARGARETE. [*Continuing*] He loves me—not—he loves me—not—

    [*Plucking the last petal and crying out delightedly*]

    He loves me!

FAUST.   Dearest, yes! Yes, let the flower be

    The oracle by which the truth is said.

    He loves you! Do you understand?

    He loves you! Let me take your hand.

    [*He takes her hands in his.*]

MARGARETE. I'm afraid!

FAUST. Read the look on my face,   3250

    Feel my hands gripping yours,

    They say what is the case,

    Can't ever to put in words:

    Utter surrender, and such rapture

    As must never end, must last forever!

    Yes, forever! An end—it would betoken

    Utter despair! a heart forever broken!

    No—no end! No end!

    [*Margarete squeezes his hands, frees herself and runs away. He*

      doesn't move for a moment, thinking, then follows her.]

MARTHE. It's getting dark.

MEPHISTO.   That's right. We have to go.

MARTHE. Please forgive me if I don't invite   3260

    You in. But ours is such a nasty-minded street,

    You'd think people had no more to do

    Than watch their neighbors' every coming and going.

    The gossip that goes on here, about nothing!

    But where are they, our little couple?

MEPHISTO.   Flew

    Up that path like butterflies.

MARTHE.   He seems to like her.
MEPHISTO. And she him. Which is the way the world wags ever.

A SUMMERHOUSE

Gretchen runs in and hides behind the door, putting her
fingertips to her lips and peeping through a crack.

MARGARETE. Here he comes!
FAUST.   You're teasing me, yes, are you?
    I've got you now! [*Kisses her.*]
MARGARETE. [*Holding him around and returning the kiss*]
                    My heart! Oh, how I love you!
                    Mephistopheles knocks.
FAUST. [*Stamping his foot*]
    Who's there?
MEPHISTO.   A friend.
FAUST.   A fiend!
MEPHISTO.   We must be on our way.   3270
MARTHE. [*Coming up*] Yes, sir, it's late.
FAUST.   I'd like to walk you home.
MARGARETE. My mother, I'm afraid. . . . Goodbye!
FAUST.   So we must say
    Goodbye? Goodbye!
MARGARETE.   I hope I'll see you soon.
                    Exit Faust and Mephistopheles.
    Good God, the thoughts that fill the head
    Of such a man, oh it's astounding!
    I stand there dumbly, my face red,
    And stammer yes to everything.
    I don't understand. What in the world
    Does he see in me, an ignorant child?

FOREST AND CAVERN

FAUST. [*Alone*] Sublime Spirit, all that I asked for, all,   3280
    You gave me. Not for nothing was it,
    The face you showed me all ablaze with fire.
    You gave me glorious Nature for my kingdom,
    With the power to feel, to delight in her—nor as
    A spectator only, coolly admiring her wonders,
    But letting me see deep into her bosom
    As a man sees deep into a dear friend's heart.
    Before me you make pass all living things,
    From high to low, and teach me how to know
    My brother creatures in the woods, the streams, the air.   3290
    And when the shrieking storm winds make the forest
    Groan, toppling the giant fir whose fall
    Bears nearby branches down with it and crushes
    Neighboring trees so that the hill returns
    A hollow thunder—oh, then you lead me to
    The shelter of this cave, lay bare my being to myself,
    And all the mysteries hidden in my depths
    Unfold themselves and open to the day.
    And when I see the moon ascend the sky,
    Shedding a pure, assuaging light, out   3300
    Of the walls of rock, the dripping bushes, float
    The silver figures of antiquity
    And temper meditation's austere joy.

    That nothing perfect's ever ours, oh but
    I know it now. Together with the rapture
    That I owe you, by which I am exalted
    Nearer and still nearer to the gods, you gave me
    A familiar, a creature whom already
    I can't do without, though he's a cold

And shameless devil who drags me down   3310
In my own eyes and with a whisper turns
All the gifts you gave me into nothing.
The longing that I feel for that enchanting
Figure of a girl he busily blows up
Into a leaping flame. And so desire
Whips me stumbling on to seize enjoyment,
And once enjoyed, I languish for desire.

Enter Mephistopheles.

MEPHISTO. Aren't you fed up with it by now,
   This mooning about? How can it still
   Amuse you? You do it for a while,   3320
   All right, but enough's enough, on to the new!
FAUST. I wish you'd more to do than criticize
   The peace I feel on one of my good days.
   Mephisto. A breather you want? Very well, I grant it;
   But don't speak so, as if you really meant it.
   I wouldn't shed tears losing a companion
   Who is so mad, so rude, so sullen;
   I have my hands full every minute—
   Impossible to tell what pleases you or doesn't.
FAUST. Why, that's just perfect, isn't it?   3330
   He bores me stiff and wants praise for it.
MEPHISTO. You poor earthly creature, would
   You ever have managed at all without me?
   Whom do you have to thank for being cured
   Of your mad ideas, your feverish frenzy?
   If not for me you would have disappeared
   From off the face of earth already.
   A life, you call it, to be brooding
   Owl-like in caves or toad-like feeding

On oozing moss and dripping stones?   3340
That's a way to spend your time?
The old Doctor still lives in your bones.

FAUST. Try to understand, my life's renewed
When I wander in communion with wild Nature;
But even if you could I know you would
Begrudge me, Devil that you are, my rapture.

MEPHISTO. Oh my! Your rapture—superterrestrial!
Sprawled on a hillside in the nocturnal dewfall,
Penetrating intuitively the bowels of the earth,
All the six days of Creation unfolding inside yourself,   3350
In your arrogance enjoying I don't know what satisfaction,
Amorously immerging with the all in its perfection,
Nary a trace left of the child born of this earth,
And then as finis to your deep, deep insight—
            [*Making a gesture*]
I forbid myself to say, it's not polite.

FAUST. Ugh! Oh ugly!

MEPHISTO.   That's not what you care for?
You're right, "ugh"'s right, the moral comment called for.
Never a word, when chaste ears are about,
Of what chaste souls can't do without.
Oh well, go on amuse yourself   3360
By duping now and then yourself.
Yet you can't keep on like this any longer,
You look done in again, almost a goner.
If you persist so, in this fashion,
You'll go mad with baffled passion.
Enough, I say! Your sweetheart sits down there
And all's a dismal prison for her.
You haunt her mind continually,
She's mad about you, oh completely.
At first your passion, like a freshet   3370

Swollen with melted snow, overflowing
Its peaceful banks, engulfed a soul unknowing,
But now the flood's thinned to a streamlet.
Instead of playing monarch of the wood,
My opinion is the Herr Professor
Should make the silly little creature
Some return in gratitude.
For her the hours creep along,
She stands at the window watching the clouds
Pass slowly over the old town walls,   3380
"Lend me, sweet bird, your wings," is the song
She sings all day and half the night.
Sometimes she's cheerful, mostly she's downhearted,
Sometimes she cries as if brokenhearted,
Then she's calm again and seems all right,
And heart-sick always.

FAUST. Serpent! Snake!

MEPHISTO. [*Aside*] I'll have you yet!

FAUST. Away you monster from some stinking fen!
Don't mention her, the soul itself of beauty,   3390
Don't make my half-crazed senses crave again
The sweetness of that lovely body!

MEPHISTO. Then what? She thinks you've taken flight,
And I must say, the girl's half right.

FAUST. Far off as I may go, still she is near me,
She fills my thoughts both day and night,
I even envy the Lord's flesh the kiss
Her lips bestow upon it at the mass.

MEPHISTO. I understand. I've often envied *you*
Her pair of roes that feed among the lilies.   3400

FAUST. Pimp! I won't hear your blasphemies.

MEPHISTO. Fine! Insult me! And I laugh at you.
The God that made you girls and boys

Himself was first to recognize,
And practice, what's the noblest calling,
The furnishing of opportunities.
Away! A crying shame this, never linger!
You act as if hard fate were dragging
You to death, not to your truelove's chamber.

FAUST. Heaven's out-heavened when she holds me tight,　　3410
And though I'm warmed to life upon her breast,
Do I ever once forget her plight?
Am I not a fugitive, a beast,
That's houseless, restless, purposeless,
A furious, impatient cataract
That plunges down from rock to rock to the abyss?
And she, her senses unawakened, a child still,
Dwelt in her cottage on the Alpine meadow,
Her life the same domestic ritual
Within a little world where fell no shadow.　　3420
And I, abhorred by God,
Was not content to batter
Rocks to bits, I had
To undermine her peace and overwhelm her!
This sacrifice you claimed. Hell, as your due!
Help me, Devil, please, to shorten
The anxious time I must go through!
Let happen quick what has to happen!
Let her fate fall on me, too, crushingly,
And both together perish, her and me!　　3430

MEPHISTO. All worked up again, all in a sweat!
On your way, you fool, and comfort her.
When dolts like you are baffled, don't know what,
They think it's hopeless, the end near.
Long live the man who keeps on undeterred!

I'd rate your progress as a devil pretty fair;
But tell me, what is there that's more absurd
Than a moping devil, mewling in despair?

GRETCHEN'S ROOM

GRETCHEN.   [*Alone at her spinning wheel*]

My heart is heavy,
My peace gone,   3440
I'll never know any
Peace again.

For me it's death
Where he is not,
The whole earth
Waste, desert, rot.

My poor poor head
Is in a whirl,
For sure I'm mad,
A poor mad girl.   3450

My heart is heavy,
My peace gone,
I'll never know any
Peace again.

I look out the window,
Walk out the door,
Him, only him,
I look for.

His bold walk,
His princely person,   3460

His smiling look,
His eyes' persuasion,

And his sweet speech—
Magicalness!
His fingers' touch
And oh his kiss!

My heart is heavy,
My peace gone,
I'll never know any
Peace again.   3470

With aching breast
I strain so toward him,
Oh if I just
Could catch and hold him,

And kiss him and kiss him,
Never ceasing,
Though I should die in
His arms kissing.

MARTHE'S GARDEN

Margarete, Faust.

MARGARETE. Heinrich, the truth—I have to insist!
FAUST. As far as I'm able.
MARGARETE.   Well, tell me, you must,   3480
    About your religion—how do you feel?
    You're such a good man, kind and intelligent,
    Yet I suspect you are indifferent.

FAUST. Enough of that, my child. You know quite well
    I cherish you so very dearly,
    For those I love I'd give my life up gladly,
    And I never interfere with people's faith.
MARGARETE. That isn't right, you've got to have belief!
FAUST. You do?
MARGARETE.   I know you think I am a dunce!   3490
    You don't respect the sacraments.
FAUST. I do respect them.
MARGARETE.   Not enough to go to mass.
    And tell me when you last went to confess?
    Do you believe in God?
FAUST.   Who, my dear,
    Can say, I believe in God?
    Ask any priest or learned scholar
    And what you get by way of answer
    Sounds like mockery of a fool.
MARGARETE. So you don't believe in God.
FAUST. Don't misunderstand me, lovely girl.   3500
    Who dares name him,
    Dares affirm him,
    Dares say he believes?
      Who, feeling doubt,
    Ventures to say right out,
    I don't believe?
    The All-embracing,
    All-sustaining,
    Sustains and embraces
    Himself and you and me.   3510
    Overhead the great sky arches,
    Firm lies the earth beneath our feet,
    And the friendly shining stars, don't they

Mount aloft eternally?
Don't my eyes, seeking your eyes, meet?
And all that is, doesn't it weigh
On your mind and heart,
In eternal secrecy working,
Visibly, invisibly, about you?—
Fill heart with it to overflowing   3520
In an ecstasy of blissful feeling
Which then call what you would:
Happiness! Heart! Love! Call it God!—
I know no name for it, nor look
For one. Feeling is all,
Names noise and smoke
Dimming the heavenly fire.

MARGARETE. I guess what you say is all right,
The priest speaks so, or pretty near,
Except his language isn't yours, not quite.   3530

FAUST. I speak as all speak here below,
All souls beneath bright heaven's day,
They use the language that they know,
And I use mine. Why shouldn't I?

MARGARETE. It sounds fine when it's put your way,
But something's wrong, there's still a question;
The truth is, you are not a Christian.

FAUST. Now darling!

MARGARETE.   I have suffered so much, I can't sleep
To see the company you keep.

FAUST. Company?   3540

MARGARETE. That man you always have with you,
I loathe him, oh how much I do
In all my life I can't remember
Anything that's made me shiver
More than his face has, so horrid, hateful!

FAUST. Silly thing, don't be so fearful.

MARGARETE. His presence puts my blood into a turmoil.

    I like people, most of them indeed;

    But even as I long for you,

    I think of him with secret dread—   3550

    And he's a scoundrel, he is too!

    If I'm unjust, forgive me, Lord.

FAUST. It takes all kinds to make a world.

MARGARETE. I wouldn't want to have his kind around me!

    His lips curl so sarcastically,

    Half angrily,

    When he pokes his head inside the door.

    You can see there's nothing he cares for;

    It's written on his face as plain as day

    He loves no one, we're all his enemy.   3560

    I'm so happy with your arms around me,

    I'm yours, and feel so warm, so free, so easy,

    But when he's here it knots up so inside me.

FAUST. You angel, you, atremble with foreboding!

MARGARETE. What I feel's so strong, so overwhelming,

    That let him join us anywhere

    And right away I almost fear

    I don't love you anymore.

    And when he's near, my lips refuse to pray,

    Which causes me such agony.   3570

    Don't you feel the same way too?

FAUST. It's just that you dislike him so.

MARGARETE I must go now.

FAUST.   Shall we never

    Pass a quiet time alone together,

    Breast pressed to breast, our two beings one?

MARGARETE. Oh, if I only slept alone!

    I'd draw the bolt for you tonight, yes, gladly;

But my mother sleeps so lightly,
And if we were surprised by her
I know I'd die right then and there.   3580
FAUST. Angel, there's no need to worry.
Here's a vial—three drops only
In her cup will subdue nature
And lull her into pleasant slumber.
MARGARETE. What would I say no
To when you ask?
It won't harm her, though
There is no risk?
FAUST. If there were,
Would I suggest you give it her?   3590
MARGARETE. Let me only look at you
And I don't know, I have to do
Your least wish.
I have gone so far already,
How much farther's left for me to go?

Exit.

Enter Mephistopheles.

MEPHISTO. The girl's a goose! I hope she's gone.
FAUST. Spying around, are you, again?
MEPHISTO. I heard it all, yes, every bit of it,
How she put the Doctor through his catechism,
From which he'll have, I trust, much benefit.   3600
Does a fellow stick to the old, the true religion?—
That's what all the girls are keen to know.
If he minds there, they think, he'll mind us too.
FAUST. Monster, lacking the least comprehension
How such a soul, so loving, pure,
Whose faith is all in all to her,
The sole means to obtain salvation,
Should be tormented by the fear

The one she loves is damned forever!

MEPHISTO. You transcendental, hot and sensual Romeo,   3610

See how a little skirt's got you in tow.

FAUST. You misbegotten thing of filth and fire!

MEPHISTO. And she's an expert, too, in physiognomy.

When I come in, she feels—what, she's not sure;

This face I wear hides a dark mystery;

I'm a genius of some kind, a bad one,

About that she is absolutely certain,

Even the Devil, very possibly.

Now about tonight—?

FAUST.   What's that to you?

MEPHISTO. I get my fun out of it too.   3620

AT THE WELL

Gretchen and Lieschen carrying pitchers.

LIESCHEN. You've heard about our Barbara, have you?

GRETCHEN. No, not a word. I hardly see a soul.

LIESCHEN. Sybil told me; yes, the whole thing's true.

She's gone and done it now, the little fool.

You see what comes of being so stuck up!

GRETCHEN. What comes?

LIESCHEN.   Oh, it smells bad, it stinks.

She's feeding two now when she eats and drinks.

GRETCHEN. Oh dear!

LIESCHEN.   Serves her right, if you ask me.

How she kept after him, without a let-up,

Gadding about, the pair, and gallivanting   3630

Off to the village for the music, dancing;

She had to be first always, everywhere,

While he with wine and sweet cakes courted her.
She thought her beauty echoed famously,
Accepted his gifts shamelessly,
They kissed and fondled by the hour,
Till it was goodbye to her little flower.

GRETCHEN. The poor thing!

LIESCHEN.   Poor thing, you say!
While we two sat home spinning the whole day
And our mothers wouldn't let us out at night,   3640
She was where? Out—hugging her sweetheart
On a bench or up a dark alley,
And never found an hour passed too slowly.
Well, now she's got to pay for it—
Shiver in church in her sinner's shift.

GRETCHEN. He'll marry her. How can he not?

LIESCHEN. He won't—he can.
That one's too smart,
He'll find a girlfriend elsewhere in a trice.
In fact he's gone.

GRETCHEN.   But that's not nice!   3650

LIESCHEN. And if he does, she'll rue the day,
The boys will snatch her bridal wreath away
And we'll throw dirty straw down in her doorway.

                                                        Exit.

GRETCHEN. [*Turning to go home*]
How full of blame I used to be, how scornful
Of any girl who got herself in trouble!
I couldn't find words enough to express
My disgust for others' sinfulness.
Black as all their misdeeds seemed to be,
I blackened them still more, so cruelly,
And still they weren't black enough for me.   3660
I blessed myself, was smug and proud

To think I was so very good,
And who's the sinner now? Me, me, oh God!
Yet everything that brought me to it,
God, was so good, oh, was so sweet!

THE CITY WALL

In a niche in the wall, an image of the Mater Dolorosa at the foot of the cross, with pots of flowers before it.

GRETCHEN.   [*Putting fresh flowers in the pots*]

> Look down, O
> Thou sorrow-rich Lady,
> On my need, in thy mercifulness aid me!
>
> With the sword in your heart,
> With your infinite hurt,   3670
> Upwards you look to your son's death.
>
> To the Father you gaze up.
> Send sighs upon sighs up,
> For his grief and your own sore grief.
>
> Who's there knows
> How it gnaws
> Deep inside me, the pain?
> The heart-anguish I suffer,
> Fright, tremblings, desire?
> You only know, you alone!   3680
>
> Wherever I go, no matter,
> The woe, the woe I suffer
> Inside my bosom, aching!

No sooner I'm alone
I moan, I moan, I moan,
Mary, my heart is breaking!

From the box outside my window,
Dropping tears like dew,
Leaning into the dawning,
I picked these flowers for you.   3690

Into my bedroom early
The bright sun put his head,
Found me bolt upright sitting
Miserably on my bed.

Help! Save me from shame and death!
Look down, O
Thou sorrow-rich Lady,
On my need, in thy mercifulness aid me!

NIGHT

The street outside Gretchen's door.

VALENTINE. [*A soldier, Gretchen's brother*]
    Whenever at a bout the boys
    Would fill the tavern with the noise   3700
    Of their loud bragging, swearing Mattie,
    Handsome Kate or blushing Mary
    The finest girl in all the country,
    Confirming what they said by drinking
    Many a bumper, I'd say nothing,
    My elbows on the table propped,
    Till all their boasting at last stopped.

And then I'd stroke my beard, and smiling,
Say there was no point in quarrelling
About taste; but tell me where   3710
There was one who could compare,
A virgin who could hold a candle
To my beloved sister, Gretel?
Clink, clank, you heard the tankards rattle
All around, and voices shout
He's right, he is, she gets our vote,
Among all her sex she has no equal!
Which stopped those others cold. But now—
I could tear my hair out, all,
Run right up the side of the wall!   3720
All the drunks are free to crow
Over me, to needle, sneer,
And I'm condemned to sitting there
Like a man with debts unpaid
Who sweats in fear lest something's said.
I itch to smash them all, those beggars,
But still that wouldn't make them liars.

Who's sneaking up here? Who is that?
There's two! And one I bet's that rat.
When I lay my hands on him   3730
He won't be going home again!

               Faust, Mephistopheles.

FAUST. How through the window of the vestry, look,
    The flickering altar lamp that's always lit
    Upward throws its light, while dim and weak,
    By darkness choked, a gleam dies at our feet.
    Just so all's night and gloom within my soul.
MEPHISTO. But me, I'm itching like a tomcat on the prowl
    That slinks past fire ladders, hugs the wall.

An honest devil I am, after all;
It's nothing serious, the little thievery   3740
I have in mind, the little lechery—
It merely shows Walpurgis Night's already
Spooking up and down inside me.
Still another night of waiting, then
The glorious season's here again
When a fellow finds out waking beats
Sleeping life away between the sheets.

FAUST. That flickering light I see, is that
Buried treasure rising, what?

MEPHISTO. Very soon you'll have the pleasure   3750
Of lifting out a pot of treasure.
The other day I stole a look—
Such lovely coins, oh you're in luck!

FAUST. No necklace, bracelet, some such thing
My darling can put on, a ring?

MEPHISTO. I think I glimpsed a string of pearls—
Just the thing to please the girls.

FAUST. Good, good. It makes me feel unhappy
When I turn up with my hands empty.

MEPHISTO. Why should you mind it if you can   3760
Enjoy a free visit now and then?
Look up, how the heavens sparkle, star-full,
Time for a song, a cunning one, artful:
I'll sing her a ballad that's moral, proper,
So as to delude the baggage the better.
[Sings to the guitar.]
     What brings you out before
     Your sweet William's door,
      O Katherine, my dear,
        In morning's chill?
      You pretty child, beware,   3770

The maid that enters there,
Out she shall come ne'er
  A maiden still.

Girls, listen, trust no one,
Or when all's said and done,
You'll find yourselves undone
  And poor things, damned.
Of your good souls take care,
Yield nothing though he swear,
Until your finger wear 3780
  A silver band.

VALENTINE. [*Advancing*]
  Luring who here with that braying,
  Abominable rat catcher?
  The devil take that thing you're playing,
  And then take you, you guitar scratcher!

MEPHISTO. Smashed my guitar! Now it's no good at all.

VALENTINE. And now I think I'll split your no good skull.

MEPHISTO. [*To Faust*] Hold your ground, Professor! At the ready!
  Stick close to me, I'll show you how.
  Out with your pigsticker now! 3790
  You do the thrusting, I will parry.

VALENTINE. Parry that!

MEPHISTO.   Why not?

VALENTINE.   And this one too!

MEPHISTO.   Delighted, I am, to oblige you.

VALENTINE. It's the Devil I think I'm fighting!—He's grinning.
  What's this? My hand is feeling feeble.

MEPHISTO. [*To Faust*] Stick him!

VALENTINE. [*Falling*]   Oh!

MEPHISTO.   See how the lout's turned civil.
  What's called for now is legwork. Off and running!

In no time they will raise a hue and cry;
I can manage sheriffs without trouble,
But not the High Judiciary.   3800

Exeunt.

MARTHE. [*Leaning out of the window*]
　Neighbors, help!
GRETCHEN. [*Leaning out of her window*]
　　　　　　A light, a light!
MARTHE. They curse and brawl, they scream and fight.
CROWD. Here's one on the ground. He's dead.
MARTHE. [*Coming out*] Where are the murderers? All fled?
GRETCHEN. [*Coming out*]
　Who's lying here?
CROWD.　　　　　Your mother's son.
GRETCHEN. My God, the misery, on and on.
VALENTINE. I'm dying! Well, it's soon said, that,
　And sooner done. You women, don't
　Stand there blubbering away.
　Come here, I've something I must say.   3810
　[*All gather around him.*]
　Gretchen, look here, you're young yet,
　A green girl, not so smart about
　Managing her business.
　We know it, don't we, you and me,
　You're a whore, privately—
　Go public, don't be shy, miss.
GRETCHEN. My brother! God! What wretchedness!
VALENTINE. You can leave God out of this.
　What's done can't ever be undone,
　And as things went, so they'll go on.   3820
　You let in one at the back door,
　Soon there'll be others, more and more—

A whole dozen, hot for pleasure,
And then the whole town for good measure.

Shame is born in hugger-mugger,
The lying-in veiled in black night,
And she is swaddled up so tight
In hopes the ugly thing will smother.
But as she thrives, grows bigger, bolder,
The hussy's eager to step out,   3830
Though she has grown no prettier.
The more she's hateful to the sight,
The more the creature seeks the light.

I look ahead and I see what?
The honest people of this place
Standing back from you, you slut,
As from a plague-infected corpse.
When they look you in the face
You'll cringe with shame, pierced to the heart.
In church they'll drive you from the altar,   3840
No wearing gold chains any more,
No putting on a fine lace collar
For skipping round on the dance floor.
You'll hide in dark and dirty corners
With limping cripples, lousy beggars.
God may pardon you at last,
But here on earth you stand accurst.

MARTHE. Look up to God and ask his mercy!
    Don't add to all your other sins
    Sacrilege and blasphemy.   3850

VALENTINE. If I could only lay my hands
    On your scrawny, dried up body,
    Vile panderer, repulsive bawd,

Then I might hope to find forgiveness
Ten times over from the Lord!

GRETCHEN.   My brother! Hell's own wretchedness!

VALENTINE.   Stop your bawling, all your to-do.
When you said goodbye to honor,
That is what gave me the worst blow.
And now I go down in the earth,   3860
Passing through the sleep of death
To God—who in his life was a brave soldier.

Dies.

THE CATHEDRAL

Requiem mass, organ music, singing. Gretchen among a crowd of worshippers. Behind her an Evil Spirit.

EVIL SPIRIT.   How different then, Gretchen,
It was when, all innocent,
Here at the altar
You babbled your prayers
From the worn little prayer book,
Half a game playing,
Half God adoring
In your childish heart,   3870
Gretchen!
And how is it now?
In your heart what
Wicked deed?
Do you pray for the soul of your mother
Who through you slept on and still on
Into pain and more pain?
There at your door whose blood is it?

—And already under your heart
A stirring, a quickening, is it,   3880
Affrighting you both
With its foreboding presence?
GRETCHEN. Misery! Misery!
    To be rid of these thoughts
    That go round and around in me.
    Accusing, accusing!
CHOIR. *Dies irae, dies illa*
    Solvet saeclum in favilla.
    [*Organ music.*]
EVIL SPIRIT. The wrath of God grips you!
    The trumpet sounds,   3890
    The grave mounds are heaving,
    And your heart,
    From its ashen rest waking
    Into billowing flames,
    Agonizingly burns!
GRETCHEN. How hateful it's here!
    I feel as if stifling
    In the organ tones!
    The chanting is shrivelling
    My heart into dust.   3900
CHOIR. *Judex ergo cum sedebit,*
    Quidquid latet adparebit,
    Nil inultum remanebit.
GRETCHEN. How shut in I feel,
    The pillars imprison me!
    The vaulting presses
    Down on me!—Air!
EVIL SPIRIT. Hide yourself, do! Sin and shame
    Never stay hidden.

Air? Light?   3910
Poor thing that you are!

CHOIR. *Quid sum miser tunc dicturus?*
Quem patronum rogaturus,
Cum vix justus sit securus?

EVIL SPIRIT. The blessed avert
Their faces from you.
Pure souls with a shudder
Snatch their hands back from you.
Poor thing!

CHOIR. *Quid sum miser tunc dicturus?*   3920

GRETCHEN. Your smelling salts, neighbor!
[*She swoons.*]

WALPURGIS NIGHT

The Harz Mountains, near Schierke and Elend. Faust,
Mephistopheles.

MEPHISTO. What you would like now is a broomstick, right?
Myself, give me a tough old billy goat.
We've got a ways to go still, on this route.

FAUST. While legs hold up and breath comes freely,
This knotty blackthorn's all I want.
Hastening our journey, what's the point?
To loiter through each winding valley,
Then clamber up this rocky slope
Down which that stream there tumbles ceaselessly—   3930
That's what gives the pleasure to our tramp.
The spring has laid her finger on the birch,
Even the fir tree feels her touch,
Then mustn't our limbs feel new energy?

MEPHISTO. Must they? I don't feel that way, not me.
    My season's strictly wintertime,
    I'd much prefer we went through ice and snow.
    The waning moon, making its tardy climb
    Up the sky, gives off a reddish glow
    So sad and dim, at every step you run   3940
    Into a tree or stumble on a stone.
    You won't mind my begging assistance
    Of a will-o'-the wisp—and there's one no great distance,
    Shining for all he's worth, so merrily.
    —Hello there, friend, we'd like your company!
    Why blaze away so uselessly, for nothing?
    Do us a favor, light up this path we're climbing.
WILL-O'-THE-WISP. I hope the deep respect I hold you in, sir,
    Will keep in check my all-too-skittish temper;
    The way we go is zigzag, that's our nature.   3950
MEPHISTO. Trying to ape mankind, poor silly flame.
    Now listen to me: fly straight, in the Devil's name,
    Or out I'll blow your feeble light immediately.
WILL-O'-THE-WISP. Yes, yes, you give the orders here, quite right;
    I'll do what you require, happily,
    But don't forget, the mountain on this night
    Is mad with magic, witchcraft, sorcery,
    And if Jack-o'-Lantern is your guide,
    Don't expect more than he can provide.
FAUST, MEPHISTOPHELES, WILL-O'-THE-WISP. [*Singing in turn*]
        We have entered, as it seems,   3960
        Realm of magic, realm of dreams.
        Lead us well and win such honor
        His to have, bright-shining creature,
        By whose flicker we may hasten
        Forward through this wide, waste region!

See the trees, one then another,
Spinning past us fast and faster,
And the cliffs impending over,
And the jutting crags, like noses
Winds blow through with snoring noises!   3970

Over stones and through the heather
Rills and runnels downwards hasten.
Is that water splashing, listen,
Is it singing, that soft murmur,
Is it love's sweet voice, lamenting,
For the days when all was heaven?
How our hearts hoped, loving, yearning!
And like a tale, an old, familiar,
Echo once more tells it over.

Whoo-oo! Owl's hoot's heard nearer,   3980
Cry of cuckoo and of plover—
Still not nested, still awake?
Are those lizards in the brake,
Straggle-legged, big of belly?
And roots winding every which way
In the rock and sand send far out
Shoots to snare and make us cry out.
Tree warts, swollen, gross excrescents,
Send their tentacles like serpents
Out to catch us. And mice scamper   3990
In great packs of every color
Through the moss and through the heather,
And the glowworms swarm around us
In dense clouds and only lead us
Hither, thither, to confuse us.

Tell me, are we standing still, or
Still advancing, climbing higher?

Everything spins round us wildly,
Rocks and trees grin at us madly,
And the errant lights, more of them ever,   4000
Puff themselves up, big and bigger.

MEPHISTO. Seize hold of my coattails, quick,
We're coming to a middling peak
Where you'll marvel at the sight
Of Mammon's Mountain burning bright.

FAUST. How strange that glow is, there, far down,
Sad and pinkish, like the dawn.
Its faint luminescence reaches
Deep into the yawning gorges,
Mist rises here and streams away there,   4010
Penetrated by pale fire.
Here, like a thin thread, the glitter
Winds along, then like a fountain
Overflowing, spills down the mountain,
And vein-like, branching all about,
Holds in gleaming embrace the valley,
And here, squeezed through a narrow gully,
Collects into a pool apart.
Sparks fly about as if a hand
Were scattering golden grains of sand,   4020
And look there, how from base to top,
The whole cliffside is lit up.

MEPHISTO. Holiday time Lord Mammon's castle
Puts on a show that has no equal.
Don't you agree? You saw it, very luckily.
I hear our guests arriving—not so quietly!

FAUST. What a gale of wind is blowing,
Buffeting my back and shoulders!

MEPHISTO. Clutch with your fingers that outcropping
Or you'll fall to your death among the boulders.   4030

The mist is making it darker than ever.
Hear how the trees are pitching and tossing!
Frightened, the owls fly up in a flutter.
The evergreen palace's pillars are creaking
And cracking, boughs snapping and breaking,
As down the trunks thunder
With a shriek of roots tearing,
Piling up on each other
In a fearful disorder!
And through the wreckage-strewn ravines   4040
The hurtling storm blast howls and screams.
And hear those voices in the air,
Some far-off and others near?
That's the witches' wizard singing,
Along the mountain shrilly ringing.

CHORUS OF WITCHES.
The witches ride up to the Brocken,
Stubble's yellow, new grain green.
The great host meets upon the peak and
There Urian mounts his throne.
So over stock and stone go stumping,   4050
Witches farting, billy goats stinking!

VOICE. Here comes Mother Baubo now,
Riding on an old brood sow.

CHORUS.
Honor to whom honor is due!
Old Baubo to the head of the queue!
A fat pig and a fat frau on her,
And all the witches following after!

VOICE. How did you come?

VOICE.   Ilsenstein way.
I peeked in an owl's nest, passing by.

VOICE.   Oh, I wish you'd go to hell, all,
Why such a rush, such an insane scramble?   4060
VOICE. Too fast, too fast, my bottom's skinned sore!
Oh, my wounds! Look here and here!
CHORUS OF WITCHES.
Broad the way and long the road,
What a bumbling, stumbling crowd!
Broomstraw scratches, pitchfork's pushed,
Mother's ripped and baby's crushed.
HALF-CHORUS OF WARLOCKS.
We crawl like snails lugging their whorled shell,
The women have got a good mile's lead.
When where you're going's to the Devil,
It's woman knows how to get up speed.   4070
OTHER HALF-CHORUS.
A mile or so, why should we care?
Women may get the start of us,
But for all of their forehandedness,
One jump carries a man right there.
VOICE. [Above] Come along with us, you down at the lake.
VOICE. [From below] Is there anything better we would like?
We scrub ourselves clean as a whistle,
But it's no use, still we're infertile.
BOTH CHORUSES.
The wind is still, the stars are fled,
The veiled moon's glad to hide her head,   4080
Rushing, roaring, the mad chorus
Scatters sparks by the thousands about us.
VOICE [From below] Wait, please, wait, only a minute!
VOICE. [Above] A voice from that crevice, did you hear it?
VOICE. [From below] Take me along, don't forget me!
For three hundred years I've tried to climb

Up to the summit—all in vain.
I long for creatures who are like me.
BOTH CHORUSES.
    Straddle a broomstick, a pitchfork's fine too,
    Get up on a goat, a plain stick will do.   4090
    Who can't make it up tonight,
    Forever is done for, and so good night.
HALF-WITCH. [*From below*] I trot breathlessly, and yet
How far ahead the rest have got.
No peace at all at home, and here
It's no better. Dear, oh dear!
CHORUS OF WITCHES.
    The unction gives us hags a lift,
    A bit of rag will do for a sail,
    Any tub's a fine sky boat—
    Don't fly now and you never will.   4100
BOTH CHORUSES.
    And when we've gained the very top,
    Light down, swooping, to a stop.
    We'll darken the heath entirely
    With all our swarming witchery.
[*They alight.*]
MEPHISTO. What a crowding and shoving, rushing and clattering
Hissing and shrieking, pushing and chattering
Burning and sparking, stinking and shaking,
We're among witches, no mistaking!
Stick close to me or we'll lose one another.
But where are you?
FAUST.   Here, over here!   4110
MEPHISTO. Already swept away so far!
I must show this mob who is master—
Out of the way of Voland the Devil,
Out of the way, you charming rabble!

Doctor, hang on, we'll make a quick dash
And get ourselves out of this terrible crush—
Even for me it's too much to endure.
Yonder's a light has a strange lure,
Those bushes, I don't know why, attract me.
Quick now, dive in that shrubbery! 4120

FAUST. Spirit of Contradiction! However,
Lead the way!—He's clever, my devil:
Walpurgis Night up the Brocken we scramble
So as to do what? Hide ourselves in a corner!

MEPHISTO. Look at that fire there, burning brightly,
Clubmen meeting, all seeming so sprightly;
You don't feel alone when the company's fewer.

FAUST. But I would like it better higher,
On the summit, where I make out
A red glow and black smoke swirling, 4130
Satanwards a great crowd's toiling,
And there, I haven't the least doubt,
Many a riddle at last is resolved.

MEPHISTO. And many another one revealed.
Let the world rush on crazily,
We'll pass the time here cozily,
And doing what customarily's the thing done,
Inside the great world contrive us a little one.
Look there, young witches, all stark naked,
And old ones wisely petticoated. 4140
Don't sulk, be nice, if only to please me;
Plenty of fun—as for trouble, hardly.
I hear music, a damned racket!
You must learn not to mind it.
No backing out now, follow me in
And find you are my debtor again.
—Now what do you think of this place, my friend?

Our eyes can hardly see to its end.
A hundred fires, in a row burning,
The people shouting, drinking, dancing,   4150
Eating, loving, oh what a party!
Where is there anything better, show me.

FAUST. To get us admitted to the revel,
You'll appear how, as magician or devil?

MEPHISTO. I travel incognito normally,
But when it comes to celebrations
A man must show his decorations.
The Garter's never been awarded me,
But in these parts the split hoof's much respected.
That snail there, do you see it, creeping forwards,   4160
Its face pushing this way, that way, towards us?
Already I've been smelt out, I'm detected.
Even if deception was my aim,
Here there's no denying who I am.
Come on, we'll go along from fire to fire,
The go-between me, you the cavalier.
      [Addressing figures huddled around a fire]
Old sirs, you keep apart, not very merry,
You'd please me better if you joined the party.
You ought to be carousing with the youngsters,
At home we're all alone enough, we oldsters.   4170

GENERAL. Put no trust in nations, for the people,
In spite of all you've done, are never grateful.
It's with them always as it is with women,
The young come first, and we—ignored, forgotten.

MINISTER OF STATE. The world has got completely off the track.
Oh, they were men, the older generation!
When we held every high position,
That was the golden age, and no mistake.

PARVENU. We were no simpletons ourselves, we weren't,
>   And often did the things we shouldn't.   4180
>   But everything's turned topsy-turvy now,
>   Just when we're foursquare with the status quo.
AUTHOR. Who wants, today, to read a book
>   With a modicum of sense or wit?
>   And as for our younger folk,
>   I've never seen such rude conceit.
MEPHISTO. [*Suddenly transformed into an old man*]
>   For Judgment Day all now are ripe and ready,
>   Since I shan't ever again climb Brocken's top;
>   And considering too my wine of life is running cloudy,
>   The world also is coming to a stop.   4190
JUNK-DEALER WITCH. Good sirs, don't pass me unawares,
>   Don't miss this opportunity!
>   Look here, will you, at my wares,
>   What richness, what variety!
>   Yet there is not a single item
>   Hasn't served to claim a victim,
>   Nowhere on earth will you find such a stall!
>   No dagger here but it has drunk hot blood,
>   No cup but from it deadly poison's flowed
>   To waste a body once robust and hale,   4200
>   No gem but has seduced a loving girl,
>   No sword but has betrayed an ally or a friend,
>   Or struck an adversary from behind.
MEPHISTO. Auntie, think about the times you live in—
>   What's past is done. Done and gone!
>   The new, the latest, that's what you should deal in,
>   The nouveau only, turns us on.
FAUST. Oh let me not forget I'm me, me, solely!
>   A fair to beat all fairs this is, believe me.

MEPHISTO. The scrambling mob climbs upwards, jostling, crushed,   4210
    You think you're pushing and you're being pushed.

FAUST. Who's that there?

MEPHISTO.   Look at her close.
    Lilith.

FAUST.   Lilith? What's she to us?

MEPHISTO. Adam's wife, his first. Beware of her.
    Her beauty's one boast is her dangerous hair.
    When Lilith winds it tight around young men
    She doesn't soon let go of them again.

FAUST. Look, one old witch, one young one, there they sit—
    They've waltzed around a lot already, I will bet!

MEPHISTO. Tonight's no night for resting but for fun,   4220
    Let's join the dance, a new one's just begun.

FAUST. [*Dancing with the young witch*]
    A lovely dream I dreamt one day:
    I saw a green-leaved apple tree,
    Two apples swayed upon a stem,
    So tempting! I climbed up for them.

THE PRETTY WITCH. Ever since the days of Eden
    Apples have been man's desire,
    How overjoyed I am to know, sir,
    Apples grow, too, in my garden.

MEPHISTO. [*Dancing with the old witch*]
    A naughty dream I dreamt one day: 4230
    I saw a tree split up the middle—
    A huge cleft, phenomenal!
    And yet it pleased me every way.

THE OLD WITCH. Welcome, welcome, to you, sire,
    Cloven-footed cavalier!
    Stand to with a proper stopper,
    Unless you fear to come a cropper.

PROCTOPHANTASMIST. Accursed tribe, so bold, presumptuous!
    Hasn't it been proven past disputing
    Spirits all are footless, they lack standing?   4240
    And here you're footing like the rest of us!
THE PRETTY WITCH. [*Dancing*]
    What's he doing here, at our party?
FAUST. [*Dancing*]
    Him? You find him everywhere, that killjoy,
    We others dance, he does the criticizing,
    Every step one takes requires analyzing,
    Until it's jawed about, it hasn't yet occurred.
    He can't stand how we go forwards undeterred;
    If you keep going around in the same old circle,
    As he plods year in, year out on his treadmill,
    You might be favored with his good opinion,   4250
    Provided you most humbly beg it of him.
PROCTOPHANTASMIST. Still here, are you? It's an outrage!
    Vanish, ours is the Enlightened Age—
    You devils, no respect for law and regulation,
    We've grown so wise, yet ghosts still walk in Tegel.
    How long I've toiled to banish superstition,
    Yet it lives on. The whole thing is a scandal!
THE PRETTY WITCH. Stop, stop, how boring you are with your
        gabble!
PROCTOPHANTASMIST. I tell you to your face, you ghostly freaks,
    I'll not endure this tyranny of spooks   4260
    My spirit finds you spirits much too spiritual!
    [*They go on dancing.*]
    I see I'm getting nowhere with these devils,
    Still, it will add a chapter to my travels,
    And I hope, before my sands of life run out,
    To put foul fiends and poets all to rout.

MEPHISTO. He'll go and plump himself down in a puddle—
     It solaces him for all his ghostly trouble—
     And purge away his ghost and all the other spirits
     By having leeches feed on where the M'sieur sits.
     [*To Faust, who has broken off dancing and withdrawn*]
     What's this? You've left your partner in the lurch   4270
     As she was sweetly singing, pretty witch.
FAUST. Ugh! From her mouth a red mouse sprung
     In the middle of her song.
MEPHISTO. Is that anything to fuss about?
     And anyway it wasn't gray, was it?
     To take on so, to me, seems simply rudeness
     When you are sporting with your Amaryllis.
FAUST. And then I saw—
MEPHISTO.   Saw what?
FAUST.   Look over there,
     At that lovely child, pale -faced with fear,
     Standing by herself. How laboriously   4280
     She pushes herself forwards, wracked by pains,
     As if her feet were shackled tight in chains.
     I must confess, it looks like Gretchen.
MEPHISTO.   Let it be!
     It's bad, that thing, a lifeless shape, a wraith
     No man ever wants to meet up with.
     Your blood freezes under her dead stare,
     Almost turned to stone, you are.
     Medusa, did you ever hear of her?
FAUST. Yes, yes, those are a corpse's eyes
     No loving hand was by to close.   4290
     That's Gretchen's breast, which she so often
     Gave to me to rest my head on,
     That shape her dear, her lovely body,
     She gave to me to enjoy freely.

MEPHISTO. It's all magic, hocus-pocus, idiot!
   Her power is, each thinks she's his own sweetheart.
FAUST. What rapture! And what suffering!
   I stand here spellbound by her look.
   How strange, that bit of scarlet string
   That ornaments her lovely neck,   4300
   No thicker than a knife blade's back.
MEPHISTO. Right you are. I see it, too.
   She's also perfectly able to
   Tuck her head beneath her arm
   And stroll about. Perseus—remember him?—
   He is the one that hacked it off her.
   —Man, I'd think you'd have enough of
   The mad ideas your head is stuffed with!
   Come, we'll climb this hill, discover
   All's as lively as inside the Prater.   4310
   And unless somebody has bewitched me,
   The thing I see there is a theater.
   What's happening?
SERVIBILIS. A play, a new one, starting shortly,
   Last of seven. With us here it's customary
   To offer a full repertory.
   The playwright's a rank amateur,
   Amateurs, too, the whole company.
   Well, I must hurry off now, please excuse me,
   I need to raise the curtain—amateurishly!   4320
MEPHISTO. How right it is that I should find you here, sirs;
   The Blocksberg's just the place for amateurs.

WALPURGIS NIGHT'S DREAM

or

Oberon and Titania's Golden Wedding

Intermezzo

STAGE MANAGER. (*To crew*) Today we'll put by paint and canvas,
    Mieding's brave sons, all.
    Nature paints, the scene for us:
    Gray steep and mist-filled vale.
HERALD. For the wedding to be golden,
    Years must pass, full fifty;
    But if the quarrel is made up, then
    It is golden truly.   4330
OBERON. Spirits, if you hover round,
    Appear, it's right, the hour;
    King and Queen are once more bound
    Lovingly together.
PUCK. Here's Puck, my lord, who spins and whirls
    And cuts a merry caper,
    A hundred follow at his heels,
    Skipping to the measure.
ARIEL. Ariel strikes up his song,
    The notes as pure as silver;   4340
    Philistines all around him throng,
    Those, too, with true culture.
OBERON. Wives and husbands, learn from us
    How two hearts unite:
    To find connubial happiness,
    Only separate.
TITANIA. If Master sulks and Mistress pouts,
    Here's the remedy:

Send her on a trip down south,
Him the other way.   4350
FULL ORCHESTRA. [*Fortissimo*] Buzzing fly and humming gnat,
     And all their consanguinity,
     Frog's hoarse croak, cicada's chat
     Compose our symphony.
SOLO. Here I come, the bagpipes, who's
     Really a soap bubble;
     Hear me through my stumpy nose
     Go tootle-doodle-doodle.
A BUDDING IMAGINATION. A spider's foot, a green toad's gut,
     Two winglets—though they hardly   4360
     Compose a living creature, yet
     Make do as nonsense poetry.
A COUPLE. Short steps, smart leaps, all done neatly
     In the honeyed air.
     I grant you foot it very featly,
     We stay planted here.
AN INQUIRING TRAVELER. Can it be a fairground fraud,
     The shape at which I'm looking?
     Oberon the handsome god
     Still alive and kicking?   4370
A PIOUS BELIEVER. I don't see claws, nor any tail,
     And yet it's indisputable:
     Like Greece's gods, his dishabille
     Betrays the pagan devil.
AN ARTIST OF THE NORTH. Here everything I undertake
     Is weak, is thin, is sketchy;
     But I'm preparing soon to make
     My Italian journey.
A STICKLER FOR DECORUM. I'm here, and most unhappily,
     Where all's impure, improper;   4380

Among this riotous witchery
Only two wear powder.
A YOUNG WITCH. Powder, like a petticoat,
Is right for wives with gray hair;
But I'll sit naked on my goat,
Show off my strapping figure.
A MATRON. We are too well bred by far
To bandy words about
But may you, young thing that you are,
Drop dead, and soon, cheap tart! 4390
THE CONDUCTOR. Mosquito's nose, gnat's proboscis,
Mind you keep the tempo.
Let be, you bugs, the naked miss—
On with the concerto!
A WEATHERCOCK. [*Pointing one way*]
No better company than maids
Like these, so kind, complaisant;
And bachelors to match, old boys,
Agog all, all impatient!
WEATHERCOCK. [*Pointing the other way*]
And if the earth don't open up
And swallow this lewd rabble, 4400
Off I'll race at a great clip,
Myself go to the Devil.
SATIRICAL EPIGRAMS [XENIEN]. Gadflies, we, who plant our sting
In hides highborn and bourgeois,
In so doing honoring
Great Satan, our dear Papa.
HENNINGS. Look there, at the pack of them,
Like schoolboys jeering meanly.
Next, I'm sure, they all will claim
It's all in fun, friends, really. 4410

MUSAGET ["LEADER OF THE MUSES"]

    If I joined these witches here

    I'm sure I'd not repine;

    I know I'd find it easier

    To lead them than the Nine.

THE OUONDAM "SPIRIT OF THE AGE."

    What counts is knowing the right people,

    Catch hold and we'll go places;

    Blocksberg's summit's more than ample,

    Like Germany's Parnassus.

THE INQUIRING TRAVELER. Who's that fellow who's so stiff   4420

    And marches so majestical?

    He sniffs away for all he's worth,

    "Pursuing things Jesuitical."

A CRANE. An earnest fisherman I am,

    In clear and troubled waters.

    And thus you see a pious man

    Hobnobbing with devils.

A CHILD OF THIS WORLD. All occasions serve the godly

    In their work. Atop

    The Blocksberg, even there, they   4430

    Set up religious shop.

A DANCER. What's that booming, a new team

    Of musicians coming?

    No, no, they're bitterns in the stream

    All together drumming.

THE DANCING MASTER How cautiously they lift their feet—

    Draw back in fear of tripping!

    The knock-kneed hop, they jump the stout,

    Heedless how they're looking.

THE FIDDLER. This riffraff's so hate-filled, each lusts   4440

    To slit the other's throat;

Orpheus with his lute tamed beasts:
These march to the bagpipes' note.

A DOGMATIST. I can't be rattled, no, by your
Doubts, suspicions, quibbles;
The Devil's real, he is, that's sure,
Else how would there be devils?

AN IDEALIST. The mind's creative faculty
This time has gone too far;
If everything I see is me,   4450
Daft I am for sure.

A REALIST. It's pandemonium, it's mad,
I'm floored, I am, dumbfounded!
This is the first time I have stood
On ground on nothing founded.

A SUPERNATURALIST. The presence of these devils here
For me is reassuring evidence:
From the demonical I infer
The angelical's existence.

A SKEPTIC. They see a flickering light and gloat,   4460
There's treasure there, oh surely;
Devil's a word that pairs with doubt,
This is a place made for me.

CONDUCTOR. Frogs in leaves, grasshoppers grass—
What damned amateurs!
Cicadas chirr, mosquitos buzz—
Call yourselves performers!

THE SMART ONES. Sans all souci we are, shift
About with lightning speed;
When walking on the feet is out,   4470
We walk on the head.

THE NOT-SO SMART ONES. At court we sat down to free dinners,
And now all doors are shut;

We've worn out our dancing slippers
And must limp barefoot.

WILL-O-THE-WISPS. We're from the muddy flats, marais,
   Such is our lowly origin;
   But now we shine as chevaliers
   And dance in the cotillion.

A SHOOTING STAR. I shot across the sky's expanse,   4480
   A meteor, blazing bright.
   Now fallen, I sprawl in the grass—
   Who'll help me to my feet?

THE BRUISERS. Make way, make way, we're coming through,
   Trampling your lawn,
   We're spirits too, but spirits who
   Have lots of beef and brawn.

PUCK. How you tramp, so heavily,
   Like infant elephants!
   Elfin Puck's stamp be today   4490
   The heaviest of tramps.

ARIEL. Or gave you wings, our loving Nature,
   Or gave you them the Spirit,
   My light trace, come, follow after,
   Up to the rose hill's summit.

ORCHESTRA. [*Pianissimo*]
   Shrouding mists and trailing clouds
   Lighten in the dawning,
   Breeze stirs leaves, wind rattles reeds,
   And all, all, gone in the morning.

AN OVERCAST DAY. A FIELD

Faust and Mephistopheles.

FAUST. In misery! In despair! Stumbling about pitifully over the   4500
earth for so long, and now a prisoner! A condemned criminal,
shut up in a dungeon and suffering horrible torments, the poor
unfortunate child! It's come to this, to this! And not a word about
it breathed to me, you treacherous, odious spirit! Stand there
rolling your Devil's eyes around in rage, oh do! Brazen it out
with your intolerable presence! A prisoner! In misery, irremedi-
able misery! Delivered up to evil spirits and the stony-hearted
justice of mankind! And meanwhile you distract me with your
insipid entertainments, keep her situation, more desperate every
day, from me, and leave her to perish helplessly!   4510
MEPHISTO. She's not the first.
FAUST. You dog, you monster! Change him, O you infinite Spirit,
change the worm back into a dog, give it back the shape it wore
those evenings when it liked to trot ahead of me and roll at the
feet of some innocent wayfarer, tripping him up and leaping on
him as he fell. Give it back its favorite shape so it can crawl on
its belly in the sand before me, and I can kick it as it deserves, the
abomination!—Not the first!—Such misery, such misery! It's inconceivable, humanly inconceivable, that more than one creature should ever have plumbed such depths of misery, that the first   4520
who did, writhing in her last agony under the eyes of the Eternal
Forgiveness, shouldn't have expiated the guilt of all the others
who came after! I am cut to the quick, pierced to the marrow, by
the suffering of this one being—you grin indifferently at the fate
of thousands!
MEPHISTO. So once again we're at our wits' end, are we—reached
the point where you fellows start feeling your brain is about to

explode? Why did you ever throw in with us if you can't see the thing through? You'd like to fly, but can't stand heights. Did we force ourselves on you or you on us?   4530

FAUST. Don't snarl at me that way with those wolfish fangs of yours, it sickens me!—Great and glorious Spirit, Spirit who vouchsafed to appear to me, who knows me in my heart and soul, why did you fasten me to this scoundrel who diets on destruction, delights to hurt?

MEPHISTO. Finished yet?

FAUST. Save her or you'll pay for it! With a curse on you, the dreadfulest there is, for thousands of years to come!

MEPHISTO. I'm powerless to strike off the Great Avenger's chains or draw his bolts.—Save her indeed!—Who's the one who ruined   4540 her, I would like to know—you or me?

[Faust looks around wildly.]

Looking for a thunderbolt, are you? A good thing you wretched mortals weren't given them. That's the tyrant's way of getting out of difficulties—strike down any innocent person who makes an objection, gets in his way.

FAUST. Take me to where she is, you hear? She's got to be set free.

MEPHISTO. In spite of the risk you would run? There's blood guilt on the town because of what you did. Where murder was, there the avenging spirits hover, waiting for the murderer to return.

FAUST. That, from you, that too? Death and destruction, a world's   4550 worth, on your head, you monster! Take me there, I say, and set her free!

MEPHISTO. All right, all right, I'll take you there. But hear what I can do—do you think all the powers of heaven and earth are mine? I'll muddle the turnkey's senses, then you seize his keys and lead her out. Only a human hand can do it. I'll keep watch. The spirit horses are ready. Off I'll carry both of you. That's what I can do.

FAUST. Away then!

NIGHT. OPEN COUNTRY

Faust and Mephistopheles going by on black horses at a furious gallop.

FAUST. What's that going on at the ravenstone?   4560
MEPHISTO. Brewing something, doing something, don't know.
FAUST. Soaring up, swooping down, bowing, genuflecting.
MEPHISTO. A pack of witches.
FAUST. Strewing stuff, consecrating.
MEPHISTO. Keep going, keep going!

A PRISON

FAUST. [*With a bunch of keys and carrying a lamp, at a narrow
       iron door*]
    I shudder as I haven't for so long—
    Oh, how it suffers, our humanity!
    She's shut up inside these dank walls, poor thing,
    And all her crime was love, the brave, the illusory.
    You're hanging back from going in!   4570
    You're afraid of meeting her eyes again!
    In, in, your hesitation's her death, hurry!
    [*He puts the key in the lock.*]
SINGING. [*From within*]
        My mother, the whore,
        She's the one slew me,
        My father, the knave,
        He's the one ate me,
        My sister, wee thing,
        Heaped up my bones

Under cool stones,
Turned into a wood bird, I sing   4580
Fly away, fly away!

FAUST. [*Unlocking the door*] She doesn't dream her lover's listening,
Hears her chains rattle, the straw rustling.
[*He enters.*]

MARGARETE. [*Cowering on her paillasse*]
They're coming, they're coming! How bitter, death, bitter!

FAUST. [*Whispering*] Hush, dear girl, hush! You'll soon be free.

MARGARETE. [*Groveling before him*]
If your heart's human, think how I suffer.

FAUST. You'll wake the guards. Speak quietly.
[*Taking hold of the chains to unlock them*]

MARGARETE. [*On her knees*] Headsman, so early, it isn't right.
Have mercy on me! Too soon, too soon!
You come for me in the dead of night—   4590
Isn't it time enough at dawn?
[*Stands up.*]
I'm still so young, too young surely—
Still I must die.
How pretty I was, that's what undid me,
He held me so close, now he's far away,
My wreath pulled apart, the flowers scattered,
Don't grip me so hard! Please, won't you spare me?
What did I ever do to you?
Don't let me beg in vain for mercy.
I never before laid eyes on you.   4600

FAUST. It's unendurable, her misery!

MARGARETE. What can I do, I'm in your power,
Only let me nurse my baby first,
All night long I hugged the dear creature;
How mean they were, snatched it from my breast,
And now they say I murdered it.

I'll never be happy, no, never again.

They sing songs about me in the street,

It's wicked of them.

There's an old fairy tale ends that way,   4610

What has it got to do with me?

FAUST. [Falling *at her feet*] It's me here who loves you, me at
      your feet

To rescue you from this miserable fate.

MARGARETE. [*Kneeling beside him*]

We'll kneel down, that's right, and pray to the saints.

Look, under those steps,

Below the doorsill,

All Hell's a-boil.

The Evil One

In his horrible rage

Makes such a noise.   4620

FAUST. [*Crying out*] Gretchen! Gretchen!

MARGARETE. [*Listening*] That was my darling's own dear voice!

    [*She jumps up, the chains fall away.*]

I heard him call. Where can he be?

No one may stop me now, I'm free!

Into his arms I'll fly so fast,

Lie on his breast at last, at last.

Gretchen, he called, from there on the sill,

Through all the howlings and gnashings of Hell,

Through the furious, devilish sneering and scorn,

I heard a dear voice, its sound so well known.   4630

FAUST. Its me!

MARGARETE. It's you! Oh, say it again.

    [*Catching hold of him.*]

It's him! Where's the torture now, it's him!

Where's my fear of the prison, the chains they hung on me?

It's you, it's you! You've come here to save me!

I'm saved!

—I see it before me, so very plain,

The street I saw you the first time on,

I see Marthe and me where we waited for you

In the sunlit garden.

FAUST. [*Pulling her toward the door*]

Come along, come!

MARGARETE.   Don't go, stay here!   4640

I love it so being wherever you are.

[*Caressing him.*]

FAUST. Hurry!

If you don't hurry

The price we will pay!

MARGARETE. What? Don't know how to kiss anymore?

Parted from me a short time only

And quite forgotten what lips are for?

Why am I frightened with your arms around me?

Time was, at a word or a look from you,

Heaven herself threw her arms around me   4650

And you kissed me as if you'd devour me.

Kiss me, kiss me,

Or I'll kiss you!

[*She embraces him.*]

Oh the cold lips you have,

Cold and dumb.

What's become of your love,

All gone?

Who stole it from me?

[*She turns away from him.*]

FAUST. Come, follow me! Darling, be brave!

Oh, the kisses I'll give you, my love—   4660

Only come now, we'll slip through the door.

MARGARETE. [*Turning back to him*]
    It's you, is it really? For sure?

FAUST. Yes, it's me—you must come!

MARGARETE.   You strike off my chains,
    Take me into your arms.
    How is it you don't shrink away from me?
    Have you any idea who you're setting free?

FAUST. Hurry, hurry! The night's almost over.

MARGARETE. I murdered my mother,
    Drowned my infant,
    Weren't both of us given it—you too its parent—   4670
    Equally? It's you, I can hardly believe it.
    Give me your hand. No, I haven't dreamt it.
    Your dear hand!—But your hand is wet!
    Wipe it off, there's blood on it!
    My God, my God, what did you do?
    Put away your sword,
    I beg you to!

FAUST. What's past is done, forget it all.
    You're killing me.

MARGARETE. No, live on still.   4680
    I'll tell you how the graves should be;
    Tomorrow you must see to it.
    Give my mother the best spot,
    My brother put alongside her,
    Me, put me some distance off,
    Yet not too far,
    And at my right breast put my baby,
    Nobody else shall lie beside me.
    When I used to press up close to you,
    How sweet it was, pure happiness,   4690
    But now I can't, it's over, all such bliss—

I feel it as an effort I must make,
That I must force myself on you,
And you, I feel, resist me, push me back.
And yet it's you, with your good, kind look.
FAUST. If it's me, then come, we can't delay.
MARGARETE. Out there?
FAUST.   Out there, away!
MARGARETE. If the grave's out there, death ready,
    Yes, come, the two of us together,
    But only to the eternal place, no other.   4700
    —You're going now?
    I'd go too if I could, Heinrich, believe me!
FAUST. You can! All you need is the will. Oh come!
    The way is clear.
MARGARETE. No, I mayn't. For me all hope is gone.
    It's useless, flight. They'd keep, I'm sure,
    A sharp watch out. I'd find it dreadful
    To have to beg my bread of people,
    Beg with a bad conscience, too;
    Dreadful to have to wander about   4710
    Where all is strange and new,
    Only to end up getting caught.
FAUST. But I'll stick with you!
MARGARETE. Hurry! Be quick!
    Save your poor child—
    Run! Keep to the track
    That follows the brook,
    Over the bridge.
    Into the wood
    Left to the plank,   4720
    There in the pool—
    Reach down, quick, catch it!

It's fighting for breath!
It's struggling still!
Save it, oh, save it!
FAUST. Get hold of yourself.
One step and you're free, dear girl.
MARGARETE. If only we were well past the hill.
There on a rock Mother sits, all a-tremble—
Not a sign does she make, doesn't speak.   4730
There on a rock Mother sits, head a-wobble—
To look at her gives me a chill.
She slept so long she will never wake,
She slept so we might have our pleasure—
The happy hours we spent together!
FAUST. If all my persuading is no use,
I'll have to carry you off by force.
MARGARETE. Let go, let go, how dare you compel me!
Your're gripping my arm so brutally!
I always did what you wanted, once.   4740
FAUST. Soon day will be breaking! Darling, darling!
MARGARETE. Day? Yes, day, my last one, dawning,
My wedding day it should have been.
Not a word to a soul you've already been with your Gretchen.
My poor wreathe!
All's over and done.
We'll see one another again,
But not to go dancing.
The crowd presses in—not a sound, nothing,
Not the cry of a child.   4750
There are too many
For square and alley
To hold.
The bell calls, staff's shattered,
I'm seized and I'm fettered

And borne away, bound, to the block.
Every neck shivers with shock
As the sharp blade's brought down on my own.
Dumb lies the world as the grave.

FAUST. I wish I had never been born.   4760

MEPHISTOPHELES. [*Appearing outside*]
Come, come, or all's up with you, friend—
Debating, delaying, useless jabbering!
My horses are trembling.
A minute or two and it's day.

MARGARETE. Who's that rising up out of the ground?
It's him, him, oh drive him away!
It's holy here, what is he after?
It's me he is after, me!

FAUST. Live, hear me, live!

MARGARETE. It's the judgment of God! I surrender!   4770

MEPHISTO. Die both of you, I have to leave.

MARGARETE. In your hands, our Father, oh save me!
You angelical hosts, stand about me!
Draw up in your ranks to protect me!
I'm afraid of you, Heinrich, afraid!

MEPHISTO. She's condemned.

VOICE. [*From above*]
                                        She is saved!

MEPHISTO. [*To Faust, peremptorily*]
Come with me!
[*He disappears with Faust.*]

VOICE. [*From within, dying away*]
Heinrich! Heinrich!   4778

End of Part One

PART
—————
TWO

Here on earth
Is opportunity enough.

PART
TWO

ACT I

A PLEASANT LANDSCAPE

Faust stretched out in a field of flowers, tired, restless, trying to sleep.

Twilight.

A circle of spirits hovering about in the air, pleasant little creatures.

ARIEL. [*Singing to the accompaniment of Aeolian harps*]
    When like spring rain blossoms drift down,
    Showering all who live on earth,   4780
    When again fields don green, doff brown,
    Promising heaped harvest wealth,
    Elves as tiny as great-hearted
    Hasten helping where they can:
    Be he good or be he wicked,
    They feel for the unfortunate man.

    You spirits hovering about this prostrate figure,
    Show yours is the kind, the noble elfin nature.
    Ameliorate the cruel strife in his heart,
    Pluck out self-condemnation's burning dart   4790
    And wash his soul clean of the horror, fright.
    Four watches make up the slow turning night;
    Take good care they pass benignly for him.
    First lay his head on pillows of cool linen,
    Then bathe him in the dews of Lethe river,
    His rigid limbs will soon relax their tension
    As he sleeps daywards and recovers vigor.
    Your kindest office, perform it, each sprite,
    Restore him to the blessed light!

CHORUS. [*Solo voice, duet, and full chorus, by turns*]

    When the scented breezes sighing   4800
    Through the green-encircled glade,
    And the mists of twilight rising
    Veil the plot in a brune shade,
    Lulling childlike the worn heart,
    Whispering peace, tranquillity,
    Soon on weary eyes is shut
    Soundlessly the door of day.

    Darkness on the wide world settles,
    Up the sky star follows star,
    Great lamps some, some flickering candles,   4810
    Glittering near, shining afar,
    Here reflected in lake water,
    Sparkling there in the clear sky,
    And sealing all in deepest slumber,
    The moon in glory thrones on high.

    Now the hours of joy and pain
    All are spent and passed away;
    Know it!—you'll be well again!
    Trust yourself to the new day!
    Hills emerge, then the green vales,   4820
    Bushes cast their cooling shadows,
    And rows of ripening wheat in fields
    Roll harvestwards in silver billows.

    To have your every wish, desire,
    Wake, regard the glorious light!
    What holds you bound is a mild power,
    Sleep's a shell, break out of it!
    Up, no lagging, boldly does it;
    Though the crowd doubts and delays,

All's possible to a brave spirit   4830
Who sees, and seeing's quick to seize.

[*A tremendous din announces the rising of the sun.*]

ARIEL. Hear the Hours' loud career
        Which only spirit ears can hear
        As once again a new day's born!
        Granite gates grind open, grating,
        Apollo's car drives up, wheels rattling,
        Oh what a din it makes, the dawn!
        Beating drums and trumpets blaring
        Dazzle eyes and ears dumbfound
        With sounds too loud for our hearing;   4840
        Creep inside a folded flower,
        Inside rocks, beneath leaves, farther,
        Where all's hushed and hidden, for,
        Once hearing it you'll hear no more.
FAUST. Life pulses in me with a quickened beat,
        Welcoming the dawn's etherial light;
        And you, Earth, too, stood steadfast through the night
        And now breath with new vigor at my feet,
        Surrounding me already with so much pleasure,
        Firing me with a purpose I'll never forswear: 4850
        To strive after highest existence always, forever.
        —Slowly the world's disclosed in the paling dawn,
        The woods ring with a thousand-throated life,
        Mist eddies through the valleys, aloft, far down,
        Yet heaven's light piercing it, reaching into the depth,
        Awakens bough and branch—they start into view
        Out of the odorous dark where they lay sleeping;
        And colors emerge from the dimness, hue on hue,

On flower and leaf the pearly dew trembles, dripping—
All around I see a paradise appearing!   4860

And look up there!—the giant peaks announcing
The solemn hour at hand. They are first
To enjoy the eternal light, which downwards creeping
Reaches us after. Alpine meadows, a patch
Of green, each, in the evergreen, show clearer,
Still, show greener, as step by step the light
Descends. And there's the sun! but brighter
Than eyes can bear—I avert my dazzled sight.

Just so when hoping, yearning, striving hard
To realize your supreme wish, and there   4870
It is, the gateway to it open wide,
Out of the eternal beyond, vast, far
Excess of light erupts, a storm of flames
Engulfing us. We thought to light the torch
Of life, a sea of fire, and oh what a fire, overwhelms
Us instead. Is it love, is it hate, the seething flames
That envelop us—pain following joy, joy pain
In awful alternation, until compelled
To turn our gaze back to the earth again
And try in her earliest veiling mists to be concealed.   4880

Then let the blinding sun shine at my back,
My face be turned to the sounding waterfall
Shooting down the wall of rock! The more I look,
The more delight I take seeing it roll
Down cliff and crag, into numberless tumbling
Streamlets breaking, with bursts of bright spray flying
High in the air. How still more glorious when
The changing-unchanging bow from the watery uproar
Springs, the tinted arch now sharply drawn,

Now blurring and fading away in a misty shower. 4890
The bow is a mirror of our human endeavor;
When you think about it, how clear the realization:
What is it, our life, but a bright-hued reflection?

THE IMPERIAL PALACE

THRONE ROOM

Awaiting the Emperor, his Council of State. Trumpets. Courtiers of every kind, richly dressed, advance to front. The Emperor ascends the throne, the Astrologer on his right.

EMPEROR. My loyal subjects, welcome all,
    Assembled here from near and far!
    —I see him, my philosopher,
    But where the devil is my fool?
JUNKER. Fell straight down as if struck
    As he came waddling at your back.
    They lugged the tub of guts away— 4900
    Drunk or dead? It's hard to say.
SECOND JUNKER. As if by magic, in a trice,
    There stood another in his place,
    Very elegantly dressed,
    Yet all start back, he's so grotesque.
    The watch with their crossed halberds bar
    The clown from coming through the door.
    —Well, I must say: the nerve, the crust!
    Here he is, right in our midst!
MEPHISTO. [*Kneeling at the foot of the throne*]
    Who's cursed roundly, then embraced? 4910
    Who's wished for first and then dismissed?
    Who's shielded always in his post?

Who's scolded harshly and denounced?
Whom mayn't you bid come again?
Whose name is greeted with a smile?
Who is it drawing near your throne?
Who's sent himself into exile?

EMPEROR. Right now spare us, please, your wit,
  This is not the place for it.
  Riddles enough these lords here pose—   4920
  I'd like to hear how you'd solve those!
  My old fool's gone, I fear, his final journey;
  Come here, fool, and take his place beside me.

[*Mephistopheles mounts the steps and stands at his left.*]

MUTTERINGS FROM THE CROWD.
    A new fool—New troubles, then—
    What's the fellow's origin?—
    I'd like to know how he got in—
    The old fool dropped—His race was run—
    A tub he was—A stick this one.

EMPEROR. And so welcome, dear companions,
  Gathered here from far and near!   4930
  The time's auspicious, say all omens,
  Good fortune's ours, the stars declare.
  But tell me why when we wish most of all
  To be diverted from our nagging cares,
  Back we should return to state affairs,
  Lay down the grinning masks of Carnival?
  Well, you admitted no objection, said
  It had to be. We're here, so go ahead.

CHANCELLOR. The highest virtue, shining halolike
  Around the Emperor's head, which only he   4940
  May make prevail by his authority,

Is—justice! What all men love, cry out for, seek
To have and sorely need—they look
To him, as loyal subjects, for it.
Yet what good is a well-intentioned heart,
Best understanding and a willing hand
When there's a fever raging through the realm
And every evil hatches out a swarm
Of yet more evils. Look out from where we stand,
Here on this height, across the wide land,   4950
And what do you see? A nightmare where grotesquely
Disorder, apelike, mocks what's right and seemly,
Where lawlessness is law, new crimes old crimes outdoing,
And everywhere about us all's misrule, wrongdoing.

One man steals cattle, one the wife of his neighbor,
A third cup and candlestick from the altar,
And talks about it for years with a grin,
Never fearing the lash, safe in his skin.
The courthouse is crowded with plaintiffs appealing,
The judge sits high up in cushioned state,   4960
While out in the street an angry mob gathering,
Threaten revolt, hearts overflowing with hate.
He can boast of his crimes, the insolent wretch,
Who's backed by accomplices even more wicked,
While "Guilty!" is the verdict you hear from the bench
Where innocence has but itself to defend it.
And thus the whole world goes to smash,
All decency outraged, derided.
How should it thrive, then, that right sense
By which our actions must be guided?   4970
An honest man is swayed in time
By flattering words and venal offers;
The judge who fails to punish crime

Allies himself with the evildoers.
The picture I've painted is black enough,
Blacker by far if I told the strict truth.   (*Pause*)
There's no avoiding the severest measures;
When all men injure, in turn are injured,
Even the throne finds itself endangered.

MINISTER OF WAR. What days of riot, murderous brawls!   4980
All strike wildly, themselves are struck,
Deaf to all of our commands.
The burgher safe behind his walls,
The knight in his castle high on a rock
Conspire to frustrate our demands,
Withhold troops pledged His Majesty.
Our mercenaries growl impatiently,
Shout from the ranks they want their pay,
If we didn't owe them so much, our army
Would long ago have melted away.   4990
It's stirring up a hornet's nest
To countermand what all are determined on;
The Reich they've sworn to defend to the last
Lies in ruins, pillaged and trampled on.
No effort's made to check these disorders,
Half the world's in a state of collapse,
And the kings around us, our neighbors,
Think, "It's got nothing to do with us."

TREASURER. There's just no counting on our allies,
The subsidies they swore to send,   5000
Like our piped water, never arrives.
Also, Sire, throughout the land
Who is it owns the property?
All over new men have moved in,
Barons who like their liberty,
And we stand by, looking on:

So many rights we've given away,
Not a right's left us, no, not one.
And as for the parties, as they are known,
It doesn't matter, their praise or blame,   5010
They're not to be relied upon,
They love us, they hate us, it's all the same.
Guelph and Ghibelline lie low,
Resting up from their latest bout.
Who lifts a hand for his neighbor now?
Me and mine, each thinks about.
No gold's to be had, search high search low,
All scrimp and squeeze, hoard every penny,
With the result our Treasury's empty.
STEWARD. The things I must contend with, too!   5020
Daily we do our best to save,
Daily we spend more than we have,
Every day brings a new woe.
The cooks are lucky, lack no provision,
Payments in kind of boar and venison,
Rabbit, chicken, duck, goose, turkey
Come in on time or very nearly.
But as for the wine, it's been drunk up.
We used to have barrels stacked to the ceiling.
From the best vineyards, the best years,   5030
But now all's gone, there's not a drop
Thanks to our noble lords' endless swilling.
The Stadtrat, too, have broached their stores,
Drawing it off by bumper and bowlful
Till the banquet finishes under the table.
It's me must deal with our arrears;
The Jew's unrelenting, today what I borrow
Devours the rents I look for tomorrow.
There's not enough time for the pigs to fatten,

The pillow's been pawned our heads rest on at night,   5040
Bread's put on the table we've already eaten.

EMPEROR. [*After a moment's reflection, to Mephistopheles*]
Fool, I suppose you, too, have got a complaint?

MEPHISTO. Me, Sir? No, Sir! All's so splendid here,
Yourself, your noble court! How should there be
A want of confidence where the Emperor
In all things is obeyed implicitly?
Where his power stands ready to rout all hostile force?
Where so much goodwill, married to good sense,
Loyally waits to serve him in every way?
How should the evildoers succeed in combining,   5050
Darkness prevail, where light so effulgent is shining?

MUTTERINGS FROM THE CROWD.
A rascal, that one—Knows all the tricks—
Talks a good line—For as long as it works—
You can't fool me, I see through his game—
So what will it be?—Some grandiose scheme.

MEPHISTO. Where isn't there something lacking on this earth?
There it's this, there it's that, here what's lacking is cash.
You don't pick money up right off the floor;
But as deep as it's buried, a wise head can find it.
Under ancient walls, inside thick veins of ore,   5060
The gold to be had, minted as well as unminted!
If you ask who's the one will unearth us this treasure?—
It's the man that's been favored with a keen mind by Nature.

CHANCELLOR. Nature! Mind! How dare you! For talking so
We burn atheists at the stake, fellow!
Language like that is dangerous blasphemy!
Nature is sin, mind rank heresy;
The two beget as their offspring
The monster Doubt, that misshapen thing.
No more, you hear!—In our Empire   5070

Two classes, orders, only are,
Which worthily uphold the throne:
Knighthood one, priesthood the other.
They shelter it from every storm,
And their reward is bench and altar.
If the rabble in their distraction
Should ever rise up in rebellion,
You'll find behind it, make no mistake,
The sorcerer and heretic.
They undermine us in town and country,   5080
And now you want, by an impudent trick,
To sneak them into this august body
—No welcome to those wicked men!
The fool with them is close akin.

MEPHISTO. Aha, those accents! That's a man of learning.
What you can't touch, be sure it has no being,
What you can't grasp, for you it counts as nothing,
What you can't put in numbers, is a cheat,
What you can't weigh, well then, it has no weight,
What you don't mint yourself is counterfeit.   5090

EMPEROR. [*To Chancellor*] Are we better off by all this arguing?
What good's all your Lenten sermonizing?
I'm sick of hearing if and when and but—
What's lacking's money, well then get me it.

MEPHISTO. I'll get you all you need, more than you need;
It's easy, though what's easy's also hard.
The stuff is there, the trick is to discover it.
So who's the one that knows the way to it?
Think how in those old centuries of fear
When mounted hordes descended everywhere,   5100
How many a one, trembling with apprehension,
Buried from sight his every dearest possession.
So it was when mighty Rome held sway,

So yesterday, and so it is today.
It's all there still, in the ground where people hid it;
The ground's the Emperor's, so he should have it!

TREASURER. For a fool he doesn't speak so badly;
By ancient prerogative it's the Emperor's legally.

CHANCELLOR. Satan's laying golden snares to seize us,
What he says is not right, not religious.   5110

STEWARD. If he's able to balance the budget, why quibble?
I don't mind overstepping the line a little.

MINISTER OF WAR. Wise fool! He promises each a piece of the pie.
But it's not for a soldier to mix in policy!

MEPHISTO. Perhaps you think I'm working a scam—
We've got an astrologer here, ask him!
He knows the heavens, their every star and sphere.
Do tell us, sir: how does it look up there?

MUTTERINGS IN THE CROWD.
                Fool and dreamer—So near the throne—
                We're tired of hearing the same old tune—   5120
                Scoundrels both—In cahoots—
                Sir Fool whispers—Dr. Stargazer spouts.

ASTROLOGER. [*Prompted by Mephistopheles*] The sun's pure gold,
        gold without alloy;
Quick Mercury bears messages for pay;
Frau Venus has bewitched you with her light
As sweetly she looks down, early and late;
The moon, the fickle moon, yet maidenly;
With his sword sheathed, Mars still looks threateningly;
But Jupiter's aspect shows best of all;
Saturn's huge but, so far off, looks small: 5130
As metal he's not held in high repute,
Although his weight is great his value's not.
When Luna is with Sol in chaste accord,

Silver with gold, general joy is the reward.

Then all else waits by you to be possessed,

Palace and garden, pink cheek and dainty breast.

All this he can command, the learned man—

What not one of us here can do, he can!

EMPEROR. I hear him, hear him *twice*, distinctly;

Nevertheless he does not convince me.   5140

MUTTERINGS IN THE CROWD.

Astrological rubbish—Alchemy—

Heard it so often—Hoped foolishly—

It means nothing—Stale stuff, a joke—

Let him show up here!—I know he's a crook.

MEPHISTO. Look at them standing there, gawping and gaping,

Refuse to believe there's treasure waiting.

Yet one will mumble about mandrakes,

The black dog another—great skeptics, you see!

Well, sneer away, make lots of jokes,

Cry work of the Devil, rank sorcery—   5150

Till there's a prickling in your sole,

Till losing your balance, you stumble and reel.

It's then all feel the secret working

Of ever ruling Nature's power,

From the lowest depths a sense of something

Upward steals, a tremor, shudder;

When your every limb aches like the devil,

When the wind blows strangely all around,

Fall to at once with pick and shovel,

The treasure's there, right where you stand!   5160

MUTTERINGS IN THE CROWD.

My foot feels a lead weight—

My arm hurts—It must be gout—

How it itches, my big toe—

And oh my back, it aches so—
By these signs you would swear
A king's ransom's buried here.

EMPEROR. Then right now, fool! No sneaking off!
Prove your words are more than froth:
Lead us to the buried hoard.
I'll lay aside scepter and sword,   5170
With imperial hands, if you're telling the truth,
Dig myself. But prove a liar
And down you go into Hellfire.

MEPHISTO. [*Aside*] In any case, I know the way there!
—I can't say it often enough:
The wealth that waits to be picked up!
The peasant plowing his strip of earth
Turns up with the sod a gold cup,
Scratching his clay walls for saltpeter,
Fearful, joyful, what does he find?   5180
Kronen hidden under the plaster.
The vaults that beg to be unsealed!
The tunnels, crevices that wind
Down nearly to the underworld
Which he who has a nose for gold
Will dare to enter unappalled!
In cellars long closed off he'll find
Golden vessels, dishes, tankards
Stacked and piled and heaped up roofwards,
Ruby-crusted cups that stand   5190
Just at the elbow. If inclined,
He can broach, from casks in rows,
Ancient vintages. However—
If you'll believe one who knows,
The staves have long since rotted away;
What keeps the wine in is its crust of tartar.

The best part of such noble liquor,
No less than gold and jewelry,
By preference dwells in night and gloom.
The wise man searches tirelessly;   5200
To see by daylight, that's child's play,
But where it's dark, there mysteries have their home.

EMPEROR. Keep your mysteries, your gloom!
Sneak thieves go undetected in the dark,
At night all cats are gray, all cows are black.
Below us pots of gold, you claim, lie hidden—
All right, then plow them up, let's see them!

MEPHISTO. Take pick and shovel and dig yourself,
Work like a peasant, it's good for the health,
And golden calves, so many, a herd   5210
Starting out of the earth, are your reward.
Immediately with what delight
You'll deck yourself and your mistress out.
Jewels that sparkle with every color
Lend beauty and majesty even more luster.

EMPEROR. Yes, yes! But quick! How long must we wait?

ASTROLOGER. [*As above (prompted by Mephistopheles)*]
Sire, I beg you, restrain your eagerness!
First we must let the Carnival season pass.
Nothing can be done to any purpose
When all are pleasure-minded, unserious.   5220
Penance is called for, sobriety, composure;
Our higher strivings license our lower.
Who craves good things, first himself be good.
Who craves delights, tame his unruly blood,
Who wishes wine, patience till grapes ripen,
Who hopes for miracles, his faith strengthen.

EMPEROR. Then let the time be passed in merriment,
And when Ash Wednesday comes, more welcome it!

Without delay we'll celebrate meanwhile
Even more joyously the riotous Carnival.   5230

Trumpets Exeunt.

MEPHISTO. Good fortune's closely linked to merit,
A thought that never enters foolish minds;
The Philosopher's Stone's there in their hands?
The Philosopher's searching everywhere for it.

A GREAT HALL

With rooms decorated for the Carnival leading off it.

HERALD. Don't expect a carnival
Conducted in the German style—
Devils, clowns that whirl and prance
And Death the Master of the dance.
The watchword now is pleasure, fun!
Our Sovereign, when he went to Rome,   5240
Served our pleasure and his gain:
Over the Alps he brought back with him
Mirthfulness to his boreal kingdom.
Kneeling to kiss the Papal slipper,
He begged his right to the Imperial power,
And as he reached to seize the Crown,
He seized the Fool's Cap with it, too.
And here to us has brought it home.
Now all are as if born anew!
Who knows the world as it is, not appears,   5250
Will pull the cap down on his ears
And look the dolt and cavort crazily,
While keeping his own counsel, wisely.
People, I see, already are meeting,
Rushing together, backwards retreating,

Knots forming here and there dissolving—
Go to it, never feeling bashful!
The world's a world of nonsense still,
A hundred thousand follies, fill
Its cup up ever till it's brimful.   5260

FLOWER GIRLS [*Singing to Mandolins*]
          We wish to please, you see how smartly
          We've arrayed ourselves tonight;
          Florentine girls, young and pretty,
          Following the German court.

          In brunette locks we have tied
          Glossy blooms of every tinct;
          Silken threads and ribbons aid
          To show them off to best effect.

          Have we not earned by our art
          Your praises, Sirs? Oh, we feel sure!   5270
          Our flowers, counterfeit,
          Blossom throughout the whole year.

          Snippets of all hues and shapes,
          Pieced together by our skill;
          Jeer though you may at such scraps,
          How attractive is the whole.

          Pretty things to look at, we are,
          Flower girls, yet modish, smart,
          For women are disposed by Nature
          To the stratagems of Art.   5280

HERALD.
          Show us, please, your baskets, girls,
          Swelling with their floral treasure
          In your arms, poised on your curls.
          Each shall pick as suits his pleasure.

With your flowers quickly make
A garden of each arbored walk.
They're worth our custom, no mistake,
These fair peddlers and their stock.

FLOWER GIRLS.

At this joyful flower fair
Buy, yes buy, but please, no haggling!   5290
A few well-chosen words declare
What the buyer shall be getting.

AN OLIVE BRANCH.

I don't envy any flower,
For all strife I have a horror,
It goes against my fecund nature.
I'm earth's archetypal yield,
The pledge of peace in every field.
Today it's my hope I may gladly
Grace a handsome head and worthy.

A GARLAND OF GOLDEN EARS OF WHEAT.

Ceres' gifts are beautiful,   5300
Wound in garlands to adorn you;
What life requires first of all,
As ornament, how it becomes you!

A FANCIFUL WREATH.

Mallowlike are these bright flowers,
Moss grown, most surprisingly!
Blooms beyond Dame Nature's powers,
Not, though, fashion's fantasy!

A FANTASTIC BOUQUET.

Theophrastus himself would not
Ever dare to try and name me,
To please all people, though I may not,   5310
Still I hope I may please many:

Her whose beauty I'd set off
If she wound me in her hair,
Her who found me fine enough
To wear upon her heart, just there.

ROSEBUDS. [*Challenging the artificial flowers*]
All very well, such fantasy,
As a fashion of the day,
Extravagantly made as never
Thing was shaped by hand of Nature,
Grass-green stems and golden bells   5320
Peeping out of tumbling curls!—

Ourselves, we're not conspicuous,
Lucky who discover us;
Come, however, summertime,
Rosebuds burst into bright flame—
Lacking them, how you would grieve!
We promise first, then timely give
To eye and mind and heart at once,
Under Flora's governance.

[*The Flower Girls dispose their stock along the arbored walks.*]

GARDENERS. [*Singing to lutes*]
Flowers wound into a wreath   5330
Binding brows, work an enchantment.
Fruits have no wish to deceive;
Taste them, that gives the enjoyment.

Sunburnt faces, smiling, offer
Cherries, peaches, fat plums—buy!
Tongue and palate, not the eye,
Judge best juiciness and flavor.

Here's ripe fruit to eat, your Graces,
With smacking lips, with great gusto!
Roses are for poets' verses,   5340
Apples you must bite into.

Please, we ask that you allow us
Fellowship with yourselves, girls,
So that we may show our produce
Heaped up side by side with yours.

Under gay festoons and wreaths
Ornamenting the green bower,
You'll find everything together,
Fruit and flowers, buds and leaves.

[*Singing alternately to guitars and lutes, the two choruses expose
their wares for sale in tiered rows.*]

Mother and Daughter

MOTHER.

Daughter, when you saw the light,   5350
Prettier none than my pet,
How your face peeped pink and white
From beneath your bonnet;
Saw you all in bride's white clothed,
To the richest man betrothed,
Saw you woman wedded.

Ach, how many years have passed
By and still what?—nothing!
Troops of suitors smartly dressed
Soon their leave take, bowing.   5360
Round you swiftly whirl with one beau,
Nudge another with your elbow,
Still it's nothing doing.

So many outings we got up, and
Parties—goodness, what work!
Playing spin-the-bottle and
Odd-man-out, with no luck.
Today's the day the fools run loose,
Uncross your legs, don't be a goose,
Catch yourself a young buck!   5370

[*Pretty young girls throng in, chattering among themselves. Fishermen
with rods and birdcatchers with nets and limed twigs enter and mingle
with the girls, the men trying to catch the girls, the girls slipping from
their grasp, all of this providing opportunities for amiable banter.*]

WOODCUTTERS. [*Entering, boisterous, hulking peasants*]
Look out there, stand clear!
Room, room, people, please!
Give way, just don't stare!
What we do is fell trees,
When they topple, take care—
Oh, the thunder, the din!
And when we lug in
The fresh-cut logs,
Look out for your ribs!
Do us the justice,   5380
Fine dames, gentlemen,
To acknowledge our service:
We're crude, but without us,
What then, what then,
Though you're ever so clever?
How you would shiver,
Freeze to death without heat,
If we didn't sweat.
PUNCHINELLOS. [*Gawkish, almost silly*]

Oh, but you're simpletons,
Born with bent backs!   5390
We are the smart ones,
Don't lug loads, no thanks!
Our jackets, our caps,
Our pants with bright stripes
Sit on us lightly,
And oh how delightfully
Idle we are,
Lounging along
As free as the air
Through the marketplace throng,   5400
Or stop short to stare,
Screeching out to each other;
Then slip off like eels
To kick up our heels
And racket together.
Praise us or blame us,
It don't please us or shame us.

PARASITES. [*Fawning, greedy*]
      You brawny woodcutters
      With your fellow laborers,
      The charcoal burners—   5410
      You're the ones we admire!
      All our bows, our curtsies,
      Eager yesses, fulsome phrases,
      Now grave, now rapt faces,
      As occasions require—
      What good would they do
      If it were not for you?
      Even Heaven's swift fire
      Striking down with a crack,
      Without logs by the stack,   5420

Without big bags of coal,
Would nothing avail
To make the hearth flame,
By which means cooks boil,
Roast, stew, and broil!
Your true trencherman
Who licks his plate clean,
Sniffing fish, smelling meats,
Is inspired to feats
You'd never think possible   5430
At his patron's long table.

DRUNKARD. [*Maudlin*]

Nothing this day can go wrong,
Wonderful I feel, so free!
Fun's the program, lively song,
Banish all care, drink with me!
Let the wine flow, what is better,
When good fellows get together?
You there, hanging back, come on!
Now clink glasses, every one!

She got mad, the little lady—   5440
"Fool, in that coat, to show off!"
Called me a poor tailor's dummy
When I strutted back and forth.
Yet I drink my wine, what's better,
When good fellows get together?
Make the crystal ring, come on,
Now clink glasses, hang back none!

Me a lost soul? Never say it,
Look at me, I'm fine and dandy.
If the Host won't give me credit,   5450
Hostess will, if not her, Betty.

So I drink on, nothing's better!
All you others, come, together—
Up the glasses, every one!
Good, good, that's the way it's done.

Pleasure I find where I can,
May it be so, Lord, forever!
Leave me lie here where I am,
I can't stand up any longer.

CHORUS.

Brothers, wine was never better!　　　　　　　　　5460
One more toast, now, to each other!
Keep hold of your benches, hang on!
—Down he goes, he's had it, that one.

[*The Herald introduces a variety of poets: poets of nature, of court life and chivalry, love poets both sweet and passionate. In the press of rivalry, none lets the others speak. But one manages to get a few words in.*]

SATIRICAL POET.

What would give me the most pleasure,
Make me, as a poet, proud?
Spite these à-la-mode performers,
Write what *doesn't* please the crowd.

[*The Night and Graveyard poets beg to be excused because of the engrossing conversation they are having with a vampire just emerged from the tomb, the result of which might be a new style of poetry. The Herald, perforce consenting, calls instead on Greek mythology, which even in modern dress retains its character and charm.*]

The Graces

AGLAIA.

>What we give to life is grace;
>
>You for your part give with grace!

HEGEMONE.

>Accept with good grace, not with poor!   5470
>
>How good to get what you wished for.

EUPHROSYNE.

>And in your quiet, bounden days,
>
>With grace give thanks, with good grace praise.

The Fates

ATROPOS.

>The eldest, I, today, though, chosen
>
>For the spinning; it demands
>
>Careful thought and close attention
>
>When life's thin thread slips through your hands.

>So it's pliable, has softness,
>
>I've looked out the best flax for it;
>
>Drawing it to the right thickness   5480
>
>Needs a finger that is expert.

>If pleasures are extravagant,
>
>Exuberant and wild the sport,
>
>Think! The yarn's strength has a limit,
>
>Strain it too much, it will part.

CLOTHO.

>Note I am in charge at present
>
>Of the shears. The past behavior
>
>Of our sister lacked good judgment,
>
>Caused a great deal of displeasure:

>Lives devoid of any good use   5490
>
>Spun out to the very end;

Lives full of hope, of glorious promise,
Cut short and dragged underground.

But I, too, with youthful brashness
Have made already many an error;
To guard against my own rashness
I keep the scissors in their holder;

I'm glad to practice self-control,
Around look with a kindly eye.
So use the time of Carnival,   5500
Enjoy to the full your liberty!

LACHESIS.

I alone am prudent, careful,
So I supervise the thread;
Round and round it goes, the spindle,
Never at too great a speed.

From the spindle comes the yarn,
Fingers guide it on the reel,
Making sure that it runs on
Smoothly, without knot or burl.

Should I ever nod, forget,   5510
How I'd fear for you, world, then!
Hours, years add without let,
And the weaver takes the skein.

HERALD. Who our next ones are you'll never guess,
Scholars though you may be of old texts;
To look at them, who cause such wretchedness,
You'd think them aimiable, quite welcome guests—

The Furies they are, though you won't believe it—
Dear creatures, handsome, friendly, and so young!

But get mixed up with them and you'll regret it,   5520
These cooing doves conceal a serpent's fang,

With poison filled. Yet since today's a time
When fools boast openly their every frailty,
They don't pretend they're angels either, own
Themselves the plague infecting town and country.

The Furies

ALECTO. A warning! Who cares? You'll still listen trustfully
To us charming kittens' flattering purrs;
Whoever's got himself a darling sweetie,
With our claws we'll gently scratch his ears
Till we can tell him to his face his sacred   5530
True love has given the eye to this one and another;
That anyway she limps, is humpbacked, stupid.
He means to marry her? Not very clever!

As for the girl, her, too, we'll torture mercilessly
With how the other day he ran her down,
The cad, to this and that one, so dishonorably!
And if they make up, still, it's never the same.

MEGAERA. That's nothing! Once a couple's joined, my turn
Arrives, and I know how to change their rapture,
By whim and caprice, into galling pain;   5540
Natures are vincible, swayed by occasion and hour.

And no one, hugging tight the love he's wished for,
Doesn't, fool, soon languish for new bliss,
His good fortune now grown stale, familiar;
Flying the sun, he sweats to warm up ice.

An expert I am in affairs conjugal,
And know the right time for Asmodeus to appear
To change love into jangle, squabble, quarrel—
In this way I wreck mankind, pair by pair.

TISIPHONE.

My way's poison, sharp-edged daggers,   5550
Not sly whispers, with betrayers;
Play around, do, break your faith,
Know that you will come to grief.

Purest ecstasy must turn
Into gall and blackest spleen;
Bargain, beg, use every plea,
For all you've done you've got to pay.

Let none whine for forgiveness!
I ask judgment from the cliff,
Echo answers—listen!—Vengeance!   5560
Who proves faithless shall not live.

HERALD. To one side, please, good ladies, gentlemen!
Approaching now's a thing beyond your ken;
Look there, a mountain moving, on each flank
Carpets bravely hang, it has a head
Furnished with curving tusks, long snaky trunk:
A mystery!—which I've the key to read.
Mounted upon its neck, a gentle lady
Wielding a baton drives the creature smartly.
Erect behind her, glorious, is another,   5570
Dazzling the eye with awe-inspiring splendor;
On either side walk two chained noblewomen,
One trembling with fear, the other cheerful, sanguine,
One longing to be free, the other sure she is.
Now let each lady speak and tell us who she is.

FEAR.

Smoking torches, lamps, and tapers
Dimly light the boisterous fest;
Among these many lying faces
Here am I, alas, chained fast.

Giggling fools, out of my sight!   5580
Untrustworthy, grinning lot!
All my enemies tonight
Hound me with their secret hate.

There's a friend turned enemy,
I can see through his pretense!
Another means to murder me,
Ha, found out, away he slinks.

Oh how I long to take flight,
Run away, here, there, wherever!
Menaced on all sides, I halt   5590
Between uncertainty and terror.

HOPE.

Sisters dear, I greet you all!
Though this time of Carnival
Gives you pleasure, yet we all know
Off the masks must come tomorrow.
And if revels by torchlight
Something lack of true delight,
We shall saunter at our pleasure
In the happy days to come,
All alone or arm in arm,   5600
By green bank and poppied pasture,
Resting, if we choose, or acting,
Always carefree, nothing lacking,
Forward striving, never doubting,
Every house whose door we knock on
Opening with warmest welcome.
All that's best must somewhere be
Awaiting our discovery.

PRUDENCE.

Hope and Fear, opposed allies,

Undermine the world with lies,   5610
So they're kept in strictest durance.
Back, all!—you're safe thanks to Prudence!

Ruler, I, of this colossus
With his swaying, castled back;
Steadily his feet plod forwards
On the steep and narrow track.

But high up, upon his summit,
Wings outspread, the goddess, see,
Hawklike looking round to fly at
Every opportunity.   5620

Glittering, splendid, bathed in glory,
All around she shoots her bright beams,
Victory's the name she's called by,
Goddess of all undertakings.

ZOILO-THERSITES. Grr, I'm just in time to rail
At this fine lot, each and all:
But the one I hate especially
Is her perched up there, Victory.
With her wings spread to the breeze
She thinks an eagle's what she is,   5630
Wherever she flies she is sure
Everything belongs to her.
But me—when worthy deeds are done,
I howl with rage and curse and groan.
—Raise up the low, pull down the high,
What's crooked praise, what's straight decry:
Only so I'm kept in health,
So I'd have things here on earth.

HERALD. For that, you whining cur, receive
The shrewdest blow my staff can give—   5640

Now twist and turn, contort yourself!
—How quick the ugly, two-faced dwarf
Contracts into a loathsome lump!
The lump becomes an egg, and what
Do I see? Bulging, ripe,
It bursts—a pair of twins falls out,
One a bat and one a viper.
The black bat flies up to a rafter,
Off in the dust it crawls, the other:
They'll meet outside. I wouldn't care   5650
To make a third of such a pair.

MUTTERING VOICES.

       Come, the dancing has begun—
       No! I wish I hadn't come—
       Can't you feel how everywhere
       Very strange things fill the air?—
       Something's buzzing in my hair—
       Oh my foot, there's something there—
       None of us is hurt a bit—
       But we've had an awful fright—
       Ugh, those things! Now our fun's ruined—   5660
       Exactly what they had in mind.

HERALD. Since at masquerades my duty
    Is the herald's, I watch duly
    At the door, keeping guard
    So that anything untoward
    Shan't pass through to mar our pleasure;
    Firm I stand and never waver.
    But I've got, I fear, some bad news:
    Entering by all the windows
    Ghostly creatures in have swarmed   5670
    Here among us; I'm alarmed,
    For over ghosts and sorcery

I have no authority.
The dwarf already was suspicious,
But now a worse thing from behind us
Bears down mightily upon us.
I'd like, as herald, to explain
What the devil these things mean,
But how explain the meaning of
Something you've no inkling of?   5680
All of you must help me out!
—Do you see that chariot,
Four strange steeds drawing it,
Speeding swiftly through the crowd,
Yet not making it divide,
Causing no stir or confusion?
Glittering colors fill the air,
Stars float through the atmosphere—
It's just like a magic lantern!
Snorting loud as a storm blast,   5690
It draws up to us at last.
Give it room! I'm scared!

BOY CHARIOTEER.   Too fast!
Coursers, slow your beating wings!
Answer to your well known reins.
When I signal stop, all stop;
When you feel the whip, speed up.
Let us honor this great palace!
Look how more and more crowd round us,
Ring on ring, in admiration.
Herald, execute your function,   5700
Come, before we leave, describe us
To the revelers, and name us.
As we are an allegory,
Our meaning's proclaimed plainly.

HERALD. What's your name? Well, I can't say.
  How you look? All right, I'll try.
BOY CHARIOTEER. Go ahead.
HERALD.   I won't deny
  That you are young, also goodlooking,
  A half-grown boy, but one the women,
  Once a man, round you'll come flocking,   5710
  A future Don Juan, I don't doubt,
  I feel sure a born seducer.
BOY CHARIOTEER. Good, very good. You'll soon find out,
  If you keep on, the riddle's happy answer.
HERALD. Eyes flashing with dark fire, locks like the night
  Made vivider by a jeweled headband's luster!
  And such a pretty robe that from the shoulder
  Falls straight down to your sandaled foot,
  With sparkling tinsel, purple hem!
  Too girlish, some might say—to tease.   5720
  Yet you are one whom, all the same,
  The girls would only be too eager
  To tutor in love's ABCs.
BOY CHARIOTEER. And what about this sumptuous figure
  Resplendently seated in my car?
HERALD. He looks a king, rich as a shah.
  Happy the man who wins his favor!
  He's got nothing more to strive for.
  Where there's a need, who spies it quicker?
  The pleasure that he takes in giving   5730
  Means more to him than all his having.
BOY CHARIOTEER. Don't stop there, keep on, describe him
  More exactly, top to bottom.
HERALD. Dignity defies description.
  However, here's the way I see him:
  Blooming cheeks, a generous mouth,

A face aglow with good health,
As bright and round as skiey Dian;
On his head a bejewelled turban,
His body robed in a rich gown.   5740
And as for how he bears himself?
Kinglike—heralds know a kingly mien.
BOY CHARIOTEER. He's Plutus, he is—god of Wealth!
    Come here himself in all his pompery,
    The Emperor needs him urgently.
HERALD. And you, tell me who you might be?
BOY CHARIOTEER. I'm poetry, that prodigal,
    Who fulfillment finds when he
    Squanders lavishly on all
    The intimacies of his soul.   5750
    I, too, am rich, immeasurably;
    My wealth, which Plutus's quite equals,
    Enlivens all his feasts and revels,
    What he hasn't, I provide.
HERALD. Your boasting doesn't ill become you.
    Well, let's see the fine tricks you do.
BOY CHARIOTEER. A snap of the fingers, far   and   wide
    All   is   flashes,   sparkles, gleams—
    Presto, strings of pearls appear!

[*Continuing to snap his fingers all around.*]

    Golden gauds for neck and ear,   5760
    Combs and pins and diadems,
    Rings set with expensive gems!
    Sparks, too, sometimes I will scatter
    Here and there, to start a fire.
HERALD. How these good people snatch and grab!
    He's nearly trampled by the mob.

It's like a dream, how the boy's power
Makes materialize such treasure
Which left and right the people rush for.
—But look, now still more magic, my!   5770
What someone seizes eagerly
Proves a worthless prize to him—
The gift flies off upon the wind;
The pearls spill from their string, transformed
To beetles crawling on his hand;
Away he flings them, the poor clod,
And now they're buzzing round his head.
Some, snatching for things solid, good,
Catch skittish butterflies instead.
The rascal tempts with wealth untold: 5780
They get what glitters, not what's gold.

BOY CHARIOTEER. Your understanding's good, I see, of masks.
But when it comes to what's beneath, one asks
A keener penetration than a herald's—
But please, I mean no ill, I don't like quarrels.

[*Turning to Plutus.*]

To you, my master, I turn now and ask:
Didn't you confide to me the task
Of managing your whirlwind chariot?
Don't I drive skillfully and take you straight
To every place you designate?   5790
By my intrepid, daring flights, don't I
Bring back to you the palm of victory?
As often as I've battled for you,
Have I ever, ever failed you?
If laurels decorate your brow,
Who's the one you owe it to?

PLUTUS. You want a testimonial? I'll give it
    Gladly, O you spirit of my spirit.
    Your actions meet my every wish,
    Rich as I am, you're more rich.   5800
    More than all my crowns as Wealth's great god,
    I prize the branch I give you as reward,
    A garland—hear me, all!—so well deserved.
    This is my son in whom I am well pleased.

BOY CHARIOTEER. [*To the crowd*] The finest gifts at my command
    I've strewn about with lavish hand.
    From the red-hot sparks I scattered
    Little fires have been started;
    The fire jumps from head to head,
    Here it burns still, there it's dead.   5810
    Sometimes, rarely, a bright flame
    Blazes up in a brief bloom.
    With many, sadly, it goes out
    And no one taking the least note.

WOMEN GABBLING.
        That one up there on the car
        Is a charlatan for sure;
        Crouched behind him's Hans the Clown—
        But so thin and wasted grown
        From thirst and hunger, I must say,
        As I've not seen him till today.   5820
        Pinch him hard, he'd never yell;
        He lacks the flesh you need to feel.

SKIN-AND-BONES. You awful women, don't you dare come near me!
    You've lost your old appreciation for me.
    When women took care of the house
    My name was Lady Avarice;
    Those were the days, and don't you doubt it:
    Lots came in, little departed.

How I guarded chest and closet—
A deadly sin, ha, ha, they called it!   5830
But nowadays when you fine ladies
No longer sinfully pinch pennies,
And as the case is with all debtors,
Have fewer dollars than desires,
Your husbands groan beneath their ills,
In every drawer they find new bills.
If spinning earns you pocket money,
For lovers you adorn your body,
With all your sorry friends you dine
More richly now, drink much more wine.   5840
So gold and still more gold I need:
My sex is changed, I am Sir Greed!

FIRST WOMAN. The dragon! Let him scrimp and scrape
With all those dragon friends of his;
A hoax, a fraud, the whole thing is!
He means to stir the men all up,
They're too indulgent—I don't think!

ALL THE WOMEN.
       The scarecrow! What he wants's a slap,
       He dares to threaten us, the stick,
       With paper dragons, just imagine!   5850
       Come on, we'll teach him a good lesson!

HERALD. My staff's raised! I'll have no feuding!
—However, I'm not needed. Why?
All are stopped in their tracks by
The monster creatures hugely spreading
Double pairs of wings and spitting
Fire from their scaly jaws—
Back the crowd falls, the place clears.

[*Plutus descends from the chariot.*]

He steps down just like a king
And signals—at his motioning   5860
The dragons lift a treasure chest
Out of the gilded chariot,
With Greediness perched on it, and
Set the box down on the ground
Before his feet. How did they do it?
It's a wonder!—I can't believe it.

PLUTUS. [*To the Charioteer*]

Now relieved of this too heavy burden.
You are free!—off quick to your own sphere
Which isn't here! Here we're surrounded by
Such turmoil, tawdriness, confusion;   5870
But you belong where all's unclouded, where
Your trust is in yourself, your own clear eye.
To where all's good, all's beautiful you're called,
To solitude!—There, there create your world!

BOY CHARIOTEER. I value myself as your worthy envoy,
And love you as the one the most kin to me.
Where you are, Plenty pours her horn, where I,
Each feels that by it he gains gloriously.
Men often hesitate, for life's contrary:
Go your way, should they, or should they go my way?   5880
If yours, they lead a happy life of leisure;
If mine, you never see an end to all your labor.
I have no secrets, nothing is concealed,
If I so much as breathe, I stand revealed.
Goodbye. You send me off to my good fortune gladly;
But whisper once, and back in a flash you'll see me.

                              Departs the way he came.

PLUTUS. It's time now to unloose the wealth.
A touch to the locks with the herald's staff
And they spring open. See there—gold!

Rising molten, bubbling up   5890
In bronze cauldrons, about to drown
Crowns and chains and rings, melting all down!
VOICES CRYING FROM THE CROWD.
        Look there, the riches welling up,
        Filling the chest, spilling over the top.
        Golden bowls and goblets fusing,
        Out of the flux gold pieces jumping,
        New-minted ducats, so they seem,
        Pour out in a glittering stream.
        How my heart leaps with excitement!—
        The money, the money loose on the pavement,   5900
        Free for the taking! Now's your chance,
        Stoop and you are rich at once.—
        Lightning quick, we'll grab together
        The chest itself with all its treasure
HERALD. What idiots you are! You think
    The stuff is real? It's just a joke
    You will soon enough find out.
    Who gives gold away like that?
    Even counters made of lead
    You'd take for gold in your blind greed.   5910
    Make a pretty show and you'll
    Swallow it right down as real.
    What's truth to you? You only crave
    Gross illusion, make-believe.
    —Disguised Plutus, hero of this night,
    Drive these people off the field in fright!
PLUTUS. The staff you've got there, that will do it,
    Lend it to me for a moment,
    I'll dip it in the boiling fire.
    —Watch out, maskers, back, retire!   5920
    What flashings, cracklings, flying sparks!

The staff's caught fire, how it smokes!
Whoever pushes in too near,
Will get himself a pitiless singeing
Around I'll go now, the torch swinging.
CROWD. [*Shouting and jostling*]
　　　Oh dear, we're dead men, that's for sure,
　　　If we don't get out of here!—
　　　Give way in back, space, give us space—
　　　He's spraying sparks right in my face!—
　　　The staff hits, too, and how it hurts!— 5930
　　　It's the end of all of us—
　　　Back, you mummers, idiots!
　　　If only I had wings I'd soar
　　　High up out of this uproar.
PLUTUS. They've stumbled back in full retreat,
　　None of them, I think, 's been hurt,
　　Only had themselves a scare.
　　We haven't any cause to fear.
　　But so as to be absolutely certain,
　　Around us I have drawn a magic curtain. 5940
HERALD. A fine action that was, on your part!
　　I thank you for it, Sir, with all my heart.
PLUTUS. My excellent friend, patience, patience!
　　There still remains a threat of violence.
GREED. Well, now at last a fellow's able
　　To get a good look at these people.
　　Who's always up front, on view?—women!
　　Nibbling pastries, staring about them.
　　I'm still not sunk into decrepitude,
　　Good-looking women, oh my, still look good! 5950
　　And seeing everything today costs nothing,
　　I'll go around, try finding me a nice thing.
　　However, where there's such a crowd

It's hard to make what you say heard,
So let's see if some pantomiming
Is able to convey my meaning—
But gestures, looks, don't do the trick here,
I've got to think of something clever.
I'll work the gold like wet clay, press and squeeze it;
Gold takes any shape you care to give it.   5960

HERALD. What's he up to, that starved monkey?
Can one so skinny think he's funny?
He kneads the gold like dough to make it
Soft enough so he can shape it.
Pinch it, punch it as he will,
It remains a great lump still.
He turns to face the women, they
Shriek and shrink back in dismay,
Hands before their faces raised,
Absolutely scandalized!   5970
The rogue's offensiveness is flagrant,
It tickles him to be indecent.
I can't stand here watching that,
Let's have my staff, I'll chase him out.

PLUTUS. He's got no notion what a storm is coming.
It doesn't matter, all his stupid clowning,
Soon he'll be pushed aside: your staff is stout,
But stronger still an onward sweeping rout.

A RIOTOUS CROWD. [*Singing*]
From hill and dale, an army, we
Press forward irresistably,   5980
Worshipping our Great God Pan,
Acknowledging no discipline.
We know a thing that none suspect.
And crowd into the ring unchecked.

PLUTUS. I know you well, I know your great god Pan.
    Oh, it's audacious, it is, what you've done.
    What none suspects, is no secret from me,
    Allowing you to come in here's my duty.
    Good luck to you, the best of fortune!
    But unexpected, strange things happen;   5990
    You don't know what you're getting into,
    Looking ahead is not what you do.
RIOTERS' SONG.
        You dressed up fops, glittering in sequins!
        Buckos us, rambunctious ruffians,
        In great strides come leaping high,
        A gross, ham-handed company.
FAUNS. We're fauns, we are,
    And whirl and spin,
    With oak leaves in
    Our curly hair,   6000
    From which two pointed ears peep out;
    A broad, a flat face we have got,
    A snub nose, too, but never mind,
    The ladies seldom prove unkind:
    Even the fairest seize the chance,
    When we put out our paw, to dance
    With us through the checkered shade
    Of the leafy woodland glade.
SATYR. Hopping after, here I come,
    A satyr with goat's feet I am,   6010
    Legs sinewy and thin, well suited
    For bounding high upon the summit
    Of rocky crags, where like a chamois
    I look down on all below me.
    By freedom's air exhilarated,

I scorn mankind that well contented
Dwell in lowland murk and mist,
Fancying their life is best—
While I, on the pure heights, alone,
Breathe a world that's all my own.   6020

GNOMES. Now our midget crew appears,
We don't care to work in pairs;
In mossy coats, with tiny lamps,
We swarm about like busy ants,
Each intent on his own business,
To and fro we zigzag, heedless
Of our fellows, who likewise
Hurry on their separate ways.

The Little People are our kin,
As rock-surgeons we're well known;   6030
We bleed the mountain's swollen veins
To draw the rich ore it contains;
With our miners' cheery hail
We pitch the metal down until
It's heaped high beneath the hill.
Really, we are friends to man
And wish to help him all we can.
The gold unearthed by us, however,
Drives him on to steal and lecher,
The proud don't lack for iron when   6040
They scheme how best to slaughter men.
Despise the three commandments, soon
None of them's respected, none.
It's not our fault that things are so;
We bear with it, and you must, too.

GIANTS. The wild men we, for so they call us,
Well-known in the Harz's forests;

Naked, strong, as made by nature,
Each of us a huge, great creature,
With pine trees gripped in our right hands   6050
And bulging girdles round our loins
Made from leaves and branches crudely tied—
A bodyguard popes lack, too citified.

CHORUS OF NYMPHS. [*Encircling Pan*]
He too has come!
The All of Earth
As figured forth
In the Great Pan!
You happy dancers, weave a ring
Around him, flitting, fluttering,
A grave god, he is also kindly,   6060
His wish is all, all should be merry.
Under this blue, vaulted roof
He tries to keep from dropping off
Into his midday sleep; however,
The brooks run with so soft a murmur,
So soft's the whisper of the breezes
That he is overcome and dozes,
And when Pan nods in the hot noon,
All the world sinks in a swoon;
No leaf stirs, the wholesome plants   6070
Fill the air with their incense;
No nymph dares to frolic, they
Drowse arrested in their play.
But if unexpectedly
His great voice sounds fearfully,
Like thunder's growl, the storm wind's shrieking,
Then all look round them, panicking;
Armies turn and run hellbent,
Heroes in the uproar faint.

So pay him homage, hail him, all,   6080
Who led us to this Carnival!

DEPUTATION OF GNOMES. [*Addressing Pan*]
      When shining veins of precious ore
      Threadlike wind through granite depths,
      Only the divining rod
      Can trace its labyrinthine paths.

      And there in hollowed caves we live
      And mine the riches underground
      So you, benignly, up above,
      May hand out riches all around.

      But now we've found before us here   6090
      A source of wealth so wonderful!
      It promises to give us more
      Than ever we thought possible.

      You know best how to use it,
      Take it, sir, into your keeping;
      Treasure, when the Great Pan has it,
      Is a universal blessing.

PLUTUS. [*To Herald*] With steady nerves, a composed mind
      and face,
We must let happen what's about to happen.
You've always shown yourself a man of courage;   6100
The shocking thing soon to take place
Will be dismissed as anecdotage,
But note it in your minutes faithfully.

HERALD. [*Grasping the staff, which Plutus still keeps hold of*]
      Gently the dwarfs conduct Great Pan
      To the fire; it boils up wrathfully
      From below and then sinks down,
      Leaving the dark mouth yawning blankly,

Only to boil up once again.
Pan, marveling, is pleased with it,
Pearly showers fall right and left;   6110
He bends down to peer inside—
How is it he's not afraid?
—Look, his beard has fallen in!
Whose is it, that smooth chin?
His hand goes up, concealing it.
And now a dreadful thing takes place:
The beard, afire, flies back on his face
Setting wreath and head and breast alight.
All our joy has turned to fright.
The crowd runs up to douse the blaze,   6120
But can't escape the flames themselves,
The more they beat and slap at them,
The more the flames leap up again.
Engulfed in fire, a whole host
Of mummers, burnt up, now are dust.

But what is it they're saying there,
Whispering it in every ear?
O unhappy night, the sorrow
You have brought on us! Tomorrow
All around the news will fly,   6130
Multitudes will groan and cry:
"The Emperor's hurt!" "His courtiers, too!"
How I wish it weren't true!
I curse those who misled our monarch,
Put on girdles of pine branches
To roar out songs, cavort in dances,
And caused this universal havoc.

O youth, O youth, will you learn ever
You must moderate your pleasure?

O Majesty, will you learn ever   6140
Reason must consort with power?

The branch-hung halls are now alight,
Sharp tongues of fire licking at
The crossbeamed roof—the danger looms
The palace will go up in flames.
How awful, how calamitous,
Where's the one to rescue us?
A single night, no more, suffices
To turn Imperial pomp to ashes.
PLUTUS. These people have had shocks enough,   6150
What they need now's some relief.
Sacred staff, do you now strike
The floorboards so they sound and shake,
You wide, embracing atmosphere, ·
Breathe around us cooling air!
You curling mists, clouds full of moisture,
Appear and spread your foggy cover
Over the all-devouring fire!
Drizzle showers, drenching rains fall
On the palace, mimic woods, all—   6160
These make-believe flames, mere pretending,
Turn them into summer lightning!
When spirits injure and abuse us,
Magic must step in to save us.

A PLEASURE GARDEN

A sunny morning.
The Emperor, Courtiers; Faust, Mephistopheles respectably
dressed in sober clothes, both kneeling.

FAUST. Do you forgive us, Sire, those fireworks?
EMPEROR. [*Signing them to stand*]
    I'd love to see a lot more of such tricks!
    Suddenly I felt a very Pluto,
    The air around me hot, with a rouge glow;
    Out of the dark as black as coal appeared
    A rock-strewn, parching plain, and as I neared,   6170
    Fierce flames by thousands from deep pits upshot
    And met above to form a swaying vault;
    The fiery tongues, flaming into the sky,
    Made and unmade a dome incessantly.
    And then through fiery columns twisting upwards
    I saw long lines of people marching forwards
    In a wide circle, on myself converging,
    Their customary solemn homage offering.
    I recognized Court faces here, there, others:
    I thought, "Why, I'm a prince of salamanders."   6180
MEPHISTO. And so you are, Sire; each element
    Acknowledges your august majesty.
    You've proved that fire is obedient;
    Now throw yourself into the roughest sea—
    At once as the tide tumbles you and swirls,
    You'll find beneath your feet a floor of pearls;
    Pale green waves bordered with royal purple
    Heave up and down about you in a circle;
    A beautiful, subacqueous dwelling
    Around you forms, its center. And as you move   6190

The palace moves, its limpid walls alive
With myriad creatures swift as arrows darting
To and fro. Out of the deep rare monsters
Rush at the strange light, all in vain, none enters
The shining precincts. Dragons with gold scales
Sport in the water flailing their huge tails.
The shark, wide-jawed, gapes at you, murderous,
You laugh into his maw, impervious.
However pleased by the courtiers that surround you,
Such company you have never had around you.   6200
Nor do you lack for the prettiest, most pleasing:
Nereids, curious, come flirting their tails, all gazing
At the palace amid the eternal waters blazing,
The young ones like fishes, wanton, but also timorous,
With the older ones, wiser, behind. The news reaches Thetis:
A second Peleus captures the heart of the goddess!
And then it is yours, Sir, a seat on the top of Olympus.
EMPEROR. That windy height! It's yours, I yield it gladly,
    Along with its throne—one goes up there too early.
MEPHISTO. And as for the earth, you possess it already.   6210
EMPEROR. What good luck brought us you with your fine arts
    As if straight out of the Arabian Nights?
    If your imagination's fertile as Scheherazade's,
    I'll load you down with honors, rich rewards.
    Stick close to me, your magic at the ready,
    For there are times, I tell you, far too many,
    When I find my life quite insupportable,
STEWARD. [Hurrying in] I never dreamt, Your Highness, I would ever
    Know such delight that's mine now as the bearer
    Of news so stunning, unbelievable.   6220
    All our debts, Sir, have been paid in full,
    The usurer's hard clutch on us is broken,

No more must I support that infernal burden,
What peace of mind is mine now, happiness!
In heaven itself there can't be purer bliss.

MINISTER OF WAR. [*Hurrying in*] A part payment's just been made
    the army,
    They're once again prepared to do their duty;
    Morale's restored, the soldiers' spirits raised,
    And tarts and tapsters do a thriving trade.

EMPEROR. How my ministers come running!   6230
    Breathing relief, their chests heaving!
    Brows unfurrowed, faces smiling!

TREASURER. [*Also making an appearance*]
    Question these two, they're the ones that did it.

FAUST. It's for the Chancellor, for him, to tell it.

CHANCELLOR. [*Coming forward slowly*]
    A glad old age is mine now, all's auspicious,
    Hear what this bit of paper says—momentous!
    Our outlook, once so black, is bright with promise.
                [*He reads.*]
        Know all concerned! This present Note is worth
        A thousand Crowns. Security: the wealth
        Of untold Treasure hidden in the earth   6240
        Of our Realm. The Bearer is assured
        Our first care will be to unearth the hoard
        Whereby this Pledge may be redeemed in Gold.

EMPEROR. I smell chicanery, a great imposture!
    Who dared to forge the Emperor's signature?
    How is it that this crime still goes unpunished?

TREASURER. *You* signed it, Sir, last night. I am astonished
    You don't remember. There you were, great Pan,
    The Chancellor spoke, all heard it, everyone:
    "Sir, on this holiday enjoy the pleasure   6250
    Of making sure of your good people's welfare

By one stroke of the pen." You signed and then,
Quite magically, those wonder-working men
Produced a thousand copies. Wishing to share
The benefit with everyone immediately,
We stamped the entire series then and there:
Tens, thirties, fifties, hundreds, all are ready.
The joy your people feel, you can't conceive,
Your city, rotting away once, half alive,
Now swarms with people carousing all the time.   6260
Though gratefully the world pronounced your name,
Never has it rung with such acclaim,
Its letters now are our whole alphabet,
In this sign all shall prosper and be blest.

EMPEROR. My people think it's good as gold, this stuff?
Don't protest loudly when you pay them off
In camp and court with paltry paper notes?
All right, approved—although I have my doubts.

STEWARD. We tried to circulate them sparingly;
Around they went quick as you blink an eye.   6270
The moneychangers threw their doors wide open,
For every note you lay upon the counter
You get hard cash (of course a discount's taken).
The next stop is the butcher, baker, vintner:
Half the world is busy eating, drinking,
The other struts around in brand-new clothing;
The clothier cuts his cloth, the tailor stitches;
In taverns wine is gushing, toast follows toast
"To the Emperor's health!" and cooks in kitchens roast
And boil and broil and rattle dinner dishes.   6280

MEPHISTO. Stroll alone on the terraces, you soon see
A lovely creature, gorgeous in finery,
Her peacock fan aflutter before her face;
A sharp, appraising eye, as bold as brass,

Sizes you up even while smirking coyly:
Perhaps this fellow's got some of that money?
And faster than smart talk, fine eloquence,
It buys you all the pleasures of romance.
Forget your purses, money bags, who needs them?
Bills tuck so comfortably inside the bosom,   6290
Folded up with perfumed billets-doux.
For the priest they are convenient, too;
Piously he slips them in his missal,
And with a lightened belt the soldier's able
To wheel about more nimbly in the battle.
Trifling matters, Sir, but not at all meant
To minimize a notable achievement.

FAUST. The great treasures that your lands contain,
Buried deep inside the earth, remain
A dead mass. Your farthest estimate   6300
Of what this wealth is worth, how it falls short!
High as winged imagination's flight is,
Nothing it is able to conceive suffices.
But minds uncommon, deep, preserved from arrogance,
Have in the infinite infinite confidence.

MEPHISTO. Paper money, unlike gold and silver,
Says what it's worth on its face, it doesn't require
Endless haggling before a person can,
If he so wishes, indulge in love and wine.
You like your money hard? There's the broker's booth.   6310
He's shut his door? Then go dig in the earth.
You decide to sell something of yours that's valuable?
The notes you're paid for it are all redeemable—
Which puts the doubting Thomases to shame.
People come to accept it, prefer it, in time,
With the result that every place in our Empire
Is well supplied with paper, gold, and treasure.

EMPEROR. We, for all the good you've done, are grateful.
Your reward should be as great, if possible.
Take charge of our subterranean riches,   6320
For who knows best their secret hiding places?
Your word decide where we should dig the earth.
Now, masters old and new of our wealth—
We call upon you to combine your forces
Whereby our upper world with our under
In happy concord may united labor.

TREASURER. Don't fear between us there'll be any friction,
I can use the help of a magician.

EMPEROR. It pleases us to give all here a gift.
Tell me what use you will make of it.   6330

A PAGE. [*Accepting bills*]
A jolly life for me, all fun and games.

ANOTHER. [*Likewise*]
I'll buy my sweetheart a gold ring and locket.

A CHAMBERLAIN. From now on I drink only the best wines.

ANOTHER. The dice have started jumping in my pocket.

A KNIGHT. [*Considering*]
I'll pay off all I owe on house and lands.

ANOTHER. It's money, so—more money in my hands.

EMPEROR. I hoped to hear bold plans for great endeavors,
But knowing you, I should have guessed your answers.
It's clear: with all the wealth you now possess
You'll do just as you always do, but worse.   6340

FOOL. [*Entering*] Handing gifts out? Don't forget your jester.

EMPEROR. Back to life? You'll spend it all on liquor.

FOOL. Magic money! I don't understand it.

EMPEROR. I believe you, seeing how you'd use it.

FOOL. You dropped some on the floor. What should I do?

EMPEROR. Pick it up, fool, it is meant for you.

Exit.

FOOL. Five thousand crowns they make—I'm flabbergasted!

MEPHISTO. O walking wineskin, are you resurrected?

FOOL. It happens often, this time best of all.

MEPHISTO. You're panting with excitement, in a sweat!   6350

FOOL. Look here, is all this paper really money?

MEPHISTO. You'll eat your fill with it, drink yourself silly.

FOOL. Can I buy land with it, a house and cattle?

MEPHISTO. Of course. Just bid away and you'll have all you want, all.

FOOL. A castle, too, woods to hunt in, fish in the river?

MEPHISTO. All, all!—oh, won't you make the perfect squire.

FOOL. Tonight I'll go to sleep in my own hall!

Exit.

MEPHISTO. Now where's the one dare say our fool's a fool?

A DARK GALLERY

Faust, Mephistopheles.

MEPHISTO. Why drag me off down these dark passageways?
   In there did you find you were bored to tears   6360
   Among that motley crowd of courtiers?
   No chance for hoaxes and flimflammeries?

FAUST. Stop your drivel, will you, it's been years
   Since I took pleasure in those tricks of yours.
   All your running here and there incessantly
   Is just so you don't have to talk to me.
   I'm at my wits' end, don't know what to do;
   The Chamberlain insists, the Steward, too:
   Produce at once, before the Emperor,
   Helen and Paris as in life they were,   6370
   The very paragon of women, she,
   Of men the very beau ideal, he.

There's no escape, the Emperor must have it.
To work! I gave my word, I've got to keep it.
MEPHISTO. To promise carelessly like that was stupid.
FAUST. You're the one, friend, who's been thoughtless
About where all those arts of yours would lead us.
First we schemed how to enrich him,
Now we're expected to amuse him.
MEPHISTO. It's not a thing done just like that,   6380
The way is winding, difficult.
You venture boldly onto strange terrain
And end up in an awful mess again.
Helen's ghost, you think, 's produced as easy
As we produced that ghostly paper money?
Oh no! For witches, specters, ghouls, a gnome
With a disgusting goiter, I'm your man;
But Old Nick's lady friends, though not at all bad,
Could never pass for heroines of the Iliad.
FAUST. There you go again, I'm sick of it!   6390
I never know where I am at with you.
You always find the matter's difficult,
Make new demands for everything you do.—
Just mumble a few words, in the next breath
There the two would stand, as big as life.
MEPHISTO. Those old pagans are none of my business.
They've got their own Hell, not at all like ours is.
Still, there's a way.
FAUST.   Quick, let's hear it, please!
MEPHISTO. How I dislike revealing mysteries!
—Goddesses there are, apart, sublime,   6400
Their throne outside of place, outside of time.
To talk about them makes me feel uneasy.
They're called the Mothers!

FAUST. [*Startled*]   Mothers!

MEPHISTO.   You're afraid?

FAUST. The Mothers! Why, it sounds so queer, the word.

MEPHISTO. Indeed it does. For they are deities
    You mortal men know nothing of, whose name
    We loathe to utter. You will need
    To dig down deep, so deep, to come on them.
    Who got us into this fix? You're to blame.

FAUST. The way, the way!

MEPHISTO.   No way! Tread, you must tread   6410
    The way not trodden, never treadable!
    The way not found by asking, it's unaskable!
    Ready and willing, are you, Dr. Faustus?
    No locks to open, bolts to slide, from emptiness
    To emptiness you'll fall, cold, shuddering.
    Can you conceive such desolation, loneliness?

FAUST. I thought you'd given up such hocus-pocusing.
    It's got the Witch's Kitchen's note, is what,
    Recalls that time of misery for me
    When I lived in the world and stupidly   6420
    Studied nonsense, then that nonsense taught.
    To speak the truth, as truth to me appeared,
    Caused noisy protests, I was hooted down.
    Such unpleasant incidents occurred
    That I ran off so as to be alone,
    Into the wilds. Utterly forsaken,
    I took at last the Devil for companion.

MEPHISTO. Even if you swam across the ocean,
    Experienced its limitless extension,
    Its boundless vacancy, you'd still see wave   6430
    Following wave, and though a watery grave
    Should gape and threaten you, you'd still see something,
    Dolphins, maybe, through the placid sea streaking,

Clouds as you sank, high in the atmosphere passing,
The sun in the day, the moon and the stars in the evening.
But in those reaches stretching emptily,
Absolutely nothing will you see,
Nor hear the sound of your own tread,
Nor find whereon to lay your head.

FAUST. Don't you sound like the worst mystigogue—   6440
Bamboozler of poor novices—you rogue!
Except you offer the exact reverse:
Nothingness—where I am to immerse
Myself so as to sharpen up my black arts,
After which you'll find me much more useful—
Just like the poor cat in the Frenchman's fable—
For snatching for you from hot ashes chestnuts.
Still, here goes! Whatever may befall,
My hope is in your Nothing to find All.

MEPHISTO. You know the Devil, I'll say that for you.   6450
Here's something you should have before you go,
A present—it's this key.

FAUST.   That key—that's nothing.

MEPHISTO. Take it. Wait and see. Don't underrate it.

FAUST. It's growing in my hand, it's shining, flashing!

MEPHISTO. I see you're learning to appreciate it.
The key will sniff out where you want to go
And lead you to the Mothers.

FAUST. [Shuddering] Mothers! That word's like a blow!
Why am I so affected by it?

MEPHISTO. Are you so narrow, hide-bound, that you fear   6460
A new thing? Only want to hear
Things heard before? Really, there's no need,
Whatever comes, for you to feel dismayed,
Who are so used now to what's strange and queer.

FAUST. That's not for me: a soul that's frozen, shut;

Awe and wonderment are man's best part.

They cost one, in the world, those sentiments,

Yet seized by them, man feels what's great, immense.

MEPHISTO. Then down, descend, or what's the same thing, rise!

Escape existing things, all that's alive,   6470

And seek to penetrate the cloudy realms

Of empty, spectral, unsubstantial forms;

Delight in what has long ceased to exist.

They'll wind around you, those wraiths, like the mist—

Swing your key so as to keep them off.

FAUST. [*Enthusiastically*] Good, good! By clasping it I gain new
strength,

My breast expands—on, on to the great test.

MEPHISTO. A glowing tripod, when you see it, means

You've reached the bottommost, deepest depth of things.

By the light it casts you'll see the Mothers,   6480

Sitting, standing some, or walking others,

As it may be. Formation, transformation—

The eternal mind in eternal self-conversation.

Surrounded by the forms of all things possible,

They see schemata only, you are invisible.

A stout heart's needed for the peril's great,

Approach the tripod, never hesitate,

And touch it with the key.

[*Faust strikes an imperious attitude with the key.*]

MEPHISTO. [*Watching him*]   That's right! Oh perfect!

It's linked itself to you, your faithful servant;

By fortune calmly lifted in the air,   6490

Up, up, you'll rise, be brought back to us here

Before they even notice. Once back, summon

From out of the night the hero and heroine—

First of all men bold enough to do it!

It'll be done and you'll have done it.

For by the magic's action, clouds of incense
Will turn into a handsome god and goddess.

FAUST. But how, I'd like to know, should I begin?

MEPHISTO. With all your being downwards strive. By stamping
Your foot hard, down you'll sink, by stamping   6500
Your foot when below, you'll rise again.

[*Faust stamps his foot and sinks from sight.*]

MEPHISTO. I trust that key works as it's meant.
Will he come back, I wonder, as he went?

BRIGHTLY LIT HALLS

Emperor and Princes. Courtiers moving about.

CHAMBERLAIN. [*To Mephistopheles*]
Where's the ghost show that you owe us?
The Emperor is getting restless.

STEWARD. A moment ago that's what he asked about.
Look here! Don't fail him or he'll be much put out.

MEPHISTO. But that's just why my colleague's gone away—
The man's an expert in this kind of undertaking;
He's in seclusion, working quietly,   6510
It demands from him continual concentrating.
Calling up the Beautiful necessitates
The magic of philosophy, arcanest of the arts.

STEWARD. Never mind about your philosophical arts!
The Emperor's impatient, wants results.

A BLONDE. [*To Mephistopheles*]
Sir, a word. My skin, as you can see,
Is clear. But summertime, distressingly,
Brownish freckles by the hundred spoil
My fair complexion. Oh, it's such a trial!
A remedy!   6520

MEPHISTO. How sad such a lovely thing
    Is spotted like a leopard in the spring.
    Take some frogs' eggs mixed with a toad's tongue,
    Distill it carefully when the moon's young,
    When it's full, apply the lotion freely:
    Next spring, you'll see, no spot shall mar your beauty.
A BRUNETTE. The crowd that is around you, smirking, mincing!
    Help me, please, I've got such a lame foot;
    Walking's hard for me as well as dancing,
    And when I bow, how clumsily I do it!   6530
MEPHISTO. Permit me, dear, to press my foot on yours.
BRUNETTE. But that's what lovers do, out of affection.
MEPHISTO. My action means a great deal more than theirs.
    Like to like, whatever the affliction!
    Foot cures foot, limb limb, all scientifically.
    Now watch, I'll do it—don't you do it back to me!
BRUNETTE. [Shrieking]
    It hurts! You stamped so hard! Enough!
    It felt just like a horse's hoof.
MEPHISTO. But it's cured you, see! Now you are able
    To dance all night, flirt, carouse, and revel   6540
    And press your lover's foot beneath the table.
A LADY. [Pressing up]
    Let me through, I'm tortured, I am, frantic!
    The rage, the boiling rage I feel inside me!
    Yesterday my smile made him ecstatic,
    Now her he talks with, ignores me completely.
MEPHISTO. A hard case, to be sure! But listen:
    Go up to him unobtrusively,
    With this lump of charcoal mark his person
    Where you can, his sleeve, his cloak, his shoulder;
    That will make his heart throb with remorse.   6550

Then swallow down the lump of coal at once,
And afterwards abstain from wine and water:
By nightfall he'll be sighing at your door.
LADY. Are you sure the coal won't poison me?
MEPHISTO. [*Indignant*] Do you question my authority?
    For coal like this you have to travel far.
    Where's it from? A burning at the stake—
    We used to do more of that kind of work.
A PAGE. I'm in love. "You're too young," she said.
MEPHISTO. [*Aside*] It's getting too much for me, I'm afraid.   6560

                      [*To the Page*]

Don't woo young ones, they will only mock you;
The well along appreciate your value.
[*Still more people crowd around him.*]
More and more! I'll drive these people off
By falling back—oh shame!—upon the truth.
But what else can I do in such a crisis?
O Mothers, Mothers, send me back my Faustus!

                      [*Looking around.*]

The torches in the brackets have burned low,
The courtiers stand up and start to go,
Passing in orderly procession through
Long corridors and distant galleries   6570
So as to gather inside the Great Hall
That's scarcely able to contain them all;
The walls are covered with rich tapestries,
Armor fills each corner, niche and bay.
Here magicking is superfluous, I'd say—
Ghosts come unbidden, need no if-you-please.

BARONIAL HALL

Dim illumination. Emperor and Court already present.

HERALD.   To announce the play has always been my duty;
　　Tonight, however, there's some difficulty
　　Because of supernatural interference,
　　So I must beg, good people, your indulgence:　　　　　6580
　　What's happening is so uncanny, I
　　Am at a loss to explain it rationally.
　　However—. Chairs and benches, as you see,
　　Have been set out; the Emperor placed so that
　　He's able comfortably to contemplate
　　The famous battles of heroic days
　　Depicted on the hanging tapestries.
　　Monarch and Court are seated close around,
　　The benches, filled with people, stand behind;
　　In the shadows shifting spectrally　　　　　　　　　6590
　　Lover sits with lover happily,
　　The coughing stops, feet cease to scrape the floor,
　　And since all's ready now: Spirits, appear!
　　　　　　　　　　　　　　　　　　　　[*Trumpets.*]
ASTROLOGER.   Let the play begin—our Sovereign's command!
　　Walls, open up! With magic you can banish
　　Every obstacle: the carpets vanish
　　As if curled up by fire, the wall parts and
　　Revolves, a stage appears, marvelously,
　　That stretches back into the obscurity.
　　An eerie light, I don't know where it comes from,　　6600
　　Illuminates the scene. I mount the proscenium.
MEPHISTO.   [*Popping up in the prompter's box*]
　　I trust, good people, I'll enjoy now your respect,
　　Prompting is the Devil's rhetoric.
　　　　　　　　　　　　　　　　　　[*To the Astrologer*]

You understand how stars move in the sky,
You'll understand my whispers perfectly.

ASTROLOGER. Here, by magic means presented, see
An ancient temple bulking massively.
Like Atlas shouldering Heaven long ago,
Its great columns hold up, row on row,
The weight of stone; two such would suffice   6610
For bearing up the biggest edifice.

ARCHITECT. So that's what's meant by classical! I can't
Say I'm impressed. Too ponderous, too squat.
What's rude's called noble, clumsy great.
Slim buttresses that soar into the sky,
Tall arches pointing to infinity—
These most uplift our souls, most edify.

ASTROLOGER. Greet reverentially this star-blest hour!
Let magic loose the tyranny of Reason
And Fantasy, fetched from afar, display her power,   6620
For it belongs to her, this great occasion.
What all here boldly asked to see, now see it!
A thing impossible—therefore believe it.
[*Faust mounts the proscenium from the other side.*]
In priestly robes, head wreathed, the wonder-working man
Now confidently consummates what he began.
A tripod from the depths accompanied his ascent,
Incense is burning in the bowl, I smell the scent,
Next comes the invocation, all's prepared;
A fortunate conclusion is assured.

FAUST. [*Grandly*] Mothers, hear me, where you throne   6630
In limitless reaches, dwelling alone,
Yet always together! Around your head
The life-forms turn, restless but dead.
All that shone once in its pride
Stirs with the wish for life eternal;

And you, omnipotent and awful,
Part the empty shapes, to some allot
The tent of day, to some the vault of night.
Send some along life's pleasant pathways wandering,
The others must be sought by fearless conjuring.   6640
Bold wizardry is able to produce
What all men crave to see, the marvelous.

ASTROLOGER. No sooner does his bright key touch the bowl
Than a gray mist begins to fill the hall,
Streaks at first, then dense cumulus;
It spreads, piles up, thins out, divides in two,
And now behold a masterpiece of magic:
The clouds as they swirl round are making music,
Sounding airy notes mysteriously!
All, all around is turned to melody,   6650
Every column, every triglyph ringing,
Why, the whole temple, I believe, is singing!
A handsome youth out of the thinning vapor
Steps forward, footing featly to the measure.
And now I'm done. No need to say who he is.
Where's the one don't know the lovely Paris?

Paris steps Forward.

A LADY. The glory, oh, of youth in bloom! As strong as douce!
SECOND LADY. As luscious as a ruddy peach, ripe, full of juice.
THIRD LADY. The finely shaped, the sweet voluptuous lip!
FOURTH LADY. From that cup you'd like a little sip?   6660
FIFTH LADY. Very pretty, yes—but not refined.
SIXTH LADY. Something lacks in elegance, I find.
A KNIGHT. You can see the shepherd boy he was;
    Nothing princely, court-bred—wants true poise.
SECOND KNIGHT. Oh well, half-naked youth has its appeal;

Just let's see him weighed down by chain mail.
LADY. Charming how he sits down, quite demurely!
KNIGHT. You'd find it pleasant on his lap, I imagine, surely.
ANOTHER LADY. He folds his arm behind his head, so prettily.
CHAMBERLAIN. How ill-bred! Behavior so unmannerly!   6670
LADY. Oh you men! With what don't you find fault?
CHAMBERLAIN. Before the Emperor to lounge like that!
LADY. The play calls for it, "Paris, at ease, solus."
CHAMBERLAIN. Plays, too, must be polite before His Highness.
LADY. Sleep's overtaken our pretty charmer.
CHAMBERLAIN. Who starts to snore—it's realistic drama!
YOUNG LADY. [*With delight*]
    What odor's that that's mingled with the incense,
    Gladdening so my soul with its fresh fragrance?
OLDER LADY. Yes, yes, I also find the smell delicious.
    It comes from him.
STILL OLDER LADY.   It is his youth in flower,   6680
    Its ambrosial scent suffusing the atmosphere.
                    Helen appears
MEPHISTO. So there she is! Well, I am not bowled over.
    Pretty, yes, but not the type I favor.
ASTROLOGER. For once I find I stand before you speechless;
    An honest man, I must confess I'm helpless.
    When she appears, even the ardenest tongue . . .
    Beauty's praises forever have been sung.
    Bereft of self he is, who sees the fabled wench,
    And who possessed her never merited so much.
FAUST. Is what I see a thing seen with the eyes,   6690
    Or Beauty's very fount and origin
    Outpouring from the depths of mind within?
    My fearful journey's gained a glorious prize.
    How nothing worth I found the world, impenetrable!
    Now I am a priest of beauty, how desirable,

How firmly based, how solid and enduring!
The breath go out of me forever if
I ever weary of you, cast you off!
That lovely form I once found so alluring
When I beheld it in the magic glass,   6700
Beside such beauty were a shadow, nothing.
To you I owe all of my vital force,
My passion's very heart and soul, to you
I give myself entirely, in affection,
Love, in worship, yes in madness, too!
MEPHISTO. [*From the prompter's box*]
    Control yourself, keep to the role that's yours here.
OLDER LADY. Tall. Good figure. But her head's too little.
YOUNG LADY. Just see those feet. Could they be clumsier?
DIPLOMAT. I've seen princesses like her, very regal;
    A great beauty, in my view, sans equal.   6710
COURTIER. Slowly she draws near the sleeper, slyly.
LADY. Beside his pure youth, doesn't she look ugly!
POET. He glows, illuminated by her beauty.
LADY. Like Luna and Endymion in the painting!
POET. Yes, yes! The goddess, as it seems, descending
    From above—and bends to drink his breath.
    A kiss. His cup is full—oh, lucky youth!
DUENNA. In front of everybody, I declare!
FAUST. A boy to be so favored!
MEPHISTO.   Silence there!
    She'll do what pleases her, don't interfere.   6720
COURTIER. Off she tiptoes and he starts awake.
LADY. I knew it—see how she is looking back.
COURTIER. He's thunderstruck—a marvel, extraordinary!
LADY. For her no marvel, a familiar story.
COURTIER. Now she is turning round, with dignity.
LADY. She's making plans for him, that's plain to see.

Men, men, what fools, what simpletons you are!
The fellow thinks he is the first, ha, ha!
KNIGHT. She's noble, queenly, don't you criticize her.
LADY. The trollop! Doing what she did—so vulgar! 6730
PAGE. Oh how I wish I stood in that man's shoes!
COURTIER. Who, tempted by her, ever would refuse?
LADY. That article has been around, I fear;
It's looking shabby, faded, quite threadbare.
SECOND LADY. At ten already she was on the downgrade.
KNIGHT. You take the best occasion may afford you;
With such leavings I'd think I was well paid.
PEDANT. I see her clearly, but I must inform you,
I can't be certain she is the right Helen—
One's judgment in a living presence's skewed. 6740
Above all else I hold by what's been written,
And what it says cannot be misconstrued:
She always pleased Troy's graybeards mightily,
Which seems to fit the facts here perfectly,
For I'm not young, and yet she pleases me.
ASTROLOGER. A boy no more, a glorious hero, daring,
He seizes her, her protests count for nothing,
His arms, grown stalwart, catch her ripeness up—
Will he abduct her?
FAUST.   Fool, what madness, stop!
How dare you? Hear me, put her down at once! 6750
MEPHISTO. It's you, I thought, arranged this weird séance.
ASTROLOGER. Excuse me, but from what I've seen, I'd say
The Rape of Helen is the title of this play.
FAUST. Rape! I'm nothing here? Rape, if you please!
Don't you see this key still in my hand
That steered me through tumultuous waves, great seas
Of utter solitude, to reach dry land?
Here I can plant my feet, securely stand,

Here all about me are realities
Enabling my spirit boldly to contend   6760
With spirits, and thus fortified create
The great, the double realm it has always sought.
So far away once, could she now be closer?
If I rescue her she's mine twice over.
Then risk it! Mothers, Mothers, let me have her!
When once you've seen her you can't live without her.
ASTROLOGER. Whatever are you doing, Faust, O Faust?
He's seized her, mad man, now she's fading fast.
The key's aimed at the youth—oh no! oh no!—
It touches him!—It's any second now!   6770

[*An explosion. Faust is knocked flat. The spirits vanish in smoke.*]

MEPHISTO. [*Slinging Faust across his shoulder*]
That's the way it is. With fools become engaged,
And even Satan doesn't extricate himself unscathed.

[*Darkness, tumult.*]

ACT II

A HIGH, NARROW, VAULTED GOTHIC ROOM

Faust's old study, unchanged.

MEPHISTO. [*Entering from behind a curtain. As he raises it and looks
back, Faust is seen lying prostrate on an old-fashioned bed*]
Lie there, poor beguiled wretch, trussed
In bonds of love not soon unloosed.
Whom Helen's blinding beauty trances
Doesn't soon regain his senses.
[*Looking around him.*]
I look around me and I see
All's just the way it was before.
The stained-glass window's dimmer, certainly,
And there are lots more cobwebs everywhere,   6780
The inkwell's dry, the paper sere,
But everything is as it used to be.
Why, even the pen's still on the table
Faust used to sign up with the Devil;
There's still a trace high up the stem
Of the drop of blood I got from him—
A find indeed for the collector who
Gets hold of such a unique curio!
Look: dangling from its hook his old fur cloak,
Reminding me of every fancy, joke,   6790
I planted in that poor boy's brain,
Notions, I bet, now he is a man,
He still nourishes himself upon.
Really, I'm inclined, wrapped in that gown,
To play the professor once again and pompously

Declare all things are as I say, infallibly,
Which your professor knows so well to do;
The Devil lost the trick of it some time ago.

[*He gives the furred gown a shake, and crickets, beetles, and moths fly out.*]

CHORUS OF INSECTS.
    Oh welcome, dear papa,
    The lord of us flies!   6800
    We hop and we flutter
    Making our eternal buzz.
    You secretly planted us
    One at a time,
    Now thousands and more of us
    Whirr round and round.
    Lice in a fur collar
    Hide deep out of sight,
    But the Devil hides deeper
    By far, in man's heart.   6810
MEPHISTO. Such a glad surprise—all these are my creation!
    Only sow, you'll reap at the right season.
    A last shake let me give to this old pelt;
    Here and there a few more flutter out.
    —Now off with you, my dears, don't ever linger!
    Go hide yourself in every dusty corner,
    Over there inside those rotting chests,
    Here inside these mildewed manuscripts,
    Among the fragments of old pots and bowls,
    Inside the staring sockets of those skulls.   6820
    Amid such ruination, rot and rust
    Bugs breed ever, in brains as well as dust.
        [*Slips into the gown.*]

Once more I don, old coat, your dignity,
Again I am the Dean of the Faculty
How fine that title is, but where's the profit
If not a soul's around to recognize it?

[*He rings the bell, with such a shrieking, piercing sound that the corridors quake and doors fly open.*]

A FAMULUS. [*Stumbling down the long, dark corridor*]
    What a clanging! What a shaking!
    Stairs are rocking, stone walls cracking!
    Through the painted panes I see
    Lightning flashing luridly,   6830
    Pavement cracks and ceiling shudders,
    Sending rubble down in showers.
    Magically that bolted door
    Is burst open, hangs ajar!
    Horrors, what is that in there?
    A giant wearing Faust's old fur!
    With a look he waves me over,
    My poor legs are turned to rubber.
    Take to my heels, should I, or stay?
    I'm scared of what's in store for me!   6840
MEPHISTO. [*Motioning to him*] Come here, my friend. Your name is
    Nicodemus?
FAMULUS. Yes, Your Honor, yes, it is!—*Oremus!*
MEPHISTO.   Spare us that!
FAMULUS.   I'm so glad you know me.
MEPHISTO. Yes, I do. Much older now, I see,
    Yet still the student, everlastingly.
    What else can he do, your man of learning,
    But study, study, keep on studying?
    He builds his house of cards with oh what labor,

But does the genius ever finish? Never.
However, he's a brainy one, your master,   6850
The well-known, much revered Herr Dr. Wagner.
In the learned world he is the brightest spark,
Without him we would still be in the dark,
Thanks to him each day the world knows more,
Around him students gather by the score,
They hang on every word that his lips utter;
He's keeper of the keys, just like St. Peter,
Both to the higher world and to the lower.
His intellect's so keen, shines with such brilliance,
All reputations pale in that effulgence.   6860
Even Faust's name has been overshadowed;
All that we know, he only has discovered.

FAMULUS. Allow me, dear Sir, if I may,
To disagree with what you say.
He's not the kind of man that you suggest;
Name all his traits, and modesty stands first.
Faust's vanishing so unaccountably
Is not a thing he's able easily
To reconcile himself to. Every day
He prays the Lord the great man may return;   6870
Only then will he feel right again.
This room's just as it was the day
That Dr. Faustus went away,
It still awaits its ancient master.
It needed all my courage, Sir, to enter.
—The time's so strange, what have the stars in store?
The very walls seem terror-stricken,
The doorposts shook, the bolts burst open,
Or you, Sir, never would have got in here.

MEPHISTO. Where does Wagner have his lair?   6880
Lead me there or bring him here.

FAMULUS. Oh, I don't know, Sir, if I dare;
    So very strict his orders were.
    The great work that he has in hand
    Requires him to live for months on end
    In solitude. Though so refined a scholar,
    He now looks like a charcoal burner,
    With a face that's black from ear to ear
    And bloodshot eyes from blowing up the fire.
    A minute wasted and he's driven frantic,   6890
    The clashing of the tongs to him's pure music.
MEPHISTO. So he won't see me? I'm the very one
    To speed the good work of his project on.

[*Exit Famulus. Solemnly, Mephistopheles seats himself.*]

    No sooner do I settle into place
    Along comes someone with a well-known face—
    A B.A. now, equipped with advanced opinions,
    There won't be any limit to his pretensions.
BACCALAUREUS. [*Striding down the corridor*]
        Every door's wide open here,
        Letting in, thank God, some air
        Where all is dry rot, fustiness,   6900
        Where life's not life but a slow death.
        It gives a fellow hope he may
        Do more than breathe dust, waste away.

        The walls are swaying, they're about
        To topple over and fall flat.
        If I'm not careful, promptly leave,
        I'll find myself buried alive.
        I'm brave as any, even braver,
        But I stop here, I'll go no farther.

But what's this I am looking at?   6910
I swear it is the very spot
Where I arrived, so long ago,
A naive freshman, keen to know
All the old heads had to teach.
How I drank in their gibberish!

Out of old tomes bound in leather
They taught the lies called by them learning—
Learning they believed in? Never!
So spent their lives and ours on nothing.
Look! Inside the study someone   6920
'S sitting in the dark, half hidden.
Coming closer, my eyes popping,
I see it's him in his old wrapping,
His fur-lined robe, just as he wore it
The last time that I saw him in it.
He seemed to me a fount of wisdom
In those old days—I didn't know him.
But now I see right through the man!
I'll have myself a go at him.

Unless, old Sir, you lack the strength to hold   6930
Your bent, bald head above the cloudy tide
Of Lethe's drowsy stream, in me behold
Your former pupil, now outgrown the rod!
You're just as I remember you, exactly;
Myself, however, you'll find changed completely.
MEPHISTO. I'm glad it fetched you here, my bell.
I held you then in some esteem;
The grub and chrysalis foretell
The brilliant butterfly to come.
You took in your curls and lace collar   6940
A childish pleasure, I remember.

You wore your hair long, I think, while
Now it's short in today's style.
You look so able, resolute,
But one must not be absolute.

BACCALAUREUS. Old man, here all's just as it was before,
But times have changed, don't you forget it, please,
So spare me professorial ironies,
We're not the innocents that we once were.
No wit was needed to mock guileless boys,   6950
But that's all past, today no one would dare.

MEPHISTO. Tell the young the plain truth honestly,
They close their ears, they have no wish to hear it.
But when on their own hides as by and by
They feel its sting and come at last to know it,
They all think it is their brains found it out.
And their old master? What an idiot!

BACCALAUREUS. Or rather rogue! Is there anywhere
A teacher who says how things truly are?
They praise, they blame, as seems expedient,   6960
Beam brightly, frown—the poor trusting student!

MEPHISTO. To be sure, there's first a time for learning,
And now, I see, you're ready to teach others.
In all your months and years of living, looking,
The rich experiences you must have gathered!

BACCALAUREUS. Experience! Why, it's just dust and bones
Compared with what the mind of man contains.
Admit it: all your hard-won learning, knowledge,
What is it? Just a lot of useless baggage.

MEPHISTO. [*After a pause*] Yes, I've suspected it. How stupid,   6970
How trivial my thinking's been, how vapid.

BACCALAUREUS. Oh very good! Now you are talking sense—
The first old-timer with intelligence.

MEPHISTO. I searched for golden treasure in the ground,
    Contemptible, base coal was what I found.
BACCALAUREUS. Confess it, your bald head is no more worth
    Than that old hollow skull upon the shelf.
MEPHISTO. [*Cheerfully*] How rude you are which you don't realize.
BACCALAUREUS. To be polite, in German, means: tell lies!
MEPHISTO. [*Who has been rolling his wheeled chair nearer and*
        nearer to the foot of the stage, addressing the audience]
    I can hardly breathe or see up here.   6980
    Is there any room for me down there?
BACCALAUREUS. What nerve, so as to hang on a while longer,
    To claim you matter still, when all is past and over.
    What's life? It's blood, and where, I'd like to know,
    Does blood, unless in youth, more freshly flow?
    In youth blood's vigorous, it throbs and beats,
    From its own vital force new life creates,
    It's active, stirring, makes things move along,
    Rejects the weak, gives first place to the strong.
    While we've been conquering half the world, tell me,   6990
    What have you done?—Dreamt your life away
    Nodding over this scheme, that scheme, and another.
    It's a fact: old age is a cold fever,
    An ague, full of fussiness and worry,
    You're good as dead when you are over thirty,
    That's when you should all be put away.
MEPHISTO. About all that the Devil has no comment.
BACCALAUREUS. No devil is, unless with my agreement.
MEPHISTO. [*Aside*] He'll lay you by the heels, though, by and by.
BACCALAUREUS. Youth's glorious calling, listen, do: what is it?
    There was no world until by me created.   7000
    I led the beaming sun out of the sea,
    I launched the moon upon her changing course,
    The day appeared, all garlanded, for me,

The earth grew green and lived in my embrace,
Upon my sign, in that creating night,
The stars, unveiled, shone gloriously bright.
Who but me unloosed your captive minds
From their confinement in philistine bonds?
Free as the air, just as the spirit prompts me,
I joy to follow where my soul's light leads me,   7010
I speed along in sheerest self-delight,
Brightness before and at my back the night.

                                                            Exit.

MEPHISTO. Go thy ways, rare genius, in your glory!
    How chagrined you'd be to know
    There's nothing wise and nothing silly
    Wasn't thought of long ago.
    —But I don't think he'll do us any wrong,
    In a few years he'll sing another song.
    The juice may seethe and sputter in the vat,
    Time passes and good wine is the result.   7020

[*To the younger section of the audience, who have refrained from
applauding.*]

    My words, I notice, leave you cold.
    Well, never mind, you're all good children.
    Remember that the Devil's old,
    When you're old, too, you'll understand him.

A LABORATORY

*In the medieval style, filled with cumbersome, intricate
equipment designed for the most fantastic purposes.*

WAGNER. [*At the furnace*] The fearful bell shakes with its boom
    The sooty walls of the dim room;
    This state of tense suspense must soon
    Be ended and the outcome known.
    The darkness lightens bit by bit;
    Deep inside the crystal vial   7030
    Something glows like a live coal,
    Like the loveliest carbuncle,
    Sending through the dark its sparkle.
    I see a clear white light appearing.
    If only this time I succeed!
    —Oh God, why is that doorlatch rattling?
MEPHISTO. [*Entering*] Greetings, Sir—don't be afraid.
WAGNER. [*Nervously*] Greetings, yes—at this momentous juncture!
    [*Softly*] But not a word, please, not a whisper.
    A glorious work is nearing its completion.   7040
MEPHISTO. [*Lowering his voice*]
    What glorious work?
WAGNER. [*Whispering*] A man's creation.
MEPHISTO. No! Have you two lovers snugly
    Tucked up there inside that chimney?
WAGNER. God forbid! Our ancient mode of breeding
    We now pronounce a clownish, coarse proceeding.
    The tender source from which sprang all of life,
    The sweet force pressing outward from within,
    Which took and gave, making itself again
    With all that it absorbed into itself

Of like and unlike from nearby, far off,   7050
According to old Nature's antique plan—
Well, it's deposed, no longer will we honor it;
Beasts of the field may still take pleasure in it,
But man, endowed so nobly, must henceforth
Use nobler, higher means to make himself.

>   [*Turning to the furnace.*]

Look how it shines! Now we can hope it's possible,
By mixing together every kind of material—
For everything depends upon the mixture—
To make out of the mixture human matter;
Then sealing up all in a limbec carefully,   7060
We redistill the contents thoroughly,
To find at last all's been accomplished quietly.

>   [*Turning again to the furnace.*]

It's working! See the mass stir, brighter, clearer!
I feel more confident in my belief than ever.
What once we lauded as great Nature's mystery,
We dare to do now by proceeding rationally.
Her way of working was organic, vital;
We synthesize men inside a glass bottle.

MEPHISTO. A man lives long enough, he learns a lot,
He's seen the world, he is surprised by nothing;   7070
Already in my traveling about
I've come on more than one synthetic being.

WAGNER. [*Who has never taken his eyes off the vial*]
It rises, shines, agglomerates,
A minute more and it is done.
A great idea seems mad at first,
But in the end the day must come
When hit-and-miss ways of begetting life
Will only stimulate our mirth,

When banished chance and accidents,
A thinking man will make a brain that thinks.   7080
                              [*Ecstatically observing the vial.*]
The glass chimes, oh how dulcet-strong its ringing!
It clouds, it clears—yes, now it's happening!
I see the delicate outline within
Of something gesturing, a manikin!
Well, there you have it, who can ask for more?
The secret now's no secret any more.
Hear how that sound becomes a human voice
That's able to form words and speak to us.
HOMUNCULUS. [*Addressing Wagner from the vial*]
Greetings, my dear Dad! That was no joke.
Come, clasp me to your bosom tenderly,   7090
But not too hard, for fear the glass might break.
It's the way things are, what more's to say?—
The universe, though big enough,
Is hardly able to find space
For all of Nature's sprawling wealth,
But manmade life you shut in a tight place.

                              [*To Mephistopheles*]
It's Brother Rascal, am I right?
You've come, I must say, very opportunely.
It's our good luck, I thank you most sincerely.
I'm alive so I must have activity,   7100
I need to buckle down to work immediately,
And you are just the one knows how to help me.
WAGNER. One word more, please. How I've blushed for shame
To find myself unable to explain
The problems with which young and old besiege me.
For instance: no one comprehends, not even vaguely.
How body and soul should fit so well together,
Cling so close a knife can't pass between them,

And yet they are eternally in contention.
And then—

MEPHISTO.   Hold on! I'd rather put this question: 7110
Why is it man and wife don't get on better?
My friend, give up, you'll never find the answer.
—But there's work here for him to do, our midget.

HOMUNCULUS. Work? There's work? Direct me to it.

MEPHISTO. [*Pointing to the side door*]
Look there. Now show us what your talents are.

WAGNER. [*Still staring into the vial*]
Such a darling boy you are, a dear!
[*The side door opens, showing Faust recumbent on the bed.*]

HOMUNCULUS. [*Astonished*] Significant!

[*The vial escapes Wagner's hands and hovers over Faust,
shedding its light on him.*]

So beautiful a scene!
I see a pool, trees round it as a screen,
With girls undressing, all so very lovely,
And lovelier still in their naked beauty.   7120
But one stands out more radiant than the rest,
Sprung from the gods or an heroic race.
She dips a foot in the transparent glitter,
Cooling the glowing life in her white limbs
In the yielding crystal of the tranquil water.
—But what's that thunder of fast-beating wings?
That plunging, splashing, splintering of the mirror?
The women flee in fear, but she, the queen,
Is unalarmed and looks on calm, serene,
And with a woman's pride, a woman's pleasure,   7130
Observes the swan prince nestling at her knees,
Submissive yet insistent, familiar and at ease.

But suddenly a mist arising, no more's seen
Of this most charming, most enchanting scene.

MEPHISTO.   The stories that you tell, you fabulist!
As little as you are, as great a fantasist!
I see nothing.

HOMUNCULUS.   Well, the North
Is where you're from. Grew up a youth
Of the Dark Ages, in the unwashed ignorance
Of chivalry and priestcraft. There's no chance   7140
You'd have eyes that see with any clarity,
Who only feel at home in cold and darkness.

                                             [*Looking around*]

Blackened buildings, mouldy, mean and cheerless,
Pointed arches, gargoyles, Gothic grotesquery!
If that one there wakes up we'll have our hands full,
He'll die right on the spot, it's all so awful.
White swans, naked beauties, a woodland stream—
There's where his desire led him in a dream.
But here—how could he possibly endure it?
Myself, at home no matter where, can hardly bear it.   7150
You've got to move him elsewhere.

MEPHISTO.   Else is where?

HOMUNCULUS.   Send a soldier off to war,
Take a young girl to the dance,
And everything's as it should be.
Just now it has occurred to me
That by a very happy chance
It's Classical Walpurgis Night—
Just his element, for him just right.

MEPHISTO.   I never heard of it.

HOMUNCULUS.   You only know about
Your romantic phantoms, but   7160
Genuine ghosts, the true goods, you will

Find without exception classical.

MEPHISTO. All right, so which way lies our route?

Classical colleagues—what a thought!

HOMUNCULUS. The northwest, Satan, is your stamping ground,

The southeast's the direction we are bound.

Through a great plain, through thicket and through grove,

Peneios flows along still, sultry reaches,

The plain extends back to the mountain gorges,

And old and new Pharsalus lie above.   7170

MEPHISTO. Spare me that, that's ancient history!

A contest between tyranny and slavery.

It's all so boring! No sooner one war's done,

They start another one right up again,

And never notice, they're so asinine,

Asmodeus it is who eggs them on.

It's freedom that they fight for, each side says;

Look close, you see it's slaves who fight with slaves.

HOMUNCULUS. Never mind that men are so intractable!

Pitched out into the world, with tooth and nail   7180

Each must defend himself as best he can—

That's the way a boy becomes a man.

But our problem here is how to cure

Our good Faustus lying prostrate there.

If you've a way, then try and we shall see.

If not, step back and leave his case to me.

MEPHISTO. I could try my Brocken dodges, but

Against me heathendom keeps its gate shut.

Light-minded, those Greeks were, without the Bible—

All that naked, sensual razzle-dazzle,   7190

That sinning with a light heart, gaily, freely!

Our sinning's serious, soul-torturing, dreary.

So what's your plan?

HOMUNCULUS.   Well, you were never shy

And if I say "Thessalian witches," I
Imagine you know what I mean.

MEPHISTO. [*Salaciously*]
Thessalian witches, my, oh my!
About them I have wondered a long time.
I doubt if it is lots of fun to pass
Night after night in their grim company,
But a short visit's worth a try, I guess.   7200

HOMUNCULUS. Fetch the cloak and wrap our knight up in it!
The rag will bear you both, it's always done it.
I'll light the way.

WAGNER. [*Anxiously*] And me?

HOMUNCULUS.   Hm, you.
Your place is here, you've still much work to do.
Unroll your parchments, diligently gather
The elements that the prescriptions call for
And mix them all together carefully;
Think hard about the *what*, about the *how* still harder.
I meanwhile about the world will wander
And maybe find the dot that dots the "i,"   7210
And so at last complete the great endeavor.
Such great effort is rewarded worthily:
Wealth and fame, a long life and much honor,
Much knowledge and much virtue—possibly.
Goodbye!

WAGNER. [*Downcast*] Goodbye. Oh I feel sad, I do,
I fear this is the last I'll see of you.

MEPHISTO. Off, off! Peneios, here we come!
My cousin here must not be underrated.
[*To the audience*] In the end we are dependent on
The very creatures we ourselves created.   7220

CLASSICAL WALPURGIS NIGHT

BATTLEFIELD OF PHARSALIA

Darkness.

ERICHTHO.

    Erichtho, I, the dismal one, come once
    Again, as oftentimes before, to this horrid feast
    Of ghosts—not so revolting as the unkind poets
    Like to picture me. Blame or praise, on and on
    They run, there is no end.—Above, below,
    The valley now shows whitish from wave on wave
    Of gray tents running all along its length—
    Afterimage of that cruellest, dreadfullest
    Of nights! How often it returns and shall return
    Eternally. For neither will let go   7230
    The Empire to the other, nor ever to him,
    Got hold of it by force, by force holds on.
    For selves unmastered are all too ready masterfully
    To make their neighbor's will bow to their own.
    Here was enacted a great example how, when force
    Confronting greater force they battle to the bitter end,
    Sweet Freedom's thousand-flowered wreath is torn to shreds
    And the stiff laurel's bent about the conqueror's brow.
    Here Pompey dreamed of former days, bright garlanded
    With victories, here Caesar waked, watching   7240
    With bated breath the swaying balance arm.
    Strength against strength! Now see, the battle's joined!
    And which prevailed the world well knows.

                Campfires blaze,
    Shooting out red flames. The ground gives off

The glimmer of long-ago-spilt blood.
And the legions of Greek legend, tempted out
By the unusual brilliance of this night,
Foregather here. Fabled shapes appearing out of
Old antiquity, haunt half-glimpsed about
The fire or recline beside them at their ease.   7250
Still not at the full yet radiant,
The moon swims up shedding its mild light,
The phantom tents all fade, the fires all
Burn blue. —But overhead, what's that
Appearing unexpectedly, a meteor?
Its light reveals a round corporeal thing.
Ha, I smell life! No, it's not good, not right
To allow it near me, being as I am
A baneful influence on all that lives.
My reputation would decline still more,   7260
To no good purpose. Down the meteor drops.
I think it best I should withdraw.

Exit.

The Aeronauts Aloft.

HOMUNCULUS.

I'll make a circle over these
Ghastly fires once again;
The valley bathed in silver haze
Presents a strange, a ghostly scene.

MEPHISTO.

It's like looking out the window
On my fearful northern gloom,
Loathsome phantoms everywhere show,
I feel, I do, right at home.   7270

HOMUNCULUS.
> Look at that tall thing departing
> With long strides, hastily.

MEPHISTO.
> It's as if she fearfully
> Spied us nearing in the sky.

HOMUNCULUS.
> Never mind. Just set your knight down
> On the ground and in a breath
> You'll see life returning to him
> Where he seeks it, in Greek myth.

FAUST. [*As he touches the ground*]
> Where is she?

HOMUNCULUS.   I've no idea.
> But this looks like a good place to inquire.   7280
> You might, before the dawn appears,
> Scout around among these fires
> And find what trace you can of her.
> What should a fellow have to fear
> Who's dared to go down to the Mothers?

MEPHISTO. I have my reasons why I've come here, too.
> So I suggest what's best for us to do
> Is go our separate ways among the fires,
> Each one looking for his own adventures.
> Then when it is time to reunite,   7290
> Little fellow, shine your tuneful light.

HOMUNCULUS. Like this—see how it rings, it flashes,
> Off to new things, strange surprises.
> [*The glass rings and lights up brightly.*]

FAUST. [*Alone*]
> Where is she?—But there's no need to fret.
> If this is not the very ground she walked on,

The wave that curled, breaking at her feet,
It's the air in which her Greek was spoken.
Here miraculously I'm in Greece!
Standing here, at once I knew the place,
A fresh spirit coursed again through me,   7300
Roused the sleeper, Antaeus-like, with its warmth.
I'll search throughout this fiery labyrinth,
Encountering its fabulous company.

Exit.

ON THE UPPER PENEIOS

MEPHISTO. [*Snooping around*] Going around these fires I find I am
    Ill at ease, it's all so strange, so foreign;
    Stark naked almost all, they know no shame,
    Only one or two have got a shirt on;
    Immodest sphinxes, bold, unblushing griffins,
    Things with wings and curling hair, queer demons
    Presenting themselves front and rear to you.   7310
    It's true that au fond we're indecent, too,
    But it's too natural, antiquity,
    It needs to be redone in modern style,
    Touched up with plaster into decency.
    Ugh, what people! Still, as a newcomer, I'll
    Behave as one should, greet all properly.
    —Fair ladies, how d' you do, and how do y' do,
    All you sage ancients, venerable gray ones!
GRIFFINS. [*Snarling*] Not gray ones, *griffins!* Mind what you say,
        will you!
    Who likes being called a doddering dodo?   7320
    Gray, grim, grouchy, grudging, grisly, gruesome,
    All etymologically alike in origin,
    Grate on our ear—we're not some grotesque relic.

MEPHISTO. Yet not to change this fascinating topic—
  You find *gr* a pleasing syllable
  In griffin, your so honorable title.
GRIFFINS. [*Who never cease to snarl*]
    Of course! You grab for gold, for gelt, for girls—
    Griffin, grab, they're cognates, it's been proved,
    Proof disputed often, oftener approved.
    Who grip and gripe and grab, on them Dame Fortune smiles.   7330
ANTS. [*A giant variety*] Gold, we heard. We've gathered lots,
      we have,
    And hid it all away in cliff and cave.
    Those Arimaspians found where it was stuck,
    Packed it off, now laugh themselves till sick.
GRIFFINS. Soon enough we'll force them to tell all.
ARIMASPIANS. Not tonight you won't. Tonight's a festival,
    And by morning we'll have blown it all.
    Ha, ha, this time we've pulled off our trick.
MEPHISTO. [*Having sat down among the Sphinxes*]
    How nice it's here, at once I feel at home!
    I understand you creatures, every one.   7340
SPHINX. We utter our ghostly sighs and groans,
    Then you lend your own sense to our sounds.
    However—as a beginning, please, your name.
MEPHISTO. The names, the names inspired by my fame!
    —Are any English here? They love to tour around,
    Survey old battlefields, view waterfalls
    And dreary classical sites and crumbling walls—
    This place would suit them right down to the ground.
    They'd vouch for me; in an old British play
    I have the part of "Old Iniquity."   7350
SPHINX. And where'd they find that name?
MEPHISTO.   I've no idea.

SPHINX. Ah well. And stars, you understand their meaning?
  What can you tell about the present hour?
MEPHISTO. [*Looking up*] I see shooting stars, a pale moon
      waning. . . .
  I like it here, it's such a cozy spot,
  You warm me with your lovely lion's pelt.
  A waste of time the stars, much rather I'd
  Hear riddles or at least act a charade.
SPHINX. Say what you are, that's riddle enough for us;
  Try, do, once, some self-analysis: 7360
      As needful to the best as to the worst:
      The best, to learn the self-denying skill
      By which to foil your wicked cut and thrust;
      The worst, a fellow helping to raise hell,
      And both, to Zeus, a comedy, a jest.
FIRST GRIFFIN. [*Snarling*] I don't like him.
SECOND GRIFFIN. [*Snarling louder*] Why's the fellow here?
BOTH TOGETHER. An ugly brute! Toss him out on his ear.
MEPHISTO. [*Savagely*] You think perhaps my nails can't do the
      damage
  Your claws can? I'm ready for a scrimmage.
SPHINX. [*Mildly*] Stay, Sir, stay, don't get into a huff,   7370
  Soon enough you'll want to leave yourself.
  At home, it may be, you cut quite a swath,
  But here you don't feel right, is my belief.
MEPHISTO. You're very tempting upwards of your waist,
  But down below—oh horrible, a beast!
SPHINX. Rascal, you'll pay dear for your rude tongue.
  Our claws are healthy ones and strong
  And you with that weak, shriveled hoof of yours
  Won't find it pleasant here, and with good cause.
              [*Sirens tuning up overhead.*]

MEPHISTO. What birds are those that I see swinging   7380
    In the poplars by the river?
SPHINX. Beware of them, their pretty singing
    'S vanquished many a famous figure.
SIRENS.
        Ah, why linger, your taste spoiling,
        With the ugly-fabulous?
        We flock here, from our throats trilling
        Sweet sounds and harmonious,
        As beseems our siren's voice.
SPHINXES. [*Mocking them to the same tune*]
        Make them come down from their perch in
        Those trees' leafy branches where   7390
        They conceal their hawks' claws, sharp and
        Long as knives, with which to tear
        Limb from limb who lend them ear.
SIRENS. Banish hatred, banish envy!
        Stranger, listen to our offer:
        Joys unmatched beneath this sky,
        Happiness the like as never.
        You will find on land or sea.
        Beckoning, as we do seldom,
        You with signs of kindest welcome.   7400
MEPHISTO. That's the latest style of singing,
    Voice and string together jingling,
    One note through the other ringing.
    I can do without such warbling.
    It titillates my ear to hear it,
    But never reaches to my heart.
SPHINXES. Hear him—heart! Oh, but that's rich,
    A wrinkled, dried up leather pouch
    Better fits with that face, much!

FAUST. [*Appearing*]

How wonderful to have sight of such creatures;   7410

Forbidding, they are, vigorous their features.

It augurs well for me, I do feel sure.

This solemn vision points the way—to where?

FAUST. [*Turning to the Sphinxes*]

Fated Oedipus on these once fixed his stare.

[*Turning to the Sirens*]

Hearing these, Ulysses fought the hemp.

[*Turning to the Ants*]

These gathered immense treasure in a heap,

[*Turning to the Griffins*]

And over it these faithfully kept guard—

My soul's revived as if by a fresh breeze.

How great these shapes, how great these memories!

MEPHISTO. Once you would have simply abhorred   7420

The likes of these, and now how much they please.

Oh but how a man is glad to have

Even monsters help him to his love!

FAUST. [*To the Sphinxes*] You she–shaped creatures surely know the answer:

Where's your Helen, tell me, have you seen her?

SPHINXES. She belongs to Greece's latter days,

The last of us were killed by Hercules.

Ask Chiron, he knows everything, he does;

This haunted night he gallops up and down and back,

If he stops to answer you, you are in luck.   7430

SIRENS.

Rather visit with us, do it!

Ulysses wasn't scornful, didn't

Hurry past with eyes averted,

Everything he knew he blurted

Out to us, and we'd be glad to

Pass on all his news, all, to you.

Only come down where we live by
Green sea water lapping softly.
SPHINX. Good gentleman, don't be enticed!
Ulysses had himself bound to the mast,   7440
You be bound by our Sphinxes' counsel.
Find noble Chiron if you're able,
He'll tell you all you want to know
Just as we have promised you.

> *Faust departs.*

MEPHISTO. [*Peevishly*]. Those croaks I hear, those whirring wings
Go by too fast to see the things;
One bird following another,
They'd prove too much for any hunter.
SPHINX.
It is the fleet Stymphalides,
Goose feet they have, a vulture's beak,   7450
Are swift as winter wind's storm blast,
The arrows of great Hercules
Hardly reach them, they're so fast.
That's a friendly hail, their croak—
They wish to demonstrate their kinship
With us Sphinxes, win our friendship.
MEPHISTO. [*Pretending fear*] There's something horrible I hear
hissing!
SPHINX. No need at all to feel such terror,
Those are the heads of the Lerneaen Hydra,
Struck off, whose cries you're witnessing—   7460
And still they think that they are something!
—But what's the matter anyway?
You seem to want to get away.
Well, go then! How you twist your neck
To eye that troupe there! Don't hold back
But introduce yourself at once,

Enjoy a bit of dalliance
With ladies of experience,
The Lamiae! whose smiling lips and bold demeanor
With all the Satyr race find favor.   7470
With Lamiae a goatfoot's able to
Do everything that he's inclined to do.
MEPHISTO. But you'll stay here in case I should return?
SPHINX. Yes, yes! But go, the merrymakers wait.
We hail from Egypt where we Sphinxes learn
To endure millennia on our stone seat.
If you examine closely our position,
You'll see we mark the months' and years' progression.
Before the pyramids our stations,
Witnessing the fate of nations,   7480
War and peace and floods go by,
We watch all unblinkingly.

ON THE LOWER PENEIOS

Riverscape with Nymphs.

PENEIOS. Sedges, stir with a soft murmur!
Sway, you reeds, and rushes whisper,
Rustle, yellow willow bushes,
Sough, you trembling poplar branches,
Lull me back to peaceful dreaming—
A strange tremor in the ground
Wakes me with its anxious sound,
Wakes me from my quiet rippling.   7490
FAUST. [*Coming to the riverbank*]
Unless I'm much mistaken, I
Hear, quite inexplicably,
Sounds I'd swear are human voices

Coming from these close-grown bushes,
The ripples seem to talk together,
The breezes play tag with each other.

NYMPHS.

    Sir, may we suggest
    You lie down and rest
    Beside the cool water
    Where you may recover,   7500
    May find the repose
    Your soul seldom knows?
    We'll murmur, we'll whisper,
    Till you sink in a drowse.

FAUST. *Now* I'm awake! How gladly I
Surrender to the matchless forms
I've called forth here by my own eye!
How moved I am, amazingly!
What are they, memories or dreams?
Once, once before I knew such joy.   7510
The water, sliding through the fresh,
Green-growing, swaying brake and bush,
Makes little noise, you hardly hear
A ripple; springs, a hundred, pour
From every side to come together
In a pool whose pure bright water
Doesn't frighten by its depth,
Affords a pleasing rustic bath.
Girls' limbs, in the liquid mirror
Glowing pink and white with health,   7520
Delight the admiring eye twice over!
Bathing happily together,
Cautiously wading, boldly swimming,
At last, like schoolgirls, wildly screaming,
They splash each other with the water.

The pleasure this affords my eye
Should really be enough for me,
But still my mind keeps searching farther,
Would like to pierce that thicket yonder:
Its foliage, so rich and green,   7530
Conceals the nymph who is their queen.

How wonderful! A fleet approaches,
Sailing in from the broad reaches,
Swans! Majestic, tender, calmly
Gliding side by side, yet proudly
Turning head and beak—oh splendid
Creatures, haughty, self-delighted!
But one seems prouder than the rest,
Boldly puffing out his breast,
Sailing swiftly through his fellows   7540
With his nobly swelling feathers,
Himself on white waves a white wave,
He swims straight to the sacred grove.
The others, plumage brightly glowing,
Quietly are to- and fro-ing,
Soon, however, make a rush at
All the flustered nymphs—they aim at
Making them forget their duty,
Only think of their own safety.

NYMPHS.

Sisters, stoop and lay your ear   7550
To the river's grassy shore.
Unless I am deceived I hear
Drumming hoofbeats heading here.
What messenger, I wonder, might
Be bringing news to us tonight?

FAUST. The ground's ringing and the cause is

Hoofs, I think, a galloping horse's.
I search in the distance,
Can it be assistance?
Can I hope it's good fortune 7560
He's bringing, that horseman?
And see, a rider's coming toward me,
As wise and brave a man as might be;
On a snow-white horse he's mounted,
I recognize him, we're acquainted—
Philyra's celebrated son!
Chiron, stop, I've got to speak to you.
CHIRON. Well, what is it?
FAUST.   Stop! How you keep on!
CHIRON. I *never* stop.
FAUST.   Then take me, please, with you.
CHIRON. Mount up and we will have a talk together. 7570
    Where to? You're standing on the riverbank;
    I'll take you over, shall I, on my back?
FAUST. [*Mounting*]
    Take me where you like, I'm in your debt forever.
    —O you great man, O noble educator,
    Who trained a hero race whose deeds are legendary:
    Jason's Argonauts, that bold and noble order
    And all those whom the poets owe their epic matter.
CHIRON. Forget that, please, I've put all that behind me!
    Even Pallas did herself small honor
    By taking on the thankless role of Mentor. 7580
    In the end they do as they see fit,
    Just as if they never had been taught.
FAUST. Profound physician, namer of all plants,
    Best of all skilled in the lore of roots,
    Who heals the sick and salves the wounded's smart,
    My arms embrace you here, so does my heart!

CHIRON. When a hero got hurt by my side,
  My science helped to mend his broken bones;
  But finally I put all that aside,
  Leaving it to priests and to old crones.   7590
FAUST. You belong among the truly noble
  Who find all praise offensive, they can't bear it,
  Modestly they close their ears, won't hear it,
  Pretending there are others just as able.
CHIRON. A clever hypocrite you seem to be
  Who flatters prince and people equally.
FAUST. Nevertheless I don't think you'll deny
  You knew the great and famous of your day
  And strove to emulate their finest deeds,
  To live as nobly as do the demigods.   7600
  But which among the heroes of the past
  In your opinion were the greatest, best?
CHIRON. In Argo's glorious company
  Each hero shone in his own way,
  Providing by his particular gift
  What in his comrades might be missed.
  The Dioscuri led all others when
  Beauty was what counted, youth, élan;
  The two Boreads when a shipmate's peril
  Demanded the most resolute, quick action;   7610
  Strong, reflective, wise, and patient in council,
  Jason, loved by women, was the captain;
  Then Orpheus: a gentle, pensive soul,
  Best of those who on the lyre played;
  And Lynceus, steering night and day, sharp-eyed,
  To bring the ship past jagged reef and shoal.
  Danger's best braved with your friends around you:
  Boldly you strike, and all your comrades cheer you.
FAUST. Nothing to say about great Hercules?

CHIRON. Don't speak that name, it wakes such memories!   7620
　　　I'd never once seen Phoebus, Ares, or
　　　Those others by whatever names they're called,
　　　When big as life before me I beheld
　　　The one men thought a god, so great their awe.
　　　A king, a born king, Hercules, he stood there,
　　　Glorious-looking in his youth,
　　　Submissive to his elder brother,
　　　To pretty women, too, I fear.
　　　His match you'll never see upon this earth,
　　　Nor Hebe lead another upwards like him.   7630
　　　Vainly verse attempts, tongue-tied, to sing him,
　　　Sculptors torture marble all in vain.
FAUST. They boast of their work, every one;
　　　How short it falls of your description.
　　　You've portrayed the fairest man,
　　　Now portray the fairest woman.
CHIRON. Ha, female beauty, what a bore—
　　　So often statuelike, cold, stiff;
　　　I reserve my praises for
　　　Beings brimming with glad life.   7640
　　　The Beautiful delights itself,
　　　To itself it's all in all,
　　　But charm is irresistible,
　　　Like Helen when I carried her.
FAUST. You carried her?
CHIRON.　　　　　　　　　I did, for sure.
FAUST. Already I've been staggered, dazed—
　　　And now I learn where she sat I sit, too!
CHIRON. She clutched my mane the way you do.
FAUST. Beside myself I am, half crazed!
　　　Helen is my heart's desire.   7650
　　　Where was this, where did you take her?

CHIRON. Your question is soon satisfied.
    Once it happened brigands seized her,
    Then the Dioscuri freed her;
    The raiders, unused to defeat,
    Rallying, rushed in hot pursuit.
    I and Helen with her brothers
    Raced along but found our course
    Barred by the Eleusinian marsh;
    The Dioscuri waded, I splashed over.   7660
    She, when we were safe, sprang down,
    Sweetly stroked my dripping mane
    And said such things, so charmingly!
    So young she was, yet self-possessed,
    Thanking me with such ease, grace—
    The joy it gave to an old man like me.
FAUST. And only ten years old!
CHIRON.   You've been taken
    In, as I can see, by the professors,
    Who've taken in themselves. For women
    In mythology enjoy a special grace: 7670
    The poet shows them as his tale requires,
    They never need endure a wrinkled face,
    They keep their slim, attractive figures;
    Carried off in youth, by crowds of suitors
    Still pursued in age. In short,
    Poets aren't subject to time's writ.
FAUST. Then why impose it on great Zeus's daughter?
    On Pherae didn't slain Achilles find her,
    Outside time's bounds. Oh what rare good luck
    From destiny's hard grip to snatch love back!   7680
    Why shouldn't I, with my fierce longing filled,
    Bring back to life that form unparalleled,
    That creature, goddesslike undying,

As dear as great, sublime as charming?
You saw her once, today I saw her, too,
As fair, as longed for, as so long ago!
Her beauty's taken my whole being captive,
I'll make her mine, without her I can't—won't—live!

CHIRON. Your rapture, you strange fellow, 's all too human,
But to us spirits you look like a madman.   7690
Now as it happens you're in luck today:
I briefly visit Manto annually,
Manto, Aesculapius's daughter,
Who prays her reverend parent fervently
That he may, for the sake of his own honor,
Teach physicians wisdom finally
And save the people from their reckless slaughter.
Of all the Sibyls she's best, I prefer her,
She's not some grotesque crone who raves and shrieks,
But kind and gentle, busy with good works.   7700
Remain with her awhile, I feel assured
That with her herbs you'll be completely cured.

FAUST. Keep your cures, my mind's in perfect order—
She'd make me like the rest, ignoble, vulgar.

CHIRON. We've reached the healing well—now quick, alight,
And drink its waters while you have the chance.

FAUST. Where have you carried me this dreadful night,
Splashing through gravelly streams? What place is this?

CHIRON. Here Rome's republic warred with mighty Greece,
Olympus to the left, Peneios right.   7710
The greatest realm the world had ever seen,
Overthrown and swallowed by the sand,
The king in flight, the citizen exulting.
Look up and see, so close at hand,
The moonlit temple, still enduring.

MANTO. [*Dreaming within*]

Clattering hoofs
Sound on the steps,
Two demigods here.

CHIRON.

Wise, oh you're wise—
Open your eyes.   7720

MANTO. [*Waking*] Hello! I see you've not failed to appear.

CHIRON. And I see that your temple is still here.

MANTO. You still race around, you never tire?

CHIRON. You love best your chair and fire,
   I love best to run round everywhere.

MANTO. It's time that circles round me—and I wait.
   —Who's this?

CHIRON.   The tides of this notorious night
   Have swept him here. The man's a lunatic,
   Wants Helen and he wants her quick,
   But hasn't got the least idea   7730
   How he should look for her or where.
   He needs some Aesculapian therapies.

MANTO. I love who wish impossibilities.

                [*Chiron is already far away.*]
   Foolhardy fellow, enter and rejoice!
   This passage follows a descending course
   Into Olympus's hollow foot, and there
   Proserpine covertly cocks an ear
   To hear an intruding footfall, living voice.
   I smuggled Orpheus down there this way once;
   So boldly does it, don't you spoil *your* chance!   7740

                                        They descend

AGAIN ON THE UPPER PENEIOS

SIRENS. Dive into Peneios river!
    Splash and swim, enjoy its sports!
    Sing out with a song, another,
    For all poor unfortunates.
    Away from water, what's life—nothing.
    If we all went down together
    To the green Aegean, bathing
    In its waters, oh the pleasure!
        [*Earthquake!*]
    Water, foaming, backwards surges,
    Cast out of its ancient bed,   7750
    In astonished, reverse flood,
    Smoke pours from the cracked shore's fissures.
    Run, run, don't delay, away all!
    It's no good, this miracle.

    Off, distinguished guests, go too, you all,
    To our gay sea carnival,
    Where the tremulous waves sigh
    Along the shingled shore and die,
    Where Luna shines with double hue
    And bathes us in her sacred dew!   7760
    There life's unconfined, and here
    Earthquakes make one shake with fear.
    If you're wise, away you'll hurry,
    Here in this place it's too scary.
SEISMOS. [*Rumbling noisily down below*]
    Once more now, use all your strength, heft,
    With your shoulders, eight, nine, ten—lift!
    When we break through, see how they will
    Stare amazed and run off, fearful.

SPHINXES.   How unpleasant, all this quaking,
             What a shiver's in the air!   7770
             How all things are swaying, shaking,
             Back and forth—such turbulence!
             Insufferable disturbance!
             But we won't stir from our place
             Even if all Hell breaks loose.

             Now the ground thrusts up, in form
             Marvelously like a dome,
             And I know who's doing it:
             It's the same Old One who built
             Delos island to give shelter   7780
             To Latona in her labor—
             Pushed it up out of the waves!
             With all his force how he strains upward,
             Arms stiff, back bent, he's no sluggard;
             Atlaslike behaving, heaves
             Green riverbank and river bed,
             Gravel, earth, and grass and reed
             Up, up, making a great gap in
             Our peaceful valley region.
             By his efforts unexhausted,   7790
             A colossal caryatid;
             Buried still up to his waist,
             He sustains the huge weight
             Of granite, marble, quartz, and schist.
             No farther, though—here he must stop.
             Sphinxes don't budge, not a step.
SEISMOS.   All this is owing to my doing
             Which in the end you must concede:
             Without my shaking and my shoving
             This world, this lovely world, how should   7800

It ever have become so fair?
Your mountains towering in the air,
Into the pure and glorious blue,
Affording picturesque views to you—
Because of my drive, push, they're there.

Before black Night and Chaos, my
Oldest forbears, boldly I
With the Titans back and forth
Tossed Pelion and Ossa both
Like two balls; and in this way   7810
We roughhoused in the joy of youth,
Till growing tired finally,
Malapertly clapped the peaks
Atop Parnassus—now he wears two caps.
You'll find Apollo up there, he amuses
Himself with the blithe and buxom Muses.
I even raised aloft Jove's seat,
From where he wields his thunderbolt.
And now once more, prodigiously,
From below up forced my way   7820
And loudly call for dwellers here
To fill these slopes with life and cheer.

SPHINXES. We'd swear these mountains were primeval
If our own eyes hadn't just
Witnessed their immense upheaval
Bursting through the planet's crust,
A forest mantling their steeps,
With rocks appearing, heaps and heaps.
But we Sphinxes pay it all no notice,
Our seat is sacred, no one dare disturb us.   7830

GRIFFINS. Gold in all forms, leaf and nugget,
Glitter in the cracks of granite.

Ants, arise, they're thieves about!
With your fingers pick it out.
CHORUS OF ANTS.
          After the giants'
          Great work is complete,
          Up we go, we ants,
          On our fidgety feet,
          Darting in, darting out
          Of the crevices where   7840
          Every grain we discover
          Adds its little bit
          Of worth to the treasure.
          We search every corner,
          Don't dawdle or slacken,
          Bring only pure gold in,
          Ignore
          The crude ore.
GRIFFINS. Heap it up here, all of it!
          We'll squat down, our claws on it,   7850
          Good strong bolts they are, none better
          For keeping safe the richest treasure.
PYGMIES. It's really true, we've found a home!
          How it happened?—no idea.
          Never ask where we came from,
          It's enough that we are here.
          All lands, great and small, provide
          Life a place where it may thrive;
          Where a cranny shows, be sure
          Soon you'll see us dwarfs appear.   7860
          Man and wife together, we
          Work in pairs exemplary
          Of untiring industry.
          Was Paradise like this?—can't say.

But here in this place we feel blest
And thank our stars, immensely grateful.
Everywhere you look, east, west,
Mother Earth is kind, is fruitful.

DACTYLS.

If she in one night
Made these little ones, 7870
She'll also beget
The littlest ones
Who looking round find
Lots more of their kind.

PYGMY ELDERS.

Move along, never stop,
Occupy this fine spot!
Speed makes up for muscle,
So let's see you hustle.
It's peace still, get busy
And build us a smithy 7880
To furnish our army
With weapons aplenty!

You ants, show you're useful,
Swarm about and discover
What we must have, metal.
And Dactyls, so tiny,
Past counting, so many,
Your orders are:
Fetch fagots here!
Fire pits will 7890
Give us charcoal.

GENERALISSIMO.

Go, valiant bowmen,
March out together,

Shoot the white heron
Nesting there, yonder,
On that pond's shore,
Puffed with hauteur!
With one quick shot
Bring down the lot,
So every gnome   7900
May flaunt a plume.

ANTS AND DACTYLS.

Who, who will save us?
We smelted the iron
And they, they did what, then?
Forged chains to enslave us.
Rebel we will, but
It's too soon for that,
So stoop in submission.

THE CRANES OF IBYCUS.

Murderous shrieks and deathly moans!
Frightened flapping of white wings!   7910
Dreadful cries of agony
Rise up to us in the sky!
All, all slaughtered, once so proud,
The lake crimson with their blood!
Greedy monsters without mercy
Rob the herons of their glory;
Now plumes nod upon the helmets
Of those fat, bowlegged midgets!
You fellow cranes in your great V's
Flying above the heaving seas,   7920
All together, come, we'll rally,
Assemble an avenging army!
We are kin, hear our appeal
In a cause concerns us all.

None must spare himself, we'll serve
These ugly brutes as they deserve!

[*They fly off in all directions, croaking.*]

MEPHISTO. [*Down in the plain*] I know how to handle Northern
    witches,
But these foreign ones give me the twitches.
The Blocksberg region's such a pleasant place,
No matter where, it shows a friendly face.   7930
Frau Ilse watches from her clifftop home,
Heinrich high up smiles down amiably;
The Schnarzers sneer at Elend, certainly,
Yet everything stays put till kingdom come.
But here! Go where you will, you never know
When there will be an eruption from below.
Upon a valley floor I saunter blithely
And suddenly there rises up behind me
A mountain—well, a hill at least, let's say—
That's more than big enough to bar the way   7940
To my dear Sphinxes.—Fires still burn brightly
Lighting up the lurid scene around me,
Revealing that pert troupe of flirts, still dancing
Towards me teasingly, then with a taunting
Laugh escaping. Careful! When you've stolen
Slyly in to snatch up sweets too often,
You push at any door you think is open.
LAMIAE. [*Drawing Mephistopheles after them*]
    Go fast, then slow down,
    Hesitate, then race on!
    Linger to chatter   7950
    Then off like birds, scatter!
    What fine entertainment,

To make the old sinner
Come hobbling after,
Come stumbling hot for
His favorite pleasure,
So as to find what?
A well-earned chastisement.
He drags his clubfoot,
As we flutter before him,   7960
Slower and slower.

MEPHISTO. [*Coming to a stop*]
Damn, oh damn! Poor johnnies all,
From Adam on led to our fall!
A man gets old—but wise? Mooncalf,
Haven't you been fooled enough?

The truth's well known, they're worthless through and through.
Rouged faces, bodies in tight corsets squeezed,
There's nothing good they have to offer you,
Take hold of them, you find their flesh diseased.
We understand it well, we caught on soon,   7970
And yet we jig when these jades call the tune.

LAMIAE. [*Halting*] Slow down, he's hesitating, he thinks twice.
Back, back or he'll escape us, the old vice.

MEPHISTO. [*Going on again*] Keep going, don't get in a tangle
Of silly doubts! For who the devil
'D be the Devil for a minute
If bewitching witches weren't?

LAMIAE. [*At their most alluring*]
Come, around our hero dance,
Love, we feel sure, shall announce
Itself in him for one of us.   7980

MEPHISTO. I'll admit in this uncertain
Light you look like pretty women,
So I will disparage no one.

EMPUSA. [*Pushing herself forward*]
    Nor me neither! So I hope you'll
    Let me join your friendly circle.
LAMIAE. Always hanging round, she seems,
    Spoiling all of our good times.
EMPUSA. [*To Mephistopheles*]
    Greetings to you, I am Empusa,
    The darling, donkey-footed loser,
    Your foot's a horse's, cousin, yet   7990
    I won't refuse you my "Well met!"
MEPHISTO. I thought I didn't know a soul here,
    And find that we are all relations.
    An old, old story, I see, we are,
    From Harz to Hellas, none but cousins.
EMPUSA. I act fast and in a flash
    Assume whatever shape I wish.
    But in your honor I am glad
    To wear my long-eared ass's head.
MEPHISTO. Kinship here means much, I see—   8000
    Such emphasis on family!
    But I'm not one who acquiesces
    In being linked to silly asses.
LAMIAE. Forget that hag, disgusting, ugly,
    She drives away all charm and beauty,
    Wherever charm and beauty dwelled,
    She arrived, they were expelled.
MEPHISTO. These other cousins, tender, luscious,
    Nevertheless make me suspicious;
    Those cheeks of theirs, blooming like roses—   8010
    Behind them I fear metamorphoses.
LAMIAE. Try, though! You can choose from many—
    Courage! And if you are lucky
    You'll walk away with the grand prize.

What good are all your amorous sighs?
For all your airs, your sneering, proud face,
As a suitor you're a sad case!
—Good, good, now he's joined the dance.
Let your masks drop, show the dunce
What you girls are really like.   8020
MEPHISTO. The prettiest is the one I pick.
                         [*Embracing her.*]
Damn it, dry as a broomstick!
                         [*Grabbing another.*]
How about her?—That face, hard grin!
LAMIAE. You're owed better? Think again.
MEPHISTO. This one's petite. Let's bargain, dear.
—A lizard, slips away so quick,
Her braid smooth and serpentlike.
Well, I'll take the tall one there.
—A thyrsus I have in my grip!
Atop a pinecone as its tip.   8030
Where will it end? Look, there's a fat one,
Perhaps it's possible with that one.
Here goes with my final try.
She's flabby, doughy, in the East
Such creatures fetch the highest price.
—Ugh! The puffball's blown away!
LAMIAE. Scatter every which way, flashing
Bat-winged, silent, like black lightning!
In a scary, shifting ring, each
Fly around that son of a witch,   8040
On the interloper sweep—
He is getting off too cheap!
MEPHISTO. [*Giving himself a shake*]
I never seem to learn, apparently;
It's stupid in the North, it's just as stupid here.

Here as there the ghosts are creepy, queer,
The people crude, the poets equally.
Here as everywhere a masquerade
Sets your pulses going till your head
Is in a whirl. I see a charming mummer,
Pursue her and catch something makes me shudder.   8050
Being fooled is just fine if
Only it lasts long enough.
[*Wandering among the rocks.*]
I'm lost. Where once there was a path,
Now all I see is rock and cliff.
I came here on a level track,
On rubble I go stumbling back.
Clambering I cry, "Halloo,
My good Sphinxes, where are you?"
It's mad, it's crazy, just imagine,
In one night to raise a mountain!   8060
A real witches' ride, I reckon:
To pack along with them their Brocken!
OREAD. [*Out of real, natural rock*]
    Climb up here, my mountain's old as
    Time, and keeps its ancient slopes,
    Its venerable granite steeps—
    The farthest-reaching spurs of Pindus.
    Unshaken I stand as I did
    When over me great Pompey fled.
    But that illusion there, false show,
    Will vanish at the first cockcrow.   8070
    I've often seen such spectacles put on,
    Hold the stage awhile, then poof, they're gone.
MEPHISTO. Honor to you, you reverend peak,
    With your great forests of stout oak,
    Whose umbrage Luna's brightest light

Strives in vain to penetrate!
—But in those bushes there I see
A spark glowing modestly.
How luckily things work out, yes,
It's him, it's him, Homunculus!   8080
And where have you been, minikin?

HOMUNCULUS. Here and there and out and in,
     Full of longing and impatience
     To smash my glass, enjoy a real existence.
     It's only that so far I've not met up with
     Any body I'd like to join up with.
     However—let me say, between us,
     I've been following two famous
     Men, philosophers the pair are,
     Whose every word is "Nature! Nature!"   8090
     I'll stick to them, I will, like glue—
     Life on earth is surely what they know;
     All that they say I'll listen to
     And learn from them the right, best way to go.

MEPHISTO. Go your own way, using your own mind!
     Where phantoms flourish, there you'll find
     Philosophers, they're always welcome,
     For they create new phantoms by the dozen.
     Don't make mistakes and you will never learn!
     You'd like to live, would you, be really born?   8100
     Well, you yourself must do that, on your own.

HOMUNCULUS. Still, good advice is not to be sneered at.

MEPHISTO. Well, go ahead, we'll see how far you get.

                                        [*They separate.*]

ANAXAGORAS. [*To Thales*]
     Your mind's stubborn, unrelenting.
     What more proof, tell me, is wanting?

THALES. The wave before the breeze runs glad enough,
   But from the bristling cliff it keeps far off.
ANAXAGORAS. Explosive gases gave this mountain birth.
THALES. In wetness lies the origin of life.
HOMUNCULUS. [*Between the two*]
   Let me go along with you!   8110
   I yearn for a beginning, too.
ANAXAGORAS. In one night, my good Thales, did
   You ever raise a mountain out of mud?
THALES.
   Nature's living stream never flows jerkily
   By day and night and hour, it runs steadily;
   She shapes all things in order, eschews quirks,
   Force she abhors, even in hugest works.
ANAXAGORAS. Do you say! Fierce Plutonic fires,
   The enormous explosive force of Aeolian vapors—
   These broke through the old flat crust of earth   8120
   And in a moment brought this mountain forth.
THALES. Yes, yes, it's there all right, fine, good, however,
   How does this advance us any farther?
   It's a waste of time, such argument,
   Patience's useless with the adamant.
ANAXAGORAS. How fast the mountain fills with myrmidons
   Who find a home in all the cracks and fissures,
   Swarming pygmies, insects, and Tom-thumbs
   And every kind of busy little creatures.
                         [*To Homunculus*]
   You've never wanted power and dominion,   8130
   You've been a recluse, living in seclusion,
   But if you're ready to take charge and govern,
   I'll have you crowned as king of this great mountain.
HOMUNCULUS. And your opinion, Thales?

THALES.   Wait!
    When you live with little people,
    The things you do perforce are little;
    Among the great a little man grows great.
    Look up and learn! See that black cloud
    Bringing down on that dwarf nation
    Chaos and disintegration—   8140
    Cranes! and they, believe me, would
    Destroy the King of Pygmies, too.
    With their sharp beaks, murderous talons,
    Down they swoop on those felons
    Like thunderbolts out of the blue.
    A crime it was to kill the herons
    Stepping round their peaceful lake.
    But those arrows which rained down
    Murder on the innocent flock
    Grew a bloody crop: in turn   8150
    The cranes, their rage excited by
    Their poor kindred's tragedy,
    Make pygmy blood pour out and soak the fields.
    What good now their helmets, spears, and shields?
    What good now his plume to every dwarf?
    How the ants and Dactyls scurry off!
    The pygmy legions waver, break, and fly.
ANAXAGORAS. [*After a pause, solemnly*]
    Till now I've praised the powers underneath,
    In this case I direct my gaze on high.
    —Eternal Lady, ageless and unchanged,   8160
    Triple-shaped and triple-named,
    My people perish! Hear, do, me,
    Luna, Dian, Hecate!
    Heart-inspiring, most profoundly serious,
    Calm-appearing, fiery, amorous,

Unclose your shadow's dread abyss,
Unconjured, bring down an eclipse!
                    [*A pause.*]
        How quick it's heard, my prayer!
        Has my loud cry
        Into the sky   8170
        Disturbed great Nature's order?
The goddess's round throne swells larger
As it nears, burns whiter, brighter,
A monstrous, frightening light whose blaze
Purplish glows in blinded eyes!
—No nearer, huge and menacing sphere,
Or you'll destroy us, us and all things here!

It's true, then, that Thessalian sorceresses,
Resorting to their wicked practices,
Once sang you down out of your monthly course   8180
And wrung from you by necromantic force
Destructive powers?—Now the disc's turned dark,
It breaks apart and rains down burning rock
With such a clatter, noise of hissing flames,
Mixed with thunder, roar of hurricanes!
Submissively I bow before the throne!
Forgive me, I called this disaster down.
                    [*Falls on his face.*]
THALES. The wonders this man thinks he heard and saw!
        What happened I am not exactly sure,
        But his ideas and mine are nowhere near.   8190
        We'll agree: the times are very queer,
        But Luna still rocks high up in her sphere
        Quite comfortably, just as she did before.
HOMUNCULUS. Look up to where the Pygmies made their home:
        The mountaintop, once round, now's a sharp peak!
        I felt a huge, a cataclysmic shock

Caused by a boulder fallen from the moon.
Down it dropped, no questions asked,
And friend and foe alike were smashed.   8200
Still, I must praise the skill, the might,
Able in a single night,
Working high up and down under,
To elevate this mountainous structure.
THALES. Calm down! All was imagining.
That nasty brood are gone, and a good thing.
Just think if you had been their king!
And now let's off to the sea festival.
They're glad when strangers come, they treat them well.

[*They leave.*]

MEPHISTO. [*On the other side of the mountain, climbing*]
Look at me—scrambling up steep rocks,   8210
Tripping on roots of wretched oaks!
In my dear pine-clad mountains of the Harz
There's a pitchlike smell, a smell I favor
Most of all, excepting that of sulphur.
But here among these Greeks there's not a trace
Of anything like that. I'm curious
To find out what they use below in their Hell
To stoke the fires with, their kind of fuel.
DRYAD. I guess you're smart enough in your own country,
Abroad you're something less than apt;   8220
Stop thinking home thoughts, try, Sir, to adapt
And show due honor to our sacred oak tree.
MEPHISTO. What you have lost, that's what you think about,
What you were used to, that seems Paradise.
—But what's that in the cave there my eye spies,
Three shapes squatting in the feeble light?
DRYAD. The Phorkyads. Why don't you go inside
And speak to them—unless you are afraid?

MEPHISTO. Well, why not?—I can't believe it, oh no!
    I've been around, I have, yet must confess   8230
    Nothing I have seen to match this trio,
    The mandrakes take a back seat to such ugliness.
    The worst, most primal sins that ever were,
    When once you've laid eyes on this triple horror,
    Will seem quite innocent, demure.
    In our most dreadful hells we'd never suffer
    Their even coming near the door.
    And here they're fixtures in the land of beauty,
    Antiquity's great home, as it's called proudly.
    They sense my presence, stir upon their mats,   8240
    Squeak and twitter like vampire bats.
PHORKYAD. Hand me the, eye, my dear, and I shall
    See who's ventured near our temple.
MEPHISTO. Esteemed ladies, have I your permission
    To come and ask your triple benediction?
    You don't know me, that can't be disputed,
    Yet I believe we're distantly related.
    I've seen a lot of ancient gods already,
    Bowed down to Ops and Rhea reverently;
    The Parcae, like you Chaos-born, I saw   8250
    Just yesterday, or was it—I'm not sure.
    But till now your like has been denied me.
    I'm overjoyed to meet your trinity.
PHORKYADS. Good sense this specter here, I think, possesses.
MEPHISTO. I'm so surprised no poet's hymned your praises.
    How has it happened, too, that I have never
    Beheld your dignities portrayed in sculpture?
    It's you the chisel should attempt to capture,
    Not Juno, Pallas, Venus, or whoever.
PHORKYADS. Sunk in solitude and quiet nights,   8260
    We've been occupied with other thoughts.

MEPHISTO. To be sure! You've been too long concealed
    From the admiring eyes of the great world.
    Your proper place is the distinguished circle
    Where Art and Splendor, gloriously united,
    High on a pedestal side by side are seated,
    Where every day produces the revival
    Of defunct heroes out of blocks of marble,
    Where—
PHORKYADS. That's enough! Don't waken wishes in us.   8270
    What good knowing such things would it do us?
    Born in the night, with nighttime things allied,
    Unknown to the world, by our own selves mystified.
MEPHISTO. Ladies, really, there's no difficulty.
        Here is my suggestion: Let your trinity
    Hand over one of you to someone else,
    With you three, one eye, one tooth suffice;
    So shouldn't it be possible for you
    To squeeze together mythologically
    And as two instead of three make do?   8280
    The extra shape you then could lend to me,
    Pro tem.
A PHORKYAD. Hm, hm—do we agree, we three?
THE OTHERS. We do.   But tooth and eye—they're out.
MEPHISTO. No, no, that's just what shows best in you women!
    To hit you off exactly I must have them.
THE PHORKYAD. Keep one of your red eyes shut,
    Let a single fang stick out,
    Seen in profile, then you would
    Look just like our sisterhood.
MEPHISTO. All right. I'm honored.
PHORKYADS.   Good!
MEPHISTO. [*A Phorkyad in profile*]   So now it's done.   8290
    Just look at me—Chaos's darling son!

PHORKYADS. And we his daughters—about *us* there's no doubt.
MEPHISTO. But dear me, when I think: the shame of it!
    They'll jeer as I pass by, "Hermaphrodite!"
PHORKYADS. A new trio we are—beautiful!
    With two eyes now, two fangs—oh wonderful!
MEPHISTO. With a face like this I'd better hide, I'll go
    And scare the Hell out of the devils down below.

ROCKY INLETS OF THE AEGEAN SEA

The moon arrested at the zenith.

SIRENS. [*Reclining on the rocks, playing flutes and singing*]
    If Thessalian hags one night
    Gave you such a dreadful fright,   8300
    Drawing you down wickedly
    From your seat high in the sky,
    Yet Dian, mild luminary.
    We implore you, look benignly
    Down upon these crisping wavelets
    Scattering their silver droplets,
    Shine upon the waters seething
    With the crowd of creatures rising
    From the waves, all at your service.
    Queen of the Night, bright moon, be gracious!   8310
NEREIDS AND TRITONS. [*Appearing as wonders of the deep*]
    Sound a shriller note to call up
    From the deep the scaly sea folk
    Hiding in the depths below!
    Down we dove for shelter from
    The wild chaos of the storm
    To the quiet bottom: now
    Your sweet song draws us from under.

See with what delight we put on
Bracelets, gold chains, jewels of wonder,
Buckles, matching belts of jadestone—   8320
To your song we owe this treasure
Got from hulks upon the sea floor
Shipwrecked following your lure
—Demons of this bay and shore!

SIRENS. We know very well you fishes
Find your life at sea delicious,
Where you dart about carefree.
But upon this festive day
Demonstrate, for such our wish is,
You are more than thoughtless fishes.   8330

NEREIDS AND TRITONS. The selfsame thought was ours, too,
Before our coming here to you.—
Sisters, brothers, off! We'll manage
It by means of a short voyage,
Furnish proof conclusive that we
All are more than fishes merely.

[*They depart.*]

SIRENS. Off they go in a race,
Heading where? Samothrace.
Out of sight soon, the wind
Blowing well from behind.   8340
What we wonder 's the object
Of such a visit
To the realm of the great Cabiri?
Gods extraordinary
That self-beget themselves continually,
With no idea ever
Of who it is they are.
Lovely Luna, be gracious,
Stay your heavenly passage,

Keep it nighttime still and thus   8350
Daylight shan't scatter us.

THALES. [*On the shore, to Homunculus*]
I'd be glad to take you to old Nereus,
His cavern's close by, too, but that old walrus
Is so difficult, ill-tempered, sour,
Grumbles that he cannot find
An ounce of good in humankind.
Yet he can see into the future,
For which he's held in general esteem;
And he's helped many, I'll say that for him.

HOMUNCULUS. So let's knock and see what happens. I'm   8360
Not afraid for my glass, little flame.

NEREUS. I hear something—human voices, are they?
Instantly I'm thrown into a fury!
Ambitious things they are, striving to be
Like the gods, yet damned eternally
To end at last just as they were at first.
I might have passed these years in godlike rest,
But felt impelled to shower all the best
With good advice and still more good advice—
And then see what they do—all wrong, all wrong!   8370
I might just as well have held my tongue.

THALES. Yet Old Man of the Sea, we've faith in you.
Your wisdom's famous, don't turn us away.
Regard this flame, seems human, it is true,
But it will do exactly as you say.

NEREUS. As I say! I *say* but do they *heed*?
It dies dumb in them, my every word!
As often as they bitterly condemn
A thing they've done, they do the same again.
How like a father I warned Paris, often!   8380
Don't, I said, seduce that foreign woman.

There he stood upon the Greek shore, boldly;
I told him what in vision I saw clearly:
The smoke-filled air, shot through with a red glow,
The roofs ablaze, murder and death below,
Troy's judgment day, fixed in epic verses
Millennially, as terrible as famous.
An old man's words made that vain puppy smile;
Lust led him on, Troy's topless towers fell:
A giant corpse, stark after its long torture,   8390
Providing Pindus's eagles a fine dinner.
Ulysses, too! Didn't I foretell him
Circe's tricks, the Cyclops' frightfulness,
His own dallying, his men's brainlessness,
And what else, heavens! What good did it do him?
Till ten years overdue, half drowned, storm tossed,
A kind wave bore him to a friendly coast.

THALES. A wise head is distressed by such behavior;
A good heart tries again because it's good.
An ounce of thanks contents the kindly mentor,   8400
Outweighs a ton of black ingratitude.
We haven't come to you to beg a trifle,
The boy longs to be born, he needs your counsel.

NEREUS. Don't spoil it when for once I'm in good humor!
Quite other things are on my mind today.
My children have been summoned, every daughter,
The lovely Dorids, Graces of the Sea.
Not high Olympus, no, not all your Greece
Shows figures suaver than my dears possess.
From water dragons with what grace they leap on   8410
The white-maned horses of earth-shaking Neptune,
With the element they're so at home,
They seem uplifted by the very foam.

Galatea, loveliest of all,
Borne on Aphrodite's scallop shell
Sparkling opal-like, comes here today.
She, since the Cyprian forsook us—
Forsook her birthplace in the sea—
In Paphos now is worshiped as a goddess;
The temple city and the chariot throne,   8420
The foam-born's once, are now my daughter's own.

Leave me! In a father's hour of such pure bliss,
Curses aren't fitting, any bitterness.
Go ask that wonderworker, Proteus,
The way one's born or changed to something else.

                                              [*Departs seaward.*]

THALES. We've not advanced a single step by this.
         If we catch Proteus he'll turn to water
         In our grasp. If he stays put, he'll mutter
         Such strange things to make our poor heads swim.
         Still, what you need's advice, the more the better,   8430
         So it's worth trying. Off we go to him!

                                              [*They go off.*]

SIRENS. [*On the rocks above*]
         What's that we see approaching
         From far out in the offing.
         White sails, they look like, bellying
         In the brisk wind blowing.
         How brightly round a light's shed—
         They're mermaids, but transfigured!
         Down, sisters, we'll go, shall we?
         Those are their voices surely.

NEREIDS AND TRITONS.
         You'll welcome with delight   8440
         Whom we bring here tonight:

Figures austere, still,
Emerging shining from
Chelone's giant shell—
And gods all, every one!
Then sing and louder sing.

SIRENS.

Short in their height,
Great in their strength,
The shipwrecked's savior,
Ancient gods, old in honor.   8450

NEREIDS AND TRITONS.

We bring you the Cabiri
To rule this happy revel,
Their presence, holy, peaceful,
Calms Neptune so he's friendly.

SIRENS.

We give way to you—
When ships break in two.
With your great strength you
Rescue the whole crew.

NEREIDS AND TRITONS.

We've brought along three,
The fourth wouldn't come;   8460
Claimed he, only he,
Was the true, rightful one
Who thought for them all—
He refused our appeal.

SIRENS.

One god may mock another,
Divinity dishonor—
Fear injury, misfortune,
All honor without exception.

NEREIDS AND TRITONS.

They're seven, all told, really.

SIRENS.

The other three, where are they?   8470

NEREIDS AND TRITONS.

We don't know, don't ask us,
Inquire on Olympus.
Also the eighth's there that
Nobody's thought of yet.
Benignant, all, to us but
Unfinished still, imperfect.

None there are like these gods,
Ever pressing onwards
With hungriness unspeakable
For the unattainable.   8480

SIRENS. Regularly lauds
We send all the gods
Of sun and moon and skies.
Piety pays.

NEREIDS AND TRITONS.

Our renown shines brightest
As leaders of this sea fest.

SIRENS.

The heroes of old story,
The bravest men of Greece,
Shall see themselves less famed.
All their efforts gained   8490
Them the Golden Fleece—
Ours, the great Cabiri!
[*All together.*]

Ours   }
Yours   }   the great Cabiri!

[*Nereids and Tritons pass off across the stage.*]

HOMUNCULUS. These misshapen things, they look
    Like old pots of clay.
    The learned break their heads to think
    What they signify.
THALES. Yes, what's old they covet most:
    The coin is precious for its rust.
PROTEUS. [*Unobserved*] Old fabulist that I am, this delights me!   8500
    The queerer something is, the more it suits me.
THALES. Where are you, Proteus?
PROTEUS. [*Throwing his voice, now sounding far off, now near*]
                        Right here!—and here!
THALES. I do forgive you your old jokes, dear fellow,
    But don't try fooling me, a friend, for I know
    You're able to sound far off when you are near.
PROTEUS. [*As if from far away*]
    Bye-bye!
THALES. [*Whispering to Homunculus*]
          He's here, right here! Now sparkle, flash!
    He's just as curious as a fish:
    Wherever he hides, whatever his shape,
    Out our light will tease the scamp.
HOMUNCULUS. There, it's brighter now, the spark;   8510
    Any brighter and the glass would crack.
PROTEUS. [*As a giant turtle*]
    What thing's giving out that pretty light?
THALES. [*Tucking Homunculus out of sight*]
    Good!—Come closer for a better look,
    But on two man-legs, hear! The change won't put
    You to much trouble, I imagine—right?
    Who wants to see what I have hidden here
    Needs our approval and consent, dear Sir.

PROTEUS. [*In noble human shape*]
    Still up to your old sophist's japes.
THALES. And you're still fond of switching shapes.
    [*He uncovers Homunculus.*]
PROTEUS. [*Astonished*] A dwarf that shines! That's something new
        for me.   8520
THALES. He needs advice, he's anxious to be born.
    The dear thing came, as I've heard him explain,
    Into the world halfway, amazingly.
    He's all there mentally, he thinks all right,
    But bodily he's null. All the weight
    He's got is in the glass. He'd like to have
    A tangible existence, really live.
PROTEUS. A real virgin's son, I see—
    He's here before he ought to be
THALES. [*Lowering his voice*]
    That's not all that's not quite right.   8530
    I think he's an hermaphrodite.
PROTEUS. All the better. He can go, whenever
    He comes into a body, one way or the other,
    As the circumstances may require.
                                            [*To Homunculus*]
    —But come, there's no need here for prolonged thought,
    The open sea is where you make your start.
    You're small, so you begin on a small scale,
    Enjoy devouring what is smaller still,
    Till growing steadily, you mount up bit by bit
    To ever higher stages, forms more complete.   8540
HOMUNCULUS. The air's so soft here, with a breath
    I simply love of wet, green growth.
PROTEUS. I believe you, dear boy that you are!
    And farther out upon this narrow tongue
    The misty sea air's even fragranter.

And look there, moving steadily along—
It is the pageant coming into view.
Let's go see it.
THALES.   I'll come, too.
HOMUNCULUS. Extraordinary, our trinity:
  Three spirits walking out in company!   8550

[*Telchines of Rhodes on hippocamps and sea dragons, flourishing Neptune's trident.*]

CHORUS OF TELCHINES. We forged the trident of Lord Neptune
  By which he rules the boisterous ocean.
  When black clouds with a loud uproar
  Are let loose by the Thunderer
  And lightning plummets down the sky,
  Neptune flings up in reply
  Wave after wave defiantly,
  And all things struggling fearfully
  Between the two, worn out and battered,
  By the deep are soon devoured.   8560
  Tonight, entrusted with his scepter, we
  Can ride the waves without anxiety.
SIRENS.
    Votaries of Helios, blest
    With days that know no rain or mist,
    Greetings to you at this time
    In which we honor midnight's queen.
TELCHINES.
  O loveliest goddess, pinnacled high in the aether,
  The delight with which you hear lauded your brother!
  Then towards our blest Rhodes cock an attentive ear where
  Our unending paeans to him fill the air;   8570
  His fiery beams look down upon us when

He begins the day's race and when it is run.
We please him, our cities, our mountains, and bays,
Which he warms benevolently with his rays;
No banks of fog overwhelm us, should a wisp creep in,
A sunbeam or wind puff, and our isle's clear again.
Numberless effigies return him his likeness
As gentle youth, giant and tremendous colossus.
We were the first to represent his god-power
Worthily, as a proud-standing man figure.   8580

PROTEUS. Let them go on singing, bragging!
      Those dead works, to the life-bestowing
      Sacred sunlight, are a joke.
      Untiringly those people work
      At smelting bronze, and when it's cast:
      See, a marvel, is their boast.
      But what's the end with all of these
      Grandly standing god-effigies?
      Along a quake comes, knocks them flat
      And all that grandeur's sold for scrap.   8590

      All men do upon dry land
      Is toil away without end—
      The eternal sea suits life much better.
      So off you go into the water
      With your uncle Proteus,
      Who changes to a dolphin—thus!
                        [*He transforms himself.*]
      There, there's just the place for you,
      Mount my back, I'll carry you,
      To the ocean marry you.

THALES. The wish to start at the beginning   8600
      Of Creation is deserving
      Of all praise. Be prepared

For working hard, at top speed,
Obedient to eternal laws,
Whirled through eons without pause,
Through more forms than head can reckon,
And endless time, before you're human.

[*Homunculus mounts the back of dolphin-Proteus.*]

PROTEUS. Bright spirit, come, we'll dive into the wet,
   Although there's nothing much of you as yet,
   Here you'll live in length and breath,   8610
   Free to choose your own path.
   But one caution: don't aspire
   To climb up Nature's ladder
   For once you reach the top, become
   A man, that's it, you're finished, done.
THALES. Maybe so. Still, I'll defend a life
   Lived worthily in its brief time on earth.
PROTEUS. A life like yours, yes—it persists
   Well past the bounds of mortal days.
   Among the crowd of pale and drifting ghosts   8620
   I've noticed you these many centuries.
SIRENS. [*On the rocks*]
   See, around the moon bright clouds
   Make a shining ring, they're doves
   Aglow with love, with wings as white
   As the clearest, purest light.
   Paphos sent them to our rock,
   Amor's amorous bird flock,
   Now our festival's complete,
   Our pleasure exquisite.
NEREUS. [*To Thales*]
   For the nighttime wayfarer   8630

The ring's a trick of light and air,
But we spirits stick to our opinion,
Never doubting it's the right one.
Doves they surely are, believe me,
Escort for my daughter's journey
On her shell. How they fly's
A marvel, learnt in the first days.

THALES. I too hold the honest faith
Of a simple man is best,
A holy sense, nursed in the warmth   8640
And quiet of the inmost heart.

PSILLI AND MARSI. [*Riding sea bulls, sea calves, sea rams*]
In Cyprus's deep caves
Where Neptune's crashing waves
Halt foaming at the sill,
Where Seismos cannot shake
The massive roofs of rock,
Fanned by the eternal breeze,
With quiet pleasure still,
As in the elder days,
We guard the Cyprian's shell—   8650
In which, when night winds whisper
Across wave-woven water,
We bring Nereus's daughter,
Most lovely Galatea,
Unseen by earth's new race
Usurping here our place,
We do our work with no fuss,
Unafraid and heedless
Of Eagle and Winged Lion,
Of Crucifix and Crescent: 8660
Thrones transitory, restless,
Now rising up ascendant,

Now overthrown and fallen,
That drive out and strike down,
Lay waste field and town.
But we as we do ever,
Bring the one none dearer.

SIRENS.

Now unhastily approaching,
Ring within ring smoothly turning
Round the chariot planetlike,   8670
Or round it coiling serpentlike,
Come the Nereids, stout figures,
Boisterous yet pleasing creatures,
Also Dorids, mere wisps, tender,
Bringing with them Galatea,
She who is most like her mother:
Olympian her gravity,
Immortal and deservedly,
But so charming, too, and winsome
In the way of earthly women.   8680

DORIDS. [*As a chorus, passing by Nereus astride dolphins*]

These blooming youths, Dian, illumine
With your shadowy moonlight,
So our father may judge right
The dear spouses we have chosen.
                              [*To Nereus*]
They are shipwrecked boys we rescued
From the clutch of the cruel surf
And on beds of moss and seaweed
Warmed them back again to life,
Who now, proving true hearts, thank us,
As they should, with fervent kisses—   8690
Your favor, Father, them vouchsafe!

NEREUS. A double boon, deserving of applause:
    You're merciful, and you enjoy yourselves.

DORIDS.

        Don't begrudge us, O dear Father,
        Our bravely won conquest,
        Grant us hold them fast forever,
        Pressed to our immortal breast.

NEREUS. Your lovely prizes, daughters, have,
    Enjoy your youths and make them men,
    —It's not my prerogative   8700
    To grant what only Lord Zeus can.
    The waves by which you're rocked and tossed
    Forbid love should for you endure,
    And when your fancy fades at last,
    Then gently set your youths ashore.

DORIDS.

        You're very dear, sweet boys, to us,
           But part we must, can't help it;
        We wished for ever faithfulness,
           The gods will not allow it.

THE YOUTHS.

        Be as you've been, we'll not repine,   8710
           Brave sailor boys as we are,
        We've never known a time so fine,
           We shouldn't wish a better.

    [*Galatea appears on her shell.*]

NEREUS. It's you, it's you, my darling daughter!

GALATEA. Oh joy! Oh joy! Stop, dolphins, my father
    I see there, it's me he's calling to, crying!

NEREUS. Past me already they sweep, spray flying,
  Care nothing about one's deepest feeling.
  How I would like it, to be with them!
  Still, I'm so pleased with this one glimpse,
  For me an entire year's recompense.   8720
THALES.
  Hurrah! And again in my loudest voice!
  How expanded my soul is, how I rejoice,
  By beauty and truth my whole being's imbued . . .
  In water all that there is has its source,
  By water all that there is is renewed,
  Ocean, your dominion forever enforce!
  If you didn't send clouds big with moisture
  To pour down rain on the brook-laced pasture,
  To keep all the streams to and fro flowing,
  To keep the great rivers forever ongoing,   8730
  For our mountains and plains, our earth, what should we do?
  Over and over life is revived thanks to you!
ECHO. [A chorus of all the voices]
  Over and over life is reborn thanks to you!
NEREUS. Swinging back, far out at sea,
  So far I can't make out my girl,
  In still wider circles they
  Turn and turn, a gay display.
  To crown the water festival.
  Again and again I glimpse the shell
  Glittering like a star-burst   8740
  Amidst the ocean-skimming host.
      She, she, so dear,
      Who though so far from me,
      Shines clear, shines near,
      Through all eternity.

HOMUNCULUS. In this delicious damp and wet,
    No matter where I shine my light
    All's simply so lovely.
PROTEUS. In this life-giving damp and wet,
    How your tiny, tinkling light   8750
    Rings out bright and bravely.
NEREUS. In the midst of the dolphin-riding host.
    What new mystery do I see manifest?
    What is it flames all round the shell, a bright jet
    Of fire that stoops at the goddess's feet,
    Now blazing up fiercely, now burning low,
    Like a heart full of love beating fast, beating slow?
THALES. It's our little fellow, Homunculus,
    Incited, inspired by old Proteus!
    What you see are the signs of imperious longing,   8760
    And aren't those anguished sounds amorous groaning?
    He'll smash himself, he will, on her throne, wait and see.
    There! A flash, a bright flame, and he's spilt in the sea!
SIRENS. What marvel of brightness transfigures the water,
    The waves as they break shooting out sparks of fire?
    Such effulgence, such bursting and flashing of light,
    Every creature aflame as it swims through the night!
    How sea, how shore's held in a burning embrace!
    Then let Eros reign with whom all things commence!
        Hurrah for the ocean! Hurrah for the waves   8770
        And their crests with the sacred fire ablaze!
        Hurrah for the water, hurrah for the fire,
        Hurrah for their union, so rare, with each other!
ALL TOGETHER. Hurrah for the gentle caressing breezes!
        Hurrah for the caves and their secret recesses!
        Lift up our voices in praise of the four:
        Water, fire, earth, and air!

ACT III

BEFORE MENELAUS'S PALACE AT SPARTA

Enter Helen with a Chorus of Trojan Women, and Panthalis, the Chorus Leader.

HELEN.

The much admired, much reprobated Helen, I
Have come up from the beach where just now our ship landed,
Still giddy from the rolling, tossing waves which, with   8780
Poseidon's favor and Eurus's stiff push, bore
Us on their heaving backs to our native shore. Below
King Menelaus with his bravest soldiery
Are celebrating their return. But you, O great house
Of Tyndareus, built near the hang of Pallas's hill
When he came home, say welcome to me who was once
Your child—house finer fitted than any in all Sparta,
Where I with sister Clytemnestra, with Castor
And with Pollux too, played happily and there grew up.
And greetings to you, great bronze double doors!   8790
It happened on a day once when you stood hospitably
Opened wide, that the light of Menelaus, picked out
Of many, shone through them in the shape of my bridegroom.
Open, doors, again so I may, as befits a wife,
Convey a message from the King. Oh, let me in!
And all the storms that fate caused to rage round me—
Let them stay behind! For since the day she crossed
This threshhold with a carefree heart to visit Cythera's
Temple, by piety enjoined, but there to be seized by him,
The Phrygian ruffian, much oh much has happened   8800
That people far and wide delight to tell, but no

Delight for her to hear, the story longer in each
Telling and now grown into a legendary tale.

CHORUS.
        Oh never scorn, great Lady that you are,
        Gift whose honor is beyond compare!
        Fortune chose you for her highest prize:
        Beauty whose fame brighter shines than all else.
        A hero's name flies on before the man
        And so his stride is proud;
        And yet the stubbornest of heroes bows   8810
        Before all-conquering beauty his stiff mind.

HELEN. Enough, yes. With my husband by ship I
    Arrived, to his city have been sent ahead,
    And what he means by it I cannot guess.
    Come I a wife, come I a Queen?
    Come I a sacrifice to appease his royal hurt
    And the long-endured misfortunes of the Greeks?
    I'm a captive, whether prisoner too, I've
    No idea. It's true, for me the Immortals have decreed
    An ambiguous fame, ambiguous destiny,   8820
    The doubtful fellows of my handsomeness,
    Who even now stand here beside me at
    The door, lugubrious and threatening.
    In the hollow ship my husband hardly looked
    At me, nor spoke one cheering word.
    Seated facing me, he seemed like one
    Who meditated evil. But once we'd passed
    Into the bay into which Eurotas's waters
    Pour, the lead ships' prows but barely scraping
    On the beach, he, as if god-prompted, spoke: 8830
    My men will debark here. I'll muster them on shore.
    But you go on ahead, up along holy Eurotas's
    Flourishing bank, your horses riding through damp meadows

Deep in flowers, until you come on Lacedaemon's
Broad and fertile, once well cultivated plain
Around which mountains, frowning, stand. Enter
The high-towered palace, call together all the servants that
I left behind, the crafty old one too I put
In charge. Let her show you the great treasure that
Your father left, treasure I have heaped and ever   8840
Higher heaped through years of war and peace.
You'll find that everything is just as it should be;
At princes' homecomings it is their droit
To know that nothing's not in its right place.
Servants have no leave to shift things round.

CHORUS.

    Eyes surely brighten, heart must swell
    To see such treasure, always more and more.
    Glittering chains and gem-encrusted crowns
    Rest there proudly thinking themselves nonpareil.
    Walk in, do, and challenge them—and   8850
    Quick as jewel's flash they array themselves!
    How I'd love to see your beauty warring
    Against gold and pearls and noble gems!

HELEN. And then my lord gave me a further charge:
  "When you've completed a thorough, point by point
Inspection of the house and stores, collect
As many tripods as you think you'll need,
Together with the other kinds of vessels
That the rites of sacrifice require: cauldrons,
Shallow basins, bowls; pour tall jugs full   8860
Of purest water from the sacred spring;
Have ready wood that's dry and quick to catch;
And finally, be sure a sharp knife's there.
All else I leave to you." Those were his words
As he urged on my going. But no word, none,

What living, breathing thing he means to offer
Up to the Olympians. Oh, I am full
Of such misgivings! But no, don't think of it.
All's as the gods dispose, who cause to happen
What they choose, let men think well or ill   8870
Of it. We mortals, we must suffer what
We must. How often has the slaughterer,
Devoutly raising high the heavy ax
Above the tethered victim's drawn-down neck,
Found himself prevented by an enemy's
Coming near or intervention of a god.

CHORUS.   What's to come, thinking can't find out.
  Queen, take heart,
  Go in!
  Good and ill befall,   8880
  No warning given, all of us.
  And when warned, do we believe?
  We saw Troy burn, we saw
  Death face to face, death ignominious;
  And yet don't we stand here
  At your side, happy servant all,
  Under heaven's dazzling sun?—For mistress
  Earth's most beautiful, most gracious you
  Our good fortune is.

HELEN.   Well, come what may! In any case what I   8890
  Must do now, dawdling no more, is go up in
  The palace I've been parted from so long,
  Missed so much, and almost forfeited
  So foolishly. I can't believe it, there
  It stands! These feet won't bear the woman
  Up the steep steps as lightheartedly
  They did the skipping child long years ago.

Exit

CHORUS. Cast away, sisters mine,
         Sad captives though we are,
         All sorrows far away,   8900
         Share Helen's happiness,
         Our Mistress' happiness,
         Now back at Father's house,
         Late-footed back indeed,
         Yet back with surer foot,
         With gladder foot
         For being late come back.

         Praise we the gods above,
         Gods bringing gladly back,
         Us bringing gladly home.   8910
         Beyond all harsh and hard,
         Upsoaring on broad-spread wings.
         She ascends free at last,
         While with arms stretched above
         Battlemented prison walls,
         The captive wastes away.

         But her, so far, far off,
         A god reached down, plucked
         Out of Ilium's rubble heap and
         Bore back here again   8920
         To the old, new-furnished
         Father's home,
         After indescribable
         Pleasures and torments—
         Bringing back memories of
         Youth's early years.

PANTHALIS. Leave off your jubilation, sisters, look:
         There at the bronze doors I see someone—can
         It be the Queen? And hurrying back to us

Upset and pale?—Queen, what's the matter, what,   8930
Inside the halls of your own house where you
Expected only smiles of welcome, has so
Unsettled you? Don't try to hide the loathing
In your face, the indignation struggling
With surprise.

HELEN. [*Who has left the doors open behind her, very upset*]
It's not for Zeus's daughter to be
A prey to common fears, I never feel
Chill fingered panic's touch. But the horrors
Creeping out of Old Night's womb
Since the first beginnings of all things,   8940
With shapes as many as the fiery vapors
Billowing from a crater's fiery mouth,
Make even heroes' hearts turn faint. When I
Went in the house, the infernal gods in
Just such fashion made their presence known,
So that my only thought was, leave, yes, gladly
Leave, with back turned on the threshold so
Familiar once and so much longed for since.
But no! I've fallen back, afraid, into
The light, but farther back than this, O you   8950
Grim powers, howsoever called, you'll never
Harry me! My care shall be to cleanse.
The house so that, made pure, the warm hearth
May give welcome to its Lord, its Lady too.

CHORUS LEADER. Tell us, Mistress, us your servants who
Stand by you always, what thing happened there?

HELEN. What I've seen, your own eyes shall see,
Unless Old Night's already swallowed her creation
Back into her monster womb. Let me
Try as best I can to put it into words: 8960
When I walked with solemn step

Into the royal house's dim interior,
My mind intent on what I must do first,
I found to my surprise that all was emptiness
And silence: no sound of hurrying feet along
The corridors, no servants running back
And forth about their work. And no one, maid
Or old housekeeper, came to greet the stranger
In the customary way. However, as I
Neared the hearth I saw, by the dying embers'   8970
Glow, a muffled figure seated on
The floor: a woman, tall, and looking more
Like someone lost in thought than napping. "Up,"
I ordered her, "go back to work at once"—
Thinking she must be the one my husband
Left to keep the palace when he sailed
Away. But still she sat there, huddled up,
Not stirring. I warned her she must rise. At last,
As if dismissing me from house and hearth, she raised
Up her right arm. Furious, I turned   8980
Away and hurried toward the steps that led
Up to the richly furnished sleeping chamber,
With the treasure vault close by. The monstrous figure
Sprang up from the floor; peremptorily
It barred my way, a tall, gaunt shape with hollow,
Bloodshot eyes, a shape to make your senses
Swim, head whirl. But it's a waste of breath,
Impossible with words to show a figure
To the life.—But there she is herself!
And bold enough to venture out into   8990
The light! Yet we're the masters here until
The King arrives. Phoebus, Beauty's worshipper,
Stops these night-born monsters in their tracks
Or sends them scurrying back into their holes.

[*Phorkyas appears at the threshold.*]

CHORUS.

So much I've lived through, although bright ringlets
Wave like a young girl's all round my temples,
Much that was dreadful, past all describing:
War's awful anguish, Troy in the night
Of its fall.

Out of the dust clouds, uproar of soldiers   9000
Hand-to-hand battling, fearfully I heard
Ear-piercing gods' shouts, heard frightful war-strife's
Brazen voice drawing near and more near
To the walls.

Oh, still high aloft Ilium's
Walls stood, but the devouring flames
Raced from neighbor to neighbor house
Setting roof after roof ablaze,
With their hot-blowing breath they raged
Over the night-shrouded city.   9010

Running, I could see dim through the murk
And the flickering fire's glare,
Full of wrath, the dread gods approach,
Giant figures of wonder
Striding on through the gloom of the
Billowing, crimson-tinged smoke.

Or did I see them? Terrified
Did I imagine it all?
But who can say, I shall never be
Sure. Yet I know for a fact,   9020
What I see now, this horrible
Creature, I see. If I were

Not so afraid, I even could
Touch the hag, seize the witch with these
Hands of mine—if I dared.

—Which of the daughters
Are you of Phorkys?
You've got the look of
One of those creatures.
Are you perhaps one of the Graiae,   9030
Born ancient and gray-haired,
With between you one eye, one tooth,
Which you pass round as needed?

Horror, how dare you
Venture where beauty is,
Show your disgusting face
Under Apollo's
Critical eye? But it's no matter—
What is ugly he never sees,
As his heaven's eye never,   9040
Looking down, sees a shadow.

Mortals, however, such is our
Hard lot, have to endure the un-
Speakable pain that all lovers of
Beauty feel when their eyes are afflicted by
What is vile and forever cursed.

Yes, so listen sharp: dare to be
Smart with us, and I promise you
The dreadfullest menaces, awfullest curses
You've ever heard, pouring out of the mouths   9050
Of us fortunate, god-fashioned figures.
PHORKYAS. The saying's old and still as true as ever:
Modesty and beauty never walk

The green earth side by side, hand clasping hand.
Their ancient loathing for each other is
So deep-rooted that if their paths should
Cross, right around they turn and rush
Apart as fast as legs can carry them,
Modesty dispirited, beauty
Insolent as always till she passes   9060
Down into the Stygian dark, unless
Old age has tamed her first. You make me think,
You cheeky, foreign things, hussies from
Across the sea, of screeching cranes that fly
Past overhead, like a trailing cloud, so clamorously
The quiet traveler lifts his head to look;
But they keep on their way, he keeps on his,
And that's how it will be with us.—Who are
You anyway to raise a racket here
Before the palace of the King, like raving   9070
Maenads or a bunch of drunken women?
How dare you howl at me, the housekeeper,
Like dogs that bay the moon? Do you
Imagine I don't know what sort you are,
Spawned in war and nursed in battle? Itching
After men, seduced and then seducing,
Sapping soldiers' strength, and citizens'
Too! A locust plague you look like, gathered
Here, that swarms down on the ripening crops
And eats up others' industry, lays waste   9080
What grew, before you came, so prosperously!
Base captured goods, for sale or for exchange!
HELEN. Scolding servants in the presence of their mistress
Is grossly to infringe on her authority.
It's her business, no one else's, to praise
Those who deserve praise, punish the remiss.

Moreover I'm content with how they served
Me when great Ilium was besieged, and fell,
And lay stretched out; and with their conduct
Too during all the ups and downs, the hardships   9090
Of our wanderings, a time when one
Was apt to think of oneself first. And I
Expect the same good service from my cheerful
Women now we are in Sparta. The master's
Not concerned with who his servants are
But with how well they serve. So hold your tongue,
And no more of those grinning looks at them,
You hear? If you have taken good care
Of the household in Mistress's absence, you've earned
Her praise. But now she's here herself. Return   9100
To your old place, or your reward will be,
Not thanks for doing well but some smart slaps.
PHORKYAS. It's her right, yes, our heaven-blessed Lord and Master's
Spouse, to chastise servant girls; she earned
It by long years of prudent management.
I recognize you now, our Queen and Mistress;
And since you have returned to occupy
Your old position, take the reins, do, slack
So long, into your hands, take full charge
Of the house, its treasure, all of us. But please: 9110
First of all protect me from this pack
Who next to you, a very swan for beauty,
Are no more than noisy barnyard geese.
CHORUS LEADER. How ugly next to beauty ugliness is!
PHORKYAS. How stupid next to good sense stupidness is!

[*From here on members of the chorus step forward singly to speak.*]

FIRST CHORIST. Do tell us of Father Erebus, Mother Night!

PHORKYAS. And Cousin Scylla, what do you hear from her?

SECOND CHORIST. The monsters, oh dear me, that swing in your
    family tree.

PHORKYAS. Take a trip down to Hades, visit your relatives there.

THIRD CHORIST. The people who live there are much too young,
    much, for you.   9120

PHORKYAS. There's ancient Tiresias, go and make love to him.

FOURTH CHORIST. Orion's nurse was your great-great-grandchild.

PHORKYAS. The Harpies had your care and feeding, right?

FIFTH CHORIST. What *do* you eat to keep your scrawny shape?

PHORKYAS. Never the blood that you're so greedy for.

SIXTH CHORIST. You hunger for corpses, yourself a revolting corpse.

PHORKYAS. Vampire's teeth shine in your nasty mouth.

CHORUS LEADER. I could shut yours if I said who you are.

PHORKYAS. Name yourself first, lo, the riddle is solved.

HELEN. It makes me sad, not angry, to have to inter-   9130
    vene to stop this violent bickering.
    Nothing damages the good order of a household
    More than a feud that festers underneath
    The surface among its master's faithful servants.
    His commands do not, like well tuned music,
    Echo back to him in the form of promptly
    Executed work; no, all is jarring
    Discord, self-will; in the confusion he
    Himself's confused and scolds away to no
    Avail. And that's not all. In your discourteous   9140
    Rage you've conjured up before me such
    Unhappy visions, horrid, crowding shapes
    That pluck at me so that I feel I'm being
    Dragged, in spite of standing here on my
    Own native ground, down to Orcus, Are
    These memories? Or is it some delusion

Gripping me? Was I that person? Am
I still her now? And shall be in the future—
The sweet dream and the nightmare of those wasters
Of proud cities? My girls tremble; you,   9150
However, an old woman, are unmoved.
Make sense, will you, of all this for me!

PHORKYAS. If one looks back on long years of good fortune,
The extraordinary favor of the gods
Comes at last to seem a dream. You
Were blessed beyond all measure in your life—hero
After hero hot to have you, ready
For no matter what foolhardy under-
Taking. Avid with desire, Theseus seized
You young, a man as strong as Heracles,   9160
With such a splendid figure, too.

HELEN. Carried me, a ten-year-old, slim
As a doe, off to Attica, where Aphidnus
Kept me for him in his citadel.

PHORKYAS. But soon enough set free by Castor and by
Pollux, after which a host of heroes,
All outstanding men, came courting you.

HELEN. But the one I favored secretly, I must
Confess, was Patroclus, Pelides' second self.

PHORKYAS. But father wanted Menclaus, bold   9170
Sea rover, also careful landlord.

HELEN. Yes, gave him me; the rule, too, of his realm.
And from our union sprang Hermione.

PHORKYAS. But when he was contesting an inheritance
In far-off Crete, and you were left alone,
A much-too-handsome visitor appeared.

HELEN. Don't remind me, please, of my half-widow-
hood and all the terrible disasters
That were its bitter consequence for me.

PHORKYAS. That trip of his cost me my Cretan freedom: 9180
    A captive, slavery was my hard fate.

HELEN. He sent you here at once, entrusting all
    To you, his palace and the wealth his bravery won.

PHORKYAS. Which you forsook, eyes fixed on many-towered
    Ilium, love's inexhaustible delights.

HELEN. Delights! Endless sufferings, bitter more
    Than words can say, were heaped upon my head.

PHORKYAS. But what they say is, two of you were seen,
    One in Ilium, also one in Egypt.

HELEN. Don't addle my poor addled wits still more!   9190
    Even now I don't know who I am.

PHORKYAS. They also say Achilles rose up from
    The empty shadow world, on fire still,
    To love you as he'd done one time before
    In defiance of the strict decree of fate.

HELEN. I married him, a phantom to a phantom!
    It was a dream, as "phantom" itself says.
    I'm fading, feel a phantom once again. . . .

[*She falls into the arms of the half chorus.*]

CHORUS.

    Silence, silence,
    Grisly glowering, evil-jabbering hag!   9200
    Out of hideous, single-toothed
    Chops, from loathsomest gorge,
    What abhorrent sounds breathed.

    Malevolence, all benevolent smiles,
    Grim wolf dressed in cozy wool fleece,
    Is fearfuller far than the three-
    Headed dog's jaws.

Here, anxious, waiting we stand:
When—how—where will it strike,
Monster at watch   9210
Deep down in malignancy's depths?

Speak the Queen so: kindly assuaging,
Lethe-inducing, gentle, consoling words—
All past and gone things you stir up instead,
More worse things than good,
Casting at once a black shadow
Over today's brilliant blaze,
Over light of hope, too,
Glowing dim in the future.

Silence, silence!   9220
So the dear Queen's aggrieved soul,
About to take flight,
May keep hold of, still hold fast to
Form fairest of all forms
Ever sun on fairest forms shone.

[*Helen, recovering, again stands among the women.*]

PHORKYAS. Come out from the passing clouds, O sun lighting
        our day,
    Who veiled, still is entrancing, shining out strikes us blind.
    How the world unfolds for you, your own eyes can see.
    Ugly thing they may call me, yet beauty know when I see it.
HELEN. Coming shakily out of the dark blank of my faint,   9230
    So bone-weary I am, what I most wish for is rest.
    But it's required of queeens, indeed required of all:
    Hold your soul in a firm grip, against peril's quick leap.
PHORKYAS. You stand there clothed in greatness, in your beauty
        stand there,

> Commanding look on your face—your command then is
>   what?

HELEN. Makes good the lost time that your bickering cost,

> Get ready the sacrifice the King ordered at once.

PHORKYAS. All's prepared in the house, tripod, flat bowl,
>   sharp ax,

> Water to sprinkle, incense to burn afterwards.

> But the name of the victim, do please tell me it, do.   9240

HELEN. The King didn't say.

PHORKYAS.   Didn't say? Oh dear me!

HELEN. "Dear me" did you say?

PHORKYAS.   Queen, it's you who is meant.

HELEN. Me?

PHORKYAS.   And these here as well.

CHORUS.   Us too!

PHORKYAS.   Queen, the ax is for you.

HELEN. Horrors! Yet foreseen.

PHORKYAS.   And no escaping, it seems.

CHORUS. For us here, what's in store?

PHORKYAS.   She shall die as a queen.

> But hung from the rooftree in there like thrushes just snared,

> You'll dance one after the other, your feet kicking the air.

[*Helen and Chorus form a single group of astonishment and terror*]

PHORKYAS. You're ghosts, all ghosts! Yet there you stand like
>   creatures

> Turned to stone, in dread of being banished

> From the day, that's not for you. It's just   9250

> The same with men: all ghosts like you, and like

> You loath to quit the glorious sunlit world,

> But no one's here to plead for, rescue them.

All know, few like, the end that always waits.
Enough! You're finished, done for. Now to work!

[*Claps her hands. Masked dwarfs appear at the door and swiftly do as they are commanded.*]

Come on, you sad-faced, paunchy freaks of nature!
Waddle over here, here's mischief to be done,
All that your hearts' desire. The altar, gilt-horned,
Set down in its place, the shining ax,
Lay it along the silver edge! Fill up   9260
The water jugs to wash away the gruesome
Black bloodstains! Now spread the costly
Carpet on the ground so that the victim
May kneel royally and then, wrapped up
In it, be buried fittingly, without
Delay, though with her head cut off.

CHORUS LEADER. The Queen's walked off to one side, thinking,
The girls are wilting like mown meadow grass.
I'm the eldest, have a solemn duty,
As I think, to talk about all this   9270
With you, who are so very, very old.
You've seen a lot, you're wise and seem to mean
Us well, in spite of the mistaken, brainless
Way these women acted toward you. Tell
Me then if you know how we might be saved.

PHORKYAS. Indeed I do. If the Queen will save herself,
She can, with you thrown in.
But resolution's called for, speed, great speed.

CHORUS. Honored most of the three Parcae, wisest of the Sibyls,
  you,
Don't unsheath the golden scissors, keep us here in light and
  life!   9280

We can feel our legs already dangling, twitching, in the air,
Limbs we'd far prefer to dance with, afterwards to rest our
    heads
On our darlings' breast
HELEN. They're scared to death, the things. Well, I am not,
    It's pain I feel. But if you know a means,
    Some way to rescue us, how grateful we
    Should be. A circumspect, shrewd head
    Is able to see possibilities where none
    Seem to exist. Say what you have in mind.
CHORUS. Tell us, yes, oh tell us quickly how we can escape the noose   9290
    That like an insidious necklace they'll draw tight around our
        throats—
    Already choking, for breath gasping, life already but a thread,
    If you, Rhea, the gods' mother, turn your face away from us,
    Wretched us!
PHORKYAS. What I propose requires a long prologue—
    Have you the patience to listen quietly to it?
CHORUS. Lots, oh lots! To listen is to live.
PHORKYAS. The one that stays at home and guards his wealth,
    Keeps his palace walls well mortared, sees
    To it the roof keeps out the driving rain,   9300
    He'll prosper all the days of his long life.
    But let him rush off somewhere irresponsibly,
    Impiously deserting house and hall,
    Yes, he may find the old place still there, coming
    Back, but changed, how changed, if not in ruins.
HELEN. What's the point of this familiar wisdom?
    Say what you have to say, but keep away
    From subjects I find painful in the extreme.
PHORKYAS. I'm recounting history, mean no
    Reproach. Menelaus coursed the sea,   9310
    From bay to bay he went in search of plunder,

Raiding islands and along the seaboard, bringing
Booty back, great heaps of it, now stored
Inside the palace. Ten long years he spent
Before the walls of Troy; how long it also
Took him to come home I do not know.
But his great house, how is it with it now?
With all of Sparta?

HELEN.   Finding fault again!
Is it so much your nature you can't move your lips
Without an accusation tumbling out?   9320

PHORKYAS. The highlands in the north, in back of which
The Taygetos ascends, have been forgotten
All these years—it's from there Eurotas
Starts out as a lively brook, and dropping
Down the valley broadens out into the reed–
Lined stream that feeds your swans. In that hill country
Back there a bold race, appearing out
Of the Cimmerian dark, have settled down and built
A stronghold none can scale, from where they harry
The whole countryside just as they please.   9330

HELEN. They did all that? It seems impossible.

PHORKYAS. They had the time, it must be twenty years.

HELEN. Have they a chief? Are they a band of brigands?

PHORKYAS. No, they're not. And yes, they have a chief.
He raided here once but I don't complain.
He could have taken all we have but only
Chose a few things—gifts, he said, not tribute.

HELEN. He struck you how?

PHORKYAS.   Not bad at all!
I liked him—cheerful, lots of spirit, a fine figure
Of a man, and sensible as few Greeks are.   9340
They're called barbarians, those people, but
I doubt there's one of them as savage, bloodthirsty,

As many a hero showed in front of Troy.
I'd trust myself to him, his magnanimity.
And you should see his castle! Not at all
The heap of clumsy stones your fathers, Cyclops-
Fashion, piling block upon unmortared
Block, haphazardly threw up. There all
The verticals are plumb, the horizontals
True. Before your eyes it soars into   9350
The sky, a close-joined structure, steely smooth.
To scale those walls—the thought itself slides helplessly
Back! And inside, oh what spacious courts,
All around which buildings stand of every
Kind and purpose, with pillars, arches low
And lofty, balconies, and galleries
That give upon the outside and the in.
And there are coats-of-arms.

CHORUS.   Coats of what?

PHORKYAS. You saw yourself how Ajax had a coiled snake
        On his shield. The Seven against Thebes each bore   9360
        A rich device on his shield, too, with its
        Own meaning: moon and stars in the night sky;
        Goddesses and heroes; ladders, swords
        And torches and whatever else with which fine cities
        Are threatened and besieged. These heroes, too,
        Bear such devices, brightly colored, going
        Back to the remotest times: lions, eagles,
        Beaks and claws, buffalo horns, roses,
        Peacock tails; and also bands of gold
        And black and silver, blue and red. They hang   9370
        In long rows in great halls that stretch
        Away into the shadows endlessly—
        What dancing you'd have there!

CHORUS.   And dancers, do
    They have them?
PHORKYAS.   Yes, the best! Golden-haired
    And lively footed, breathing sweet youth
    Just as Paris breathed it once when he
    Approached too near to Helen.
HELEN.   Keep, please, to
    The story you were telling!—finish it!
PHORKYAS. *You* finish it—by saying clearly, in a firm
    Voice, yes! Upon which I will set you safely   9380
    Down inside that castle.
CHORUS.   Say it, yes,
    One little word, and save us all!
HELEN.   What—should
    I fear the King would overstep the bounds
    So far as to do me harm?
PHORKYAS.   Do you forget
    The unheard-of cruelty with which he butchered
    Fallen Paris's brother, your dear Deiphobus,
    Who recklessly grabbed up the widow—you—
    For his blissful concubine? He sliced his nose
    And ears off, Menelaus did, as well
    As other parts—oh, it was horrible.   9390
HELEN. Because of me he did that, yes.
PHORKYAS.   Because
    Of him he'll do the same to you. Beauty's
    Not divisible; who's possessed her for
    His own is not about to share her out.
    He'd sooner kill her, cursing less than all.

[*Trumpets sound in the distance, the Chorus shrinks in fear.*]

    As cruelly as the trumpets pierce your ear and grip

Your bowels with anguish, just so jealousy's

Sharp claws grip his heart: he can't forget

What once was his and isn't any more.

CHORUS. Don't you hear the bugles blowing, see the flashing of

    bright arms? 9400

PHORKYAS. Welcome, Lord and Master, I will gladly render my

    account!

CHORUS. And ourselves?

PHORKYAS.   You know already. Witness your eyes shall her death,

    Then inside your own, no, nothing can be done, and so it is.

                                                                     [*Pause.*]

HELEN. My mind's made up, I know what I must do.

    An evil spirit I'm afraid you are,

    Who turns what's good into its opposite.

    All the same I'll do it, go with you.

    And afterwards? That's as it may be, what

    The Queen's thoughts are is locked inside her bosom,

    And may it stay so.—Woman, lead the way! 9410

CHORUS. Oh how glad to be going,

      On scurrying feet,

      Death behind,

      Before, a

      Towering fortress's

      Unassailable ramparts.

      Safe keep us, we pray you,

      As safe as Ilium's did,

      Which in the end by low cunning

      Only, was brought down. 9420

[*A mist springs up gradually obscuring the scene.*]

What is happening, oh!

Look, sisters, about you,

Wasn't day sunny and clear?
Now plumes of mist, see, streaming up
From Eurotas's sacred flood;
Vanished already the lovely
Reed-engarlanded banks;
And the graceful-proud, free, to-and-fro
Suave gliding swans
That delight to swim side-by-side—   9430
Oh no more, they are gone!
Never the less,
I hear their call, their hoarse crying,
Foretelling death, so it's said;
Please let it not, instead
Of promised deliverance, be
Foretelling the death
Of us lovely, long-white-
Necked, swan-resembling dears,
Or of her, our swan-engendered Queen—   9440
No, no, oh no!

Mist has blanketed all,
All that is around us,
I can't see a soul.
What is happening, what?
Do we walk on the ground or
Float, half-tip-toeing, along?
You see nothing? What's that
Hovering in front? Is it Hermes,
Oh dear? That blink his gold staff   9450
Bidding us to go back
To disagreeable, dreary, dawn-gray old Hades,
Crammed, overcrammed, with its unbodied forms,
Hades empty always.

Yes, abruptly all's dreary, mist's lifting brings no brightness,
Walls granite-gray, brick-brown, block the straining eyes'
     seeking,
Their roving brought up short. A castle yard, is it, or a deep
     cavern?
In any case, odious—sisters, again we find ourselves captives,
As captive as before.

COURTYARD OF A CASTLE

Surrounded by ornate, fantastic medieval buildings.

CHORUS LEADER. Exactly, like women, making your minds
     up at once,   9460
     Slaves of the moment, the weather, every turn
     In our fortunes—whether good, whether bad, never
     Calmly endured. One of you always contradicting
     The other and being contradicted right back.
     When with joy you exult, pain loud howl and weep,
     Then, only then, do your voices sound the same note.
     Quiet, I say, wait to hear what our sovereign
     Mistress shall decide for herself, for us too.
HELEN. Pythoness, where can you be—if that is how you are
     called?
     Come out from inside this castle's gloom-breathing vaults.   9470
     Perhaps you went off to inform that simply marvellous
     Lord of yours that he has Helen waiting outside here
     Until he should come and give her proper welcome. If so,
     I thank you. Take me to him at once now without any delay.
     Long enough I've been wandering about, it's rest that I want.
CHORUS LEADER. It's no use, Queen, your searching every corner,
     hole,

The nasty creature's disappeared. It may be she
Is still there in the dense mist we emerged
From so abruptly, who knows how, for not one foot,
No, not one did we stir. It may be she is wandering blindly   9480
Round the labyrinthine halls of this most extra-
Ordinary place that looks like many castles huddled
Into one, to find its master and request him to appear—
Appear and greet us in a way that is befitting royalty.
Already there above I see people bustling in, and out
Of galleries, past high windows, open doorways—
A great reception, it appears, is being prepared for us.

CHORUS. Oh look over there, it makes my heart leap,
          Lovely boys in procession descending the stairs,
          So decorously stepping with ceremonious tread—   9490
          Not one out of step! Who can it be that arranged
          This and did it so soon? What is most to admire
          In these good-looking boys? Their lightness of foot?
          Or locks of hair that curl round their radiant brows?
          Or downy cheeks blushing like peaches in pairs?
          I'd be tempted to bite one, but shrink back in fear,
          Remembering how, in a similar case—
          How disgusting the thought is!—eager mouths chewed,
          Instead of ripe fruit, bitter ashes.

          But here the dears come,   9500
          And what's that they have?
          A carpet, a throne,
          Steps to mount it,
          An embroidered canopy
          Billowing softly,
          Drawn, like a heaven
          Of garlanded clouds,
          Over our Queen's head.
          For, begged to be seated,

She has taken her place   9510
In the sumptuous chair.
—Women, advance,
Range yourselves silently
Row on row, on the steps.
Fitting, yes, fitting, entirely fitting,
I gratefully say it, her welcome here is!

[*The Chorus's words accompany the action on the stage. When the last of the long line of pages and squires have arrived below, Faust appears at the head of the stairs, dressed like a medieval courtier, and descends with dignified, slow steps.*]

CHORUS LEADER. Unless the gods, as they so often do,
    Have lent this man his wonder-waking figure,
    Noble bearing, affable air for a brief moment
    Only, everything he undertakes   9520
    Must end in triumph, over soldiers in grim
    Battle or pretty ladies in the little wars
    Of love. I like him better, I do, yes,
    Than many a much-admired one these eyes
    Have seen. And look, the Prince approaches, with a slow
    And reverential step. Queen, turn your head!
FAUST. [*Advancing, with a man in chains beside him*]
    Instead of welcoming you with proper ceremony,
    With the reverence that you are owed, I bring
    You this man bound in chains: failing in his duty,
    He made me fail in mine. Down, fellow, on   9530
    Your knees, confess your guilt before the queen
    Of women! A man with eyes extraordinarily
    Keen, his post was in the tower, to scan
    The sky and earth for anything that showed
    Itself between the valley's boundary

Of hills and our castle here: moving herds
Upon the plain, perhaps, or armed men
On the march—protect the one, we do,
The other we confront. But today, what
A fiasco! You arrive and up above all's mute,   9540
Which makes us fail to greet so eminent
A guest with all the honors due her. By
His negligence he's forfeited his life
And already would have met the bloody death
He well deserves, except it's you alone
Shall punish or shall pardon, as you will.

HELEN. How high a dignity I am allowed—
To be the judge, the ruler here, though it
Should only be (for so I must suppose)
By way of trial. Very well, then, as   9550
The judge my first duty is to give
The accused a hearing. Prisoner, speak!

LYNCEUS THE WATCHMAN.
Let me kneel down, let me look on,
Let my end come, let me live on,
Mine's already such devotion
To this by-god-given woman.

Watching for the light of morning
Eastwards, where its pale path lies,
Miraculously, without warning,
Southwards the sun seemed to rise!   9560

Turning that way, what I see is
Neither high hill nor steep canyon,
Neither heaven's, earth's expanses,
Only her, unrivaled woman.

Mine are eyes that see as sharply
As a lynx's, hence my name,
Yet I found that all around me
Seemed a dark and cloudy dream.

I was lost, could make out nothing,
Neither towers, parapets;   9570
Then the mist abruptly offing,
Forth a golden goddess steps!

Dazzled, I could only stand there
Drinking in her glorious sight,
As her beauty blinds us all here,
So, wretch, I was blinded quite.

I forgot my watchman's duty,
Unblown my horn idle hung—
Must I fear death? Surely beauty
Softens justice's harsh tongue.   9580

HELEN. How should I be chastiser of offenses
    I'm the cause of? Unrelenting, my fate
    Is, to turn men's heads so violently
    They nothing care, not for themselves, for honor, any-
    Thing! They ravish, they seduce, fight wars, run here,
    Run there. Both gods and heroes, demigods and even
    Evil spirits have dragged me all about,
    I don't know where. When I was simply one,
    The turmoil that I caused; more turmoil still
    When there were two of me; now I am three,   9590
    Am four, trouble after trouble, endlessly.
    This good man's blameless, set him free!

FAUST. In wonder, Queen, I look at the unerring
    Shooter, him who's shot. I see the bow

That sped the arrow, him brought down by it.
Still you let fly, and who's the mark now?—Me!
In court and castle, everywhere, is heard
The hiss of feathered shafts. I, once lord
And master here, what am I now? My faithfullest
Troops you make forswear their duty, my   9600
Stout walls make a doubtful shield. I fear
It's you my army will obey, all-conquering,
Never conquered Lady, you!. There's nothing
For it but to yield myself and all
That I in my delusion thought was mine.
At your feet, reserving nothing, I
Acknowledge you my Queen, who soon as she
Appeared, my throne and all's that mine were hers.

LYNCEUS. [*With a chest, followed by men carrying more chests*]
    I'm here again, Queen, I've come back
    A rich man, see, who begs a look!   9610
    He looks at you and feels at once
    A beggarman and a rich prince.

    The man I once was, am I now?
    What's there for me to wish for, do?
    It's no use now my piercing sight,
    Back it's beaten by your light.

    Out of the East we came, a host,
    And it was all up with the West;
    So vast a multitude we were,
    The van knew nothing of the rear.   9620

    The first line broke, the second held,
    The third came on with sword and shield;
    Behind each man a hundred waited,
    The thousands slaughtered went unheeded.

We drove ahead and conquered all,
Imposing as we went our rule,
And where I gave the orders Sunday,
Another robbed and stole on Monday.

We looked for booty on the run,
Grabbed up the prettiest girls, each one,   9630
Grabbed up the fattest, best livestock,
And every horse there was we took.

But I, what's choicest I looked for,
For things extraordinary, rare;
What others seized on as a prize
Was dust, was dry straw in my eyes.

The treasure in deep caves concealed
My sharp vision soon revealed;
No pocket but I saw into it,
No chest so stout but I saw through it.   9640

Great heaps of gold coin I now own
And every kind of precious stone;
The emerald's celestial green
Is only fit for your breast, Queen.

Now let this pearl fetched from the floor
Of ocean, dangle from your ear!
Red rubies, paling, scared, must yield
Before your blushing cheeks the field.

So riches beyond all compare
I bring the one who is most fair,   9650
And set them humbly at your feet,
The spoils of many a bloody fight.

As many chests as I have brought,
As many iron-bound ones got.
Admit me to your company,
I'll stuff with gold your treasury.

No sooner do you mount the throne
Than reason, wealth, the royal crown,
Surrendering their powers, stoop
Before your unexampled shape.   9660

All, all that I rejoiced was mine
Is gone from me, is now your own.
The things I thought most rare, most precious,
I now disdain as odious.

No rich man am I any more,
What's wealth, it's only dust and straw.
Oh, give it back by one glad glance
The worth that was its proud boast once!

FAUST. This precious freight, so bravely won, away
    With it! Uncensured you are, yes, but un-   9670
    Rewarded too. Everything this castle
    Holds is hers already, offering her now
    This, now that, is meaningless. Go and in
    Good order lay the riches out; with their
    Still unseen splendor compose a sublime scene:
    Vaulted halls a-sparkle like the sky,
    Lifeless things enlivened to compose bright
    Paradises. Carpets, flowered like the spring,
    Unroll before her feet so that they may
    Encounter only tenderest ground, her eyes (that only   9680
    Gods' don't dazzle) supreme magnificence.

LYNCEUS.
    It's little enough that you, Sir, ask,

A pleasure for me, not a task.
Gladly wealth and blood, knees bent
Submit to beauty's government.
Our swaggering soldiers meekly stand
With blunted sword and nerveless hand.
Let her appear, even the sun
Suffers by comparison;
The rich garden of her face   9690
Makes all else a waste place.   *Exit*

HELEN. [*To Faust*] I'd like to speak to you—but come up here
Beside me, do! Your Lordship's occupying
His royal place assures me of my own.

FAUST. First let the homage offered you upon
My knees find favor, Lady, in your eyes;
And let me kiss the hand by which I am
Exalted to your side. Make me co-regent
Of Beauty's boundless realm and you shall have
A servant, worshiper, protector, all in one!   9700

HELEN. The marvels that I see, I hear—astonishing!
The questions I should like to ask you! Why
Did that man's speech, I wonder, have so strange
A ring, strange and yet agreeable.
One sound seemed to suit itself so sweetly
To another, one word entering the ear,
Another came caressingly on its heels.

FAUST. If you like our people's way of speaking,
You'll surely be delighted with our song,
Which so delights the mind as well as ear.   9710
What we should do now is to practise using it.
The to and fro of lively conversation
Gives verse encouragement and draws it out.

HELEN. Oh, it seems hard to speak with so much art.

FAUST. It's easy when the words come from the heart.

And when your heart's so full you cannot bear it,
You long for someone, somewhere who—
HELEN.   will share it.
FAUST. Now we look neither back nor forward, we
Find in the present—
HELEN.   our felicity.
FAUST. Our joy's our treasure, kingdom, our all,   9720
And who will promise, swear it's so?—
HELEN.   I shall!
CHORUS. Who would blame our Princess
            Showing so much favor
            To this castle's lord?
            Remember, everyone of us's
            A captive, as so often
            Since Troy's ignominious fall
            And the fearful, maze-like
            Windings of our bitter trek.

            Women used to many lovers   9730
            Are connoisseurs, yes,
            Choosers, no.
            A shepherd boy with golden curls,
            Or it may be a bristling black faun,
            As occasion offers,
            With equal right possesses
            Their lush, languid limbs.

            Close and closer sitting,
            Shoulder against shoulder,
            Knee against knee, hand holding hand,   9740
            To and fro they sway
            On the throne's
            Thick-upholstered magnificence.

Under the people's eyes,
Wantonly,
Majesty denies itself
No private joys.

HELEN. So far away I feel, and yet so near,
And glad, yes, more than glad that I am here.

FAUST. I tremble, gasp for breath, it's all a dream.   9750
I'm speechless, in what place am I, what time?

HELEN. I feel so finished, over with, and yet newborn,
At one with you, true to my dear unknown.

FAUST. Our high, rare fate, don't search how to explain it!
Being is duty, if only for a moment.

PHORKYAS. [*Rushing in*]
Waste the time, do, dillydally,
Telling over your love's story,
Kiss and cuddle blissfully,
Brood upon love's mystery!
Don't you feel the storm that's coming,   9760
Hear an army's trumpets blowing,
Know that your destruction threatens?
Menelaus and his legions
March on you in hot pursuit—
Arm, arm for the bitter fight!
If they catch you, oh my goodness,
Cut you up, they will, in pieces,
Just as they did Deiphobus.
You'll pay dear for your light ladies,
Those sluts soon will dance on air.   9770
As for you, you're well aware
A sharpened ax, its edge aglitter,
Is lying ready on the altar.

FAUST. Outrageous, bursting in like this, how in-

Supportable! Even when great danger threatens,
To act impetuously is stupid. The most
Handsome messenger, if he comes bearing
Bad news looks unlovely, and you who's
Ugliest of all, delights in it.
Well, not this time; your empty breath disturbs   9780
The air, is all. No threat exists, And if
One did, it's no threat really—see!

[*Signal calls. Explosions from the tower. Trumpets, bugles,
martial music. A mighty army marches in. Its chiefs, advancing
from before their columns, assemble in a group.*]

Look where my captains stand together,
Their might by no division marred.
He only's worthy woman's favor
Whose hero's arm is her safeguard.

[*Addressing the commanders.*]

With disciplined, with fierce, mute anger,
Unconquerable battle lust,
O Northern manhood's finest flower,
O nonpareil youth of the East,   9790

Who wear the lightning of bright armor,
Who break great empires like a reed—
You pass, and thunder follows after,
The earth shakes underneath your tread.

We came ashore at Pylos, Nestor,
Its old king, had died long since;
The legions ranging over Sparta
Make mincemeat of each petty prince.

Drive Menelaus in disorder
Back from these walls into the sea!   9800
There let him roam, waylay, and plunder,
A pirate's what he's meant to be.

I'm bidden by the Spartan Queen
To name you dukes. At her feet offer
The provinces that your arms win,
As vassals keep them at her pleasure.

Germans! Corinth and her bays
Is given you, as yours defend it.
Goths! Achaia's your share, seize
Its rocky ground and proudly hold it.   9810

Messenia, Saxons, is your prize!
Our Frankish forces, yours is Elis!
Let Norman galleys sweep the seas
And make her great again, Argolis!

There make your homes, alert to meet
The challenge of an enemy;
But Sparta, Helen's ancient seat,
Shall still own the supremacy.

Enjoying under your Queen's eye
This land which nothing lacks in goodness,   9820
You'll look to her authority
For confirmation, counsel, justice.

[*Faust descends, the dukes make a circle around him the better to hear his commands.*]

CHORUS. Who wishes to possess the paragon
         Of beauty, let him act promptly to lay

In all the arms he'll soon find he will need.
Was flattery his way to earth's first prize? It isn't
One to be possessed in perfect peace.
Other flatterers may slip her smoothly from
His grasp, bold raiders striking with
No warning make away with her.   9830
How to thwart these needs some taking thought.

I therefore praise the Prince,
Esteem him over others,
For the bold, shrewd way he has enlisted
Allies, big strong men
Who watch out his least sign
So as to execute his orders instantly—
Each serving his own interest, at the same time
Earning his commander's thanks,
And both together gaining glorious fame.   9840

For who can snatch her now,
Out of her protector's keep?
She's his, to him she's given,
And given doubly, for by us given too—he keeps
Us safe, with her, inside these walls, and
Safe by his great host outside.
FAUST.   To every chieftain we have given
A rich and overflowing land;
Let each march now to his own region,
The center's ours to command.   9850

Each shall vie with each defending
This wave-washed, deep-bayed all-but-island,
Whose chain of hills runs northward, joining
Europe's mountainous southward mainland.

Our wish is all the tribes may find
A happy home here, long existence,
Where Helen now is Queen—the land
That was the first to know her presence,

When from the broken shell she crept
Amid Eurotas's rushes' whispers,   9860
And by her bright eyes blinded quite
Her mother, sister, and her brothers.

—All Hellas turns to you, you only,
It offers you its flowering breast,
The earth itself is yours entirely,
But oh, let your own home come first.

And though its mountain range's jagged peaks
Beneath the sun's chill rays are snowy still,
A thin green's showing on the rocky flanks
Where the goat wanders cropping his scant meal.   9870

The flowing springs pour down in rushing brooks,
The gorges, slopes, and meadows have turned green;
Upon the broken uplands woolly flocks,
Spreading across the pastures, can be seen.

The scattered cattle moving cautiously,
Approach the edge of the steep cliffside's fall,
But there is shelter for the herd close by
In caves that honeycomb the granite wall,

Where Pan protects them. In the cool, wet places
Of bushy clefts, nature's nymphs live hidden,   9880
The crowding trees reach upwards with their branches
Longingly, after a higher region.

This old, old forest! Mighty oaks unbending
Stand, their gnarled limbs spreading crookedly;
The gentle maples, big with sweet sap, lifting
High their leafy heads, toss playfully.

From heavy udders, in the quiet shade,
Warm mother's milk flows down for lamb and infant,
A step away fruit ripens in the field,
From hollow tree trunks honey flows, gold, fragrant.   9890

Here ease and comfort are the legacy,
The round and glowing cheek, the red, ripe mouth,
Here each possesses immortality
In his descendants' happiness and health.

And thus in pure contentment, cloudless days,
The child grows up and fathers in his turn.
Amazed, we never cease to ask: Are these
High gods descended here or are they men?

Apollo, when he kept sheep, looked completely
The handsome shepherd in both form and face: 9900
Where Nature uninsulted rules serenely,
All worlds commingle, gods and men change place.

[*Sitting down beside Helen.*]

And all this we have made our own, we two;
We'll quite forget the past, unhappy, wrong!
Think what great god it was engendered you!
The first world, there, there, is where you belong.

It's not for you, immurement in a castle!
Quite near to Sparta there's a place

Where youth keeps all its vigor, is eternal:
Arcadia, our bower of bliss!   9910

Oh, fly with me to those blest fields, discover
The happiness that's your true fate!
There these thrones turn into a leafy arbor:
Be ours Arcadian freedom and delight!

ARCADIA

The scene changes to show enclosed arbors standing against a row
of rocky caverns. A shady grove stretches to the surrounding cliffsides.
Faust and Helen are nowhere to be seen. The Chorus lie sprawled
about asleep.

PHORKYAS. How long these girls have been asleep I've no
    Idea, nor do I know if in their dreams
    They saw what I saw, bright and clear, in front
    Of me. I'll wake them up and quite astonish
    The young things—Astonish you, too, sitting down
    Below there, all you whiskered ones who wait   9920
    With breathless faith to see the outcome of these wonders.
    —Wake, sleepy heads, and shake your tangled locks!
    Sit up, don't blink so, listen to my words!
CHORUS. Tell us, oh do, yes, the wonders that you say have taken
      place,
    Best of all we'd love to hear things unbelievable and strange,
    For how boring just to sit here staring at a lot of rocks!
PHORKYAS. Hardly rubbed your eyes, my children, and already
      bored to death?
    Listen, then: Inside the shelter that these arbors, grottoes give,

Our lord and our lady live a lovers' idyll.

CHORUS.   What,

Inside there?

PHORKYAS.   Retreating from the public world, their wish was I,   9930
I alone should wait on them. And very honored I was, though
As became a trusted servant, my gaze I turned quickly
    elsewhere—
Elsewhere looked for roots, bark, mosses in whose virtues I am
    skilled,
Leaving them all to themselves.

CHORUS. Why, you talk as if a whole world were inside there, woods
    and meadows,
Brooks and lakes: the tales you spin!

PHORKYAS.   Yes, it's so, you know so
                                         little!

In there there are depths unfathomed, long halls, courts and
    courts and long halls,
Which my sharp wits, searching, found out. Suddenly however
    laughter
Echoed through the caverns' reaches; looking, I saw a boy
    jumping
From his mother to his father, from one lap into the other.   9940
So much coddling and caressing, silliness and fondest teasing,
Shrieks of fun and shouts of pleasure, mirth that seemed to have
    no ending;
I was deafened by the din!
Naked, the bright spirit, wingless, like a faun but nothing
    brutish,
Sprang down to the ground—responding, it flung him high in
    the air,
Then a second, third leap bore him up, up till he touched the
    vaulting.
Worriedly, his mother shouted, "Leap as often as you want to,

But take care, you hear, no flying! Flying in the air's forbidden!"
And his father likewise warned him, "In the earth, the good
    earth lies the
Mighty force that throws you upwards—with the tip of your
    toe only   9950
Touch the ground and like Antaeus, son of earth, you'll find
    you're strong."
So he bounded up the rock wall, bounced from one ledge to
    another
Like a smartly driven ball—till abruptly he's gone, vanished
In a crevice of the cavern. Oh, I thought, we've surely lost him!
Mother tearfully wept, father did his best to reassure her,
I stood there with shaking shoulders. Then he reappeared,
      I marveled—
Had he come on hidden treasure? For he now was nobly,
    grandly
Dressed in robes trimmed with bright braid.
Tassels dangled from his wide sleeves, ribbons fluttered on his
    bosom,
In his hand a golden lyre—just like a petit Apollo!   9960
Cheerfully he walked up to the overhanging ledge's brink;
We're amazed, the happy parents rapturously hug each other.
Round his head what's that that's glowing? What shone so is
    hard to say.
Gold, perhaps, or luminescence of a great mind's supreme
    power?
In his boyish acts and gestures is already told his future
Mastery of all of beauty's overflowing store of wealth,
One whose every member pulses with the eternal melodies.
Just so you'll now hear him, see him, to your uttermost
    amazement.
CHORUS.
        Call that a wonder,

Cretan-born woman?   9970
Never listened when poetry
Sang its sweet lessons?
Ionia's and Hellas's
Ancientest legends
Of a gods-and-heroes abundance,
Never heard them?

Nothing that's done today's
More than a pitiful
Echo of glorious
Ancestral days;   9980
Nothing, your story is,
Compared with the lovely lie,
More trustworthy than truth,
That is sung about Maia's son.

Newborn, the baby, trig and
Tricksy already, was swaddled in
Purest down, wrapped tight in royal stuff
By the little-suspecting crowd of
Tongue-wagging nurses.
But the sly little rascal drew   9990
Limber limbs out from their purple
Confinement and left the tight
Bindings to lie where they were—
Like the butterfly cleverly slipping its
Chrysalid bondage to wave its wings
Impishly in the sunshiny air.

Nimblest of spirits, not delaying
A moment, he showed by the cunningest
Ruses he was patron of rascals,
Thieves, all those who study

What will gain them advantage—he stole   10000
From the sea god his trident, the sword out of
Ares' sheath, bow and arrows from
Under the nose of bright Phoebus,
Hephaestus his fire tongs; he even
Had made off with Zeus's dread thunderbolt
But for fear of the fire. Eros,
However, he tripped up and beat
In a wrestling match; and the Cyprian's
Girdle, while she petted him fondly,
He quietly lifted.   10010

[*The charming music, pure and melodious, of stringed instruments sounds from the cavern. All listen, seeming deeply moved. From here till the pause marked below, with full orchestral accompaniment.*]

PHORKYAS.

Listen to that lovely music,
Better than mythology!
Your gods, elderly and antique,
Give them up, they're now passé.

Those old tales have lost all meaning,
We aim at a higher goal:
From the soul must come the feeling
That can move another's soul.

[*She retreats back to the cliffs.*]

CHORUS.

If a monster like yourself feels
Moved by these seductive airs,   10020

We, recovered from dire trials,
May allow ourselves some tears.

Let it go out, the sun's fire,
If light dawns inside our souls,
In our own hearts we'll discover
What the outer world withholds.

[*Helen, Faust, and Euphorion dressed as above.*]

EUPHORION.

Hear a child sing, full of laughter,
And its mirth becomes yours, too;
See me leaping to the measure,
And your parent's heart leaps, too.   10030

HELEN.

Love's delight's a human rapture
When it joins two happily;
Its delight's divine, however,
When another makes it three.

FAUST.

All, all we possess together,
I am yours and you are mine;
By love bound one to the other,
May it be so for all time!

CHORUS.

Year on year of purest pleasure,
Basking in the boy's warm glow,
Await the pair in their blest future—   10040
Oh their union moves me so!

EUPHORION.

I'll leap and jump, I will,
Up, up, I'll fly until

I touch the sky!
Immense the longing
I am seized by!

FAUST.

Careful, oh careful!
If you're too rash you will
Crash to the ground,   10050
And by your fall pull
All of us down.

EUPHORION.

No, I won't stay here,
An earthbound creature,
Let go of me;
My hands, curls, clothing—
They're mine, I say!

HELEN.

Think, think whose child you are,
Don't make us suffer more
Than we can bear,   10060
By your destroying
The threesome we are!

CHORUS.

Shortlived, your threesome,
Is what I fear!

HELEN AND FAUST.

Bridle that violence,
Curb such extravagance
For love of us;
Bless with your presence this
Pastoral peace.

EUPHORION.

For your dear sakes, yes,   10070
I acquiesce.

[*Winding in and out among the Chorus and drawing them into a dance.*]

> Round and round, see how I
> Float feather-light,
> Have I the melody
> And the step right?

HELEN.

> Yes, darling, so well done!
> Lead them, each pretty one,
> Round and around.

FAUST.

> I'm not amused by this
> Whirling round, giddiness—   10080
> How will it end?

[*Singing and dancing, Euphorion and the Chorus turn in an intricate dance.*]

CHORUS.

> When you sway your two arms
> So gracefully,
> Tossing your shining curls
> So charmingly,
> When with so light a foot
> You turn and turn about,
> Forwards and backwards go,
> Now spinning fast, now slow,
> Then you have gained your goal,   10090
> Enchanting child:
> All of us heart and soul
> By you enthralled!

[*Pause.*]

EUPHORION.

>Fleet-footed does, each one,
>You seem to me,
>Ready for sport, to run
>Shrieking away!
>I am the huntsman,
>You are the prey.

CHORUS.

>No need to race like mad
>In a wild chase,
>Captured, the doe, she's glad,
>A willing prey,
>For we so long to kiss
>You, pretty boy!

EUPHORION.

>Off through the woods pellmell,
>Over hill, over dale!
>I find it tedious,
>An all-too-effortless,
>Quick victory—
>Only what's seized by force
>Ever suits me.

HELEN AND FAUST

>What frolicking, wild racing round,
>Small hope they will sober down.
>Are those horns that we are hearing,
>Through the woods and valleys blaring?
>What an uproar, what shrieks, cries!

CHORUS. [*Running in one by one*]

>Like an arrow he shot past us,
>Turned his nose up, he did, at us,
>Chased the one who's most rampageous.
>There he comes now with his prize.

10100

10110

10120

EUPHORION. [*Carrying in a young girl*]
>> See the amazon I've got here,
>> I will make her serve my pleasure,
>> Hug her, squeeze her, though she's loath,
>> Kiss her on her shrinking mouth—
>> Show the creature who is master.

GIRL.

>> Let me go! Inside me find
>> A hardy spirit, strength of mind,
>> With a will nobody tames.
>> Caught, am I? Well, wait a minute,   10130
>> This struggle, we'll soon see who'll win it.
>> Listen, if you don't unloose me,
>> I'll singe you, I will—dare abuse me!
>> Ready, fool? Oh fun and games!

[*Fire envelops her and she flames upwards.*]

>> Follow me where breezes blow,
>> Or where caverns yawn below,
>> Catch if you can your lost quarry!

EUPHORION. [*Shaking off the last of the flames*]
>> I feel imprisoned here,
>> Pent in by bush and cliff,
>> It's not for me whose youth   10140
>> Needs room, needs light and air.
>> I hear the winds' shrill cry,
>> Waves roaring, far away—
>> Would I were there!

[*He springs higher and higher up the rocks.*]

HELEN, FAUST, AND CHORUS.

> Daring as a mountain goat!
> If you fall?—oh dreadful thought!

EUPHORION.

> I must keep on climbing higher
> So I'm able to see farther!
> Yes, I see now just where I am,
> In the middle of an island,   10150
> Pelops's isle: on one side water,
> And the mainland on the other.

CHORUS.

> Wouldn't you rather stay
> Here where it's peaceful?
> We'll go about each day
> Searching the fruitful
> Hillsides where grapevines grow,
> Apple trees, fig trees, too.
> Here where all's pleasing, still
> Remain, please, as well.   10160

EUPHORION.

> Dreaming of peace, are you?
> Dream if it pleases you!
> The watchword's war, the cry
> Unstopping, "Victory!"

CHORUS.

> If when there's peace,
> You wish for war instead,
> Then you confess
> All your brave hopes are dead.

EUPHORION.

> Men whom this land has taught
> By its unhappy plight   10170

Courage and hardihood,
Men prompt to shed their blood,
Casting off servitude
With unbowed mind—
May they again prove, as anciently, proud,
Foe in dust grind.

CHORUS.

See how high he's climbed, no longer
Does he seem, though far up, small,
Cased in armor, keen to conquer,
Glittering in bronze and steel!   10180

EUPHORION.

Trust no more to walls for shelter,
In yourselves place all your trust,
There's no citadel securer
Than a brave man's steel-ribbed breast.
Do you long to live in freedom?
People arm, into the field!
Amazons be all your women,
And a hero every child!

CHORUS.

Let sacred poetry
Upwards soar, higher fly,   10190
Shine, shine, O fairest star,
Ever more distantly,
Yet always reaching us,
Here on earth, with a voice
Lovely to hear.

EUPHORION.

No, not a little child any more—
A young man armed, a soldier to fear.
Side by side with the bold I'll march boldly,

The deeds that I've done in my mind already!

Now I am off,   10200

Feet on the path

Of glory stretching onwards before me!

HELEN AND FAUST.

Barely born into the light,

Blinking still in the bright morning,

You look from your dizzy height

And long for scenes of strife and suffering.

We mean nothing,

It would seem.

Was our union just a dream?

EUPHORION.

Far out at sea the cannons thunder,   10210

The valleys echo with the din,

Afloat, afield, the hosts encounter

Each other, hear the groans of pain!

Death is duty,

So it must be,

Useless for you to repine.

HELEN, FAUST, AND CHORUS.

Oh, how dreadful! Grief, oh grief!

Death you think's your duty? You?

EUPHORION.

Should I stand aside, aloof?

No, I'll share men's pain and woe.   10220

HELEN, FAUST, AND CHORUS.

O spirit rash, alarming!

We fear a tragic ending.

EUPHORION.

I will, I will!—Now watch and see

How my wings spread gloriously!

There I'll go. I must, I must!
Don't forbid what I wish most!

[*He throws himself out into the air, his garments sustain him for
a moment, his head, illumined, leaves a trail of light behind.*]

CHORUS.
Icarus, Icarus!
Oh, but how sad it is!

[*He falls, a handsome youth, at his parents' feet, resembling in
death a well-known figure; his mortal part instantly fades, but the
aureole rises cometlike into the heavens. Dress, cloak, and lyre are left
lying on the ground.*]

HELEN AND FAUST.
Soon after gladness
Grimly comes pain.   10230
EUPHORION'S VOICE. [*From below*]
Mother, in drear darkness,
Don't leave me alone!

[*Pause.*]

CHORUS. [*Elegy*]
No, you'll never be alone, for
Knowing you as we think we do,
How should we forget you ever?
Always in our hearts we'll keep you.
Mourning, here, seems hardly called for.
Your hard fate we envy rather:
In sunny days or desolate,
Fine your song was, courage great.   10240

Blessed with all good things by birth,
Noble forebears, health, and strength.
Soon the hold lost on yourself,
Killed the bloom of your brave youth.
Felt with every warm heart warmly,
Saw the world sharp-eyed and quick,
Loved fine women passionately,
Had a voice that was unique.

Scorning law and moral custom,
Rushing onwards recklessly,   10250
Boldly you cut yourself off from
Recognized society.
But at last a great endeavor
Braced your soul with a high goal,
Glory now was what you strove for,
But you failed, death ended all.

Who succeeds? A futile question,
Fate is mute and gives no answer
On this desolate occasion
When all here in silence suffer.   10260
—Sing, however, new songs, don't
Droop your heads disconsolately.
Earth is song, and from that fount
Song pours out incessantly.

[*Complete pause. The music stops.*]

HELEN. [*to Faust*] The truth of an old saying is once again borne out
    In me: happiness and beauty rarely manage
    A long partnership. The bond is cut uniting
    Me to life, to love. Bewailing both, in grief
    And pain I utter my farewell, and once again,
    For the last time, throw myself into your arms.   10270
    Persephone, hear! Receive my boy and me.

[*She embraces Faust, her corporeal shape fades, and he is left holding her dress and veil.*]

PHORKYAS. [*To Faust*] Keep a good, firm grip on what is still
     left here.
  That dress there, don't let go of it. Already they've
  Begun to tug at it, the demons have, would like
  To drag it down, down to the underworld. Hang on!
  No longer does it clasp the goddess that you lost,
  Yet it is godly still, a boon impossible
  To estimate. Use it, it will bear you quickly
  Up into the higher air, high above all that
  Is commonplace, as long as you endure.   10280
  —We'll meet again but far, oh very far, from here.

[*Helen's garments, dissolving into clouds, envelop Faust, carry him aloft, and pass away into the distance. Phorkyas gathers up Euphorion's dress, cloak, and lyre from the ground, comes forward to the foot of the stage, holds them up, and speaks.*]

      A lucky find! No matter that
      The flame's no more, the fire out,
      It's not the death of poetry.
      With these I still can consecrate
      Many a tin-eared laureate,
      Whole schools, all green with jealousy.
      So if I can't supply the sacred fire,
      Yet I can furnish the correct attire.

[*She sits down beside a column at the front of the stage*]

PANTHALIS

  Girls, hurry, hurry! Aren't we now free at last   10290

Of the old Thessalian witch's barbarous sorcery—
Free, too, of that jingle-jangle music so confusing
To the ear and still worse to the mind?
—Now down to Hades! Down our Queen has hurried there
Already, with a solemn tread. Her footsteps show
Her faithful servants immediately the way. Before
The throne of the Inscrutables you'll find her, there.

CHORUS.
Wherever they are, it's fine for queens, oh yes!
Even in Hell their place is first,
Mixing proudly with their peers,   10300
Familiars of Persephone;
We however—far back, lost
In sickly fields of asphodel,
Straggling poplars, barren willows
Our sole company—how are we
Supposed to pass the time?
Squeaking miserably like bats,
Uttering ghostly whimpers, sighs?

PANTHALIS. Who's won no name nor nobly strives
Belongs to Nature's elements—depart!   10310
It's with the Queen I long to be—not great
Works only, loyal hearts preserve us in our person.

ALL.   We're given back into the light of day!
No longer persons, to be sure,
We know it, feel it, yet—
Never to go back to Hades, never!
Ever living Nature
Claims us spirits as her own,
As we claim her.

A PART OF THE CHORUS.
In these thousand trembling branches   through which
there's a rippling, rustling,   10320

Wooingly we coax the springs of   life from roots where
    they lie buried,
To the twigs which we dress first with   leaves then blossoms
    prodigally;
In the breezy air all's free to   grow and ripen, swelling
    plumply.
Ripe fruit falling, right away a   glad and merry crowd of
    people,
Herd of cattle too, come here, the   throng to gather, cattle
    nibble,
And about us all bow down as   all bowed down to the first
    gods.

ANOTHER PART.

To these mirrorlike sheer cliff sides   that throw light far in
    the distance
We cling close, in waves move round them,   giving stone
    our soft caress;
Ears attuned to every bird note,   reedy piping of the rushes,
Even to Pan's frightful outcry   our answer's ready, prompt.   10330
Rustling, is there? back we rustle,   thundering? our rolling
    thunder
Rumbles after, shaking, growling,   twice, thrice, ten times
    through the sky.

A THIRD PART.

Sisters, we, less sedentary,   run on with the running
    brooks in
Eagerness to reach those lush hills   stretching far away
    below;
Downwards tumbling, then meandering,   watering sloping
    meadows, later
Level pastures, lastly gardens   that surround the people's
    homes.

Towering high above the landscape   slender tops of
    cypresses
Mark the course of our waters   down to the broad sea's
    bright mirror.

A FOURTH PART.

Go you others where you please but   here on these
    close-planted hillsides
We will whisper round the grapevines   greening on their
    stakes and watch   10340
Vintagers who daily give their   heart and soul, intense
    devotion,
To a task whose outcome's always   plagued by such
    uncertainty.
Using hoe and sharp spade, heaping   up the earth and
    pruning, binding,
All the gods they supplicate but   the bright sungod most
    of all.
Flabby Bacchus, languid, little   cares about his faithful
    servants,
Nods in arbors, lolls in grottoes   babbling nonsense to
    a faun.
What he needs for his half-drunken   reveries he has about
    him,
Stored in wineskins, jars, all sorts of   vessels standing right
    and left
In the coolness of deep caves which   keep the wine through
    the long ages.
When, however, all the gods but   chiefly Helios have
    breathed   10350
On the vines, have wet them, warmed them,   shone with
    summer's heat upon them.
Heaping cornucopias up with   ruddy grapes to overflowing,

Suddenly there's coming, going: where the lone vinedresser labored,

Vines are shaking, men are running   up and down among the rows.

Baskets creak and buckets clatter,   panniers groan and all move towards the

Great vat and the treaders' dance. And   so the sacred vine's pure wealth of

Fruit is rudely trampled to a   foaming, splashing, nasty pulp.

Now ear-piercing cymbals' brazen   clashing's heard and Dionysus

From the mysteries comes unveiled and   after him goat-footed satyrs

Whirling their goat-footed women   while the long-eared beast Silenus,   10360

Frantic braying, rides among them   not a thing or person sparing,

All that's moral cleft hooves trampling,   all the senses whirling, swirling,

Hearing deafened hideously!   Drunken creatures grope for bowls,

Heads and bellies filled to bursting,   and though here and there some cry out

Apprehensively, it only   makes the tumult louder, madder,

For to lay up new wine the old   wineskins must be emptied fast.

[*The curtain falls.*]

[*Phorkyas, seated stage front, stands up giantlike in her buskins, steps out of them, and takes off her mask and veil, revealing herself as Mephistopheles—who is ready if required to offer as an epilogue his comments on the action.*]

ACT IV

HIGH MOUNTAINS

Grim, jagged peaks.
A cloud appears, draws up to the cliffside, and settles on an
overhanging ledge. The cloud parts and Faust steps out.

FAUST. Gazing down into the solitary depths beneath
    My feet, I quit the carrier–cloud that bore me over
    Land and sea and through fair skies and cautiously
    Step out onto this summit's brink. The fleecy mass,   10370
    Unscattered, draws back and slowly passes eastwards,
    My eyes straining after it in wonder how
    It changes and divides in wavelike movement as it drifts
    Away.—But trying, isn't it, to give shape to itself?
    My eyes don't play me false! On sun-suffused cloud-cushions
    I see a woman's figure stretched out—beautiful,
    Magnificent! Huge, too, indeed, but goddess-like,
    Like Juno's, Leda's, Helen's. How majestically
    It sways before my eyes, but soon breaks up
    Into a formless mass that is arrested   10380
    In the eastern sky—distant alps of ice,
    It seems, that dazzle me with their reflection
    Of the profound meaning of the days but just now passed.

    Yet round my breast and brow a wisp of gleaming
    Vapor hovers still, exhilarating, cool—
    Enchanting me! Now it floats lightly, hesitantly
    High and higher up as it contracts into a shape.
    —What? Deceived, am I? A ravishing image, isn't it,
    Of what to me when youngest was most good, but long,

So long deprived of, lost? The first, the richest treasure   10390
Of my heart pours up. Morning love, it is.
That lift, rush of delight at the instantly felt,
Little understood first glance which if it were
Kept hold of, would outshine all else of dearest, best.
As beauty of the soul, the lovely figure, undissolved,
Intensified, ascends up, up into the aether
And bears along with it all that is best in me.

[*A seven-league boot comes thumping down, another following it
immediately. Mephistopheles climbs out of them and steps down. The
boots go striding off.*]

MEPHISTO. I call that making tracks, I do!
    But tell me what possessed you to
    Light down in this horrid place   10400
    Of ghastly rock and vast abyss.
    How well I know it—from elsewhere;
    Actually, it's Hell's old floor.
FAUST. You're always ready with some stupid story!
    It's got no end, your Devil's repertory.
MEPHISTO. When the Lord God—and I know why—
    From Heaven hurled us down into Hell's pit,
    Whose central fire flamed eternally
    And gave off more than enough light and heat,
    We devils found ourselves uncomfortably   10410
    Packed close together. All began to sweat
    And huffed, from top, from bottom, to blow the fire out.
    Hell filled to bursting suffocatingly
    With a sulfurous stink. Oh my, the gas!
    Expanding with immense Tartarean force,
    It went off, shattering with a thunderous blast,
    Thick as it was, earth's flat, granitic crust.

This made a change, it did, in terra firma:
What once was infra, raised up, now is supra.
It also showed how right it is, the theory   10420
That holds things need to be turned topsy-turvy;
Which theory following, we escaped our prison
Underground to exercise dominion
In the air. An open secret, well concealed,
That only recently has been revealed.   [*Eph. 6:12*]

FAUST. Do I ask mountains what and where they came from?
Enough they're there, so noble, brooding, awesome.
When Nature made herself out of herself,
With a fine hand she shaped the rotund earth,
In soaring peaks and steep rock falls rejoiced;
Linking mountains in great ranges first,
She then formed hills that all might slope down gently,   10430
By slow declension to the fertile valley
Where all is a green garden. Kindly Nature
Has no use for eruptions, violence, fire.

MEPHISTO. You don't say! for you it's all so plain—
But we know better who were on the scene.
The abyss boiled over, flames shot in the sky,
And Moloch's hammer, lifted up on high,
Pounded crags and cliffs into rock piles
And scattered lumps of mountain round for miles.
Odd-shaped boulders are strewn about, all over;   10440
What hurled them there? Try and explain such power!
Philosophers cannot account for it,
The huge rocks sit there and that's that;
We rack our brains and all to no result!
But common people, sturdy and upright,
Hold fast to their traditional understanding,
Their wisdom's old, goes back lo the beginning.
They have no doubt it is a miracle

For which great Satan is responsible.
Upon their crutch of faith, in pious pilgrimage,   10450
They hobble to the Devil's Rock, the Devil's Bridge.
FAUST. I needn't now rely upon conjecture:
I know the Devil's point of view on Nature.
MEPHISTO. Nature! Nature! She's as it may be.
It's a point of honor, this, with me—
I was there! We people had the means
For pulling off the most tremendous schemes!
Unreason, turmoil, violence—behold the signs!
But never mind, I have a question for you:
Does everything on our earth simply bore you?   10460
You've looked far out from this height, seen unfurled
The glory of the Kingdoms of this World.   [*Matt. 4:8*]
Though you're so hard to please, so fussy.
There must be *something* suits your fancy.
FAUST. Yes, and very great it is.
Guess if you can what it is.
MEPHISTO. Easily done, I am sure.
Myself, I'd find some city where
The center swarms with people scrambling
Every which way to make a living,   10470
Crooked alleys, pointed gables,
In the close-built market square
Stands heaped high with vegetables,
Bloody butchers' counters where
The blowflies hover, feasting on
Fat sides of beef and venison—
We'd find there, no matter when,
Such a jostling, stinking din!
To avenue next and wide square
To stroll about with lordly air;   10480

And lastly through the city gate
To where the spreading suburbs wait,
With chaises dashing recklessly
And great crowds strolling ceaselessly—
A busy antheap overflowing
With people's restless to- and fro-ing.
Driving, riding, one would be
A magnet drawing every eye,
By thousands with doffed hats saluted.

FAUST. No, not by me desiderated.   10490
I'd like to see the people prosper,
In their own fashion have some pleasure,
Learn to read, be educated
(So know how to foment rebellions).

MEPHISTO. And then to build, to suit one's greatness,
An ostententious pleasure palace,
Surrounding it with splendid gardens
Where copses, meadows, hills, hedgerows
I would in formal style dispose;
Smooth lawns, cool, shaded arbors I'd   10500
Take care to have, allées provide;
Cascades from fall to fall descending;
A noble fountain, its jet shooting
High in the air, while round it squirting,
Petty ones are hissing, pissing;
And tucked away for pretty mistresses,
I'd put up the most charming cottages,
There to while away the hours
Happily, safe from intruders.
"Mistresses," I said: you must remember   10510
For me the feminine's a plural gender.

FAUST. Vicious, lewd—a modern Sardanapal!

MEPHISTO. No telling your wish, no, at all.
 Your ambition aims, so it would seem,
 At something highflown, bold, sublime.
 You who lately voyaged through the sky,
 Perhaps, moonstruck, now turn your eyes that way?
FAUST. Not up but down! Here on earth
 Is opportunity enough.
 My strength, my energy's unbounded,   10520
 I'll make the world sit up, astounded!
MEPHISTO. So fame is what you're after? One can see
 That you've been keeping heroic company.
FAUST. Wealth, property I'll win, and power!
 The doing's all and fame mere vapor.
MEPHISTO. Yet there'll be poets, never tiring,
 To sing your posthumous fame, inspiring
 By folly more folly, ever and ever.
FAUST. Condemned to sneer and jeer and taunt,
 How should you know what men want?   10530
 Your hateful nature, hostile, bitter,
 How should it know what men require?
MEPHISTO. Oh well, Doctor, do just as you please.
 Let's hear how far they go, your mad ideas.
FAUST. My glance wandering to the open sea,
 I saw the proud waves towering in the air,
 Then roaring fall upon the level shore
 In furious assault, presumptuously.
 And I was vexed—a mind that's free and prizes
 Respect for rights, highhandedness arouses   10540
 Passionate indignation in the soul.
 Was it an accident? I looked more closely:
 The tide, at flood, now ebbed, having gained its goal,
 But on the hour back it will come surely.
MEPHISTO. [*To the audience*]

For me the tides are nothing new,
For eons I have seen them ebb and flow.

FAUST. [*Continuing passionately*]

The water creeps up, flooding stealthily,
Sterile itself, it spreads sterility.
It flows along, rising to inundate
The lowland bogs, brackish and desolate.   10550
The waves come rolling in again and again
And then recede—and where, tell me, is the gain?
Running uncontrolled, the element
Wastes itself in vain flux and ferment.
Oh, it's enough to drive one to despair!
But I'm resolved, in spite of all, to dare
To meet the challenge of the ocean's power
And force it to acknowledge me its master!

It can be done, I know. The water flows
Around, not over, any sort of rise;   10560
A height defeats it, shallows draw it down.
The which observing, I've devised a plan
Whose execution, let success but crown it,
The satisfaction I should have! I'll bar
The lordly sea out from the lowly shore,
Restrict its power, for so long unlimited,
And drive it back upon itself defeated!
I've thought it out, the whole thing, step by step.
That's what I wish. I challenge you to help!

[*Drums and martial music in the distance, from behind the
audience's right.*]

MEPHISTO. Easily done.—Drums, did you hear, afar?   10570
FAUST. War again! What man of sense wants war?
MEPHISTO. War or peace, the wise thing is to try

And get what you can out of it, say I.
You keep a sharp eye out for any profit
Chance affords. *Your* chance is now—Faust, seize it!

FAUST. Spare me obscure twaddle, say straight out
Exactly what it is you mean by that.

MEPHISTO. Well, coming here, with my sharp eye I noticed
That our good Emperor looked dreadfully harassed.
You know the man—when we put on our shows,   10580
All that fake money led him to suppose
The world was his to do with as he would.
A beardless youth when he came to the throne,
He drew the false conclusion that he could
Amuse himself and at the same time reign,
Agreeably uniting "would" and "should."

FAUST. What a wrong idea! A ruler must
In rulership find all his satisfaction,
Nurse a lofty purpose in his breast,
But keep it hidden from all those about him.   10590
What privately in trusted ear's forecasted,
Is done—and the whole world's flabbergasted.
And so his august will remains supreme,
To frolic with familiars lowers him.

MEPHISTO. That's not our one! For he had fun, he did,
While into anarchy the whole realm slid:
Great and small in every region warring,
Brother brother banishing and killing,
Castle against castle, town against town,
Guild and nobility at daggers drawn,   10600
And the bishop feuding with his diocese.
Let eye meet eye, at once you're enemies,
Throats cut in church, merchants and travelers
The prey of roving bands of highway robbers.

Bolder and bolder all grew, living meant:
"On guard! Defend yourself!"—And so it went.

FAUST. Yes, went—it staggered, fell, lurched to its feet,
Stumbled a step, collapsed into a heap.

MEPHISTO. You dared not say how dreadful these things were.
Each could and did claim full rights for himself,   10610
The humblest acknowledged no superior,
Till it proved too much for the men of worth
Who rose up in a body and declared:
"We've got to have for our sovereign lord
A man who's able to keep order.
The Emperor cannot and he won't,
So let us put it to a vote
And choose the realm an abler ruler,
A man to infuse it with fresh spirit,
Assure each subject's safety in it;   10620
Create a new world, one in which
Peace and righteousness embrace.

FAUST. I hear the priestly note.

MEPHISTO.   And right you are!
The priesthood's bellies were their biggest care;
More than any, they provoked the tumult,
Archiepiscopally blessing revolt and riot.
And now the monarch whose life we made merry
Prepares to fight his last fight, as it may be.

FAUST. I pity him, the man was open, kind.

MEPHISTO. Well, while there's life there's hope, so we must find   10630
A way out for him from this narrow valley.
Save him now, he'll never need to worry.
The dice fall who knows how, if fortune favors,
In droves he'll see come back all his deserters.

[*They cross a lower spur of the mountains to observe the disposition of the army in the valley. Drums and martial music sound below.*]

MEPHISTO. He's taken up, I see a good position;
　　With our help his victory is certain.
FAUST. What's the point of it, tell me?
　　Tricks! Illusion! Sorcery!
MEPHISTO. The point? The point, dear sir's, to win.
　　Keep in mind your great aim   10640
　　And lay your plans accordingly;
　　Put him back upon his throne
　　And be rewarded generously.
　　You'll kneel before him: grateful for his kingdom,
　　He'll grant you endless shoreland for your fiefdom,
FAUST. So much you've done already, so
　　Go on and win a battle too,
MEPHISTO. That's your job, not mine at all!
　　You're the Commanding General.
FAUST. That would really take some gall—   10650
　　Command where what I know is null!
MEPHISTO. Leave matters to your staff's care,
　　That way the Marshal's fame's secure.
　　Aware no battle goes as planned,
　　I've been at pains to be forehand,
　　Enlisted fighters none more brave,
　　Picked from ancient, primitive
　　Mountain folk. Such heroes on your side,
　　The Marshal needn't ever feel afraid.
FAUST. Who are those there, great armed fellows?   10660
　　Roused up, have you, all the heights and hollows?
MEPHISTO. No, like Mister Peter Quince,
　　Picked from the lot the quintessence.

[*Enter the Three Mighty Men (2 Sam. 23:8)*]

And here they are, my bold bravoes,
One young, one middle-aged, one ancient.
Armed differently, in different clothes,
You won't find them a disappointment.

[*To the audience.*]

Today we're so delighted, all,
By medieval knights in armor;
And as these brutes are also allegorical,   10670
It adds a something extra to our pleasure.

RAUFEBOLD. [(*"Bullyboy"*) *Young, lightly armed, gaily dressed.*]
If someone only looks at me,
I black his eye and punch his nose for him,
And when the funker turns to flee,
I grab his long hair streaming after him.

HABEBALD. [(*"Grab-quick"*) *In his prime, well armed, richly dressed*]
A useless business, war-making,
A waste of time, of precious effort,
Unless you take and keep on taking—
All else can wait till there's time for it.

HALTEFEST. [(*"Hold-fast"*) *Old, heavily armed, not wearing mail.*]
You don't end up winning that way either,   10680
You live, you spend, and all's soon gone.
It's fine to take, but keeping is much better,
So to this old one give your booty over!
That way you will lose nothing to no one.

[*They all descend together.*]

IN THE FOOTHILLS

Drums and martial music below. The Emperor's tent is being pitched.
Emperor. Commander-in-Chief. Imperial Guard.

COMMANDER-IN-CHIEF. Our battle plan still seems a good one
    to me:
  I'm confident it's a good choice.
  Inside the narrow confines of this valley
  We'll draw back our entire force.
EMPEROR. Soon enough we'll see if you are right.
  But I dislike what looks like a retreat.   10690
COMMANDER-IN-CHIEF. Only observe our right flank, Sire:
  Terrain exactly as you would desire.
  Not steep, but not ground easy to traverse,
  Better for us, and for the enemy worse.
  Its hummocks half concealing our force,
  They'll think twice before they risk their horse.
EMPEROR. What can I say? I give it my approval.
  On this field our arms must prove their mettle.
COMMANDER-IN-CHIEF. Here in the center where the ground is flat
  You see the phalanx, cheerful, full of fight,   10700
  Their tall pikes flashing in the morning haze
  Through which the bright sun darts its golden rays.
  How the close-martialled dark square sways and heaves,
  Its thousands all on fire to do great deeds!
  Judge for yourself our strength, with your own eyes;
  I don't doubt it will split the enemy's
EMPEROR. It's the first time I have seen it, really;
  A force like that could cope with twice as many.
COMMANDER-IN-CHIEF. From our left no signals come, all's quiet,
  A picked force occupies the rugged height   10710

From which—look—you can see their weapons flash.
The cliff controls the gorge's crucial pass;
There, I suspect, the foe will meet defeat—
Caught unawares, be routed bloodily, complete.

EMPEROR. See, there they come, false kinsmen all, who called
Me uncle, nephew, brother, themselves allowed
Ever more rights, ever more liberty,
Stole from the throne its strength and sanctity,
Fell out among themselves, laid waste the Empire,
And now rebelling, march on me together.   10720
The people waver, don't know what to do,
And where the current carries them, they go.

COMMANDER-IN-CHIEF. I sent two men I trust out spying,
And down cliff here one comes—good news, I'm praying!

FIRST SPY.
            Brave and cunning as we are,
            We succeeded in our mission,
            But our news is bad, I fear:
            Many princes swear devotion
            To Your Highness, but extenuate
            Their inaction by the reason   10730
            Of the turmoils in their state.

EMPEROR. To play it safe, they reckon, is being shrewd;
Who cares for honor, duty, gratitude?
They see their neighbor's house catch fire, burn,
And never think it might soon be their turn.

COMMANDER-IN-CHIEF. And here's the second one descending
            slowly;
Exhausted, he is, legs so weak and wobbly.

SECOND SPY.
            First we saw, with much delight,
            Wild confusion everywhere,
            Then were startled by the sight   10740

Of a new-crowned Emperor.
Forming up in close order,
All the crowd marched out in step
Following their lying banner
Like a flock of docile sheep.

EMPEROR. I'm pleased with this false emperor, believe me;
At last I feel myself the Emperor really!
I donned my armor as a thing required,
But now I wear it as a man inspired.
Our brilliant festivals, where nothing wanted,   10750
Yet wanted danger—the only thing *I* wanted.
You had me tilting tamely at a ring—
With pounding heart, I imagined the real thing.
You vetoed wars, or otherwise my name
Would now shine starlike with a hero's fame.
When round about me the hot fire burned,
Mirroring me to myself, I felt confirmed
In my full manhood; the flames furiously
Leapt at me, and although sham, they seemed
Fierce enough in truth and real to me.   10760
The dreams I dreamt of glorious victories!
Today I'll redeem my shameful delinquencies!

[*Heralds are sent off to challenge the rebel Emperor. Enter Faust
in armor, with visor half-raised, and the Three Mighty Men, armed
and dressed as above.*]

FAUST. We trust our coming here, Sir, 's not unwelcome.
Though all look well, "Take care!" is a safe dictum.
It's well known to you that the mountain folk
Are skilled in rocks, read deep in Nature's book.
Abandoning the flatland ages past,
And finding mountains much more to their taste,

They toil in labyrinthine caverns, dense
With gases that are metal's noble source; 10770
They separate, combine, test, trying to
Discover things undreamt of hitherto.
By spirit power, subtly, they construct
Forms clear and crystalline, without defect;
Then in the crystal's eternal silence peering,
Perceive what in the upper world is occurring.

EMPEROR. So I have heard, and do believe, M'sieur,
But fail to see how it concerns us here.

FAUST. The Sabine sorcerer from Norcia, remember,
Is your devoted servant, staunch supporter. 10780
How grim the doom that threatened him that time:
The kindling crackled, at once leapt the flame
Up the dry logs close around him stacked,
Smeared with pitch, with sticks of sulfur packed,
Nor man nor god nor even devil able
To save the poor magician in his dire peril—
Till snatched by Majesty from a fiery burial!
In Rome that was. He feels eternally
Indebted to you, watches anxiously
Your fortune's course, its windings and its turns, 10790
Forgetting since that hour his own concerns.
For you he studies what the bright stars mean,
The secrets that the depths of earth contain.
He bade us hurry, not delaying, hither
To stand by you. Great is the mountain's power;
There Nature mightily works, supreme and free;
The priests, thick-witted, say it's sorcery.

EMPEROR. On feast days do we welcome every guest,
All enter with high spirits, full of zest,
It gladdens us, the gay throngs crowding, jostling, 10800
That fill our palace halls almost to bursting.

But doubly welcome that stout friend must be
Who rallies to our standard loyally
In the anxious hour when the foe's defiance
Is trumpeted, and our fate hangs in the balance.
Yet keep your good sword in its sheath, respecting
This moment when, the trial of arms impending,
Men by the thousands for me, against me, are marching—
Oneself's the one now, throne to him belong
Who's worthy of it, in himself is strong!   10810
And may this specter who now haunts our Empire,
Claiming the rule as his, a vile pretender
To land, to crown, our barons' duty, all,
Be by this fist of mine sent straight to Hell!

FAUST.   However that may be, Sir, it's not wise
To risk your own life, though so great the cause.
Your helmet, golden crest, and plume protect
The head that incites us to smite the landsknecht.
Without the head, what good are limbs, tell me?
Let the head nod, the limbs sink drowsily;   10820
If it is struck, all are struck together;
When it recovers, all at once recover.
The arm is quick to see and claim its right
To raise the shield and save the head from hurt;
The sword, its duty knowing, nothing slack,
The foe's stroke parries and returns the stroke;
The foot, partaking in its partners' luck,
Treads briskly on the adversary's neck.

EMPEROR.   Just so I'd like to exercise my rule:
For my wrath their heads have as my footstool!   10830

HERALDS.   [Returning]
          Insolently, rudely, curtly
          They received us, coarsely mocking
          Our challenge, noble, courtly;

      Scornfully asked were we joking:
      "Your man's had his day, his story
      'S now a fading echo, dying
      Weakly out here in this valley.
      'Once there was . . .' they'll soon be saying."
FAUST. It's as we should have wished, who faithfully
      Will stand with you against the enemy!   10840
      And there they come, our soldiers never waver!
      Sound the attack! The moment's in our favor.
EMPEROR. Here I supreme command resign:
                   [*To the Commander-in-Chief*]
      It's in your hands now, Prince, not mine!
COMMANDER-IN-CHIEF. Then right wing forward, meet their left
         wing climbing
      Up the slope! Our fellows, young, stout-hearted,
      Driving hard, will send the rash foe reeling
      Helter-skelter back, completely routed.
FAUST. [*Pointing to the man on his right*]
      Allow this dashing hero here
      To join your ranks. And never fear—   10850
      Among your troops, you'll see, he'll prove a brave knave
      And show both friend and foe the stuff he's made of.
RAUFEBOLD. [*Presenting himself*]
      Whoever meets me head on won't retire
      Without his jaw smashed, upper also under;
      Whoever turns his back on me, poor noddy,
      Will find his head's been parted from his body.
      And if your men pitch in while I
      All about me ruin spread,
      I guarantee the enemy
      Will drown, each one, in his own blood.   10860
                             Exit.

COMMANDER-IN-CHIEF. Now let the center move and join the
          action,
     Deploying its full strength, but with due caution.
     On the right already by the fierce onset
     Our men made, their battle plan's been upset.
FAUST. [*Pointing to the one in the middle*]
     And here's this one. I'm glad to recommend him.
     He's quick, he is, and drives the foe before him.
HABEBALD. [*Presenting himself*]
     The fighting spirit of the Imperial soldier
     Now be united with the thirst for plunder,
     All spirits fired with the same ambition:
     To seize the upstart emperor's pavilion.   10870
     He won't, we swear, sit long on his high horse!
     I'll lead the phalanx—in front's my place—of course!
EILEBEUTE. [*("Snatch-the-Loot") Canteen woman, snuggling up
          to him*]
     Although we've not been hitched, we two,
     He's still for me my dearest beau.
     Oh what a harvest waits here for us!
     A woman when she robs is ruthless,
     She knows no mercy once she's started,
     Then victory, hurrah! And all's permitted.

                                                    Both exit.

COMMANDER-IN-CHIEF.
     It's just as we foresaw, they've thrown their right
     Against our left with all the strength they've got.   10880
     Our men must beat back their headlong advance,
     It threatens our possession of the pass.
FAUST. [*Pointing to the one on the left*]
     Then, Sir, remark this fellow. It can't hurt
     To make a strong force even stronger yet.
HALTEFEST. [*Presenting himself*]

About your left you needn't fear;
Let me be there, all's warranted secure.
The grip this old man's fingers take
Not even thunderbolts can break.

MEPHISTO. [*Descending from above*]
Now look behind you where from every
Rocky cavern pours an army   10890
Crowding all the paths with hordes
In helm and harness, fiercely flaunting
Spears and shields and ancient swords:
A back-up force on its bit chomping
Till our signal sounds the assault

[*Aside, to the knowing ones in the audience.*]

Where are they from? Top secret, but—
I will tell you. I've cleared out
The dusty armories here about
Where rusting they stood or they sat
Their horses, still believing that   10900
They were the earth's almighty rulers,
Lordly knights and kings and kaisers—
That now are only empty shells
(As empty as those once housed snails)
Which phantoms dress up in to resurrect
Old chivalry and bring the Middle Ages back.
If devils, too, have got into the act—
No matter, what counts here is the effect.

                                        [*Aloud.*]

Hear them furiously working
Themselves up into a temper, bumping   10910
Into one another with a
Tinny sound of rattling armor.

Their tattered ensigns restlessly await
The freshening breeze to make them stand out straight.
Remember, these are an old race of people
Who long once more to breathe the dust of battle.

[*A shattering trumpet blast from above. Noticeable wavering in the enemy's ranks.*]

FAUST. The heavens lower, in the murk
        Here and there there's a red spark
        Ominously flashing out;
        Already arms gleam bloodily,   10920
        The rocks, the forest, and the sky,
        The air around, are gules throughout.
MEPHISTO. Our right wing's showing lots of firmness;
        The giant Raufbold in their midst,
        Towering high above the rest,
        Goes workmanlike about his business.
EMPEROR. Where I saw one arm before,
        Twelve I now see, even more,
        Not only Nature's at work here!
FAUST. You've never heard of the mirages   10930
        Seen on Sicilian shores and marshes?
        Visible in the bright day,
        They hover halfway up the sky,
        Reflections in the atmosphere.
        Very strange these visions are—
        Cities floating in the air,
        Gardens, too—it's all true, Sir!
        Image image following,
        Appearing and then disappearing.
EMPEROR. But I'm uneasy, I can see   10940
        The tips of spears eerily

Ablaze, and little flames that dance
Along the phalanx' every lance.
It's too uncanny, much, for me.

FAUST. Excuse me, Sir, those are what's left of
Spirits now defunct, inactive:
The antique twins, the Dioscuri,
Whom all that sail the salt sea swear by—
The fire's their last spark of life.

EMPEROR. I'd like to know who we owe Nature's 10950
Kindly doing us such favors,
Performing prodigies in our behalf?

MEPHISTO. Why, who else? The necromancer—
As anxious for you as a mother.
Distressed to see you threatened by
So powerful an enemy,
The grateful magus harbors only one wish,
To see you saved though he himself should perish.

EMPEROR. Rome cheered me through the streets: now someone to
Be reckoned with, I meant to show it, so, 10960
Without considering, on seeing that
The ancient fellow found his seat too hot,
Commanded his release. This spoiled a pleasure
Dear to priests, gone was the Church's favor.
And now long after that impulsive act
Do I experience its good effect?

FAUST. A rich reward attends all generous deeds.
But upwards, Sir, direct your gaze!
I think he's sending you a sign
Whose meaning soon will be made plain. 10970

EMPEROR. I see an eagle soaring in the heavens,
Hard after it one of those frightful griffins.

FAUST. Watch, do! I am sure the omen's favorable!
The griffin after all is just a fable,

So how should he imagine himself able
Ever to trade blows with a real-life eagle?
EMPEROR. Circling each other warily,
    At the same instant suddenly
    Hurtling through the air, they close
    And feathers fly from under claws.   10980
FAUST. The wretched griffin, mauled, discomfited,
    His lion's tail abased, has plummeted
    Down into the trees upon the height
    And disappears ingloriously from sight.
EMPEROR. As you read the sign, so be it!
    Struck with wonder, I accept it.
MEPHISTO. [*Looking to the right*]
    One hard assault after another
    Has made the enemy retire,
    Putting up a scattered fight
    As he is forced back on his right   10990
    So that his ranks, dismayed, confused,
    Leave his main troops' left exposed.
    And now our phalanx, moving rightward,
    With lightning speed drives its spearhead
    At his weakest spot. And just as
    Waves the howling storm wind raises
    Mountain high, contend together,
    The two sides have at one another.
    It couldn't have been better planned,
    The day is ours, a famous victory gained!   11000
EMPEROR. [*Looking left, to Faust*]
    Look that way, over there, however;
    Our position looks in danger.
    I can't see stones being pitched
    At the foe, who has reached
    The lower height; above, the cliff

Looks abandoned, without life.
The foe is mounting near and nearer,
Overwhelming in his number,
The pass, I fear, may have been taken—
A fitting end to godless efforts!   11010
What good have they been, all your black arts?

[Pause.]

MEPHISTO. I see my two grim ravens coming:
    What kind of news might they be bringing?
    It's not looking good in my opinion.
EMPEROR. What do they want, those ugly things,
    Sailing here on their black wings
    From the hot fighting on the mountain?
MEPHISTO. [*To the ravens*]
    Sit at my ear, close to me,
    Your advice is trustworthy,
    Whom you protect won't soon be beaten.   11020
FAUST. [*To the Emperor*]
    You've heard of pigeons, I am sure,
    Who find their way back from afar
    Unerringly to their home roost.
    Now these birds, too, from a far place
    Fly home with sure intelligence,
    Except there is this difference:
    The pigeon post we have for peace,
    For war we have the raven post.
MEPHISTO. Very grave this news is!
    Look there at the precipice: 11030
    The foe swarms up, our heroes waver;
    They've seized, I see, the neighboring height,
    And if they take the pass, good night!
    We'd find ourselves in hot water.
EMPEROR. So you deceived me after all!

I feel myself such a fool,
All along I feared a trap.

MEPHISTO. Courage! Never give up hope.
Patience, cunning, till all's won!
It's always darkest before dawn.   11040
I'll take command, just say the word;
My messengers wait at my side.

COMMANDER-IN-CHIEF. [*Meanwhile approaching*]
Oh but it gave me pain to see
You take these rogues for an ally.
Jugglery is a weak friend,
Full of smiles, false in the end,
All's bright at first and then all's black.
It's looking bad for us and I can't change it;
They began it, well then, let them end it.
I resign, here's my staff back.   11050

EMPEROR. Keep it till our luck improves,
As I hope. That grinning rogue's
Leering face and raven friends
All my sense of things offends.

[*To Mephistopheles.*]

I can't allow you the baton,
It's not for you, you're the wrong man.
But yes, take charge of things here, and
Try to save us if you can.

[*Retires into the tent with the Commander-in-Chief.*]

MEPHISTO. His great defense, that stumpy mace!
It's no use to the likes of us: 11060
It had a thing, a cross, it looked like, on it.

FAUST. So what do we do now?

MEPHISTO.   Why, we have done it!
    —Off you go, my dear dun cousins, quick
    And serviceable, to the lake
    Upon the mountain, greet with my best wishes
    The Undines sporting with the fishes,
    And borrow from them their flood trick.
    They are women, have the knack,
    Which we can't understand, to sunder
    Seem from *be* so that the former   11070
    You would swear was the latter.

                                                 [*Pause.*]

FAUST. The water maidens must have yielded promptly
    To our ravens' flattering tongues; already
    I see water has begun
    To trickle down the bare rock, soon
    The trickling turns into a stream—
    Foe's hopes of winning now a dream.

MEPHISTO. They didn't expect for welcome being doused,
    Their boldest climbers drenched and soused.

FAUST. Streams unite with streams, in a great surge   11080
    Pour out of gulleys doubled in their size;
    One torrent, high up, in a great arc leaping
    Falls on level rock, the water gushing,
    Rushing this way, that, and so by stages
    Down into the valley the flood plunges.
    All resistance, never mind how brave,
    Surely must be drowned in the huge wave.
    I'm scared myself, so frightful such deluges.   11090

MEPHISTO. I don't see it, for it's all a hoax,
    A sham I'm proof against, it only works
    On human eyes; but its bizarre result
    I see with pleasure: hordes of men that bolt

Away in panic fearing they'll be drowned,
Ridiculously gasping, coughing, stumbling
And making swimming motions as they're running,
When all the while what's underfoot's dry ground!
Ha, ha, confusion's rampant all around!

[*The ravens return.*]

Well done, and I will tell the Master so.   11100
But if you wish to show you're masters, too.
Off at once to where the Little People
Are busy striking sparks from stone and metal
At their smithy. Make your handshake warm,
Your croaking cheery, exert your sooty charm
So as at last to beg from them some fire—
Glowing, flashing, bursting, their best manufacture.
On any summer evening you can see
Lightning glimmering in the distant sky,
Stars shooting through the heavens, high, so high.   11110
But lightning darting through dense underbrush,
Stars on the wet ground sparking with a hiss,
You don't see often, they're not commonplace.
It doesn't call for great exertions, just
Ask politely first; if no, insist.

[*The ravens leave. All happens as above.*]

Blindly stumbling in thick gloom,
The foe don't know who is whom,
Lights flashing all about, here, there,
Then suddenly a blinding glare—
Good, good, but some noise, too, to scare   11120
The living daylights out of the numskulls.

FAUST. The empty armor from the musty halls
  Take, in the fresh air, a new lease on life
  And clank and rattle on the cliff:
  How strange the noise is, unreal, false.
MEPHISTO. Right, right! There was no holding them back longer,
  And now they whack away with knightly ardor
  As in the good old days of chivalry.
  Greaves and brassarts locked in bloody strife
  Renew, as Ghibelline and Guelf,   11130
  Their everlasting enmity.
  For them it's a time-honored custom,
  You can't ever reconcile them;
  Already far and wide, my, what an uproar!
  The Devil likes his revels animated,
  He's found that what works best is party hatred,
  Which ends at last in dreadfulness and horror.
  Hear it now, the panic, screams of fright,
  And mixed with them a shrill, satanic shout
  Which through the valley sends a violent shudder.   11140

[*A warlike din sounds from the orchestra, passing over into lively martial airs.*]

THE RIVAL EMPEROR'S TENT

Throne. Sumptuous interior.
Habebald. Eilebeute.

EILEBEUTE. And here we are, the very first!
HABEBALD. Show me a raven flies as fast!
EILEBEUTE. The riches here! Man, such a lot!
  Where to begin? Where to stop?

HABEBALD. So crammed with fine things, this whole space,
   I have trouble with my choice.
EILEBEUTE. I'll take this carpet. How I've had
   To make, on bare boards, my hard bed!
HABEBALD. Here's a spiked club, just the kind
   I've wished for so long, couldn't find.   11150
EILEBEUTE. A stunning scarlet cloak, gold-trimmed,
   Of the kind I've always dreamed!
HABEBALD. [*Picking up the club*]
   With this the business is soon done,
   You bash his head in, then move on.
   Your sack's already bulging but
   It's not the right stuff you have got,
   So leave it lay. Instead take hold
   Of one of these chests crammed with gold.
   Gold, all gold! the army's pay—
   Yes, the right stuff—on our way!   11160
EILEBEUTE. Murder, for me much too heavy
   To lift up, much less to carry!
HABEBALD. Quick now, stoop, duck, will you, duck!
   I'll heave it up on your stout back.
EILEBEUTE. It's slipping off, it's falling down!
   You've gone and broken my backbone.

[*The box falls and breaks open.*]

HABEBALD. The gold's all spilt, a yellow mound—
   Down, woman, quick, down on the ground!
EILEBEUTE. [*Crouching*]
   I'll scoop up an apronful.
   We'll have a nice pile, we will, still.   11170
HABEBALD. Enough. Now off you go, my girl.
                                       [*She straightens up.*]

> Damn! Your apron's got a hole!
> With every step you take you scatter
> Riches round in a gold shower.

IMPERIAL GUARDS. Nosing around the tent, are you?
> All here's the Emperor's—taboo.

HABEBALD. We risked our skins, by God, we'll have
> Our share of what is owed the brave.
> We are soldiers, custom grants
> To us as spoils the foeman's tents.   11180

IMPERIAL GUARDS. That's not our way, no, not at all:
> To be a soldier and to steal!
> Only an honest soldier may
> Fitly serve His Majesty.

HABEBALD. Your honesty's a well-known thing,
> Its name is requisitioning.
> We all of us ply the same trade
> And "Hand it over!" 's the password.
>   [*To Eilebeute*]
> Get going, girl, with what you've got.
> For us here's no welcome mat.   11190
>   [*They leave.*]

FIRST GUARD. What, I wonder, held you back
> From giving that smart rogue a whack?

SECOND GUARD. Suddenly I felt so weak,
> The two of them seemed so ghostlike.

THIRD GUARD. Spots danced before my eyes, the light
> Was strange, I couldn't see things straight.

FOURTH GUARD. I'm at a loss what to say:
> So very hot it was all day,
> Oppressive, sultry, thick with fear,
> Men staggering here, toppling there;   11200
> Groping for the foe, you struck,
> And down each fell beneath your stroke;

A veil, it seemed, your eyes obscured
And in your ears it buzzed, hummed, roared.
And so things went and now we're here.
What happened? We have no idea.

[*Enter the Emperor with four Princes. The Guards fall back*]

EMPEROR. However it was, we've won, the enemy scattered
    Back across the plain, his army shattered.
    There stands the empty throne; the traitor's treasure,
    Bundled in carpets, hardly leaves room to enter.   11210
    With our brave bodyguard around us, we await
    The nations' envoys in imperial state.
    Glad news come pouring in from left and right,
    The people's allegiance restored, the state saved from its plight.
    Perhaps we had some unorthodox help—however,
    We won in the end thanks to our own endeavor.
    Strange things happen that stand one in good stead,
    A stone falls from the sky, blood on the enemy's head;
    Out of caverns of rock came the fearfullest cries
    That lift up our spirits, the enemy's otherwise.   11220
    Defeated, he falls, jeered at, derided, despised—
    By the victor in gratitude God is exalted and praised,
    Which the people unbidden echo in thunderous shouts:
    "We thank thee, O Lord," sounds from thousands of throats.
    But most devotedly I look in myself, within me,
    In pious acknowledgment—a thing I have done rarely.
    A happy-go-lucky prince squanders his days,
    The years adding up warn him, mend, Sire, your ways.
    For house, court and realm we have decided therefore,
    Not delaying, to unite ourselves with you praiseworthy four.

                                                    [*To the first*]

You, it was, Prince, disposed our forces skillfully,
And at the decisive moment struck heroically.
Now we have peace, do as the time demands;
I name you our Marshal, with the office place its sword
    in your hands.
LORD HIGH MARSHAL. Till now our business has been only war.
    Once frontiers and throne are at last made secure,   11230
    Grant me, on the days in which we make merry,
    To see that the Castle's table is set properly.
    Before you I'll go, raising high the bright sword,
    Majesty's escort and its shining safeguard!
EMPEROR. [To the second]
    And the brave man known as well for his courtesy,
    You, Sir—our Lord High Chamberlain be.
    Take charge, our wish is, of the household staff
    Who serve us so slackly, so outrageous their strife;
    Your noble example, to whom this post's now allotted,
    Shall instruct them how Lords and Ladies are to be treated.   11240
LORD HIGH CHAMBERLAIN.
    How earn your favor? Fulfill your every purpose and wish,
    Help the good, with the bad be not overly harsh;
    Plain-spoken, not falsely-plain, not falsely calm.
    My hope is you will perceive me just as I am.
    Anticipate, shall I, the scene in the Hall?
    You come to the table, I hand you up the gold bowl,
    Hold your rings as you dip your fingers in for the feast;
    Delighted your look is, as by your look I am blest.
EMPEROR. My thoughts are too earnest to think of enjoyment.
    No matter—it helps, does a festive commencement.   11250
                            [To the third]
You I appoint our Lord Steward—in your care
Our game preserves, poultry yard, manor farm are!
As the season is, duly, know, Sir, I expect
To dine on my favorite dishes, expertly cooked.

LORD HIGH STEWARD. I'll make it my pleasant duty to fast
    Till you find it a feast, your every repast.
    I'll toil side by side with the cooks in the kitchen
    To bring near the far off, the lagging season hasten.
    But exotic things, first fruits, are not to your taste,
    What's simple, what's wholesome is what you like best.   11260
EMPEROR. [*To the fourth*]
    Since feasting must soon occupy our whole day,
    Young hero, Cupbearer be, and your sword put away.
    As such give your closest, most earnest attention
    To stocking our cellars with the wines we delight in.
    However, you yourself must observe moderation;
    When the toasts go around, Prince, beware of temptation!
LORD HIGH CUPBEARER. Only entrust the youth with duties,
        and then
    Under your eyes see how quick they grow into men.
    In my mind's eye I, too, see the grand spectacle, Sire:
    On the sideboard I lay out glittering silver- and goldware,   11270
    Reserving the noblest cup, the loveliest goblet
    For His Highness's use at the boisterous banquet:
    Rich glass of Venice aglow with the promise of pleasure,
    In it the wine is robuster yet the drinker stays sober.
    But the goblet's miraculous virtue is trusted too often;
    Your Majesty's temperate nature's a surer protection.
EMPEROR. All I have promised on this solemn occasion
    You may with full confidence, Princes, depend on;
    What the Emperor promises, none shall countermand.
    Still, a written confirmation is needed, signed by our hand.   11280
    And here is the very one to draw up the document.
    Archbishop, welcome! You come at just the right moment.

[*Enter the Archbishop-Chancellor.*]

A keystone fixed in an arch braces the structure
So the masonry holds, keeps it standing forever.
Here my four Princes are! We have proclaimed
How household and court henceforth must be maintained.
But now with respect to the realm as a whole: I give
The responsible power into the hands of you five.
I mean to make your quintet preeminent in property,
And so with the lands from the foe we have now won   11290
I am pleased to enlarge those your lordships already own.
Thus to my faithfullest I each award a fair seigniory;
Also vouchsafing the right of further extension
Of the properties granted, by purchase, exchange, and
       succession.
As a Peer of the Realm, each shall possess without let
All the prerogatives appertaining to it.
As judges your verdict is final, pronounced once for all,
No question nor challenge allowed, nor right of appeal;
Yours be all levies, rents, tolls, taxes, and fees;
From saltworks, mines, mints, all their royalties.   11300
How grateful I am, these high honors are proof
By which you are raised to be nearest our self.
ARCHBISHOP. I thank Your Majesty on their, on my own behalf;
    It strengthens us greatly, also yourself.
EMPEROR. I intend you five an honor still higher yet—
    My life is my realm's, and I rejoice in it,
    But even as I strive and I struggle ambitiously,
    I think of the many who have preceeded me.
    I, too, must part from dear friends in due course;
    And that day arriving, on you falls the choice   11310
    Of my successor. —May it bring, his election,
    To these turbulent times a good, a peaceful conclusion!
ARCHBISHOP. With pride our hearts glow, princes first of the world,
    Knees humbly bent, faithful to your every word.

As long as the blood courses through our veins,
We are the body your least will commands.

EMPEROR. So in conclusion: let what we have ordained
Be set down in writing, for all time confirmed.
As lords hold absolute what you have been granted,
Except that in no case must your lands be divided;   11320
However you add to what you presently own,
All, all must pass unabated to the eldest son.

ARCHBISHOP. I'll gladly see to it so important a statute
To the realm, to ourselves, is inscribed upon parchment
By my Chancery's clerks, with the seal affixed to it,
So Your Majesty's sacred hand duly may sign it.

EMPEROR. And now, sirs, depart so each one of you may
Ponder the matters we have decreed this great day.

[*The secular Princes withdraw; the spiritual one remains.*]

ARCHBISHOP. [*Pompously, unctuously*]
The Chancellor departs, the Bishop must not stir,
A warning spirit drives him to seek your ear!   11330
So anxious his fatherly heart is, so deeply concerned.

EMPEROR. When all is rejoicing, what should trouble your mind?

ARCHBISHOP. It bitterly grieves me, Sire, at this hour,
To see your person leagued with Satanic power.
Your throne is now safe, to be sure, or so it may seem—
Alas, in contempt of the Lord and His Vicar in Rome!
If the Pope should get wind of it, his dread anger
Would utterly shatter your iniquitous Empire.
He doesn't forget how Your Grace, newly crowned,
All Christendom contumaciously scorned.   11340
Your first act of mercy chose whom to set free?
A damnable practicer of sorcery!
But beating your breast now, from your ill-gotten treasure

Devote to things holy a trifling, small measure:
This region of hills in which you erected your tent
(Where evil spirits banded to serve your intent,
In whose Prince of Lies you were only too glad to believe)
For the Church's holy endeavors, piously give—
With mountains and forests as far as they reach,
And broad, upland pastures, grassy and rich,   11350
Lakes crowded with fish, brooks, kills, streamlets that flow
Tumbling and winding to the valley below,
And the valley as well with field, dale, and chase!
That will show your repentance, restore you to grace.

EMPEROR. Oh how I've offended, I am filled with horror!
Fix the boundaries yourself, as you think proper.

ARCHBISHOP. Firstly, proclaim it your holy, fixed purpose
To devote this profaned place to Heaven's service.
Already I see stout walls rising high in the air,
The light of the morning sun filling the choir,   11360
The transept on either side building well out,
The great nave completed, making glad the devout,
Who stream through the doors, full of glowing faith, all.
The first sound of bells rings across hill and dale,
Loud pealing from spires that heavenwards strain,
The sinner returns to the fold, born again.
The day, may it dawn soon, that we hallow God's house
Your Majesty's presence shall make glorious!

EMPEROR. By this work may my pious intention be shown
To glorify God, cleanse my soul of its stain.   11370
This is well! It has raised up my spirits mightily.

ARCHBISHOP. There remains, Sir, a final formality.

EMPEROR. Yes, the official conveyance of the lands to the Church—
Present me the deed and I'll sign it at once.

ARCHBISHOP. [*Takes his leave, but then turns back*]
Also, allow the income that these lands will produce—

Tithes, taxes, rents—for the cathedral's full use.
The money we'll need to keep it up worthily!
The outlays required to run the place properly!
Also, to push on the work in this desolate spot
We should want a small share of the gold from your loot.   11380
Moreover, I must not conceal the fact that
From far off we'll have to cart timber, lime, slate.
The hauling's the people's, urged on from the pulpit,
The Church blesses all those who devoutly support it.

> *Departs.*

EMPEROR. The sin that I laid on my soul, Lord, is heavy!
  Those wretched magicians are costing me plenty.
ARCHBISHOP. [*Again coming back, with a deep bow*]
  Your Majesty, pardon! But now I remember:
  You granted that scoundrel the shores of the Empire.
  These, too, must fall under the ban, Sir, unless
  Penitently you assign all their income to us.   11390
EMPEROR. [*Exasperated*]
  But the land isn't there yet, it's still under water!
ARCHBISHOP. If the right's on one's side one can wait with
      composure.
EMPEROR. I might as well sign the entire Empire over!

ACT V

COUNTRYSIDE WITH SEASHORE

TRAVELER.

> There they stand, each dark, old linden,
> Hardy still, still flourishing—
> To see them once again, imagine,
> After years of voyaging!
> It's the same old place, same cottage
> Sheltered me when, overwhelmed
> By the stormy billows' upsurge,   11400
> I was shipwrecked on this strand.
> I would like to thank the worthy
> Couple who took care of me;
> But so old then, is it likely
> They're alive to welcome me?
> They were such kind, pious people!
> Knock, should I, or call aloud?
> —Are you there still, hospitable,
> Happy always to do good?

BAUCIS. [*A little old woman*]

> Hush, hush, Sir, my man is resting!   11410
> Quietly, for his dear sake!
> Long sleep lends him strength for working
> In the hours he's awake.

TRAVELER.

> Mother, is it you, the one I
> Owe such thanks, your man, too, both?
> By the mercy that you showed me
> In my youth, you saved my life.

> Are you Baucis, who refreshed my
> Brine-parched lips, gave me back breath?

[*Enter Philemon.*]

> Philemon, you! Who so bravely   11420
> Dragged my goods out of the surf,
> Who so quickly lit the beacon,
> Rang the silver-sounding bell!
> Providentially it was given
> You to save me from the gale.
>
> I must walk out to the seashore,
> View again the watery waste,
> Fall upon my knees in prayer
> To relieve my too charged breast.

[*He walks down to the dunes.*]

PHILEMON. [*To Baucis*]

> Hurry now and set the table   11430
> Mid the garden's greenery.
> What a shock he'll get, he'll marvel,
> Swear it's all some sorcery.

[*Joining the Traveler.*]

> Where the waves broke fiercely on you,
> Where you weltered in cruel seas,
> See, a garden now receives you,
> As if into Paradise.
> Older grown, I lacked the vigor
> To pitch in, assist the work;

My strength ebbed as in like measure,   11440
Grudgingly, the sea fell back.
Led by skillful masters, hardy
Workmen came, they diked and dammed,
Drove back waters once unruly:
Rulers where the sea had reigned.
Verdant meadow upon meadow,
Wood and garden, field and town—
Look, look, let the sight delight you,
For the sun will soon go down.
Far away white sails are making   11450
For their haven and night's rest,
Birdlike knowing for them's waiting
At the port their marine nest.
Only at the far horizon
Can you glimpse the azure sea;
Roundabout are peasants, townsmen,
Agriculture, industry.

[*The three at table in the garden.*]

BAUCIS.

Speechless, are you? Though you're starving,
Letting the good soup grow cool?

PHILEMON.

What he saw wants some explaining,   11460
You're a talker, tell him all.

BAUCIS.

Well, it was a wonder, no doubt,
But I'm troubled by it still.
For the whole thing didn't seem right,
Had about it something ill.

PHILEMON.

> Did the Emperor do wrong leasing
> That man the great sweep of shore?
> Didn't heralds this way passing
> Cry the news outside our door?
> Close by the first steps were taken,   11470
> Tents and shacks raised near our dunes;
> Soon a gleaming palace stood on
> Sand now turned into green lawns.

BAUCIS.

> In the daytime workmen sweated
> Fruitlessly with pick and spade;
> In the night where blue lights flitted
> Next day a dam stood there made.
> Men were sacrificed, I'm certain,
> Through the dark you heard them wail;
> Seawards fiery torrents spilt down,   11480
> Dawn came, there was a canal!
> Godless, he's a man who itches
> To possess our cottage, trees;
> Overbearing in his riches,
> He imagines we're his slaves.

PHILEMON.

> Yet he offered us good farmland
> On the soil that he reclaimed.

BAUCIS.

> Put no trust in what was swampland,
> Stick where you are, on high ground!

PHILEMON.

> Come, we'll walk out to the chapel,   11490
> Watch the sun sink to its rest,
> Ring the bell and kneeling, pray, all,
> Our old God in whom we trust.

FAUST'S PALACE

A large, formal garden. Broad, straight canal. Faust, now very old, walking about and thinking.

LYNCEUS THE WATCHMAN. [*Through a megaphone*]
    The sun declines, the last ships cheerly
    Homeward steer upon the tide,
    And in the canal a bulky
    Cargo ship has just arrived.
    Her colored pennants flutter gaily,
    Upon her yards swell her white sails;
    The sailors speak your name devoutly,   11500
    Now brightest fortune on you smiles.

[The bell sounds across the dunes.]

FAUST. [*Giving a start*]
    That damned ringing, I can't stand it—
    Like a gunshot in the dark!
    Before, my realm without a limit,
    Behind, a bell drives me berserk.
    Its derisive chiming taunts me—
    My estate, though huge, yet boundless
    You can't call it; how it haunts me
    Knowing that what I possess is
    Less than all. The mouldering kirk,   11510
    Dun cabin, linden grove—not mine,
    Not mine! And should I seek its shade
    For comfort, shadows queer, malign,
    Would make me quail, recoil afraid—
    A thorn stuck in my foot, my side.
    It's torture—far from here I'd fly.

WATCHMAN.   The beflagged ship, borne gently by
　　　The evening breeze, draws near the quay!
　　　Piled high upon its crowded decks
　　　Are chests and boxes, bales and sacks.   11520

　　　[*A fine craft loaded with goods from the four corners of the earth.*
Mephistopheles. The Three Mighty Men.]

CHORUS.
　　　　　Home, home at last,
　　　　　The harbor won!
　　　　　Hurrah the Master,
　　　　　Our Patròn!

　　　[*They disembark; the cargo is unloaded.*]

MEPHISTO.   Very well our venture went.
　　　Let him approve and we're content.
　　　With only two ships we sailed forth,
　　　Now twenty scrape against the wharf.
　　　The story of our deeds is told
　　　By what comes pouring from the hold.   11530
　　　Far out at sea your soul is free,
　　　Who stops to think there, uselessly?
　　　A ship is caught as you catch fish,
　　　What's called for's action, spirit, dash,
　　　And when you've bagged a catch of three,
　　　You grapple a fourth presently;
　　　As for the fifth one—well, good night!
　　　When yours the power, yours the right,
　　　No questions asked, what counts is what
　　　You're able to draw in your net.   11540
　　　If I know maritime affairs,

What they consist of, first, are wars,
Then trade, and lastly piracy:
Inseparable trinity.

THE THREE MIGHTY MEN.

No grateful word,
No smiling welcome!
You'd think the treasure
We have brought him
Smelt bad, such a
Face he pulled.   11550
A king's ransom
Leaves him cold.

MEPHISTO.

Don't expect
More out of him.
And recollect—
You helped yourselves already.

THE THREE.

Only to
Relieve our ennui.
We want, we do,
The loot shared fairly.   11560

MEPHISTO.

First carry it
Up to the hall,
Display the lot,
The whole rich haul.
When he lays his two eyes on
All that plunder,
He will reckon
Up things better
And show himself
No skinflint, he   11570

Will entertain us
Royally.
Tomorrow brings our dear jills here,
I'll see to it they're well cared for.

[*The cargo is carried off.*]

MEPHISTO. [*To Faust*] With beetling brows, a black expression,
Is how you welcome your good fortune,
Although your wisdom's been confirmed
And peace made between sea and land.
The flood, restrained, lets willingly
Your ships pass swiftly out to sea;   11580
You can boast that from this beach
The whole world lies within your reach.
Right here the project had its start,
Right here the first rough shack was built:
Where oars now make a busy splash,
The first picks scratched a shallow ditch.
Your great purpose, your men's toil,
Have won the prize of earth, sea, all.
From here—
FAUST.   Enough! How you go on.
Your *here* is why I'm so cast down.   11590
Resourceful man that you are, listen:
It stabs me, it does, to the heart,
Unbearable, a mad obsession
I blush with shame to speak about:
They must go, that poor old couple—
I'll have those lindens, won't be foiled!
They're few, yet not mine, how they rankle,
Spoil my possession of the world.
I mean to fix a scaffold to

The branches so that I may view   11600
All I've accomplished, comprehend
This great achievement of man's mind
In a glance: the broad lands won
For men to build their dwellings on,
Where teeming nations now may have
The space they need to work and thrive.

This, this, is the worst torment,
To have so much, yet still to want!
That bell's sound, the lindens' smell
Oppress, churchlike, tomblike, my soul.   11610
My will that's free and brooks no let
A patch of sand can bring up short.
Where's the cure for this deep ache?
The bell tolls and I go berserk.

MEPHISTO. Of course, of course! Yes, such vexation
Exasperates one out of reason.
Dear me, yes! That dinging, donging
Grates on every man of feeling,
Spoils the quiet of the evening
With its bimming and its bamming,   11620
Mixes into everything
From christening to burying—
As if between the *bam* and *bim*
Life were a mere interim.

FAUST. Their obstinacy, stubbornness,
Spoils for me my great success,
And heartsore I find that I tire
Of wishing to be a just squire.

MEPHISTO. Your tender conscience! I am startled—
The populations you've resettled!   11630

FAUST. Then clear them out, this very hour!

—You know the pretty house and garden
I picked out for them to live in.
MEPHISTO. I'll move them there and in a twinkling
They'll be happily housekeeping.
Set them up in a nice cottage,
They'll forgive us the rough usage.

[*He whistles shrilly. The Three appear.*]

You hear his Lordship! Go on, do it!
Tomorrow we will have our banquet.
THE THREE. The old boy greeted us so sourly;   11640
A lively feast is our due, surely.
MEPHISTO. [*To the audience*]
How humankind keeps on and on!
It's Naboth's vineyard once again.   [*1 Kings 21*]

DARK OF NIGHT

LYNCEUS THE WATCHMAN. [*Singing from the watchtower*]
Born sharp-eyed and called
To watch from this tower,
I look at the world
With such delight, pleasure.
Afar off I peer,
Look down at things nearer,
The moon and pale star,   11650
The deer crossing the pasture.
In all things my eyes see
Their eternal beauty,
And as all things please me,
With myself, too, I am pleased.
O fortunate eyes,

Whatever you've seen,
Let it be what it was,
Always lovely it's been.

[*Pause.*]

But I've not been posted up here   11660
Only for my own delight—
What is that there, there, that horror,
Glaring in the dark of night?
I see bright sparks upwards streaming,
From the grove of linden trees,
Fire ever redder flaming,
Fanned to fury by the breeze.
It's the cottage, fiercely blazing,
Damp and mossgrown though it stood.
Help! Help! But it's useless screaming   11670
When there's no one by who could
Those good people help—they took
So much care for fear of fire,
Now they're gasping in its smoke—
What, oh what misfortune—dire!
Worse and worse! There's little hope,
Trapped inside the flaming timbers,
The old people can escape
The inferno of hot embers.
Fire licking upward scorches   11680
Leaves and twigs into a blaze
Which, igniting the dry branches,
Limb after limb the hot flames raze.
Why must my eyes have to witness
Such things? Have so far a sight?
There! The chapel now collapses
Under all the crushing weight,
Writhing tongues of flame mount higher

To the lindens' very tops
And the hollow trunks, afire,   11690
Crimson glow down to their roots.

[*Long pause, then concluding.*]

What delighted our eyes once,
With all our yesterdays gone hence!
FAUST. [*On a balcony overlooking the dunes*]
That mournful strain! It is my watchman
'S grieving song, come tardily.
Oh, I repent me of my action,
It was done too hastily.
If the lindens now are only
A charred waste, well, I'll have built
A lookout place from where serenely   11700
I'll contemplate the infinite;
See the house, too, the old couple
Occupy now happily.
There they'll pass their last days, grateful
For my magnanimity.
MEPHISTO AND THE THREE. [*Speaking from below*]
At top speed we've come running here!
Excuse us, it went badly, sir.
We knocked and banged and knocked again,
Still no one came to let us in.
We shook the old door so hard that   11710
It gave and at our feet fell flat.
We shouted, threatened, cursed till hoarse—
In vain, there was no answering voice.
It's that way always, people don't
Hear a thing because they won't!
So not delaying the least bit,

In we went and cleared them out.
They didn't suffer much, the pair,
Fright carried them off then and there.
A stranger hiding in the place   11720
Put up a fight—for a short space.
In the mêlée embers from
The hearth were scattered round the room;
Some straw ignited and the fierce fire
Now makes those three their funeral pyre.

FAUST. You didn't hear a word I said!
Exchange, I meant, thugs, not a raid.
I curse your mindless violence—
The three of you can share my curse!

CHORUS. How they din it in to you: 11730
What the Master wants, you do.
But when you show your mettle, zeal,
You risk house, home—and life as well.

[They go off.]

FAUST. [*On the balcony*] The stars put out their light, the fire
Dies down, soon it will expire;
A chill wind still is fanning it,
Blows wisps of smoke this way from it.
So quick commanded, done so quick!
—What shapes are these, dim, shadowlike?

MIDNIGHT

Four gray women appear.

THE FIRST. The name that I'm called by is Lack.
THE SECOND.   Mine's Default.   11740
THE THIRD. The name that I'm called by is Care,
THE FOURTH.   Mine is Dearth.

LACK, DEFAULT, DEARTH.

    The place is locked up, there's no getting in there;

    The fellow is rich, so he's not our affair.

LACK. In there I'm a shadow.

DEFAULT.   I'm a nothing, a nought.

DEARTH. The pampered don't even vouchsafe me a thought.

CARE. You mayn't, my sisters, go in, you're denied.

    By the keyhole Care slips without hindrance inside.

                                  [Care disappears.]

LACK. Here is no place for us, gray sisters, away!

DEFAULT. I'll walk by your side, keep you close company.

DEARTH. And hard on your heels follows both of you, Dearth.   11750

LACK, DEFAULT, DEARTH.

    Above pass the clouds, the stars dim their brilliance,

    Behind, look, look behind, far away in the distance,

    There he comes, our brother, there he comes—who but Death!

FAUST. *[In the palace]*

    I saw four come, three only went.

    I've no idea what their words meant—

    One echoed faintly, was it . . . dearth?

    Then rhyming dismally came . . . death.

    It had a hollow, ghostly note.

    I've still not won my freedom yet.

    If only I could give up sorcery,   11760

    Unlearn my spells, put magic by entirely,

    And face you, Nature, simply as a man,

    It would be worth it being human then—

    As I was once, before I tampered with

    The things of darkness, cursed the world, myself,

    Impiously. Now ghosts so fill the air,

    No matter where we turn, right, left, they're there.

    The day dawns smiling, rational and bright,

We're tangled in a net of dreams at night.
From green fields we come home contentedly,   11770
A bird croaks: meaning what?—catastrophe!
Bedeviled by superstitions, we imagine
The least thing is a sign, a portent, omen.
And so we tremble, feeling lost, alone.
The door creaks and we stiffen—there's no one.

                                                    [*Stiffens.*]

—Is someone there?
CARE.   Yes, since you ask, dear Sir.
FAUST. Who are you then?
CARE.   Enough that I am here.
FAUST. [*Enraged*]
    Clear out, you hag!
CARE.   My place is here, where else?
FAUST. [*Mastering his rage, to himself*]
    Remember, you've renounced your magic spells!
CARE.
        Stop your ears so you don't hear me,   11780
        You can't shut your heart against me,
        Taking this shape, then another,
        I exercise my grim power,
        No matter where, on land, at sea,
        I dog your heels anxiously,
        Never sought and always found,
        Cosied up to now, now scorned.
        Never known, have you, Dame Care?
FAUST. I've rushed about the world for many a year,
    Seized what I had a mind to, everywhere.   11790
    It didn't please me?—goodbye, did I care!
    On what escaped me didn't waste a tear.
    My sole wish has been what?—to desire,
    Sate my desire and desire again, all over.

I stormed through life in grand style, mightily,
But wiser now, I act more thoughtfully.
I've learned enough about the world we live in,
What lies beyond is closed to human vision.
The man's a fool who, gazing up, imagines
Above the clouds his like dwell in the heavens.   11800
With feet well planted let him look about the earth,
This world speaks volumes to a man of worth.
What business has he with eternity?
What he perceives, let him make his its truth,
And living life so, walk his earthly path.
If teased by ghosts, march forwards imperturbably,
In pressing onwards always, find his joy, his torment,
A being never satisfied, not for a moment.

CARE.

    Whom I once get hold of, he will
    Find the whole world pointless, futile.   11810
    Over him gloom casts its dun net,
    Blinding him to sunrise, sunset,
    Though possessing all his senses,
    Inwardly there's only darkness,
    Let him own great heaps of riches,
    It's as if they're someone else's,
    To him fortune and misfortune
    Only are some queer, strange notion,
    Although plenty's rich horn over-
    Flows for him, he faints from hunger,   11820
    Everything he puts off, whether
    He likes it or not, till later;
    Always waiting, hesitating,
    Nothing ever consummating.

FAUST. Enough! You'll get nowhere with me!
    I shut my ears against such rubbish.

That stupefying litany
Would make the wisest man turn foolish.

CARE.

Come or go? He can't decide, he's
At a loss, he shilly-shallies,   11830
On a straight, well-trodden pathway
Stumbles, bumbles, makes no headway,
More and more confused, he can't see
Anything as it is clearly,
Trouble to himself, to wife, all,
Breathing hard, afraid he'll stifle,
Neither stifling, neither living,
Obstinately persevering,
Keeping on and on, feet dragging,
Crossly yielding, duty lagging,   11840
Now he's free, oppressed now, quaking,
Sleeping badly, dully waking,
Stuck fast where he is until he's
Ripe for sending down to Hades.

FAUST. Damned specters! This is just what you've done to
Poor suffering mankind time and time again,
Turned even the most routine, dull day into
An ugly nightmare of confusion, pain.
It's hard, I know, to send our demons packing,
The bond with them is stringent, who can break it?   11850
Your power, Care, is great, insidious, cunning,
Yet I refuse to recognize it!

CARE.

You do, do you? Well, as I vanish,
Feel it in my parting curse at last.
The human race is blind from start to finish:
Blindness strike you down, too, Faust!

[*She breathes on him and leaves.*]

FAUST. [*Blinded*]
The night seems darker, presses closer round me,
Yet all is clear, as bright as day, within.
If I'm to get the work done I must hurry,
It needs the Master's voice to move things on.   11860
—Wake up, you fellows, turn to with a good will,
Let me see realized all that I designed;
Get busy now with mattock, pick, and shovel
And make the earth fly in the plot you have been assigned.
With discipline and diligence, I promise,
You'll earn yourselves a very handsome bonus.
To get a great work done one mind's
Enough to rule a thousand hinds.

GREAT FORECOURT OF THE PALACE

Torches.

MEPHISTO. [*As overseer leading the way*]
Get a move on! Move, come on,
You wambling, shambling creatures!   11870
You makeshift things of skin and bone,
Poor patched up, half-made natures!
LEMURS. [*In chorus*]
At once before you here we stand,
And best as we can grasp it,
What it's about's a lot of land
And we're supposed to have it.

We've brought a stack of sharp stakes here,
Surveyor's chains for measuring;

But why you called us to appear
We've trouble in remembering.   11880

MEPHISTO.   It's not an engineering job we've got,
Just use as measure your own length and breadth.
The tallest one of you, let him lie flat,
You others mark his outline in the turf.
Then dig a rectilinear hole with the same shape
Was digged for our fathers, longish, deep.
From palace to a narrow room,
That's the stupid end to which things come.

LEMURS.   [*Digging with clownish gestures*]
In youth when I did love, did love,
Methought it very sweet,   11890
From where the reed shrilled, reel spun round,
I could not keep my feet.

But stealing age put out his crutch
And tripped me so I fell flat,
I stumbled through death's open door—
Why, why was it not kept shut!

FAUST.   [*Coming out of the palace, feeling his way by the doorposts*]
I hear the clink of spades, how happily!
It is my men, their labors plying,
The land and water reconciling
By fixing for the waves their boundary,   11900
Confining in strict bonds the flooding tide.

MEPHISTO.   [*Aside*]
Yet your exertions only serve our side:
Those dikes and dams, they're only something good for
The demon Neptune to gulp down with pleasure.
No matter what you do, it's hopeless,
Your schemes, your energy, all useless;
The elements work with us in close union

Whose end result is death, destruction, ruin.

FAUST. Overseer!

MEPHISTO.   Here!

FAUST.   Use every means

To round up more and more construction gangs.   11910
Encourage them with smiles, drive them with curses,
Push them, press them, promise them higher wages.
Daily let me have a full report
How far along with the ditch the men have got.

MEPHISTO. [*Under his breath*]

From the report my people gave,
It's no ditch, it's a grave.

FAUST. At the foot of the hills there's a fen
Befouling the good work so far done.
To drain that pestilential swamp would be
A final, crowning victory.   11920
It would open up to millions space
In which to work, possess a dwelling place;
If not entirely safe, yet safe enough
For men to lead a free and active life.
Fields green and fruitful! Men and beasts at ease
Upon this newest earth, a second paradise,
Whose shelter is the massive looming barrier
A bold, industrious people raised by their hard labor,
A veritable Eden here inside,
Although the flood foam at the brink outside!   11930
A crack appearing, the sea leaks in, then each
By common impulse race to repair the breach.
Yes, I believe, uphold as my fixed faith,
As the ultimate truth we human creatures know:
He only earns his freedom, life itself,
Who daily strives to conquer it anew.
So, so we'd pass, amid the dangers here,

As child, grown man, and ancient, the busy year.
To see such life, such glad activity!
To stand with free men on ground that is free!   11940
Then, then, I might say to the passing moment,
"Linger awhile, you are so fair!
The footprints of my earthly passage cannot
Even after eons disappear."
Foreseeing such scenes of unmatched contentment,
I now enjoy the highest, supreme moment.

[*Faust collapses; the Lemurs catch him and lay him on the
ground.*]

MEPHISTO. No pleasure was enough for him, no happiness,
    Forever running after this, that, anything,
    And the poor wretch, imagine, wants to cling
    To this last moment, empty, meaningless.   11950
    Mightily he withstood me, I allow,
    But Master Time has laid the old man low.
    His clock has stopped—
CHORUS.   Stopped, yes. As midnight still.
    The hands drop off—
MEPHISTO.   Drop off, and all is nil.
CHORUS. Over, done!
MEPHISTO.   That's stupid—*over, done!*
    What's been and what has never been—they're one,
    The same! What point is there in all of this creating
    When back created things are dragged to nothing?
    "It's over, done!" Really, what does that mean?
    It means it just as well might not have been.   11960
    Yet round and round it goes, Creation, as if real!
    For me the Eternally-Nothing has more appeal.

BURIAL

LEMUR. [*Solo*]
>> Who built this house, so illy made
>>> With a rude spade and shovel?

LEMURS. [*Chorus*]
>> For you, lank guest, in burlap dressed,
>>> It's good enough, it's ample.

LEMUR. [*Solo*]
>> Who furnished it? So bare the place,
>>> No table, chairs nor bedstead.

LEMURS. [*Chorus*]
>> Its things were held on a short lease,
>>> Time ran, the lease expired.   11970

MEPHISTO. Here's the body, if the soul should try
> Eluding me, I will instantly whip out
> The bond he signed in blood. Alas, today
> There are so many ways by which to cheat
> The Devil of his due. Things tried and true,
> Our ancient practice and procedure,
> Is frowned upon, and our new
> Has not, it seemed, found overwhelming favor.
> I could have managed things all by myself once,
> These days I need to send down for assistance.   11980

> No, it's a bad time now for us.
> Old customs, ancient rights in us invested,
> You can't rely on. Once it was the case,
> The last breath breathed, why then the soul departed.
> I watched and waited like a cat,
> Then pounced, claws out—snap, mine, mine—caught!
> But now it hesitates, it hangs back, nervous,
> And doesn't want to leave the loathsome carcass,

Whose elements, in fierce war with each other,
Finally compel it to make an ignoble departure.   11990
Day and night I'm plagued, not knowing where
Or when or how the damned thing will appear.
Death's grown feeble, lost his old dispatch,
Has he come, you wonder anxiously
As you watch the stiffened members greedily—
Deceived! Again the body stirs, limbs stretch.

[*Conjuring with fantastic, drill-sergeant gestures*]

Come on, step lively, rally here to me,
You straight- and crook-horned lords of the dark below,
You devils of the old, true pedigree,
And bring the jaws of Hell along with you!   12000
It has a lot of jaws, Hell, needless to relate,
For swallowing souls according to their standing;
From now on, though, we shan't differentiate:
All's liberal now and so must be man's ending.
                    [*Hell's jaws yawn horridly on the left.*]
The tusks unclose, from the gaping gullet
A raging flood of flames pours out furiously,
And in the boiling clouds of smoke behind it
I see the Fiery City, burning eternally.
The red surge beats right up against the teeth,
The damned swim up it, desperate to escape,   12010
The huge hyena jaws shut with a snap
And once again they flounder in the surf.
There's lots more going on, too, in the corners—
The horrors crammed inside so little room!
You're right to terrify the stubborn sinners
Who still think all is dream, deception, sham.

[*To the fat devils with short, straight horns.*]

You demons with your great guts, flaming cheeks,
How your fat shines with the true sulfurous sweat!
You blocks, you stumps, with short, unmoving necks,
Look, do you see a phosphorescent glint?   12020
Know that's winged Psyche, that's the little soul:
Pluck off its wings, what is it, just a worm!
When it creeps out, I'll stamp it with my seal,
Then down with it into Hell's fire storm.

Your duty, fat fiends, is to mount
A guard upon the lower region.
Whether the soul has its preferred resort
Below the waistline, no one can be certain,
But in the navel it feels right at home—
Take care or whish! right past you it will zoom.   12030

[*To the lanky devils with long, crooked horns.*]

You clowns who sway on thin shanks, giantlike,
Reach up and with your sharp claws rake
The air above, about him, keep right at it
So as to catch the fluttering, fleeting spirit!
In its decaying old house, I will bet,
It's not so pleasant, soon it must fly out.

[*Burst of light* (Gloria) *from above.*]

The Heavenly Host.
        Envoys of heaven,
        Angelic beings,
        Follow us flying,

Slowly, unhurrying,   12040
Bringing sinners forgiveness.
Dust restoring to life!
With loving-kindness
Staying your passing,
For all natures tracing
The celestial path!

MEPHISTO. What jarring, jangling tones are those I hear,
Accompanying that unwelcome glare?
The sort of inept, unsexed, shrill falsetto
The godly's pious, sniveling taste delights so.   12050
You know how in our wickedest hour we sought
To cut mankind off right at its primal root.
Well, the most shameful thing we could devise
Is just what in their piety they prize.

Hymn-singing here they come, the frauds, so unctuous!
They steal souls from us, lie, cheat, plagiarize
Our own methods which they use against us:
They're devils, too, but wearing a disguise.
Let them win here, your shame shall know no end,
So stand fast round the graveside, every fiend!   12060

CHORUS OF ANGELS. [Scattering roses]
Roses that dazzling show,
Roses that crimson glow,
The air perfuming
With life-giving balm!
Fluttering, hovering,
As if, leaf-winged, flying—
Your petals unfolding,
Burst into bloom!

Appear now, appear, Spring,
In red and green dressed,   12070

Paradisiac joys bring
To him here at rest!

MEPHISTO. [*To the devils*]

You duck, you flinch! Is that what devils do?
Get back, fools, into your places!
Never mind them and their roses!
It's plain to see the angels mean to snow
You hot fellows under their pink drift,
But your foul breath makes tender petals shrivel,
So huff and puff with all your lungs, each devil.
—Enough! The swarming blossoms, fading, wilt;   12080
Go easy! Clap your mouths, your noses shut!
It's too hard, too hot, all your huffing, puffing;
You're so infernally immoderate!
The stuff's not only dried up, it is burning,
And drifts down on us as bright, stinging sparks—
Hold steady, never waver, close up ranks!
—Their courage fails them, gone from them's their strength,
The devils feel a strange, seductive warmth.

CHORUS OF ANGELS.

Blessed blooms shower,
Dancing flames scatter   12090
Love all about,
Bliss without stop,
All that hearts wish for—
Like words of truth burning
Bright in the sky,
For all our host making
Eternal day!

MEPHISTO. Oh damn these dolts, befuddled, woozy!

The lot of them knocked topsy-turvy,
They backward somersault and tumble   12100
Tail first down to Hell, each devil.

Enjoy your steambath which you well deserve!
But as for me, I'm here and I won't swerve.

[*Flailing his arms wildly to repel the roses.*]

Away, false lights, for all your brilliancy
What are you, caught?—nasty, jellyish matter.
Go flutter somewhere else and let me be!
—They stick to my neck, burn like pitch and sulfur.

CHORUS OF ANGELS.

What has no part in you,
You must avoid it,
What agitates you so,   12110
Never endure it!
If you are hard beset,
Our strength is stronger yet,
Love only lovers leads
Upwards to us the blest.

MEPHISTO. My head, my heart, my liver, they burn so!
It's superdiabolical, this power,
Much sharper, fiercer, hotter than Hellfire,
Oh it beats anything below!
So this is why the despised lover   12120
Screws his neck round to spy out
The least sign of his sweetheart—

As I do, too! Why should my head be turned
By enemies that I have always scorned,
The sight of whom used to arouse my fury?
What thing's got hold of me, what unknown force,
So that I'm tongue-tied, can no longer curse,
And look with longing at boys who are pretty?
If I'm made a poor fool of, in my folly,

They'll call me fool forever, don't I know it!   12130
And though my hatred for them has no limit,
They seem, the imps, so tempting, teasing, lovely!

You darling children, tell, me, do—
Don't you belong to Lucifer's tribe too?
I'd like to kiss each pretty one of you!
Just at the right time, it seems, you appear,
So natural it feels, no strain or fuss,
As if we got together every year.
So sly you are, tom cat-ish, lecherous,
Each time I look at you you're looking better.   12140
Come nearer, let me have a closer look!
CHORUS OF ANGELS. We're coming, yes, but why do you draw back?
Stay where you are, unflinching, if you're able.

[*The angels, filling up the stage, force Mephistopheles to the front.*]

MEPHISTO. Spirits damned we are, you say,
But you are the real witchery,
Indifferently seducing male and female.
—What a bleak, unsatisfactory affair!
Call this the right romantic atmosphere?
My whole body's in a sweat, a fever,
I hardly notice how my burned neck pains me   12150
—You flutter this way, that way, come down lower
And swing those hips a little more profanely.
It suits you fine, your gravity,
But do smile once, just once, at me.
How I would be delighted by it—
I mean the way that lovers do it—
A softening around the mouth, no more!
You tall one, I like you the best, beshrew me!

That priestly air detracts from your allure,
Do look at me, please, just a little lewdly!   12160
Also, that long shirt's much too modest for you;
You're overdressed, more nudity's more fitting—
Around they turn and offer me a rear view!
Those young devils are just too, too fetching!

CHORUS OF ANGELS.

    Towards celestial clarity
    Each loving flame turn,
    Let truth the self-condemned
    Heal finally,
    So that from evil
    They are redeemed,   12170
    And with the troops of blest
    Also are blest.

MEPHISTO. [*Getting a grip on himself*]

What's happened to me?—Joblike I've been struck
From head to foot with boils so that I shudder
To see myself. Yet still when I look deeper,
Farther, in—unbeaten! trusting ever
To my descent from Hell's old hardy stock:
The Devil's parts still full of pith and grit,
He's got a rash, that's all, from his love-fit.
The horrid flames have burnt down, flicker out,   12180
And as the Devil should: I curse you, the whole lot!

CHORUS OF ANGELS.

    O sacred fire!
    Round whom you hover
    With the good life discover
    Celestial bliss.
    Together all rise,
    Let sound your praise!

Air now is pure,
Spirit breathes clear.

MEPHISTO. [*Looking around*]

What's happened?—All gone, disappeared, they have!   12190
You youngsters caught me, you did, off my guard
And made off with the booty heavenward!
So that's why they were hanging round this grave.
I've lost a rare prize, long looked for reward;
From under my nose they stole craftily
The great soul that was pledged me solemnly.

And where is there a court I can appeal to,
Restore to me what I'm owed rightfully?
In my old age to let myself be fooled so—
And who's to blame for the fiasco, me!   12200
Oh, I have made a mess of things, I have;
All that great effort simply thrown away,
And why? A vulgar itch, absurd desire—love!—
Which turned the tough old Devil shamefully
Into a poor milksop. For me to carry
On like that, the shrewd, all-knowing Fiend,
Shows it was no small thing, the childish folly
That got the better of me in the end.

MOUNTAIN RAVINES

*A wilderness of forest and rock, with holy anchorites living in
clefts up and down the mountainside.*

CHORUS AND ECHO.

Woods sway and lean toward us,
Cliffs beetle over us,   12210
Roots clutch crags in their grip,

Trees crowd trees on the slope,
Wave, splashing, follows wave,
Deep, deep caves shelter give,
Lions forget to growl,
Like tame cats round us prowl,
Honoring this sacred seat,
Heavenly love's retreat.

PATER ECSTATICUS. [*Floating up and down above the ground*]

Fire of endless bliss,
Love's searing spirit-kiss,   12220
Heart filled with scalding blood,
God-joy a foaming flood!
Arrows, transfix this flesh,
Lances, defeat this flesh,
Clubs, fall and smash this flesh,
Lightnings, make ash this flesh,
Till all things valueless
Dwindle to nothingness
And the pure love alone
Starlike forever burn!   12230

PATER PROFUNDUS. [*Far below*]

The chasm at my feet, dark, yawning,
Rests on a chasm deeper still,
A thousand streams, their waters joining,
In a cascade terrific fall;
The tree's own life, its strength from nature,
Its trunk lifts skywards straight and tall—
All, all, show love's almighty power
That shapes all things, cares for them all.

The storm breaks round me, fiercely howling,
The woods, ravines, all seem to quake,   12240
And yet, swelled by the deluge falling,

The torrent plunges down the rock
To water lovingly the valley;
The lightning burns the overcast
And clears the air, now smelling freshly,
Of all its foulness, dankness, mist—

All love proclaim! the creating power
By which the whole world is embraced.
Oh kindle, too, in me your fire,
Whose thoughts, disordered, cold, depressed,   12250
Inside the cage of dull sense languish,
Tormented, helpless, hard beset!
Dear God, relieve my spirit's anguish,
My needy heart illuminate!

PATER SERAPHICUS. [*Midway up*]
What, a rosy dawn cloud is it,
Above the grove of pines' fringed crown?
I believe I know what's in it,
Souls upgathered when just born.

CHORUS OF BOY SOULS.
Where, where will it end, our journey?
Tell us, Father, who we are.   12260
Our existence is so happy,
Weighs on us as light as air.

PATER SERAPHICUS.
Boys born at the stroke of midnight,
Snatched away as life began;
For their parents a sad forfeit,
For the angel host, pure gain.
—You can feel love's presence near you,
Venture closer, nothing fear;
Life's hard ways have never scarred you,
Lucky spirits that you are!   12270

Children, come and enter into
My old earth-accustomed eyes;
Through them you can look about you,
View the world that round you lies.

[*He takes them into himself.*]

These are trees, these precipices,
Over which with awful force
Water in a torrent rushes,
Shortening its downward course.

BOY SOULS. [*From inside*]
Yes, a scene sublime, impressive,
But too gloomy, is our thought,   12280
Makes us tremble, apprehensive—
Noble sir, may we depart?

PATER SERAPHICUS.
Higher rise, still higher, growing
Stronger imperceptibly,
Near the Divine Presence gaining
A more perfect purity!
What is it the spirit thrives on,
What fills the ethereal space?
Endless love whose revelation
Blitheness brings, eternal bliss.   12290

BOY SOULS. [*Circling the highest peaks*]
All join hands, turning
Round in a ring!
Your voices raising,
Holily sing!
Divinely schooled at last,
You can feel sure

You will behold at last
Him you revere.

ANGELS. [*Hovering in the upper air, carrying Faust's immortal part*]
The spirit world's most noble soul
Is saved from deathly Satan.   12300
"Who strives, and keeps on striving still,
For him there is salvation."
And if love, pinnacled on high,
Has also watched out for him,
The angelic legions of the sky
Will fly round him in welcome.

THE YOUNGER ANGELS.
With the roses we were given
By much-loving, holy women—
Penitents—we won the battle
For this soul against the Devil: 12310
Our great work is now completed.
Taking to their heels, the wicked
Spirits scattered when we pelted
Them with rosebuds: not their wonted
Hellish torments but the tortured
Anguish love inflicts, they suffered.
Even their old captain, Satan,
Winced to feel himself love-smitten.
We've prevailed! Exult, all Heaven!

THE MATURER ANGELS.
This human scrap, we find,   12320
'S painful to carry,
Even if bleached and burned,
Still impure, earthy.
Once spirit has been joined
Fast to gross nature,
Parting them, that are wound

So close together,
Is something far above
Angelic power:
Only Eternal Love   12330
Can the two sever.

THE YOUNGER ANGELS.

All round that rocky height
Cloudlets are sailing:
Can they be spirits that
My eyes are spying?
Yes, it's becoming clear,
I see a troop appear
Of blessed children,
Who, freed from earth's sore weight,
Turn in a ring,   12340
Uplifted with delight
In the new spring
Weather of Heaven.
Let him begin with them
Upwards to mount,
Rise with them, reach with them
The crowning height.

BOY SOULS.

We welcome gladly
This new, unfledged soul!
The angels' assurance   12350
Embraces us all.
All earthly remnants
Strip away from him—
Soon, look, how lovely
Holiness makes him!

DOCTOR MARIANUS. [*In the highest, barest, purest cell*]
Here nothing blocks the view,

The mind is uplifted,
Women float skywards, to
Heaven exalted.
In their midst, glorious,   12360
The Queen of Heaven,
Star-crowned, victorious,
Sublimest woman.

[*Ecstatically.*]

Under the stretched tent of sky,
Empress, Mother, Virgin,
Let me view your mystery,
Grant my eyes such vision!
Solemn, tender feelings move
In my man's breast for you,
Don't, oh don't refuse the love   12370
That I offer to you.

Our courage nothing daunts,
By your glory summoned,
Milder burn our zealous hearts,
By your pity softened.
Purest maid that's ever been!
Womanhood's example!
This world's Mistress, chosen Queen!
The gods' peer and equal!

Small clouds float round her   12380
In the blue heaven:
Penitents they are,
Too-loving women,
At her knees crowding,
Her atmosphere breathing,
For grace imploring.

Immaculate and sacrosanct,
Yet it's not forbidden
That rejoicing you are thanked
By these fallen women.   12390
How should they, compliant, weak,
Not yield to temptation?
Who by his own strength can break
Out of lust's close prison?
On slippery ground how easily
The foot meets with mischances,
Who's not seduced by flattery,
By amorous sighs and glances?

[*The Mater Gloriosa floats by.*]

CHORUS OF PENITENTS.
As up to Heaven
You pass, Mary, listen,   12400
Hear our petition!
Lady beyond compare,
Full of grace, hear, O hear!
MAGNA PECCATRIX. [*Luke 7:37*]
By the dear love which, defiant
Of the Pharisees' derision,
Bathed your son's feet in its fragrant
Balsam tears as in a fountain,
By the jar which generously
Dripped sweet-smelling unction on them,
By the hair which rapturously   12410
Rubbed his sacred limbs to dry them—
MULIER SAMARITANA. [*John 4*]
By the well where Abraham led
Flocks of sheep and goats to water,

By the pail which, when he thirsted,
Cooled the lips of our Savior,
By the streams of living water
Pouring out from that pure fountain
Prodigally and forever,
Flowing through all of creation—

MARIA AEGYPTIACA. [*Acta Sanctorum*]

By the sacred place in which they   12420
Laid our Lord to rest in earth,
By the unseen arm that pushed me
From the door and warned me off,
By the forty years I dwelt in
Desert wastes, my sins atoned,
By the blessed farewell written
With my finger in the sand—

ALL THREE.

You who never turn away from
Sinners overwhelmed by scandal,
Who the comfort penance brings them   12430
Augment into bliss eternal,
Pardon, too, this girl who only
Fell once, hardly conscious of it,
Lavish on her your sweet mercy,
Surely, good soul, she deserves it!

ONE OF THE PENITENTS. [*Formerly called Gretchen, pressing up
to her*]

Look, Lady without peer,
Shining resplendently,
Down at me happily
Kneeling here,
Look!   12440
He's been restored to me

Him I adored, now free,
He has come back!

BOY SOULS. [*Circling nearer*]
He's bigger grown, stronger than
We are, already,
For our faithful care of him,
We'll be repaid amply.
How soon in our innocence
Death came to snatch us,
But with his experience,   12450
How much he can teach us.

THE PENITENT. [*Gretchen*]
A novice in the spirit chorus,
His newborn self he hardly knows,
How renewed life within him courses,
How soon one of the blest he grows!
See how the last threads still attaching
His striving spirit to the earth
He breaks, and clad in celestial clothing
Appears in all of youth's first strength!
Oh let me, Mary, be his teacher,   12460
He's dazzled still in the new dawn!

MATER GLORIOSA.
Rise up to higher spheres and higher!
With you before, he'll follow soon.

DOCTOR MARIANUS. [*Fallen on his face in adoration*]
Look up, chastened, contrite hearts,
To those saving features,
Thankful for the bliss awaits
All transfigured natures!
Every better purpose turn
To her sacred service!

—Be, O Virgin, Mother, Queen,   12470
Goddess, to us gracious!

CHORUS MYSTICUS.

Everything transitory
Is symbolic only;
All insufficiency
Here is made good;
The not expressible
Here is pure word;
Woman eternally
Shows us the road.   12479

NOTES

The Faust legend originated in sixteenth-century Germany. It is that very rare thing, a modern myth. Myths are stories that made part of pagan systems of religious belief. When belief declined, many remained current as traditional tales; in the modern era these were kept alive as matter for poetry, as they still are in some degree to this day. A rough definition of myth is: stories that account for primary things, such as the beginning of the world and other beginnings, life and death, natural and unnatural phenomena, the lives of gods and goddesses, heroes and heroines.

Mythic stories, whether in prose or verse, are told poetically, by image and metaphor. The idea of myths as delightful or frightening fictions—entertaining lies—is the misunderstanding of a time for which the only kind of truth is scientific truth.

The original, primitive Faust myth concerns a scholar and magician of the sixteenth century who makes a pact with the Devil by which he is granted a term of twenty-four years in which to know "the grounds of all things in heaven and on earth," at the end of which term, in return, his body and soul become forfeit to Hell. The theme of Faust was seized on by sophisticated, mainly German poets, and also opera composers, and variously interpreted. English literature's one important Faust work is Christopher Marlowe's *Tragical History of Doctor Faustus,* distinguished by its impassioned blank verse. Goethe's play (or play/poem) is one such version of the myth, and its greatest.

In his very early twenties Goethe wrote a Faust composition that was lost or discarded, a manuscript of which turned up near the end of the nineteenth century. That is known as the *Urfaust.* A notable feature of the *Urfaust,* not present in the original legend, is Faust's seduction of Gretchen (Margarete). Most of the *Urfaust* was taken up into *Faust: Part One.*

Three compositions precede the start of the work: "Dedication," "Prelude in the Theater," and "Prologue in Heaven." These were introduced after the completion of *Part One*, in Goethe's middle age. The work proper begins with the scene "Night," in Faust's study. Placed first and read first, the prefaces have come to represent its commencement.

Dedication. Composed in 1797 when the no longer young Goethe determined to resume work on his Faust play, which he had begun to write more than two decades earlier.

PART ONE

Line

(1) *figures shifting, spectral.* Characters remembered from his first attempts.

(27) *Aeolian harp.* Wind harp. A traditional image expressing inspiration's coming (or seeming to come) from without to awaken imagination, as the wind awakens the harp into sound.

(39) *The posts are up.* Manager, poet, and clown are members of a traveling theatrical troupe which must erect a temporary stage whenever there is no building that will serve.

(44) *a fix like this one.* The fiction is that curtain time is fast approaching and the company is still without a script.

(before 249) *Mephistopheles.* Derivation of the name is uncertain. It first appears in 1587 in Germany in a popular narration *(Volksbuch)* of the Faust legend, followed soon after (1588) in England in Marlowe's *Doctor Faustus.*

(249–50) *The sun . . . sounds his music . . . brother sphere.* The music of the spheres. "There's not the smallest orb which thou beholdest / But in his motion like an angel sings, / Still quiring to the young-eyed cherubims." *Merchant of Venice,* V.i.60 ff.

(288) *Earth's little god.* The Renaissance in its reborn confidence exalted humanity to the skies. ("What a piece of work is man, how noble in reason . . . how like a god." *Hamlet* II.ii.300.) To the jeerer Mephisto he is a "queer fish" (289), a "grasshopper" (295), whose little leaps are futile attempts to attain a height from which to gain comprehension of the world he lives in.

(307) *Doctor.* Of philosophy.

(307) *My good servant.* Job 1:8.

(320) *Would you care to bet on that?* Mephistopheles' challenge, that he can seduce Faust, is modeled on the testing of Job by Satan. God agrees, not to a

bet but to a test. For the All-knowing, who knows all, to bet with Mephisto would make Him what at the racetrack is called a tout. But the underminer of divinity will have it that it's a bet. For Faust, too, later, it is a bet.

(343) *Dust he'll eat.* Gen. 3:4.

(364–66) *philosophy / Law . . . medecine . . . theology.* The four pillars of medieval learning that continued to stand as late as to the end of the nineteenth century.

(389) *magic.* Faust has turned to white magic, which seeks to know the ultimate source of things. With Mephisto, he turns to black magic.

(398) *words, words, words.* A contemptuous dismissal of the scholastic mind of medieval Christianity and its contending terminological dogmatics (e.g., homoousia, homoiousia, heteroousia).

(439) *Nostradamus.* Sixteenth-century French physician and astrologer whose book of prophecies enjoyed widespread credence.

(bef. 449) *Sign of the Macrocosm.* Sign of "all" that "is woven one" (465). It is a sign only, not an existing spirit; Faust rejects it.

(479) *Spirit of Earth.* Spirit of the physical world, of Nature. A being, not an abstract sign: it rejects Faust.

(507) *superman.* One whose ambitions exceed all human measure. It has nothing of the racist meaning given it by the Nazis.

(538) *famulus.* Academic assistant.

(600) *seven-sealed book.* Rev. 5:1.

(668) *Care.* The enemy of aspiration, venturesomeness, joy. She figures more largely—quite sinisterly—in *Part Two*, lines 11741ff.

(701) *old scrolls.* Old indeed. Scrolls went out of use long before Faust's time.

(902) *St. Andrew's Night.* November 30, when young virgins might have visions of delight and glimpse their destined husbands.

(965) *Here I am human.* Some read this line as expressing Faust's feeling, not the people's.

(1065–67) *Lion . . . White Lily.* Chemical substances as poetically named in the alchemical lore, mixed together ("wedded") in a retort.

(1072) *young Queen.* The precipitate obtained by heating the mixture and passing the vapor through a series of vessels ("from one bridal chamber to another"). Goethe himself dabbled in alchemy when young.

(1248) *the original.* In Greek.

(1252) *Word.* John 1:1. For Faust, whose first words (398) say how tired he is of words, the beginning of things is no word.

(1289) *Solomon's Key.* "Clavicula Salomonis," a sixteenth-century book of conjurations.

(1304-7) *Salamander, Undine, Sylph, Kobold.* Elemental spirits (in that order) of fire, water, air, and earth.

(1320) *Incubus.* Here, unusually, like kobold an element of earth. Usually, a demon that attacks women sexually when they are asleep.

(1330) *symbol.* Of Christ crucified.

(bef. 1354) *traveling student.* A student on the way afoot to his university town.

(1355) *poodle.* An appropriate canine embodiment of Mephistopheles. Poodles, clever creatures, think of themselves first. For that reason they are rejected as seeing-eye dogs; they will swerve aside fastidiously from puddles and let their charges splash ahead.

(1366) *Lord of the Flies.* A translation of the Hebrew "Beelzebub," the name of a Philistine god who figures as "the prince of demons" in the New Testament.

(1383) *the dark out of which light burst.* The Mephistophelian idea is: light, born of the eternal dark, is a usurper. The Jewish idea is: And God said, let there be light. Gen. 1:3.

(1428) *witch's foot.* The pentagram or five-pointed star. Its points figured the five letters of Jesus and so possessed the power to ward off evil spirits.

(1471) *Spirits.* Mephisto claims they are *of my order* (1651), i.e., infernal. The glowing picture they present of an ideal landscape of human delight (which is presented "really" in *Part Two*) is a dream vision of what Faust desires in his soul, exploited by Mephisto.

(1553) *say it still a third time.* The demonic, which is fundamental disorder, insists on ceremony—i.e., on presenting a face of order.

(bef. 1629) *Spirit Chorus.* They flatter Faust as a demigod and urge a new life on him, following which Mephisto proposes a master (Faust)–servant (Mephisto) relationship.

(1724) *I'll bet you.* In the Prologue in Heaven, added after *Part One* was written, it is Mephisto who proposes the wager over Faust's soul, to God. Here Faust is the proposer, to Mephisto; he wagers his life that he will never be tempted into a moment's contentment, never rest, however briefly, from pursuing experience after experience.

(1740) *dinner for the . . . Ph.D.s.* A doctorate got one a dinner in those days. We hear no more of the dinner.

(1832) *Mr. Microcosm.* Mephisto is mocking Faust's ambition to "encompass everything human" in his "single person" (1801).

(1851) *balls. Hoden* in German. Most German editions print only the initial letter *H—. Hoden* is an emendation. There is no record of what word

Goethe meant. The most frequent suggestion is *Hintern* (backside). Was poor humble "backside" an improper word in late eighteenth-century Germany? Perhaps. But "backside" poorly fits Mephisto's exhorting Faust to throw himself into a life of sexual pleasure.

(1943) *Spanish boot.* A Spanish Inquisition instrument of torture.

(1973) *Encheiresis naturae.* A term used by Goethe's chemistry teacher at the University of Strassburg belonging to the effort to understand life by analysis of an organism into its constituent parts—as Goethe mockingly describes it in the preceding six lines. But the inorganic ("dead") parts when combined in the laboratory failed to unite into a living organism, and have failed ever since. Lacking is the mysterious force (or "soul," as Goethe puts it) that unites dead parts into an organic whole. Wordsworth expressed the same criticism of modern science—for the method is that of modern science—in a famous line, "We murder to dissect."

(2035) *No jot or tittle.* Matt. 5:18.

(2084) *Eritis sicut Deus, scientes bonum et malum.* "You shall be as God, knowing good and evil." Gen. 3:5.

(2090) *mix with little people, then with great.* In *Part One* with little people, in *Part Two* with great.

(bef. 2111) *Auerbach's Cellar in Leipzig.* An old students' hangout Goethe knew well when he attended Leipzig University, not very studiously. On one painted wall Faust is drinking with students, on another he is riding a barrel.

(2131) *Holy Roman Empire.* Succeeding the Carolingian in 936, it lasted until 1806.

(2142) *What a man must do to sit on that throne.* What he must do is drink everybody else under the table.

(2155) *Brocken.* The highest peak of the Harz Mountains, where witches fore-gathered for their sabbath on Walpurgis Night (Apr. 30–May 1). Also called Blocksberg.

(2358) *free for the taking.* Sorcerers were outside the law.

(2610) *Three-in-One and One-in-Three.* Mephistopheles is mocking the Trinitarian dogma.

(2626) *Sibyl.* Since ancient times a prophetess, in eighteenth-century Germany a witch.

(2805) *How close, oppressive it's in here.* The air is rank from the intrusion of the infernal.

(2810) *What a foolish, frightened girl I am.* A premonition.

(2811) *There was a king in Thule.* Not a folksong but Goethe's invention, in style and feeling very like one; and something like, in feeling, not in subject, the impending tragedy. Ultima Thule was the northernmost part of the habitable world, according to the ancients.

(2886) *Who overcometh is repaid.* Rev. 2:7.

(2893) *From a King to a Jew.* From highest to lowest. The Jews, kept apart in the Christian world of medieval Europe, stood lowest on the social ladder; or rather had no place on it at all. Goethe's birthplace, Frankfurt am Main, like many European cities had a ghetto, a single street into which its Jews were crammed; at night behind locked gates.

(3035) *Till the day he died he felt it still.* Felt the effects of syphilis.

(3090) *Sancta simplicitas!* What simplicity!

(3280) *Sublime Spirit.* The Spirit of Earth.

(3325) *But don't speak so.* Mephisto warns Faust his wanting a little "peace" and quiet risks losing their wager.

(bef. 3439) *Gretchen [Alone at her spinning wheel].* Set to lovely music, like many of Goethe's poems, by Schubert.

(3479) *Heinrich.* The Faust of the legend has Johann for his first name.

(3500) *Don't misunderstand me.* All about us and within us, Faust is saying, is a mysterious sustaining force. Call it what you please, for it's unnameable. But you feel it—"feeling is all." Which is perhaps the first principle of Romanticism, in its most succint statement.

(bef. 3621) *At the Well.* Still as in oldest times the well serves as a meeting place.

(3669) *with the sword in your heart.* The Mater Dolorosa is portrayed with a sword literally piercing her heart. Cf. Luke 2:35.

(3766) *What brings you out before.* Adapted from the song mad Ophelia sings in *Hamlet* IV.v.48.

(3783) *ratcatcher.* The Pied Piper.

(3800) *High Judiciary.* Court that judged in matters of life and death; empowered by the Emperor who was empowered by God, against whom Mephistopheles is helpless.

(bef. 3863) *Evil Spirit.* Gretchen's tortured conscience. Moral self-consciousness, the recognition of one's actions as good and bad—i.e., conscience—is an essential if not the essential attribute of humanity, yet here it is called an evil spirit. In I Samuel 16:14 "an evil spirit from the Lord troubles" Saul after he had disobeyed God. The torment suffered by a bad conscience is recognized as a divine evil—torment is torment, is suffering, and suffering is evil, even if justly incurred.

(3877) *pain and more pain.* In purgatory.

(3887) *Dies irae.* "Day of wrath, day that shall consume the world in ashes."

(3901) *Judex ergo.* "When the Judge takes his seat, all that is hidden shall be revealed, nothing shall go unpunished."

(3912) *Quid sum miser . . . sit securus?* "What shall a wretch like me say then? Whom beg to be my advocate when even the righteous shall hardly be saved?"

(3921) *smelling salts.* Swooning was common before the twentieth century, for which salts were carried in purses. It was a culture-inspired reaction like the once common hysteria.

(bef. 3922) *Walpurgis Night.* Walpurga was an eighth-century saint who protected against the wiles of witches. See note to line 2155. Walpurgis Night has no connection with the Faust legend. Schierke and Elend are nearby villages.

(3943) *will-o'-the-wisp.* As a misleading light (*ignis fatuus*), it was associated with the Devil.

(4005) *Mammon.* The god of gold, money, riches. In Milton's *Paradise Lost*, one of the fallen angels, "the least erected spirit that fell."

(4049) *Urian.* An old Germanic name for the Devil.

(4052) *Baubo.* An obscene witch stemming from the classical mythology.

(bef. 4067) *Warlocks.* In the centuries of witchcraft, as Americans know well from our own history, it was almost exclusively attributed to women. Goethe was no feminist, but in these lines he tries to equalize superstition's one-sided condemnation.

(4097) *unction.* Witches greased their broomsticks with a horrible embrocation to make them fly.

(4113) *Voland.* Another old Germanic name for the Devil.

(4158) *Garter.* Knighthood's ancient and highest order in Britain and the world.

(4159) *split hoof.* One of the marks of the Devil.

(4171ff.) *General.* Not only witches but generals, ministers of state, parvenus, and authors also foregather atop the Brocken, untraditionally introduced as satirical targets.

(4187) *For Judgment Day all now are ripe and ready.* Mockery of those for whom the present is always in a state of decline from a glorious past, whose own decline heralds the world's. Goethe was a modernist in upholding the present age and its advances. "America, you have it better"—a poem of his goes—for not being encumbered by crumbling castles, etc., all the obstructive traditional litter of a long, long past.

(4213) *Lilith.* In Talmudic tradition, a female night demon. In Jewish legend and medieval popular belief, Adam's first wife and a lustful witch.

(4238) *Proctophantasmist.* A word Goethe made up from the Greek for anus (*proktos*) and phantom. The target here is Friedrich Nicolai, a writer-publisher of the time who had parodied Goethe's *Sorrows of Young Werther* by writing *The Joys of Young Werther.* Nicolai was an Enlightenment rationalist who abhorred all superstitious credulity and overwrought emotionalism. But the enemy lurked within: he himself started seeing ghosts. When the apparitions persisted, believing them caused by "congestion" of the blood, he had his blood let; this was done by sticking leeches on his backside. The treatment was successful. Nicolai lectured on the subject before the Berlin Academy, recommending his science of leeches applied to the hinder parts for dealing with evil visitations.

(4255) *Tegel.* A place near Berlin where ghosts were reported to have been seen, cited by Nicolai in his disquisition.

(4263) *add a chapter to my travels.* Nicolai published, over a span of thirteen years, a twelve-volume work, *Description of a Journey through Germany and Switzerland in 1781.*

(4288) *Medusa.* A classical monster, serpent-haired, the sight of whose face turned one to stone. The hero Perseus, viewing her reflection in the borrowed shield of Athena, decapitated her.

(4310) *Prater.* The Vienna amusement park.

(4314) *Servibilis.* One who serves zealously, officiously.

(bef. 4323) *Walpurgis Night's Dream.* Satirical verses mocking contemporary literary figures and tendencies which Goethe had written for Schiller's journal *The Almanac of the Muses.* They were meant to follow an earlier set of derisive couplets that the two poets had done in collaboration (with the Greek title of *Xenien* or "parting gifts" or better still "parting shots"), but Schiller called off their publication, leaving Goethe with the quatrains on his hands. Instead of filing them in a drawer, he tacked them on to *Faust* with little apparent excuse. Do they have a place in the work? The standard opinion is, no. Nicholas Boyle says yes, appealing to the example of modernist poetic practice. *Oberon, Titania, Puck.* Names borrowed from *A Midsummer Night's Dream.*

(4324) *Mieding.* The Weimar court and stage carpenter J. M. Mieding, whom Goethe memorialized in a poem on his death in 1782.

(4339) *Ariel.* Another Shakespearian name, borrowed from *The Tempest*, seemingly with no more point than those above.

(4355) *Solo.* These verses of the bagpipes soloist, like other verses that follow, hide a satirical allusion that has proven too obscure for elucidation.

(4367) *An Inquiring Traveler.* Nicolai again.

(4371) *A Pious Believer.* Count Friedrich Leopold zu Stolberg, who attacked Schiller's poem "The Gods of Greece" for its "paganism."

(4378) *Italian Journey.* Goethe made *his* Italian journey in 1786–88.

(4407) *Hennings.* One of the targets of the Xenien; a minor literary figure.

(bef. 4411) *Musaget.* The title of a collection of poems by Hennings.

(4415) *Quondam "Spirit of the Age."* A journal published by Hennings at the end of the eighteenth century. Its name was changed to "Genius of the Nineteenth Century" after 1800.

(4420) *Inquiring Traveler.* Nicolai yet again, but now spoken about, not speaking.

(4424) *Crane.* Johann Kaspar Lavater, the Swiss preacher, physiognomist, and religious poet with whom Goethe had a more than ten years' friendship. The self-described "non-Christian" poet broke it off when he tired of his friend's piety.

(4428) *A Child of This World.* Goethe himself.

(4447) *Else how would there be devils.* Mockery of the ontological proof of God.

(4468) *The Smart Ones.* Those who shift with every shift in power. This quatrain and the four following describe types drawn from the French Revolution.

(4472) *The Not-So-Smart Ones.* Those who, like the French aristocrats, expelled from their high places and country, wander about as emigrés.

(4476) *Will-o'-the-Wisps.* Parvenus who come up from the social depths in revolutionary upheavals.

(4480) *A Shooting Star.* A revolutionary figure who rises briefly to the heights of power (e.g., Danton, Robespierre) and then falls.

(4484) *Bruisers.* The common people in rebellion (e.g., the sans-culottes).

(bef. 4500) *An Overcast Day.* Goethe let this scene stand in prose.

(4507–8) *the stony-hearted justice of mankind.* Is Faust, as so often, speaking for Goethe here? As an expression of pity for Gretchen by the young poet (for the phrase appears in the early written *Urfaust*) surely yes. But as a protest against the law decreeing death for infanticide, which is what the words literally express, no. Goethe did not oppose the law, early or late. When a servant girl in Saxe-Weimar was convicted of infanticide, the ruler, Duke Carl August, humanely requested the Privy Council to abolish the death penalty. The middle-aged Goethe, one of the three privy councilors and now an actor in a second, flesh-and-blood Gretchen drama, voted down the Duke's request along with the other two. The penalty was cruel, the servant girl's fate was pitiful, but Goethe believed it was right—as Gretchen's was right, and as Gretchen finds it right, finds it just, when she comes to accept her execution as a divine judgment. Young Goethe and old Goethe upheld the death penalty, but the one was full of pity and the other was pitiless.

(4560) *ravenstone.* Place of execution, specifically its paved ground. The raven is the bird of death: "Prophet . . . thing of evil!"—Edgar Allen Poe. The witches are conducting a diabolical death service.

(4573) *My mother, the whore.* Based on the fairy tale of the Juniper Tree, a version of which is to be found in the Brothers Grimm collection.

(4608) *They sing songs about me.* In a time before newspapers, ballads and songs reported crimes (usually local) and notable events.

(4688) *Nobody else shall lie beside me.* Infanticides were denied burial in consecrated ground.

(4754) *The bell calls, staff's shattered.* A bell summons to execution, a staff is broken over the condemned's head in sign of final judgment.

(4760) *I wish I had never been born.* Leagued with the Devil, Faust wishes death.

(4763) *My horses are trembling.* Spirit horses must vanish on the crowing of the cock.

(4772) *In your hands, our Father, oh save me! . . . / I'm afraid of you, Heinrich, afraid.* Gretchen embraces her tragic death in hope of life eternal, rejecting life on earth with death-companioned Faust, who ignominiously disappears in obedience to Mephisto's peremptory summons.

(4776) *She's condemned . . . she is saved!* Gretchen is condemned by the Devil. By a Voice retorting from Above, which is heard as that of the Father to whom she has just appealed, she is saved. But for the unbelieving poet there was no saving Father. If Gretchen was to be saved, he was the one must do it. But could a poet save, did he have such authority? It seems it was a question. Therefore he borrows from religion a Voice from Above.

NOTES TO PART TWO

ACT ONE

The change of scene in passing from *Part One* to *Two* is shocking: from a night-shrouded death cell to an Alpine field of flowers bathed in a soft twilight. Recumbent on his floral bed, Faust is restless nevertheless, as well he might be having as his last act abandoned Gretchen to the executioner's ax. But remorse, if that is what is troubling him, is not the subject here but rather its dispelling: a kindly troop of elfin sprites—nature spirits—come showering him with their care, as they shower care on all unfortunates without distinction, like the rain from heaven on the good and bad. Nature judges not, holding the whole world in her arms. Relieved of the burden of his crimes, Faust falls into a regenerative sleep from which he wakes reborn. He is delighted by the dawning landscape all about him. His infernal companion is nowhere to be seen, the stage is entirely his.

Exhilarated, all memory of his deeds expunged—unhappened!—he vows to live his life at the highest level of existence, in the paradisal world illuminated by the rising sun. But its dazzling rays are too much for him and he must avert his eyes. The very highest level of being, the divine (a word that has a very loose signification in the Goethean vocabulary), is symbolized by the heavenly disc so far away—and so immediate in its blindingness that he is forced to turn away, to turn back to the earth. Is it a defeat? Yes, but—. For the earth that he returns to is "glorious." Over it a rainbow arches, brilliant in its colors. The rainbow is a "mirror," an "image," of our human endeavor. When we hope and yearn and work to achieve an end, fulfillment finally opens before us an astonishing prospect, a sea of flames, an excess of fire and light, and we are overwhelmed. Again we are compelled to turn back to the earth, to find refuge in its mistiness and vapors. Unmediated vision blinds. But the vaporous misty earth is metaphorical; if we can't see into the essence of things, we can see into it sideways, by similitude, by likenesses that the things we know afford of it. In the eddying mists we make out images and reflections that seem to signify a great deal, and so they do. What indeed is our whole life, rainbow-like, but a reflection? Goethe's poem *Prooemion* ("Preface") expresses it, this stanza succinctly:

> Your ear, your eye, as far as they may stretch,
> It's only known things like Him that they reach,
> And upwards as your spirit strives in fiery flight,
> You have already in His likenesses sufficient light.

The earth suffices. *Faust II*'s scene is the earth, glorious and bewildering. The common reader, turning to it from *Part One,* is dismayed, the uncommon reader as well. Whatever is going on? It defies all rules, with royal indifference. No genre accomodates it, it is its own genre. It is all indirection—but what is the direction the indirections diverge from? Goethe is reported by J. F. Eckermann, his Boswell, as saying: "It would have been a fine thing indeed if I had strung so rich, so varied and diversified a life as I have exhibited in *Faust* upon the slender string of one pervading idea." "What does it mean," people came and asked him. "As if I knew myself," was his reply. Knowingness is an enemy of poetry, and much else. But we do know one thing: the immediate pleasure of his verse.

After the short scene bringing Faust back to life, we find ourselves in the German Emperor's Throne Room, in the great world Mephistopheles promised Faust would follow the little one of *Part One.* The Empire is staggering under its troubles; our two magicians will apply their talents to them. The Emperor is glad to postpone business in favor of Carnival entertainments, to be conducted in the lively style of Rome he came to know there during his coronation. The long act concludes, more amusing than amazing, with the conjuring by Faust of the ghosts of Paris and Helen of Troy.

Line
(bef. 4779) *Ariel.* See note to line 4339.
(4792) *watches.* The night between 6:00 pm and 6:00 am was divided into four vigils in antiquity.
(4795) *Lethe.* The river in Hell whose waters gave forgetfulness. In Dante it purifies.
(4832) *Hours.* Goddesses of the Seasons. In Homer gatekeepers of Olympus.
(4898) *Junker.* Young nobleman.
(5000–5001) *Subsidies . . . like our piped water.* Promised troops and funds, like the defective plumbing, fail.
(5013) *Guelph and Ghibelline.* The two warring "parties" of the early middle ages, the first supporting the pope, the second the German emperor, in Italy.
(5064) *Nature! Mind!* Orthodoxy, based on the dogma of original sin, abominates the acceptingness of Nature, the criticalness of mind.
(5085) *man of learning.* Mephisto often, here plainly, serves Goethe as a mouthpiece.

(5123) *The sun's pure gold.* In astrological lore, each planet (sun and moon being thought planets) had an associated metal. Mercury's was quicksilver, the moon's silver, Saturn's lead.

(5126) *early and late.* Venus shines as the morning and evening star.

(5137) *the learned man.* Mephistopheles is recommending the services of Faust.

(5147) *mandrakes.* Herbs superstitiously credited with all kinds of powers.

(5238) *Death the Master.* The translation borrows from Paul Celan, "Der Tod ist ein Meister aus Deutschland."

(5240) *Sovereign . . . went to Rome.* The German kings were crowned Emperor by the Pope.

(5242–43) *brought back with him / Mirthfulness.* Goethe on his Italian journey was delighted by Italy's sun and the Italians' sunniness. He returned gloomily to the overcast northern skies and other gloom of German lands.

(5279–80) *Nature . . . Art.* The question of their relation is eternal.

(5300) *Ceres,* The Roman goddess of grain, all agriculture.

(5308) *Theophrastus.* Greek philosopher of the late fourth–early third centuries B.C. whose writings on plants are regarded as the first systematic botany.

(bef. 5389) *Punchinellos.* Clowns in the commedia dell'arte, the once traditional Italian farce.

(bef. 5408) *Parasites.* Hangers-on of the rich in ancient comedy.

(bef. 5468) *Night and Graveyard poets:* The first sort dealt in Gothic horrors, the second in meditations on human mortality. These were eighteenth-century English literary fashions that crossed over to the Continent in the nineteenth.

(bef. 5468) *Graces.* Goddesses who lent social life agreeableness and grace.

(bef. 5474) *Fates.* The goddess Clotho spins the thread of life, Lachesis decides its length, Atropos cuts it off. Of course Atropos is much complained about, so in keeping with the holiday spirit the kindlier Clotho changes places with her.

(5490–5493) *Lives . . . spun out . . . / Lives cut short.* Wordsworth expressed the very same sentiment: "The good die first, / And they whose hearts are dry as summer dust / Burn to the socket."—*Intimations of Immortality.*

(5518) *Furies.* The classical avenging spirits, here changed from the hags of tragedy into fomenters of marital strife and punishers of infidelity.

(5547) *Asmodeus.* A demon of Persian origin who in the apocryphal book of Tobit murders seven husbands successively on their wedding nights.

(5613) *Ruler, I, of this colossus.* Elephantine power, guided by prudential wisdom, is able to keep to the difficult narrow track, despite the lies of Fear and Hope. And crowning his great strength is Victory, goddess of Doing.

(5625)*Zoilo-Thersites.* Mephisto disguised. The name combines those of two vituperators of classical times: Zoilus, a philosopher famous for his railing against Homer, and Thersites, the foul-mouthed insulter in the *Iliad* of the Greek army leaders.

(5713) *Boy Charioteer.* The personification of poetry, reappearing in Act III as Euphorion, child of Faust and Helen.

(5743) *Plutus.* Faust playing the part of the god of wealth.

(5749–50) *Squanders . . . intimacies of his soul.* A self-revealing (romantic) poet, like Goethe. Poetry drives the chariot of Wealth—i.e., directs riches' right use. Wealth supports Art, and is elevated by it in turn. *A snap of the fingers* offers a display of the brilliancies of poetic art; *sparks* too are scattered starting the poetic fire in others, with more or less success.

(5781) *They get what glitters, not what's gold.* The riches of poetry are worthless in ignorant hands.

(5823) *Skin-and-Bones.* Formerly Lady Avarice, her sex changed when housewives abandoned careful housekeeping for pleasure's profligacies and she was renominated Sir Greed.

(5970) *Absolutely scandalized.* By the indecent shape Greed has given the gold.

(bef. 5979) *A Riotous Crowd.* The court people gallivanting in their Carnival costumes.

(5981) *Pan.* The Emperor as the god of All. "Pan" was understood by a common etymological misinterpretation to mean "all."

(6042) *three commandments.* Those against theft, adultery, and killing.

(6180) *salamanders.* Mythical creatures able to live in fire.

(6202) *Nereids.* Daughters of the sea god Nereus, one of whom, Thetis, was won in marriage by a mortal, Peleus, by whom she had Achilles.

(6206) *A second Peleus captures the heart of the goddess.* Mephisto's flattery of the Emperor as a second Peleus promises him Olympian immortality after he dies. The latter prefers to stay alive.

(6244) *chicanery.* The Emperor sees paper money as a scam; the text too is so inclined.

(6396) *Those old pagans are none of my business.* Mephisto, from the Gothic Christian north, has been formed at the opposite pole from the pagan classical south. This polarity is one of the themes of *Part Two.*

(6403) *the Mothers.* Goethe developed his (unusually unclear) idea from a hint in Plutarch's *Life of Marcellus.* Deities that are the shades of everything that ever was and will be, but as shades nothing. Their realm is Nowhere, Nothingness. Faust on his descent (or ascent) will pass into a blank with "nowhere to rest his head." The Mothers are the "eternal mind" in eternal self-deliberation; about them throng absolute (not Platonic) forms. Faust hopes in Nothing to find All; more specifically the specters of Paris and Helen that he must produce for the Emperor's amusement. Mephisto, very solemnly, gives Faust a potent key. Some interpret the potency as sexual in meaning.

(6446) *Frenchman's fable.* The Frenchman is the great eighteenth-century fabulist La Fontaine. His fable concerns a monkey that persuades a cat to pluck chestnuts out of the fire for him.

(6656) *Paris.* The Trojan prince whose abduction to Troy of Helen, wife of the Spartan king Menelaus, caused the Greeks to attack Troy. He had grown up as a shepherd on Mount Ida.

(6699) *That lovely form. See Part One,* line 2479.

(6714) *Luna and Endymion.* The moon goddess, smitten by the beauty of Endymion, descended from the skies to steal a kiss from the sleeping youth.

(6735) *At ten already.* Theseus stole Helen when she was ten years old.

(6743) *She always pleased Troy's ancients.* The elders of Troy, seeing Helen below from the walls, exclaim:

> We cannot rage at her, it is no wonder
> that Trojans and Akhaians under arms
> should for so long have borne the pains of war
> for one like this.—*Iliad*, Book III (Fitzgerald trans.)

(6762) *double realm it has always sought.* Faust has sought to live in the actual world and the ideal world at the same time.

ACT TWO

(6795) *play the professor . . . pompously.* Goethe did not esteem the professoriate.

(6842) *Oremus!* "Let us pray!"—to ward off evil spirits.

(6851) *Dr. Wagner.* Faust's old famulus in *Part One.*

(6896) *A B.A. now.* The freshman who sought academic advice from Faust in the second Study scene in *Part One.*

(6979) *To be polite, in German means, tell lies.* Goethe said, "Germans lack tact because they lack euphemism and speak too bluntly."

(7000) *There was no world until by me created.* Baccalaureus is echoing Schopenhauer: "The world is my conception."—*The World as Will and Representation.*

(bef. 7025) *A Laboratory.* An alchemist's laboratory.

(bef. 7089) *Homunculus.* Little man, all brain and wanting a body. A chief figure in this act, and the most charming one of *Part Two.*

(7097) *Brother Rascal.* Perhaps Homunculus recognizes Mephisto as a brother because they are both unnatural (if in a different sense).

(7121) *But one stands out.* Leda, whom Jupiter as a swan descends on from the air, courteously in this account, and begets Helen and her brothers Castor and Pollux, called the Dioscuri. In Yeats's poem ("Leda and the Swan") violently: "A sudden blow: the great wings beating still / Above the staggering girl . . ."

(7157) *Classical Walpurgis Night.* To quote Mephisto: what a thought! North and South confounded!

(7168) *Peneios.* A river flowing through Thessaly that empties into the Aegean. On the plain below the town of Pharsalus, Caesar defeated the once mighty Pompey.

(7221) *Erichtho.* A Thessalian witch described by the Roman poet Lucan in his *Pharsalia,* an epic poem on the war between Caesar and Pompey.

(7301) *Antaeus-like.* Like the giant who drew his strength from contact with the earth and was helpless when lifted off it.

(7313) *modern style.* The nineteenth century turned prudish in recoil from the immodesties of the eighteenth. The modern style today is the opposite of prudish.

(7319) *griffins.* Legendary winged creatures with lion bodies who were the guardians of treasures of gold; the first of Act II's fabulous bestiary.

(7331) *Ants.* A giant kind, gatherers of gold stored in caves that the griffins stand guard over.

(7333) *Arismaspians.* A fabulous people whom Goethe has steal the gold watched over by the griffins.

(7345) *[The English] love to tour around.* The English were known as great tourists in the early nineteenth century.

(bef. 7384) *Sirens.* Half bird, half woman, they sang sailors to their destruction.

(7415) *Ulysses.* Curious to hear the sirens' song, he had himself lashed to the mast,

> and if I shout and beg to be untied,
> take more turns of the rope to muffle me.
> —*Odyssey*, XII (Fitzgerald trans.)

(7428) *Chiron.* A centaur, the wise and kindly tutor of heroes. Physician, botanist, herbalist.

(7449) *Stymphalides.* Monstrous birds whom Hercules destroyed as one of his twelve labors.

(7459) *Lernaean Hydra.* Another of Hercules' labors was to exterminate the many-headed serpent of the Lernaean swamp.

(7469) *Lamiae.* Female demons who lusted after human flesh and blood.

(7510) *once before I knew such joy.* When he dreamt of Leda and the swan, as divined by Homunculus (line 7117ff.).

(7531) *the nymph who is their queen.* Leda, again being pursued by Jupiter (the one who *seems prouder than the rest*). First the dream and then its enactment.

(7576) *Argonauts.* Heroes named after their ship, the *Argo,* in which they sailed in search of the Golden Fleece.

(7580) *Mentor.* Telemachus's teacher, whose shape Pallas Athena assumes in the *Odyssey.*

(7609) *Boreads.* Winged sons of the north wind Boreas.

(7630) *Hebe.* Goddess of youth and wife to Hercules after he was made immortal.

(7678) *Pherae.* A story about Achilles unites him and Helen, after their deaths, as lovers on the island of Leuca, which name Goethe replaced with that of the Thessalian town of Pherae.

(7692) *Manto.* A Sibyl or prophetess whom Goethe makes the daughter of Aesculapius, the physician god.

(7711) *greatest realm.* The Macedonian empire, defeated by republican Rome in 168 B.C. at Pydna (which lies north of Olympus, in Macedonia, not south).

(7739) *Orpheus.* Sweetest singer ever who, Shakespeare said, "with his lute made trees / And the mountain tops that freeze / Bow themselves when he did sing" (*Henry VIII*, III.i.3.). Sang Eurydice free from the nether world then lost her when he looked back against the prohibition when preceding her on the return.

(bef. 7741) *They descend.* Goethe did not, following the example of Homer and Virgil, accompany his protagonist underground.

(bef. 7765) *Seismos.* The earthquake personified.

(7781) *Latona* (Leto). When she was big with Apollo and Diana by Jupiter, Neptune raised Delos out of the sea as a refuge for her from Juno's anger. Goethe substitutes Seismos for Neptune.

(7806) *Black Night and Chaos.* Out of the two the world issued, the first parents. Gambolling before them, Seismos and the Titans play catch using for balls the peaks of the mountains Pelios and Ossa.

(7853) *Pygmies.* Earth accomodates all life, smallest and biggest.

(bef. 7869) *Dactyls.* Also the *very* smallest—dactyl means finger in Greek.

(bef. 7909) *Cranes of Ibycus.* Cranes were traditional enemies of the pygmies. In a ballad by Schiller they avenge the murder of the poet Ibycus.

(7929) *Blocksberg region.* The region of the Brocken where the witches celebrate Walpurgis Night in *Part One*. Ilse (*Ilsenstein*), Heinrich (*Heinrich-shöhe*); the Schnarchers ("snorers") are rock formations; Elend ("misery") is a poor village.

(bef. 7984) *Empusa.* A demon able to assume many shapes.

(8029) *thyrsus.* The staff carried by Dionysus and his fierce female followers, the Maenads.

(bef. 8063) *Oread.* A mountain nymph.

(bef. 8104) *Anaxagoras, Thales.* Early Greek philosophers whom Goethe makes represent the opposing sides of a contemporary geological controversy between the so-called Vulcanists and Neptunists. The Vulcanist Anaxagoras attributes the origin and progress of life to fiery explosions and sudden convulsions. The Neptunist Thales sees life arising out of water and advancing by steady, patient evolution.

(8126) *myrmidons.* Here, ants.

(8176) *huge and menacing sphere.* Anaxagoras mistakes a meteor for the moon.

(8219) *Dryad.* A tree nymph.

(8242) *Phorkyads.* Gray-haired from birth, they personify ugly old age. Also called the Graiae. They must share one eye among them.

(8249) *Ops and Rhea.* Ops (Roman), the wife of Saturn; Rhea (Greek), the wife of Cronos.

(8250) *The Parcae.* The Fates.

(8296) *With two eyes now, two fangs.* The merger with Mephisto gives the Phorkyads a second eye and fang.

(bef. 8311) *Nereids and Tritons.* For the Nereids, see note to line 6202. The Tritons were fish-tailed sons of Neptune.

(8343) *Cabiri.* Primitive deities whose obscure mystery cult was centered in Samothrace. Like Castor and Pollux, rescuers of shipwrecked sailors.

(8407) *Dorids.* Also daughters of Nereus, named however after their mother, the nymph Doris.

(8414) *Galatea.* Nereus's best-loved daughter, here described as the successor to foam-born Venus on Cyprus.

(8419) *Paphos.* A Cyprian city.

(8420) *chariot throne.* Aphrodite's "scallop shell" (line 8415).

(8424) *Proteus.* Another ancient sea god, famous for his quick changes.

(8444) *Chelone's giant shell.* Chelone was a nymph whom Mercury changed to a tortoise.

(8473) *the eighth's there that / Nobody's thought of yet.* Goethe is mocking the speculations of contemporary scholarship about the little known Cabiri.

(bef. 8551) *Telchines.* A legendary race of Rhodes. Skilled smiths, they were credited with forging Neptune's trident and erecting the Rhodian Colossus and many other bronze statues.

(bef. 8551) *hippocamps.* Sea horses.

(8563) *Helios.* The sun god.

(bef. 8642) *Psilli and Marsi.* Names of primitive races that Goethe appropriated for his nymphs that guard Venus's sea car.

(8659) *Eagle and Winged Lion, Crucifix and Crescent.* Romans and Venetians, Crusaders and Turks, all rulers of Cyprus at one time or another.

ACT III

(8781) *Eurus.* The east wind.

(8785) *Tyndareus.* Husband of Leda, Helen's mother. The children of Leda and Tyndareus were Clytemnestra, Helen, and Castor and Pollux, the last three fathered by the Jovian swan. See note to line 7121.

(8785) *Pallas's hill.* A hill on which stood a temple to Pallas Athena.

(8798–99) *Cythera's temple.* The temple of Venus on Cythera, a Mediterranean island off the southern Peloponnesus.

(8828) *Eurotas's waters.* Sparta, on the river Eurotas, lay upstream of where it flows into the sea.

(bef. 8995) *Phorkyas.* Mephistopheles, disguised as a Phorkyad.

(9116) *Erebus.* The undermost part of the underworld. *Mother Night.* See note to line 7806.

(9117) *Scylla.* A monster that is a composite of writhing serpents and ferocious dogs. Her opposite number, across the Strait of Messina, is Charybdis, a whirlpool that sucks down everything in reach. Past these dangers Ulysses must maneuver his ship.

(9121) *Tiresius.* The blind, ancient Theban soothsayer who figures often in classical tragedy.

(9122) *Orion.* Hunter changed into a constellation at his death.

(9123) *Harpies.* Monstrous bird women who fouled food with their excrement.

(9145) *Orcus.* Hades.

(9159) *Theseus.* The Attic hero who among his many exploits slew the Minotaur. He kidnapped Helen of Troy (she was not yet "of Troy") when she was ten years old.

(9160) *Heracles.* Hercules.

(9169) *Patroclus, Pelides.* Patroclus is Achilles' (Pelides') close comrade in the *Iliad.*

(9188–89) *two of you were seen . . . in Ilium . . . in Egypt.* A post-Homeric legend has Paris abducting a phantom Helen to Troy, while Mercury saves the real one by carrying her off to Egypt.

(9192–93) *Achilles rose up from / The empty shadow world.* See note to line 7678.

(9206–7) *three-headed dog's jaws.* Jaws of Cerberus, Hades' watchdog.

(9342) *bloodthirsty.* Achilles, to Hector fallen in the dust:

> Would god my passion drove me
> to slaughter you and eat you raw.

> —*Iliad*, XXII (Fitzgerald trans.)

(9449) *Hermes* (Mercury). Conductor of dead souls to Hades (psychopompos). See note to line 9984.

(9469) *Pythoness.* Prophetess, witch.

(9499) *bitter ashes.* The apples of Sodom, fair appearing but proving otherwise when bitten. See *Paradise Lost* X, 564–66.

(9588) *simply one:* The first Helen. *two of me:* The Helen in Troy and Egypt at the same time (see note to line 9159). *three . . . four:* The third and fourth Helens are the one come back to Sparta and the one now translated to Faust's medieval castle.

(9795) *Nestor.* Oldest of the Greek captains who fought at Troy, ruler of Messenian Pylos.

(9859) *broken shell.* Swan-begotten Helen was born from an egg.

(9910) *Arcadia.* A region in the Peloponnesus that Virgil established in poetic tradition as the ideal place of pastoral peace and beauty.

(9939) *a boy jumping.* Euphorion. See note to line 5713.

(9984) *Maia's son.* Hermes, the trickster god, fathered by Zeus. His first trick
was to steal Apollo's cattle and shoe them in bark so that they left no
tracks; the sun god Phoebus Apollo was baffled (for a while). Zeus made
him his herald, with winged sandals for speedy delivery of Olympian
messages. As the inventor god Hermes was prodigious in the number of
his creations. He invented Apollo's lyre (before inventing the shepherd's
pipe), helped the Fates invent the alphabet, devised astronomy, the musical scale, weights and measures, started boxing and gymnastics, the cul-
tivation of the olive tree, and still more—the god of the arts and sciences
of civilization. Among his sons was Autolycus, clever thief like his father,
assured immortality (apart from being child of a god) by his having a
namesake in Shakespeare's *The Winter's Tale.* See note to line 9449.

(10163) *The watchword's war.* Alludes to the Greek war of independence
against the Turks in the 1820s, to which Byron gave all his efforts, including his life.

(10189) *sacred poetry.* Byron's poetry, greatly admired by Goethe; also poetry
in general. "I could not make use of any man as the representative of the
modern poetic era except him, who is undoubtedly the greatest genius of
our century"—Goethe to Eckermann.

(bef. 10229) *well-known figure.* Byron, figured in Euphorion as the spirit of
poetry, is memorialized in the elegiacal stanzas that follow.

(10271) *Persephone.* Queen with King Pluto of the infernal regions. She was
abducted as a girl by Pluto but allowed to pass part of the year in the upper world. The Romans called her Proserpine.

(10297) *the Inscrutables.* Pluto and Persephone.

(10309) *Who's won no name nor nobly strives.* Goethe to Eckermann: "How
people have philosophized and philosophized about immortality!—and
with what result? I don't doubt of our immortality, for Nature can't do
without entelechy [without teleological drive]; but we aren't all immortal
in the same way, and whoever wishes to manifest himself in the future as
a great entelechy must be one here."

(10310) *Nature's elements.* To Eckermann earlier: "The idea that the Chorus
doesn't go back down to the underworld, instead disperses itself among

the elements on the happy surface of the earth, is one I am really a bit proud of."

(bef. 10320) *A Part of the Chorus.* The Chorus has melted into the elements. This first part into trees, and as tree spirits, Dryads. The second part into mountain cliffs, and as mountain spirits, Oreads. The third part into running brooks, and as water sprites, Naiads. The fourth part as nameless spirits of viniculture whose celebration of the grape becomes a celebration of the "mysteries" of Dionysus, called Bacchus by the Romans, god of wine (and also of the drama), and worshipped by drunkenness and sexual abandonment (line 10362) *All that's moral . . . trampling.*

(10360) *Silenus.* Bacchus's tutor, always drunk and always riding a donkey.

ACT IV

Goethe said about Act IV that "it neither possessed an entirely individual character . . . nor had much connection with what came before it and was to follow." Carried by the cloud into which Helen's garments have been metamorphosed, airborne Faust returns from Greece to German lands. The opening lines describing cloud formations reflect Goethe's intensive meteorological studies. Faust, more poet than meteorologist, sees them as a metaphorical reflection of his Greek experience, and more specifically as Juno, Leda, and Helen of Troy, with a suggestion of non-Grecian Gretchen.

(10425) *Eph. 6:12.* The devils of Hell, once confined below in darkness, now occupy the "high-places" of the world.

(10432–33) *Nature / Has no use for eruptions.* Faust is a Neptunist like Thales, Mephisto a Vulcanist like Anaxagoras. (See note to line 8104.) Goethe, a gradualist, through Faust favors the Neptunist geology.

(10437) *Moloch.* In the Bible a fearsome pagan god; in Milton's epic a rebel angel, one of Satan's crew.

(10451) *the Devil's Rock, the Devil's Bridge.* Striking rock formations, so named by popular superstition. For Satan evidence of ancient chthonian wisdom.

(10512) *Sardanapal*[us]. Greek name for Ashurbanipal, suggesting Oriental depravity.

(10570) *Drums, did you hear?* Faust's exposition of his grand scheme of land reclamation is interrupted by a war over rulership of the Empire.

(10662) *Mister Peter Quince.* A two-level allusion. The first to a German comedy by Andreas Gryphius which made its own use of the character Quince from *A Midsummer Night's Dream.* The second directly to Quince the carpenter, bumpkin director in Shakespeare's play of the bumpkin play-within-the-play of *Pyramus and Thisby.*

(10668–69) *Today we're so delighted all / By medieval knights in armor.* Medievalism was both a fad and a passion in nineteenth-century Europe, and especially in Germany.

(10902–3) *Lordly knights and kings and kaisers— / that now are only empty shells.* Goethe is mocking the pretensions of the old aristocracy. But it is a question whether, up until World War II, they were only empty shells.

(10942) *little flames.* St. Elmo's fire, the flames or fireballs seen on ships' spars in storms, called Castor and Pollux by the Romans. They light up the tips of spears, Faust says, as the last effort of that fading pair of gods.

(10953) *necromancer.* The Sabine sorcerer of lines 10779ff.

(11012) *my two grim ravens.* Messengers of Wotan (Odin) in the Teutonic mythology. They were reassigned to the Devil by Christian superstition.

(11055) *I can't allow you the baton.* Because it has a cross on it.

(11066) *Undines.* Water spirits; already encountered in *Part I,* line 1305.

(11102) *Little People.* Dwarfs were traditionally associated with mining and metallurgy.

(11215) *Perhaps we had some unorthodox help,* So the Emperor, minimizing the diabolical help provided by Faust and Mephisto.

(11388) *You granted that scoundrel the shores of the Empire.* We learn that Faust's ambitious reclamation project is at last in the way of realization.

ACT V

No papal ban has stopped Faust's project; we find him in the last act ruler of a latifundium of shoreland reclaimed from the sea, and now a prince of trade and wealth. How the work got done we learn from the account a peasant couple give a traveler whom they had rescued from drowning some years before, who has returned expressive of his gratitude. There is a difference of opinion between husband and wife about Faust's project. The happy scene changes abruptly in the succeeding one.

(bef. 11410 and bef. 11420) *Baucis . . . Philemon.* The poor pious couple in Ovid's *Metamorphoses* who welcome Zeus and Hermes, disguised as travelers, into their cottage. The two gods, testing human charity, had been refused by the rich. They reward the old couple by changing their dwelling into a temple and the pair into its priest and priestess; when they die they are turned into trees. The classical names ring incongruously here. But explicitly and inexplicitly there is much "incongruity" in *Part Two* between Gothic and Classical; it is indeed a theme of the work.

(11510) *Less than all.* Faust's project has turned into a murderous imperialism.

(11643) *Naboth's vineyard once again.* King Ahab, coveting Naboth's vineyard, offered to buy it and was refused. The upshot was as one may imagine—or better, read in the Bible, as cited in the margin of the text by Goethe.

(11741) *Care.* Tormenting anxiety. See note to Part One, line 668. Not pathological angst calling for psychiatric treatment but oppressive anxiousness. Extinguisher, suffocater, smotherer of living life; nothing-maker of the present, magnifier of the future into a monster worshipped in terror and desperation.

(11858) *Yet all is clear, as bright as day, within.* What is bright as day in Faust's end-of-life blindness? The vision of "stand[ing] with free men on ground that is free" (11940).

(bef. 11873) *Lemurs.* Specters of the dead still possessing skeletons and shreds of skin and sinew, as believed by the Romans; depicted as oafish creatures. (No relation to the monkey-like creatures found on Madagascar.)

(11889) *In youth when I did love, did love,* etc. Compare *Hamlet* V.i.61.

(11941–42) *Then, then, I might say to the passing moment, / "Linger awhile, you are so fair."* See Part I, 1724–32. Faust presumably does not lose the wager because he speaks conditionally not declaratively. Mephisto's exclamation a few lines later: "Alas, today / There are so many ways to cheat the Devil of his due," is his chagrined comment on his sophistical defeat.

(11963) *Who built this house so illy made.* Compare *Hamlet* V.i.92.

(12037) *Envoys.* Literal translation of the Greek *angeloi.* The Heavenly Host's song is self-addressed.

(12054) *Is just what in their piety they prized.* The Church prized the emasculated sopranos of castrati for her choirs.

(12061–62) *Roses.* Symbolic of divine love.

(12191) *You youngsters caught me, you did, off my guard.* Mephisto is almost seduced to coming over to the side of heavenly love. One of Goethe's boldest "serious jokes"—Evil swayed by the power of love becomes flustered and is rendered helpless, or nearly so.

(bef. 12209) *holy anchorites*. Hermit saints of the early period of Christianity; disposed at different levels on the holy mountain.

(12215) *Lions forget to growl*. "The wolf and the lamb shall feed together, and the lion shall eat straw like the bullock: and dust shall be the serpent's meat. They shall not hurt or destroy in all my holy mountain, saith the Lord."—Isaiah 65:25.

(bef. 12219) *Pater Ecstaticus*. In his ecstacy he has put away his flesh so far that he floats weightless in the air.

(bef. 12231) *Pater Profundus*. His place is below, in the depths of the holy mountain's profundity of love; his own profundity is one of anguish, his needy heart straining upwards to the heavenly love.

(bef. 12255) *Pater Seraphicus*. The seraphic—angelic—one, as St. Francis was called. He is a station on the way of the Boy Souls, born and dead at the stroke of midnight; therefore free of sin, but not of Original Sin. The view he gives them of earthly life they find "too gloomy"; they don't feel they have missed anything.

(12301–2) "Who strives, and keeps on striving still / For him there is salvation." Goethe put quotation marks around these words for emphasis; they are not a quotation. They hold "the key of Faust's salvation," he told Eckermann. He felt he needed to provide a key to unlock the work's obscurity. In much the same way that Coleridge, feeling that *The Ancient Mariner's* shadows needed moral illumination, appended the famous lines "He prayeth best who loveth best / All things both great and small."

(bef. 12356) *Doctor Marianus*. Highest placed of the anchorites, so high that he can see into Heaven; especially devoted to the Mater Gloriosa (Glorious Mother).

(bef. 12404) *Magna Peccatrix*. The woman who "sinned greatly" in Luke 7:37–38.

(bef. 12412) *Mulier Samaritana*. The Samaritan woman in John 4:7ff., whom Jesus met at Jacob's Well and asked for a drink of water. Her sinning was the many men she lived with unmarried.

(bef. 12420) *Maria Aegyptiaca*. Mary of Egypt, also a repentant sinner, whose story is told in the *Acts of the Saints* (April 2), a Catholic calendar of saints' lives.

(12475) *Here*. The Goethean beyond; the transcendental eternal and divine.